D0951604

KEN ARMSTRONG & NICK PERRY

Scoreboard, Baby

A Story of College Football, Crime, and Complicity

UNIVERSITY OF NEBRASKA PRESS   LINCOLN & LONDON

Library of Congress Cataloging-
in-Publication Data
Armstrong, Ken, 1962–
Scoreboard, baby : a story of college football, crime, and complicity / Ken Armstrong
and Nick Perry.
p. cm.
Includes bibliographical references
and index.
ISBN 978-0-8032-2810-8 (pbk. : alk. paper)
1. Washington Huskies (Football team).
2. University of Washington—Football.
3. College sports—Washington (State).
4. Football—Corrupt practices—United
States. I. Perry, Nick, 1970– II. Title.
GV958.U5865A76 2010
796.332'6309797772—dc22
2010002008

Set in Sabon by Kim Essman.

CONTENTS

ILLUSTRATIONS

Following page 174

CAST OF CHARACTERS

Players

JEREMIAH PHARMS: A top recruit, he came to the University of Washington (UW) in 1996 from Sacramento, California. A linebacker and a devastating hitter, he hoped to go pro after the 2000 season—assuming he didn't face serious criminal charges first.

JERRAMY STEVENS: A standout tight end from Olympia, Washington, he joined the Huskies in 1997 while facing a felony assault charge. At the UW he wowed professional scouts but repeatedly found trouble off the field.

ANTHONY KELLEY: An outside linebacker, Kelley came to the UW in 1998 from Pasadena, California. Because of his poor academic record in high school, he couldn't play his freshman year.

CURTIS WILLIAMS: When he came to the UW in 1996 from Fresno, California, he was already married and a father. A fifth-year senior in the 2000 season, he played strong safety and anchored the defense.

ANTHONY VONTOURE: A gifted cornerback, he played high school ball with the celebrated De La Salle program in Concord, California. After coming to the UW in 1997, he struggled to keep it together off the field.

Other Players

SAM BLANCHE: A linebacker from Pomona, California, he was good friends with Pharms—and became entangled in a police investigation of his fellow player.

ROCK NELSON: An offensive lineman from north of Seattle, he struggled to play because of a back injury suffered while lifting weights.

J. K. SCOTT: A quarterback from suburban Los Angeles, he never managed to crack the starting lineup. He was Vontoure's roommate their freshman year.

GREG CAROTHERS: Recruited from Helena, Montana, he became a starting safety in 2000 even though he was just a true freshman.

Coaches

RICK NEUHEISEL: At the University of Colorado, he became a head coach at the age of thirty-four. After going 33-14 in four years there, he took over as the UW's head coach in 1999.

TOM WILLIAMS: He coached the outside linebackers, including Anthony Kelley. The team's youngest assistant coach, he had played at Stanford, where Bill Walsh was his mentor.

CHUCK HEATER: He was the cornerbacks coach and the team's recruiting coordinator. One of his players was the troubled and volatile Anthony Vontoure.

DON JAMES: He was the UW's head coach from 1975 to 1992, recording the most wins in school history. His 1991 team went undefeated and won the national championship.

JIM LAMBRIGHT: As the UW's head coach from 1993 to 1998, he recruited Stevens, Williams, Pharms, Vontoure, and Kelley, among many other players on the 2000 team.

University of Washington Administrators

BARBARA HEDGES: The university's athletic director, she came to Washington in 1991 from USC. She hired Neuheisel to run the football program.

ROBERT ARONSON: A law professor, he was the university's faculty athletic representative from 1993 to 2004.

ERIC GODFREY: As financial aid director, he chaired the committee that determined whether an athlete could retain his scholarship. He was later promoted to vice-provost for student life.

RICHARD MCCORMICK: President of the UW from 1995 to 2002, he left Seattle to become president of Rutgers.

MARK EMMERT: A UW alumnus, he became president of the university in 2004. He was previously chancellor at Louisiana State University.

Police

MARYANN PARKER: A detective with the Seattle Police Department's Special Assault Unit, she investigated an alleged rape on Greek Row.

JEFFERY MUDD: A detective with the Seattle Police Department's Gang Crimes Unit, he became the lead investigator when a drug dealer near campus was shot and robbed.

MIKE MAGAN: A celebrated robbery detective with the Seattle Police Department, he helped investigate the case involving the drug dealer. A former football player at the UW, Magan remained close to the team, counseling players and coaches.

Prosecutors

NORM MALENG: Respected for his integrity and nonpartisan approach to law enforcement, he became head of the King County Prosecuting Attorney's Office in 1978 and kept the job for nearly thirty years.

DAN SATTERBERG: He was Maleng's chief deputy, the office's No. 2 position.

MARK LARSON: He was chief of the criminal division in Maleng's office.

ACKNOWLEDGMENTS

Our thanks to David Boardman, Jim Neff, Suki Dardarian, and other editors at the *Seattle Times* for giving us the time and support to do so much of the reporting that went into this book. Investigative reporting may be in jeopardy nationally, but the *Times'* commitment to doing tough stories hasn't wavered. Thanks also to Jim for helping us navigate the world of books.

Thanks to Jill Marsal, our agent; the Sandra Dijkstra Literary Agency; and Rob Taylor, our editor at the University of Nebraska Press, for their faith in this story and for taking a chance on first-time authors.

Many friends, colleagues, and associates were kind enough to read drafts and offer invaluable insight, or to offer help in other ways. Our thanks to Jerry Holloron, Cara Solomon, Danny O'Neil, Rose Moss, Don Nelson, Jacqui Banaszynski, Jonathan Martin, Craig Welch, Justin Mayo, William Downing, and Paul Dorpat.

Jean Sherrard was kind enough to let us use his terrific photo of Husky Stadium for free. Thanks, Jean.

And a special thanks to our wives—Ken is married to Ramona Hattendorf, Nick to Amy Beliveau. Sorry about all the weekends and evenings spent writing and reporting. Thank you for reading the same passages three, four, and five times. And for catching mistakes. And for doing double duty with the kids.

Prologue *Hush-Hush*

After rolling through the end zone, he stood, military straight, and shot his arms out to each side, his body a cross, his palms up, the football cupped in his left hand. The crowd's love washed over him—74,000 fans, in purple and gold, Microsofties, elementary school teachers, doctors, nurses, students, bankers, Boeing engineers. He pumped his head twice—yes, yes—and hugged his teammates as they jumped into his arms. The stadium siren sounded. Gold pompons waved. "They are hot right now," said the color man, up in the broadcast booth. "Are they ever," said the play-by-play man. The cheers kept coming as more players ran to him, to join the celebration.

The crowd knew what he was accused of, yes. But did that matter now?

Did it matter to ABC, which was broadcasting this game nationally? If it did, the announcers kept it to themselves. Not a word was said of how he had been arrested six weeks before on suspicion of rape. The broadcasters knew about it, of course. Bob Griese knew. Brad Nessler knew. Lynn Swann knew. *Everyone* knew. Jerramy Stevens had been arrested by a SWAT team—and an arrest like that makes the newspapers. But ABC treated the whole thing hush-hush. "A great tight end," Nessler said early on. Then, as Stevens racked up the receptions, the play-by-play man tacked on the praise. "He is some kind of target. . . . The big fella rumbles. . . . Ace in the hole."

Before the game, the crowd had buzzed about how he might be charged any day, about how maybe this time, the county's long-time prosecutor would pull the trigger. In the last two years, the prosecutor had taken a pass on charging six other players with assault. But maybe this time . . .

From the newspapers, the fans knew a few details. The woman was a freshman. Whatever happened, happened on Greek Row. But for now, the crowd erupted in cheers. A chain saw registers 100 decibels. A Husky crowd hits 135. The stadium rocked. What mattered was that Stevens had scored, putting Washington up 21–3. What mattered was that the Huskies were pounding one of the best teams in the country—and they were doing it on national TV, the broadcast a postcard of the Pacific Northwest, the greens and blues and grays, with glorious shots of Lake Washington, Douglas firs, and Mount Rainier.

The judges in King County knew what mattered. Sentencing one of Stevens's teammates to a month in jail, a judge wrote in her order: "To be served after football season." When another teammate faced a felony charge of assaulting a police officer, a judge released him without bail so that he could play in the next game. Yet another teammate, convicted of T-boning a car in an intersection, sending a woman to the hospital, was sentenced to 150 hours of community service—and allowed to perform every hour at football camps, serving as a role model to younger kids.

In the end zone, the Husky players converged on Stevens, to slap his shoulder pads, to pat his helmet. Two months before, they had turned out for his bond hearing to show their support. Who were they to judge? Innocent until proven guilty. Besides, quite a few had troubles of their own. At least three had warrants out for their arrest. They were playing in front of all these fans while wanted. Another player, a star linebacker, was under investigation by Seattle police—only in his case, the public didn't know. But the DNA results on that bloody fingerprint could be back any time now. Like Stevens, he could be charged any day.

Mike Hunsinger, a season-ticket holder, knew about that linebacker. He knew lots of things the public didn't know. An unimposing man—150 pounds, glasses, a voice more alto than bass—Hunsinger made little impression in a crowd. In Seattle, support for the University of Washington often becomes a family affair—something passed down—be the family's name Nordstrom, Gates, or Hunsinger. For three generations, the Hunsingers had owned a lumberyard in Seattle. In the 1980s, Mike's father, D.W., joined a group of thirty-four businessmen—bankers, architects, car dealers, beer distributors—who called themselves the "Endorsers," and who took it upon themselves to pad the salary of then-coach Don James with an extra $100,000 a year. They wanted to make James happy, to keep him from being swept away by the NFL or by some other school. Mike's brother Bill gave summer jobs to Husky football players at the family lumberyard. Sometimes, a quarterback and wide receiver would practice routes amid the fir and molding. Of course, the players weren't allowed to operate the saws. Nobody wanted them to get injured.

Instead of selling lumber, Mike had become a lawyer. He had built a successful practice in Seattle, doing high-end civil work, mostly. Still, he managed to do his part for the football program. In Husky Stadium, Hunsinger could look down on the field and pick out clients, past and present. In time, he would represent at least fourteen players on this team, mostly against criminal charges. He would charge each player a few hundred dollars and let him pay over time. Sometimes, he could get prosecutors to drop their charges with a single telephone call.

Washington's head coach, Rick Neuheisel, removed his headset and ran his fingers through his hair. The announcers talked of how he was resurrecting hope in Seattle. Sure, he was only thirty-nine. But he had already emerged as a new kind of coach, a coach for a new century, a gold-banged, rosy-cheeked, guitar-playing friend of the player and the fan, with nicknames like Skippy and Coach Kumbaya. Slick Rick, too. And Rookie. And Sneus—because he was a Sigma Nu, back at UCLA, back when he was a walk-on quarterback who dated all the prettiest girls and who overcame food poisoning to become Rose Bowl MVP. He was Coach Fun Fun Fun. Hear it? It's the Beach Boys, in the background, playing along.

Neuheisel was also a lawyer, which is why he used words like exonerated. *I hope the truth will exonerate you*, he had told Stevens after his arrest. Stevens had the makings of Washington's best tight end ever—and this, at a school known for great tight ends. "Not having him would change who we are," Neuheisel told reporters.

Sportswriters, high up in the press box, could feel the stadium shake, as sound waves crashed into concrete. Ever since his arrival on campus, Stevens had charmed them. Even when he had landed in trouble before, they had assured readers that he'd learned his lesson, that he was a "good-natured giant," that he would be getting the last laugh, you could be sure of that. Then he went and found trouble again.

But really.

Did that matter now?

Bow down to Washington,
Bow down to Washington,
Mighty are the men
Who wear the purple and the gold,
Joyfully we welcome them
Within the victors' fold.

The opening to "Bow Down to Washington,"
the school's fight song

Freeze

1

March 14, 2000: Six Months before the Season Begins

Kerry Sullivan tried to be careful. Sometimes, when customers would telephone, he'd turn them away. Not today, he'd say, or at least not right now. He wanted to space things out. He wanted to avoid heavy traffic. His rule was: Don't push it. A typical house does not have people lined up out front—people who knock, enter, and leave in five minutes, one after the other. If a cop sees that, he'll catch on.

That was one consideration—when to sell. Another consideration was, who to sell to. On occasion, he sold marijuana to UW football players. Sam Blanche, a backup linebacker from California, was a customer. "Sam B" is how Sullivan knew him. Blanche would call maybe once a month and drop by for $40 worth. Another customer was Curtis Williams, a starting safety and one of the team's best players. Everybody knew him as "C.W.," or "C-Dub." But for the most part, Sullivan steered clear of the football team. He figured players, with their high profile, stood a better chance of getting caught and fingering him as their source.

Customers came to Sullivan's home—to apartment 101, in the slate gray house, set back from the street, atop a rise, with a thicket of trees offering some semblance of privacy. Sullivan lived on Twenty-second Avenue Northeast, a block north of the UW campus. Two houses down was Tau Kappa Epsilon, a fraternity that might have been reminiscent of New England—the gabled roof and classic dormers—were it not for the aluminum siding.

Ten months earlier, Sullivan could have gazed upon the TKE house—it was right there, out his kitchen window—and gotten all the warning he needed about dealing with football players. On back-to-back nights, members of the football team attacked the fraternity, kicking in the front door, smashing out windows, busting up furniture. They had been turned away from a party there—that's what started it all. Not that it took much to get football players and fraternity members sideways with each other. The second night, the football players didn't exactly try to sneak up on anybody. They called ahead of time and said: We're coming to settle this. They arrived after midnight—ten of them, at least—and set upon the house. One Teke was grabbed around the neck and slammed into a wall. Another was hit on the head from behind, then kicked while down. Prosecutors refused to bring felony charges, a result that seemed to suit everybody except some of the Tekes' parents, who complained of athletes getting special treatment and talked of how their kids feared retaliation and didn't want to get the football team in trouble.

That kind of drama, Sullivan would just as soon avoid. Now twenty-four, he had been selling marijuana for about a year. He also went to school, at Seattle Central Community College. His criminal record extended back to his juvenile years and included charges of theft and misdemeanor assault. He had been popped for possession, but not for dealing. The key was to be careful. He had maybe twenty regular customers. Others came his way through campus word of mouth. He charged $40 for an eighth of an ounce—enough, maybe, for seven or eight joints. Bulk rates were cheaper. He was often paid in twenties, which he would fold in half and tuck between his mattress and box springs.

On March 14, 2000—a Tuesday, while the university was on spring break—Sullivan got a call from a football player who'd been a customer for about six months. The player asked if Sullivan would be willing to sell a half ounce to a friend called "J.P." Sure, Sullivan said. Half an hour later, a guy identifying himself as J.P. called, to confirm. No problem, Sullivan said. A half hour after that, J.P. called back. His girlfriend didn't have the $140 he needed for a half ounce, he told Sullivan. Could he buy a $40 bag instead? Sullivan said sure.

Sullivan made a practice of splitting his stash up and moving it around, one day here, another day there. That was another rule: Don't be predictable. On this day, he had a quarter pound of marijuana in his bedroom closet, in a clear plastic bag. He had another half pound in a safe, hidden away in a locked hallway closet. Add it up, and he had about $3,000 worth of marijuana in the apartment.

At about 8 p.m., Jeremiah Pharms showed up at the door, alone. He wore gray sweatpants and a white T-shirt. He looked intimidating—athletic, muscular, with shoulders that could have been quarried. Sullivan took Pharms through the apartment, which he shared with three roommates. Inside was a pool table, with dirty dishes on top. Above the fridge, a poster of Jim Morrison. On the walls, a mishmash homage to desires and aspirations—a drawing of a marijuana leaf, a Heineken label, a photo of a fighter jet, a photo of a woman, smiling, wearing not a lot. Sullivan reached into his bedroom closet and pulled out the bag with a quarter pound of marijuana, worth $1,000 or so. He kept Ziplocs on a desk, next to the closet. While Sullivan measured out an eighth of an ounce, Pharms talked about how he was failing his classes at the UW.

Pharms was twenty-one, and married with kids. He was finishing his fourth year of school at the UW, but he had another year of football eligibility left. The 2000 season would begin in six months. Pharms needed to play—and play well—to improve his standing for the 2001 NFL draft. Football was his future; he'd left himself few other options. But now his grades were so bad that he faced the threat of flunking out. In a land of 1,200 SAT scores and 3.7 GPAs, Pharms was a football mercenary, a guy who arrived ill-equipped for the university's academic demands and who just wanted to get by, to stay eligible, to keep playing, to attract the NFL's notice, and to move on.

Coming out of high school, in Sacramento, Pharms was 6-1, or 6-2 or 6-3 or 6-4, depending upon which newspaper or scouting service you read. He weighed 210 pounds—or 220 or 225 or

227—and ran the forty in 4.5 or 4.55 or 4.6 or 4.62 or 4.65. He bench-pressed 320 pounds. He had 10-inch hands and 32½-inch arms, and if you wanted to know how much he could squat or how high he could jump, those numbers could be obtained, too. He had a thick neck and a soft voice. *Blue Chip Illustrated* named Pharms a prep All-American, calling him the best high school linebacker in the western United States.

In college, Pharms just got bigger and stronger; he weighed 250, bench-pressed 405. He had started every game the last two years, emerging as one of the defense's best players. He sported a tattoo of a pit bull on his arm; his initials ran across his stomach. He refused interviews. "A man of mystery," the *Seattle Post-Intelligencer* called him. A fearsome hitter, Pharms roamed the opposing team's backfield. By game's end, he wouldn't have the most tackles. But he would often have the most memorable—the one that jarred the ball loose or elicited gasps from the crowd. Sometimes, in games, he'd lock eyes with an opposing lineman and proceed to urinate, the stream darkening his pants. He did this to intimidate, to make the other guy think he was crazy. Sometimes he'd come off the field so emotional his teammates would see tears. They were thankful they played with him, and not against him.

The transaction with Sullivan lasted only minutes. Pharms paid his $40 and left. Sullivan put the plastic bag back in the closet.

The same night—three hours later, at about eleven—someone knocked at the door of Sullivan's apartment. A roommate, Nick Banchero, went to answer, holding a cup of beer. His girlfriend had left minutes before.

Banchero owned a hardwood-flooring business. He had moved into the apartment two years earlier, after answering a shared-housing ad.

On the other side of the door was a guy with a red jacket and a distinct upper lip, looking at Banchero, saying nothing.

Can I help you? Banchero asked.

A second guy—a big guy, muscular—charged into the apartment, holding a pistol. A black ski mask covered his face. Banchero watched him run toward Sullivan's room. When Banchero looked back, he saw that the man in the red jacket had pulled a gun of his own, a black semiautomatic.

Take whatever you want, Banchero said.

The man in the red jacket still said nothing. He pointed the gun at Banchero's face, from a foot away. He backed him up against a wall, put an index finger to Banchero's lips, and whispered, "Shhh."

Sullivan was on his bed, studying for a calculus exam, when he heard someone yell: "Freeze. Don't turn around. Don't look at me." Sullivan turned around. He saw a masked man with a silver automatic. He jumped up and grabbed for the gun. The two wrestled, then the masked man pulled the pistol away and whipped Sullivan over the head with it. As Sullivan fell back onto the bed, the gunman fired. The bullet sliced through Sullivan's right thigh and thudded into his chest.

The gunman went to Sullivan's closet, grabbed the quarter pound of marijuana, and ran out. Outside Sullivan's room, the masked man tripped over a telephone cord and slammed into a wall, denting it. He fell at Banchero's feet, knocking the beer out of his hands. To Banchero, it looked like the robber cut his hand or maybe his elbow. The robber scrambled out the door, on his hands and knees. The other gunman went with him, and the two disappeared into the night.

Sullivan staggered out of his room. Holding his chest, he managed to get out the words "I've been shot." Banchero grabbed Sullivan and laid him on the pool table, amid all the clutter.

The night had shattered into blood and confusion. Only one bullet had been fired, but Sullivan had been shot in both the leg and the chest. The slug had skimmed his diaphragm and punctured a lung. He had a head wound, too, from being whipped with the gun. Sullivan knew he was hurt bad. Shock eased his pain but not his fear. Lying there, he thought he might die at any moment.

A third roommate was in his room, watching TV. He had heard

the shot, but figured it was a backfire. Banchero called out to him: Charles! Kerry's been shot! Charles came out to help. If someone who's just been shot can be called lucky, then Sullivan was lucky. Charles was a nursing assistant at Harborview Medical Center, Seattle's leading trauma hospital. He applied pressure to Sullivan's chest wound while Banchero called 911.

Detective Mike Magan was at home, sleeping, when he was paged. He called the chief dispatcher at 11:10 p.m. and learned that there had just been a home-invasion robbery on Twenty-second Avenue. One victim had been shot and was being treated by paramedics. Magan called his sergeant. Then he picked him up, at home, and headed for the University District.

Magan was only thirty-seven, but his hair had long since turned gray, and he had already become a mythic figure in police circles. In 1997 the Seattle Police Department named him the North Precinct's Officer of the Year. The Police Guild went one better; Magan's peers voted him Officer of the Year for the whole city.

Back when movies depicted the police as good guys, the typical on-screen detective looked a lot like Magan. Irish, of course. A fourth-generation cop. Talks a big game—and backs it up. When Magan was in the academy, he rubbed some of his fellow recruits the wrong way. They considered him a legend in his own mind. "The story according to Mike," they'd say. But Magan became the real deal. His personnel file, an inch thick with commendations, recounts hunches he played, good-cop bad-cop routines, shootouts with Glocks and Berettas. He kept up with a fleeing car for eight blocks—while riding a bicycle. He talked a guy off the ledge on Christmas Eve. He wrestled a gun away, he drove a little old lady home. He even received letters of praise from defense attorneys. "He did everything correctly," one lawyer wrote to the police chief. "He was careful and polite—even though he had his gun pointed at my client's head."

Magan made his biggest mark taking down bank robbers: the Abe Lincoln Bank Robbers (they dressed as Honest Abe), the Hollywood Robber (he wore wigs and theatrical makeup), the Buck Knife Robber, the Briefcase Bandit, the No Joke Bandit ("This is no joke," he wrote in his notes to tellers). In three years Magan solved eighty-five holdups. He was in a bank, investigating a robbery, when along came another robber, holding the place up. Magan chased him down. While he was driving to an awards luncheon—where he was to be honored for taking down one robber—a call came in, and Magan caught another robber on the way. Once, he bumped shoulders with a guy on a sidewalk, apologized, and stopped cold. He had matched the face with an old FBI flier. "I guess you could say I have a photographic memory," Magan told a newspaper reporter. "But just when there's film in it." In 1999 Magan achieved a special fame peculiar to law enforcement officers: Ann Rule, the nation's premier chronicler of true crime, wrote a book about the Hollywood Robber case and Magan's role in cracking it.

Magan was also an athlete. In the early 1980s he played football at the UW under Coach Don James. Notre Dame had courted him as well, but Magan wanted to wear purple and gold, not green and gold. He was an offensive lineman before a back injury cut his playing days short. Years later, whenever Magan bumped into James, beads of sweat would form on the detective's back: "Because he laid down the law. If you fucked up, you were gone."

As a cop, Magan stayed in touch with the football program. Sometimes he would address the team on staying out of trouble. Sometimes he would just hang out and chat up the players. Jerramy Stevens, he says, "stayed away from me like the plague."

Magan knew Pharms, of course. A year earlier, Magan had even played a role in keeping Pharms on the field. Neuheisel had consulted Magan about some fight involving Pharms, and Magan had checked around and concluded Pharms wasn't at fault. The details about the incident went into a court file, and the whole court file wound up being sealed. The sealing order didn't comply with the legal requirements governing secrecy. But who was to know? Pharms's case simply joined hundreds of other files that had been illegally sealed in King County Superior Court. A newspaper investigation later found it in a pile of secrecy orders that provided shelter to the prominent and the powerful: doctors, lawyers, bankers, judges, software giants, professional athletes.

By the time Magan arrived at Twenty-second Avenue, it was 11:40 p.m. The Gang Crimes Unit was already there. They'd been in the neighborhood and were first to arrive.

The Gang Crimes detectives had already learned about the two gunmen, the stolen marijuana, the nature of Sullivan's work. And they'd already caught a break. After the shooting, a neighbor had looked out his apartment window and seen two men running north on Twenty-second Avenue. Both jumped into a car and stayed there for about a minute. Then they ran off. One of the men returned within seconds, fumbled around in the car, then ran off again. The neighbor flagged down police when they arrived and pointed them to the car, a white Chrysler LeBaron.

Magan walked around the car. He saw what appeared to be a blood smear on the driver's side door, near the handle. He looked closer and saw what appeared to be a fingerprint in the blood. Through a rear passenger window he saw a glove with blood on it. The glove was gray, with a gold and black Nike swoosh on the back. Magan recognized it. It was the same kind of glove the uw football team wore. He thought the glove might even be unique to the team, an exclusive issue from Nike. Magan took pictures of the car, the blood, the glove. Then he took an envelope and taped it to the car door, so that it covered the blood smear. He wanted to make sure the print wouldn't be destroyed when the car was towed to the police department for processing.

Magan went into the apartment and interviewed Nick Banchero, Sullivan's roommate. Banchero said he didn't know what Sullivan did in his free time, or why anyone would shoot him.

I'm having a real hard time believing you, Magan told Banchero. Looks to me like your roommate sold marijuana and was shot for his stash.

Banchero described what happened—the knock at the door, the gunmen on the other side.

Describe the masked man for me, Magan said.

Linebacker size, Banchero said. Six three, 240 pounds, muscular build.

As the two talked, Banchero said something about "J.P."

What was that? Magan asked.

Oh, nothing, Banchero said.

Magan recognized the initials.

You know Jeremiah Pharms? he asked.

Yeah, I know J.P., Banchero said. But that wasn't him.

When Pharms's name came up, Banchero started acting nervous. Magan thought he was holding back—afraid, maybe, of retaliation. The detective asked him again: You know Pharms?

Yes.

Was the masked man Pharms?

I couldn't tell, Banchero said. The guy was masked and the other guy had a gun at my head.

Magan had been at the scene for only an hour, but he knew who the shooter was, or at least he had a real good idea. The physical description fit. The initials fit. The glove fit. If ever a case begged to be closed—and closed quick—it was this one. Careless robber meets clever cop. This was no whodunit; it was more like a who-he-dun-it-with. Then the case took a turn. Sergeants from the robbery and Gang Crimes units talked it over, and it was decided that Gang Crimes would take the case. They got there first, and, as Magan says, "You catch, you clean." Magan pulled aside the lead detective, an officer named Jeffery Mudd.

Your suspect is going to be Jeremiah Pharms, Magan told Mudd.

Who's that? Mudd asked.

UW linebacker. No. 4. Goes by the initials J.P.

The Gang Crimes detectives processed the apartment. Mudd collected a bloodstained blanket from Sullivan's bed and found $940 under the mattress. But the detectives missed the safe in the locked closet, the one with all the marijuana inside. Sullivan would laugh about that later.

Magan helped out a bit more before moving on. The following afternoon, he told the UW's head trainer about the investigation. The shooter might be a football player, Magan said. Let me know if you see any suspicious injuries to an elbow or hand. Magan also talked to the UW's equipment manager, who provided a pair of the team's gloves for comparison. They matched the one found in the car. Nike later confirmed that the glove was custom-made for the UW football team.

Sullivan's luck didn't end with having a roommate who could handle gunshot wounds. The bullet had narrowly missed his liver. If it hadn't, he could well have died. Sullivan spent two and a half days in Harborview before being released. Doctors were unable to remove the bullet. In months and years to come, Sullivan would continue to suffer shortness of breath and an ache deep inside his shoulder.

Within days of the robbery, police collected all kinds of other evidence. Pieced together, it blinked like a neon arrow, pointing to one very large suspect. Sullivan told police he was 90 percent sure the shooter was Pharms. The shooter had the same build, the same thick neck. Sullivan also explained how he moved his stash around—under the bed, in a drawer, hidden away in some corner. But the shooter knew just where to go. That, too, tied in Pharms, since he had been in the bedroom three hours before and watched Sullivan retrieve the bag. When they processed the car used by the robbers, police found an empty gun holster on the floor behind the driver's seat. Police also tracked down the car's owner. The Chrysler belonged to a girlfriend of Pharms.

Police also had forensic evidence, just waiting to be tested. Some criminals leave a fingerprint. Some leave blood. Whoever shot Sullivan appeared to have left both. This case was no CSI candidate; there was nothing whiz bang about it. Somebody eyeballs the fingerprint under a microscope. Somebody else extracts a DNA profile from the blood. They compare the evidence with the suspect, assuming there is a suspect, and in this case there was, thanks to Magan. Now it was up to Detective Mudd to see if Pharms and the physical evidence matched, and to put the case to bed.

Marie 2

She grew up with the same friends, in the same suburb, in the same home, right on the golf course, twenty minutes east of Seattle. Her country-club neighborhood enforced its covenants and offered a bridge club and garden club, along with views of Lake Sammamish and the Cascade Mountains. She could have gone to just about any university. Her transcript shimmered with a 3.97 GPA from one of the country's best high schools. She was captain of the volleyball team. Captain of the tennis team. President of the student body. But she didn't apply to Harvard or Duke or Smith. Why bother? Some decisions get made before you know there's a choice.

She grew up watching football at Husky Stadium. "Ever since I can remember, we would go to games," she says. "My dad went to the U. My grandpa was in the Tyee Club—he gave the school tons of money every year." Her grandfather held season tickets on the 50-yard line, the best seats imaginable to watch Billy Joe Hobert and Steve Emtman and Mario Bailey, to watch Washington when Washington couldn't be beaten, winning five in a row, 10 in a row, 15, 20. "It was just a special day, to always spend it with grandpa and my dad," she says. "Usually the three of us would go, and get all bundled up, and bring hot chocolate." She was ten years old when Washington won the national championship. In high school, she went to the UW for summer volleyball camp.

She could have gone just about anywhere. But there was only one college she wanted to attend, so there was only one college where she applied. She was accepted, of course. She had made a pact with a friend that neither would say anything until both received word. Weeks later, her friend got in, too.

Tall and blonde, she managed to be both striking and sweet.

"The most innocent girl I know," one friend would later tell police. At the U, she was pre-med, determined to become a pediatrician. "I rushed, and did the sorority thing," she says. "I met new people, and they were great, the girls were great." She became a member of Pi Beta Phi, a sorority with white columns and red brick and brass letters. Her sorority sister Sunny Rockom says the house attracted women who were, "for lack of a better word, popular. I don't like that word, because it reminds me of high school. Just popular in the sense that they attracted smart, intelligent, beautiful, outgoing women." A touch of the old-fashioned remained. Male visitors would wait in the reception area while an announcement was made, over the intercom, that a particular sister had a gentleman caller, and the sister would come down to greet him.

Her friend Megan threw the javelin on Washington's track team. While working out Megan would run into football players. They'd say, we're having a party, why don't you come, and why don't you bring your friends?

That's how she met them, this group of football players who became such good buddies her freshman year. There was Wilbur, Geoff, Andy, Todd, Spencer, and Jerramy. Spencer had a crush on her, but she had a crush on Geoff, so Spencer became more like a big brother, someone she felt would protect her. Although she had a crush on Geoff, she didn't have sex with him, she didn't have sex with anyone, she was a virgin, and when the players learned about that, she heard it plenty. "They would tease me like a little sister," she says. The players lived in a split-level rental house four miles north of campus, and in the front yard she played catch with Jerramy, a player who was going to be a star. She threw a tight spiral, too. "I could throw and catch the ball pretty well," she says. Her roommate at Pi Beta Phi was seeing Jerramy, but it was casual, nothing too serious.

Her mom worried about her spending so much time with these football players. Her mom would say, "I just want you to be careful." Her mom would say, "Sweetheart, you just have to remember that they may be thinking something different than you are." And she would answer, "Oh, mom, they're not like that. . . . Mom, they're really nice guys. In fact, Jerramy makes sure what guys I should talk to, to make sure they're nice guys."

She looks back and says, "It was fun at the time." She looks back and says, "I was naive." Someday, when she's not so afraid anymore, she wants to warn other young women to be more aware than she was. She wants to go into sororities at the UW and say, "This is me, and I'm exactly like you." But it's been years now—and there's no telling when that day will come.

Fragments

3

June 4, 2000: Three Months before the Season Begins

Returning to his dorm after a night with friends, Chris, a freshman, walked south on Eighteenth Avenue, through the heart of Greek Row. He walked past Delta Kappa Epsilon, past Chi Omega, past the rhododendrons in bloom, all pink, white, and purple, past the oaks and maples and evergreens. He walked through the garbage that collects along Greek Row's sidewalks and gutters—broken glass, barbecue tins, gum wrappers, beer cans, flattened cups from Dick's Drive In. It was about 2:30 in the morning, maybe 2:45. Saturday night had rolled into Sunday. He walked past one fraternity or sorority after another—built in the 1920s or '30s, mostly—a mix of Collegiate Gothic and Georgian Revival, with stately columns, leaded windows, coats of arms, the occasional statue of a white lion. The breaks between buildings offered a view of the alley that runs behind Eighteenth Avenue. Lined with about two dozen dumpsters, the place reeks of beer, eggs, and urine. Music thumped at the end of the block. The Sigma Chi fraternity's "Jacked Up" party—an end-of-the-school-year blowout that draws hundreds of students—was still in swing.

As he approached the Kappa Sigma house, Chris saw them, off to the right. It was a man and a woman—up against the side of the fraternity house, between the avenue and the alley. The woman leaned against the wall, arms to her side. She was white, tall, with long blonde hair. She was wearing only a white bra and maybe underwear. The music was so loud that Chris could hardly hear anything else. The area was dark, but still he locked eyes with her. She just stared at him, eyes glazed. She looked drugged or drunk, like she was half passed out. "No one home" is how he would later describe it. "She didn't look like she was all there." To Chris, the situation didn't look right: "The male was controlling things. It wasn't a two-person interlude." The woman didn't even try to cover up. She just stared at Chris. The man was black and tall—a head taller than the woman, maybe more. He wore a white T-shirt and baggy pants, and was facing the woman, with his back to the freshman. Then he turned. When he caught sight of the passerby, he moved the woman behind some bushes, out of sight.

Chris didn't know what to do. He walked across the street and pretended to knock at an apartment building. Then he crossed back, to see if the two were still there. They were gone. Chris hurried back to his dorm, ten or fifteen minutes away, and called 911. His call came in at 3:14 a.m. He told police that what he'd seen looked like rape.

Greek Row, located just north of the university, belongs to the jurisdiction of the Seattle Police Department, not the campus police. The Seattle PD dispatched officers to look for the man and woman, but they were nowhere to be found.

Later that day, at about noon, Marie awoke in her bed at the Pi Beta Phi sorority. She had a headache and stomach pains. Her ribs were sore, her left knee bruised, her right ankle scratched. She could barely move. Her bra and tube top were around her waist, and the bra, usually white, was covered with dirt. Her underwear was missing. "What happened to me?" Marie asked her roommate.

About the same time—at noon, maybe one—Jerramy Stevens emerged from his room. He lived with several other football players in a rental house north of campus. Stevens pulled a pair of women's underpants out of his jeans pocket and said, "Look what I have."

Marie, a nineteen-year-old freshman at the UW, could remember only fragments of the previous night. She remembered having three beers with a couple of friends at her sorority. She remembered going to the Sigma Chi party, a block away, with the same two friends. They had taken the alley that connects the sorority and fraternity. Her sorority was on Seventeenth Avenue, on the alley's north end; Sigma Chi was on Eighteenth Avenue, on the alley's south end. Kappa Sigma was halfway between. In the alley, she bumped into Jerramy Stevens, a football player she knew. She said "hi" and continued on. She remembered getting to the party at around 11:30 p.m. She felt fine when she got there. She had a drink—a Tequiza, a sweet syrupy beer with lime, tequila, and nectar flavors thrown in. Some fraternity member in the kitchen area was handing them out. The first one she had, the bottle's cap was still on. Later, she got a second one—this time, with the cap off. After that, things got fuzzy. She remembered a friend asking her to go to the bathroom. She remembered talking to some people on the patio, where the band was playing. She remembered bumping into Spencer Marona, another football player she knew. She remembered thinking how drunk some of the girls were.

But she couldn't remember how she got home. She couldn't remember climbing into bed. She had no idea why her bra was dirty, or where her underwear was. Sitting there, in bed, her face bright red, her body layered in sweat, she kept telling her friends: "Look at my bra." She kept asking them: "What happened to me last night?"

Marie's friends searched the sorority's grounds for her underwear. They searched the alley behind the sorority—canvassing the block to the Sigma Chi house. They even searched a path through campus. But they came up empty.

Marie talked to friends who went with her to the party, or who saw her there. She talked to her roommate. She talked to Molly, Katie, Megan, Sterling, Jennifer. What some friends had seen offered little comfort. At the party, Marie seemed fine, at first. Then, all of a sudden, her speech became slurred. She started to stutter. She began to lean against people. To Molly, Marie acted drugged, "out of character," "out of control." She had never seen Marie like that before. Jerramy Stevens and Spencer Marona were at the party. Both were hitting on Marie, according to Molly. Marona said things like, "How about you and me?" One friend said Marie had her back to Stevens, and appeared to be rubbing against him. Another friend said Stevens had his hands on Marie's waist, and Marie leaned into him, unable to keep her balance. Alarmed, this friend called Marie away.

Marie's roommate tried to get her to leave; she asked Marie for her keys. Marie refused. So two of Marie's oldest friends took charge. Marie had known Maggie since first grade, Molly since sixth. "I don't know what's wrong with her, but we need to get her back to the house," Maggie told Molly. Marie's sorority was but a short walk away—two hundred steps, at most—but Molly and Maggie decided to drive her there. In back of Sigma Chi, a police officer drove up and saw the three, walking to Molly's car. Marie was in the middle, supported by her friends. The cop asked if Marie was all right. We're just taking her home, the friends said. They drove down the alley and, on the way, came across Stevens and Marona. The two football players were walking to a store, to buy some beer. Marie's friends told them that they were going to drop Marie off at her sorority. Then they drove on. In back of the sorority, Maggie offered to walk Marie in. But Marie said she saw some other friends in the alley and walked off, toward some other girls. Thinking Marie was safe, Molly and Maggie took off.

What happened after that, no one knew. How did Marie's clothes get dirty? Who were the friends she was walking toward? Where did she go afterwards? No one knew. Her memory all but gone, Marie began to worry. She couldn't understand it. She'd had that much to drink before, and without feeling like this, without blacking out. She began to fear that maybe she had been "roofied," or slipped a date-rape drug. She'd heard stories of that happening at fraternity parties, but had no idea if the stories were true.

Marie stayed in bed most of the day. "She looked like hell," one friend said. Marie tried to make herself vomit, but couldn't. When she had a bowel movement, it was painful. On a chair in Marie's room, a friend spotted a fleece jacket, cream colored, covered in dirt and maybe blood. This was the same jacket Jerramy

Stevens had been wearing the night before. Marie's roommate told Marie: "Maybe Jerramy walked you home."

Fliers posted at Marie's sorority had advertised the party: "Countdown to Jacked Up, 8 p.m., June 3." Guys needed invitations. Girls just needed to show up. About three hundred people attended the party, with two girls for every guy.

Regulations governed parties like this, but the Sigma Chi house frequently ignored them. Fraternities were supposed to register parties with the university. This helped to alert police and liquor-control agents, who could conduct spot inspections. Fraternities were also supposed to control access to parties—and make sure underage kids didn't get served.

Sigma Chi violated these rules time and again, with little in the way of punishment. The fraternities and sororities sat north of campus, in an eight-block area that included houses and apartments. The university held the Greek system at arm's length, saying it bore no legal responsibility for what happened there. The university also claimed its student code of conduct did not apply there, freeing individuals from the threat of expulsion. The worst the university would do was withhold official recognition from some fraternity—meaning the fraternity wouldn't get the names of incoming freshmen, a list useful for recruiting. The UW and the Interfraternity Council sometimes imposed lesser penalties, but to little effect. Here was the pattern at Sigma Chi, established in the years prior to the 2000 Jacked Up party. The fraternity would fail to register a party. Minors would be served alcohol. The fraternity would be warned, or reprimanded, or fined ($1,000), or placed on probation (for two weeks). Sigma Chi would pledge to take steps to make sure it wouldn't happen again. Then it would happen again.

Sigma Chi received a reprimand for not registering the Jacked Up party in June. But it had done the same thing five months before, and would do the same thing three months later. University records and police reports detailed other incidents as well. Shooting fireworks at a man's house nearby. Throwing bottles at a student walking past. Beating a guest, unprovoked, throwing him down the stairs, and dragging him back for more. Belittling cops who showed up. One member, drunk, called an officer "Einstein." Sigma Chi fined him $100 and placed him on social probation for a month. Witnesses saw pledges duct-taped to chairs and smeared with food. At other times, pledges would be refused inside the house; they'd stand in the rain, two by two, as music played, Gregorian chants or The Doors' "The End." Sometimes violence erupted at Sigma Chi parties, with the occasional member getting hit over the head with a beer bottle. One time, three members were shot and wounded when someone opened fire on the fraternity, blasting out the windows to the bar and dance room.

That Sunday afternoon, while Marie and her friends at the sorority tried to piece together what had happened, Jerramy Stevens divulged details to teammates at his house.

When Stevens pulled out the pair of women's underwear, Spencer Marona asked him: Who'd you get laid with?

Marie, Stevens said.

No you didn't, Marona said. No way.

Yeah, Stevens said. I did.

Marona couldn't believe it. That's because he knew Marie was a virgin. With friends of hers, she would often come over to the house and hang out. One time, they all played this drinking game, called "I Never." Someone says something like, "I never kayaked before." Whoever has kayaked, has to drink. When someone said I never had sex before, Marie didn't drink. Bullshit, the guys said, calling her out. But she told them: No, really. I'm a virgin. Her friends said it was true. One night, Marie slept over at the football players' house—but even then, it hadn't led to sex.

How'd you get her panties, man? Marona asked.

She didn't give a shit, Stevens said.

Later the same afternoon, Marona, a defensive lineman from

Oregon, asked for details. Stevens said they'd had vaginal intercourse, and that he had also put his finger in Marie's anus.

Were you wearing a jimmy? Marona asked, using a slang term
for a condom.

No, Stevens said.

What the fuck? Did you bust in her?

No, Stevens said. He had pulled out before ejaculating.

Word of what Stevens was saying started to get around. When
one football player asked another, *Did you hear that Jerramy fucked
Marie in the dirt outside Sigma Chi?*, one of Marie's friends overheard. She carried the story back with her to the sorority.

Late that afternoon, Marie's roommate went to campus for a study
session. Stevens was there, too. The roommate sat next to him.

Thanks for walking Marie home last night, she said.

You're welcome, Stevens said.

By evening, the story circulating among Stevens's teammates made
it back to Marie. It was Katie who told her. Marie's eyes got huge.
She had a look of complete horror on her face, Katie recounted later.
Marie worried that maybe she'd been sexually assaulted. She worried about sexual disease. She worried about being pregnant.

Should I get a morning-after pill? she asked Katie.

Let's wait and see what Jerramy has to say, Katie told her.

Katie called Jerramy's house, pressing *67 to bypass caller
ID. No one answered. That night, at about 9:30, Marie called the
players' house. Marona answered.

Do you know what happened to me last night? Marie asked.
She was crying.

No, Marona told her.

It's not my business to say, he figured. He handed the phone
to Stevens. Stevens took the phone into his room and shut the
door.

What happened to me last night? Marie asked Stevens.

I walked you home, Stevens said.

Marie asked the question again.

We kissed and some stuff, Stevens said.

Did we have sex?

No. Don't trip. It's nothing. Don't worry about it.

So we didn't have sex?

No.

Then why are you telling your friends that you fucked me in the dirt?

Stevens denied saying any such thing.

Stevens walked out of his room.

She was fucking crying, Stevens told Marona.

Why?

She claimed she didn't remember having sex with me, Stevens said.

Bullshit. No way, dude, Marona said.

Stevens told Marona what he'd said to Marie on the phone.

You need to call her back, Marona said. You need to fucking let her know you had sex. You at least owe her that.

Late that night Marie still ached, and by now she was vomiting, lime green. She called Molly and asked for a ride to the university hospital, across from Husky Stadium. Marie puked in the parking lot. Inside, she was given a shot for nausea and told she needed to go to another hospital for a sexual-assault exam. Marie called her mother and said she'd been hurt.

I think I've been assaulted, she said.

I'll be right there, Marie's mother told her.

Marie's parents jumped in their car, with Marie's dad asking question after question, and Marie's mother saying, "I don't know, we just have to get there."

When they got there, Marie's mother looked into her daughter's eyes and saw how lost she was. "I'll never forget that look. Her eyes were just empty." Answers? Marie didn't have any. She didn't know what had happened to her. They left for Harborview Medical Center, Dad driving, Mom and Marie in the back-seat. "I just held her, and she just cried and cried and cried." Her mother's mind raced. Who would do this to her daughter? Her daughter, without an enemy in the world; her daughter, who always worried about everybody else's feelings. If she was going to be out late, she'd call and say, "Mom, I don't want you to worry," and her mom would say, "Sweetheart, you can stay out another half hour." Marie's mother put her daughter's face in her hands and said, "Sweetheart, we will get through this, we will get through this together."

At Harborview, Marie's mom called Marie's brother and said Marie had been attacked, and the brother's heart fell, he thought for a moment his sister was dead, and the mom said, no, no, she's at Harborview. The brother rushed to the hospital in such a fog that he later wouldn't even remember driving there.

Marie's family waited while Marie was in the back, with doctors, nurses, kits, tests, procedures, pills, concerns about pregnancy, syphilis, gonorrhea. They took a urine sample. They drew her blood to test for HIV.

Medical personnel recovered semen from Marie's vagina—and from her rectum.

A doctor told Marie that her anus had been torn.

Stirrings

4

Anthony Kelley wanted it all. Put something in front of him, and he'd lunge for it. On the football field, he wanted to play wide receiver, and tight end, and safety, and linebacker. He wanted to play both sides of the ball, just like he did in high school. The coaches at Washington would say, Anthony, pick one, learn the position, settle in, then we'll see. But all his life he'd had so little to choose from. Settle in? When had he ever been allowed to settle in to anything? No, Kelley didn't want to pick just one. He wanted it all.

In the summer of 2000, not long before the season's first game, Kelley sat in the office of Tom Williams, an assistant coach in charge of Washington's outside linebackers. Williams, a coach who knew something about wanting it all, was about to put something else in front of Kelley—something that had nothing to do with football, something that would change Kelley's life in ways the young player could hardly imagine. Sometimes, inspiration comes by design, in words chosen for a select audience and a singular moment. This wasn't one of those times. This was a chance conversation—one that would lead Kelley to discover the world and his place in it.

Sitting there in Williams's office, Kelley's eyes happened upon a picture on the wall. The photo was of Williams, running with a bunch of bulls.

What's that about? Kelley asked.

Williams was thirty years old, the youngest of Washington's nine assistant coaches. But he seemed wise beyond his years. He had *always* seemed wise beyond his years. That's one reason his college teammates nicknamed him "Old Man"—that, and the way he got grumpy when he didn't have enough to eat. His résumé included two degrees from Stanford—a bachelor's and master's—and four varsity letters in football, at inside linebacker. He was twice a First-Team Academic All-Pac-10. And he was a Rhodes Scholar candidate. Williams had also traveled, using school or work to take him somewhere new. A Texas native—in high school, he was All State in football, basketball, and baseball—Williams had spent three summers in Alaska, working eighteen-hour days in a salmon cannery; five months in Japan, as defensive coordinator for the semi-pro Fujitsu Frontiers; and three years at the University of Hawaii, helping coach the Rainbow Warriors.

His mentor was one of the brainiest coaches in the sport's history. Bill Walsh looked like a professor (silver hair, craggy face), talked like a professor (versed in mythology, fond of words like "salient"), and was treated like a professor, forever tagged a genius. After leading the San Francisco 49ers to three Super Bowl victories, Walsh returned to Stanford in the early 1990s. Williams was a captain on Walsh's 1992 team, which blew up all the football stereotypes. With sterling SAT scores and a collective graduation rate of about 90 percent, Stanford finished 10-3, ranked ninth in the country, with wins over USC, Penn State, and Notre Dame. While Jackie Sherrill, the Mississippi State coach, fired up his players by having a bull castrated before their game against the Texas Longhorns, Walsh lectured his players about the Wildebeest Syndrome, describing how wildebeests go into shock before being devoured, to prevent pain. "We will not be a wildebeest," Walsh told his players.

One of Stanford's three losses that year was to Washington, and it was ugly. The UW drubbed Stanford, 41–7, the Huskies' twenty-second straight win over three seasons.

After getting his bachelor's degree, Williams played briefly with the 49ers. He considered law school, but Walsh convinced him to try coaching and hired him as a graduate assistant.

Now Williams was in his second year at Washington—a bit ironic, given his mentor's feelings toward the school. To Walsh, Washington in the 1980s and early '90s had become the anti-

Stanford, a university that said student-athlete but really meant the student part to be silent, sort of like the "p" in pneumatic, a word that means full of gas or wind. In 1993, Walsh lit into Washington during a speech to Stanford alumni, saying: "The football players there have almost no contact with the rest of the student body. They have an athletic department compound, and that's where they spend their time. When they use up their eligibility and are expected to return to society, they have none of the skills you are supposed to gain in college." Walsh decried how Washington loaded up with players unprepared for college, and expected them to manage.

He later apologized—with one of those *sorry about that, I shouldn't have said it, even if it was true* numbers—but the statistics backed him up. Only a third of Washington's players graduated. More than four of every five failed to meet the uw's minimum admission standards—the second-worst showing among ninety-five universities in a national survey.

In Seattle, Williams tried to instill some of Walsh's philosophy into Washington, however discreetly. Williams believed his role didn't end with teaching defensive schemes and how to use a swim move to reach the quarterback. He didn't want players to get so caught up in the demands of football—training, drilling, lifting, studying film, running some play over and over—that they never saw the world outside. When he played at Stanford, Williams also sang in the gospel choir and studied the piano. In years to come he would leave a coaching job in the NFL to become the head coach at Yale, the first African American to hold that position.

Williams liked Kelley, this kid sitting in front of him, twenty years old, forever jabbering, smiling, longing, wanting something else or something more. To Williams, Kelley had a touch of Muhammad Ali, the infectiousness, the way he could draw people to him and make them laugh.

That picture? Williams said. That's me in Spain. In Pamplona.

Williams told Kelley how he had traveled to Europe the year before and run with the bulls. It was a return trip, a chance to revisit places he'd seen in college. When he was a junior, Williams had studied abroad in Florence, Italy, a city bursting with history, art, and ideas—conquered by Charlemagne, home to Michelangelo's *David*, the birthplace of Machiavelli's *The Prince*.

It was one of the best things I've ever done, Williams told Kelley. An amazing experience.

You should consider doing something like that yourself, he said.

But keep this between us. This is unofficial.

Kelley was both mystified and drawn. How could Williams have managed such a thing? How could he have played football in one of the country's elite conferences and studied in some city across the ocean? The very idea baffled the young player. But Williams had placed something in front of Kelley—a challenge of sorts, complete with a warning. This isn't something you can lunge for, Williams told Kelley. This is something you have to work for, prepare for, apply for, something you have to want today and tomorrow and months from now.

Nothing in Kelley's background prepared him for the possibility of something so fantastic. To study abroad, you need a passport, right? Kelley didn't even have a driver's license. He didn't have a bank account, either, because what was the point, he had no money to put in it. He was sure he had a birth certificate, but he'd be damned if he knew where to find it.

Before attending Stanford, Tom Williams had gone to a private prep school in Fort Worth, on a campus with seventy-five acres, with advance-placement classes and teachers and counselors who excelled at preparing kids for the demands of college. Kelley wasn't so fortunate. His parents split before he reached elementary school, and ever since he had moved from parent to parent and place to place, picking up and putting down in San Diego, in Flint, Michigan, in Pasadena. With his mom he was homeless for maybe half a year, living out of the family car. Another time, he lived in an apartment above a pawnshop. He seemed always to be between worlds: his mother white, his father black; a child pushed into the role of parent, taking care of his young sisters; a teenager living in a Bloods neighborhood, not wanting to join, not wanting to piss them off, either. He bounced around high schools in Michigan and California before landing for good at John Muir High in Pasadena, living with his dad, in a rough neighborhood, attending a school that was half black, half Hispanic, with a lousy track record for academics. From the roof of his dad's home he could see the Rose Bowl Stadium, with its whitewashed walls and that neon rose, a tease in the night.

In school, Kelley struggled, and was eventually diagnosed with attention deficit disorder. But he excelled in track and football. He played tight end on offense (34 catches, 824 yards, 9 touchdowns his senior year) and linebacker on defense (102 tackles, with 15 sacks). "Football was an outlet," Kelley said. "When I played, I was tired of my life, and football was the type of therapy poor people could afford. At John Muir High School, me and guys like Sultan McCullough, we were playing for our life. When you are dead broke, winning is all you have." McCullough, a running back, went on to USC and then to a professional career in the NFL and the Canadian Football League. Kelley aimed to do the same.

In the spring of 1997, his junior year, Kelley received a recruiting letter, and not just any recruiting letter, but one from Nebraska, the best team in college football. The Cornhuskers had gone undefeated and won national championships in 1994 and 1995, and would do the same in 1997. Now, more than ever, Kelley needed to bear down in class, to take advantage. "My father was like, 'You need to get good grades so you can get this football scholarship.' My coaches were like, 'You need to get good grades so you can get this football scholarship.'" Learning wasn't what mattered. What mattered was finding a way to stay on the field, to get to the next level, to keep to the path leading to professional ball.

The NCAA requires incoming student-athletes to meet a set of requirements, dictated in the language of numbers, with particular attention paid to core classes taken, GPA, and college-board score.

Kelley had to round up transcripts from all these high schools just to figure out where he stood. He wound up taking a heavy class load his senior year in hopes of catching up. His learning disability complicated matters, with questions raised about particular classes and whether they passed NCAA muster. His GPA, which hovered around 2.0, didn't inspire hope. Nor did his SAT score—a dismal 770, a far cry from that year's national average of 1,017.

This didn't deter the football powerhouses from courting him. Washington joined the hunt. So did Michigan, a team that went undefeated in 1997 and shared the national championship with Nebraska. Kelley looked at the star of that Michigan team—the wondrous Charles Woodson, a star on defense, star on offense, star on special teams, winner of the Heisman Trophy—and saw a player who wanted it all and got it all, a player Kelley could model himself after.

In January 1998, Kelley gave every indication that he would be heading to Washington, making him one of the Huskies' most prized recruits. But in February, he said he had picked Michigan instead. Then, within a day, he changed his mind back, saying he had settled on Washington. "I don't know what I was thinking," he told a Seattle newspaper. Pick one? He didn't want to pick one. He wanted to please his mom, who lived in Flint, and wanted Michigan. But picking Michigan didn't sit well with his dad, out on the West Coast. In the end, Kelley went with his gut, and his gut said Washington.

But after Kelley finished his final year of high school, the NCAA ruled that his transcript didn't cut it. He couldn't suit up. Washington decided to stick with him anyway. He became the football team's first partial qualifier—a so-called Proposition 48 player, meaning he couldn't play for a year, but if he did okay in classes, he could play the next. At Washington, some students already looked down on football players, knowing they wouldn't have been let in without athletics. For Kelley, being a partial qualifier carried a stigma beyond even that, like someone had slapped a sticker on his back that said "Stupid."

Once he reached campus, Kelley buckled down. He struggled with taking notes, but asked for help, and got better. He struggled with essays, but asked for help, and got better. All these basics that other students had picked up years before, Kelley picked up now. But he swung it. He managed to get by, to do enough, to earn his way back onto the football field.

He became eligible to play in 1999, his second year on campus. In the season's first game, against BYU, Washington threw him in at linebacker. Called to blitz, Kelley, a bundle of nerves, had "like a thousand things" going through his head. "I stood there for five seconds pounding my feet," he says. Before the play even started, he was out of breath. As a backup linebacker and special-teams player, Kelley appeared in every game in 1999, and earned his first letter. He didn't set the field afire, but he showed flashes, enough to be named a starter for the 2000 season.

In many ways, Kelley epitomized how sports can bring a measure of social justice to campus, drawing students from backgrounds that don't typically lead to top universities. Some of his teammates on the 2000 squad could relate. Hakim Akbar's father was in prison for armed robbery. Omare Lowe, at age eight, saw his mother killed by a drunk driver. As a child he bounced from one foster home to another, skipped classes, stole. But hardship wasn't universal. One player's father was a police chief, another's a rodeo star. One's was a football coach, another's a minister. J. K. Scott, a backup quarterback, came from the Los Angeles suburbs, looking like a surfer, with a 3.97 high school GPA.

A football team tends to be about as diverse a group as you'll find on any campus. Ossim Hatem, a Muslim, observed Ramadan. Ben Mahdavi, a Jew, became a first-team All-American selection by the *Jewish Sports Review*—and who even knew there was such a team? Some players grew up on farms, some in rough neighborhoods like Compton. Some were married. A few had kids. Thirty-eight of the 107 players on the 2000 team were from California. Used to sunshine, many hated the Seattle gray. Downpours were rare. But did the sky have to keep spitting like that?

Some players were blue-chip recruits who had been courted by dozens of schools. Others were happy to play without a scholarship, walk-ons like Jason Simonson, an offensive lineman. In five years he played only one down that wasn't in mop-up time—and on that play the opposing player dropped back in pass coverage, leaving Simonson with no one to block. "I sat there, with the nicest-looking pass protection, but I never touched a soul," he says. Simonson could have played more at a smaller college, but doesn't second-guess his decision to walk on at the UW. "It is the greatest sport you can ever play or be a part of. Nothing in life is so grand. It's football, what can I say? And on top of that, it's Husky football. To me, I was basically living the dream."

The football program threw all these kids together—in dorms, in the weight room, on the field—and offered them up to the university, with its promise of a world-class education.

In the center of the UW campus, the soaring Suzzallo Library tells any new student that this is a place where academics are taken seriously. Built in grand Gothic style, the library has eighteen terracotta statues that greet visitors: Moses, Dante, Shakespeare, Herodotus, Beethoven. Inside, the reading room's sixty-five-foot-high ceiling can inspire—or intimidate. The UW president who built the library in the 1920s, Henry Suzzallo, talked about it being the soul of a "University of a Thousand Years." For a place like Seattle, with its short and gritty history, the building represented something solid, something of substance.

The students began living up to its grandeur. Over the years, the UW became a public school where locals found it harder and harder to get accepted. On the south side of campus, across the hand-laid bricks of Red Square and past Drumheller Fountain—where, legend has it, upperclassmen once tossed freshmen into the pool—the UW medical school became so celebrated that it was named the nation's best for primary care. Other programs flourished, too. Computer scientists created one of the country's top-ranked graduate programs, in a building paid for by Paul Allen.

When Allen was a teenager at Lakeside High School, he would visit the UW to tinker on the old mainframe computers with his buddy, Bill Gates. Together, the two would later start Microsoft.

But at the UW, there has always been the upper campus and the lower campus. The Suzzallo Library and the Paul Allen Center are on the upper campus. Go down the hill, to the shores of Lake Washington, and you find the lower campus. That's where the gymnasium is, and the baseball fields, the basketball pavilion, the football fields. That's where the athletes study when they're not in class, and that's where they play on Saturdays in Husky Stadium.

By the time Anthony Kelley arrived, thousands of would-be freshmen were being turned away from the upper campus. The average GPA of those accepted had reached 3.65, the average SAT score, 1,155. Kelley's numbers—a 2.0 or thereabouts, and a 770—didn't come close to measuring up. But he wasn't alone. Plenty of other players also got admitted on an entirely different set of numbers—ones that measured potential on the football field, not in the classroom. Like how many times they could bench-press two hundred pounds. How many inches they could jump straight up. Whether they ran 40 yards in 4.4 seconds or 4.6. Lots of players would have had no prayer of being admitted to the UW based on their academic performance. But, like most schools competing in Division 1, the UW has created a loophole. It ignores its own academic floor in the case of thirty or so athletes each year, allowing them in as "special admits."

At the UW, Kelley found a small army of people waiting to help him and the other struggling athletes. There were the four academic coordinators, the two academic advisers, the learning specialist, and the supervisor. There was the team of eighty part-time tutors, working five to twenty hours a week, attending the players' classes, taking lecture notes, and explaining concepts to Kelley and the others in study sessions.

When Bill Walsh had called out Washington in the early 1990s, his words stung. So did the NCAA reports that detailed how poorly Washington's football players fared in the classroom. So did the newspaper stories, with headlines like "A Matter of Degree— Husky Football Program Coming Up Anything but Roses Academically." One NCAA report looked at all athletes, regardless of sport, and found that at Washington, 62 percent of the white athletes graduated, compared to 37 percent of the black athletes. Ron Sims, a King County councilman, bristled at the disparity: "You get angry at a program that uses kids up. We can't have them coming back into the neighborhoods without degrees because the little kids look up to them."

Barbara Hedges, who became Washington's athletic director in 1991, made clear that she wanted these academic measures to improve. By 2000, she had her wish. Upwards of 60 percent of the football players now graduated, a figure comparable to the student body as a whole. But what kind of education were they getting? Robert Aronson, a law professor, served as faculty representative to the athletic department. He watched as Stan Chernicoff, the director of student-athlete academic services, clashed with coaches. Chernicoff's view was: I'm an educator. My goal isn't just to meet minimum NCAA rules. It's to prepare students for life. But if Chernicoff steered some player toward difficult courses, he might get blowback from the athletic department. "The coaches would say, 'Why would you put him in a program where he might not remain eligible?'" Aronson says. To compound matters, Aronson saw the athletic department put "undue pressure" on the admissions office to accept players who were not up to the UW's academic challenges.

To new players, the team's upperclassmen whispered which classes were easy. Stick with Sociology, they would say. Or Dinosaurs. Or Paper Science, which is the science of making paper, not science *on* paper. Some players found a teacher they liked and simply made up their own major, studying in their own time, not needing to go to any particular classes. Forget about a degree in history or biology. These players majored in "Sports Management," or "Multicultural Leadership," or "Media Presentation."

When the university wrote a report on its special admits, it found they did okay for a quarter but then began to flounder. The athletes tended to cluster in the same classes, but at a certain point, those classes would run out.

Of course, Washington was hardly alone in catering to athletes. Lots of universities pile up the credits for student-athletes without offering an actual education. The *Washington Post* found nearly three dozen universities that award credits—as many as four—to athletes simply for playing their sport, for going to practice, for showing up for games. The University of Georgia offered a class, "Coaching Principles and Strategies of Basketball," that had only one exam, with twenty questions, multiple choice. The questions included: How many halves are in a college basketball game? How many quarters in a high school game? How many points is a 3-point field goal worth?

For his major, Kelley initially picked sociology. It seemed to be what the others were doing. But there was something different about Kelley. In the athletes' study hall, down in the Conibear Shellhouse where the crew team launched its boats onto Lake Washington, Kelley was hanging around and getting involved. Some players avoided that place, in case anybody noticed how much they were slacking. Others came in exhausted, demoralized, even in tears. But Kelley, he was diving into academics, even though he didn't have any idea how to swim. Sarah Winter, she noticed.

At twenty-four, Winter, an academic adviser, was barely older than some of her students. But she had grown up in a world where books mattered. As a girl in Connecticut, she'd fallen in love with reading. Grades came easily to her, and she'd decided she wanted to teach. Before graduating from Indiana University, she had finished a stint as a student teacher at a boarding school on the giant Navajo reservation, which sprawls across Arizona, Utah, and New Mexico. For a time, she'd found out what it was like to be in the racial minority. She'd seen firsthand the poverty and lack of resources that drove parents to leave their five-year-old children at the school for a week at a time.

Later, when she taught at a high school in Bloomington, Indiana, she noticed that the advanced classes were stacked with kids whose parents were professors, while the remedial classes were full of kids from rural areas. In Goshen, Ohio, it was the same sort of thing. There were kids who were pregnant, kids who were addicts, kids who had fewer chances because of their backgrounds. Winter decided she'd had enough of the classroom. She wanted to work more one-on-one, to help students succeed no matter their background or baggage.

She took the UW job in 1998, the same year Kelley started. Winter noticed the way Kelley seemed so full of life, how he made friends wherever he went. Everyone loved him, and it wasn't hard. Sometimes he would stay behind in her office, just chatting, taking it all in. With his learning disabilities he struggled those first two years, confronting academic demands that were beyond him. But he'd kept going, he'd made it through.

Then he came to her with his idea. After the football season, he wanted to study abroad. Winter almost broke down in tears. It was madness. It was absurd. It was wonderful. It was thrilling. It had never been done before. Football players just didn't do that sort of thing. And he was a starter. A big part of the team. The team that all those people talked about on sports radio and read about in the newspapers, the team that all those thousands of people paid so much money to come and watch. The coaches wouldn't like it. Kelley knew it. Winter knew it. But yet.

There was so much to think about. Anthony had missed out on so much growing up. He had never been out of the country. Could he round up the records needed for a passport? Where would he get the money for a plane ticket? And what would people think? How would the other players react? And the coaches, the coaches. They weren't going to like it. No way. Winter said she was going to help Kelley. Through every step, through every turn. She was going to get him on that plane. But they both realized they had to keep it all quiet. Real quiet.

Louisville Slugger 5

Detective Maryann Parker opened the case file to find only four pages inside. There was an incident report—a fill-in-the-blank form, one page, with the words "Sexual Assault" written in the box for Incident Classification. And there was a follow-up report, three pages, drawn up by an officer who had talked to Marie and her mother. For Parker, these four pages offered both promise and foreboding. The follow-up report listed a possible suspect: Jerramy Stevens, "BM, approx. 20, 6-7, 250." That was the encouraging part—starting with a suspect. The discouraging part was reading Marie's account, which was notable mostly for what was missing. Marie's whereabouts for ten or eleven hours were a mystery. Whatever happened between the Sigma Chi party and when she awoke at noon in her sorority, Marie couldn't say. She was with someone, but did she tell him no? Yes? Anything at all? Marie couldn't say.

It was 9 a.m. on June 6 when Parker received the case. Marie had called Seattle police the previous evening, one day after her trip to the hospital. An officer had met Marie and her mother in a parking lot in the University District. Marie's mother handed the officer the bra and pants Marie had been wearing the night of the party, along with the fleece jacket that belonged to Stevens and which had been found in Marie's room. The officer placed each item in a separate bag.

As thin as it was, the file sketched the case's essential elements, generating a list of questions that would occupy Parker for months to come. Was Marie drugged? Did she have sex with Stevens? If she did, was it consensual or forcible? Was Marie in any condition even to be capable of consent? And if she wasn't, did Stevens know that? The report said Marie had talked to Stevens before going to the hospital, and that he'd tried several times since then to reach her again. Marie had refused to answer his calls. Parker started putting out calls and rounding up paper. When she called to arrange an interview with Marie, Marie's mother answered, and talked of how distraught her daughter was. Parker faxed a release form to the hospital to get Marie's medical records. She also ran Stevens's name through a criminal-history index—and got a hit, for a previous charge of felony assault.

As a police officer, Parker knew she couldn't rely on muscle. She was five foot five and 125 pounds, maybe 130, hardly enough weight to throw around. She couldn't brace people—she couldn't intimidate—so she found other ways. She always carried a pack of gum or Life Savers. If some guy was going ballistic, spitting in her face, she'd pull the gum out and ask if he'd like a stick. Casual as can be. Want some gum? Just the question—the gesture, an act among friends—would defuse the situation. How do you accept a piece of gum and then start throwing punches? The guy would calm down. Then Parker could start over.

By the summer of 2000, she had been a Seattle police officer for fourteen years. She had worked her way up to detective in the Special Assault Unit, where she investigated rape cases and crimes against children. This was no unit for the cartoonish detectives of hardboiled fiction, all hard edges, grim, as though they alone had seen the truth, and the truth did not abide solace or hope. Detectives in the Special Assault Unit could be as much counselors as cops, comforting victims who often struggled with embarrassment or shame. For Parker, this came easy. Some cops kick ass, take names, move on. Parker liked to stay behind, look around, and see if maybe she could help put the pieces back together.

Parker's mother, Thelma, was ahead of her time—a successful businesswoman, single, in the 1920s and '30s. Her business happened to be keeping the books and selling illegal slot machines for criminal types in Chicago and San Francisco. The mob? Maybe, probably, it's hard to say now. Thelma was a looker—her picture graced a matchbook cover—and a flashy dresser. During the Depression, she drove a twelve-cylinder Lincoln convertible and bought her own house. Later, she didn't say much about those years, at least not to her children. But she kept the photographs. And in every one, it seems, she's wearing a fancy hat and sitting in the lap of some gangster.

In her early thirties, Thelma settled down with John Parker, a military man. Maryann, their third child, grew up on the family's farm in Redmond, Washington, riding, from the age of three, quarter horses through woods that would later become the campus for Microsoft. At twenty, Maryann got married. Her husband had gone to high school with her, in Seattle. He'd been on the football team. Running back, she thinks, but she isn't sure. They had a boy and a girl, but, after ten years, divorced. Single, without a degree to fall back on, Parker needed a career to raise her kids. She joined the police force at the age of thirty-three. At the time, few officers were women, not even 1 in 10. Parker liked the idea of being outside, of helping people, meeting them under all circumstances, good and bad, of doing something different every day.

The job didn't disappoint. She worked patrol, the night shift, 8 p.m. to 4 a.m. Then she joined the anti-crime team, serving search warrants on crack houses. Once, amid the litter and stench, a woman charged at her with a knife. The woman also held a baby, which she just tossed away, like some teenager flinging off a backpack. Luckily, the baby landed on a mattress, unharmed, and another officer took the woman down.

In other assignments, Parker worked undercover, doing drug buys and playing decoy, looking to lure some robbery suspect. She did community policing, back when it was something new. Weed and seed. Weed out the drug dealers, seed the neighborhood with drug-treatment programs and shelters from violence. She worked narcotics, mounted patrol, gang prevention. She was tapped for an FBI task force. Parker received good assignments and was often the only woman in her unit. She knew what some people whispered:

Who'd she sleep with to get that job? She received praise from sergeants, lieutenants, captains, and assistant chiefs for her fairness, compassion, dedication, and instincts. "An excellent patrol officer . . . an outstanding investigator . . . a real professional."

"Maryann Parker was one of the best cops I met during my 34 years in policing," says Norm Stamper, Seattle's police chief from 1994 until February 2000. "She had all the basics: smarts, diligence, determination, exceptional observation skills, an admirable work ethic, and impeccable ethical standards. Her BS detector was especially acute. And she was absolutely fearless in the face of personal danger or the lazy or unethical behavior of peers, superiors, or outsiders from other agencies or institutions. I never saw her get holy or self-righteous about it, but if someone was doing something wrong—or not doing what needed to be done—she'd be in their face. Justice mattered."

In Parker's personnel file, it is the letters from the community that stand out, the letters from parents of troubled kids whose lives she helped reclaim. Before joining the Special Assault Unit, Parker worked on the department's Team for Youth, trying to save kids from themselves and the streets. Without Parker, one mother wrote, "I would not only have lost my son, but my own soul." Another mother wrote a five-page letter, describing Parker's commitment to her daughter. Before tenth grade, the woman's daughter, Sarah, could recite long passages from *Macbeth* and did honors math. Then she began shooting crystal methamphetamine into her veins. Her boyfriend beat her, busting her nose, breaking a rib. She dropped out of school. She got hepatitis, types A and C, and her weight plummeted to eighty-five pounds, her arms like chopsticks, her neck so weak she could barely lift her head. She communicated in growls. She was close to dying. For hours on end, Parker searched streets and houses, looking for Sarah. She convinced a court commissioner to hold Sarah long enough in detention to dry her out. When Sarah escaped from drug treatment, Parker hunted her down at a bus depot, and started over. She drove Sarah to assessment appointments, arranged meetings with a case manager, and showed up at her court hearings. She won Sarah's respect and her mother's gratitude. When Sarah's mother wrote the letter, Sarah's weight had returned to 125 pounds. She was at home, obeying curfew. She'd been clean for four and a half months and had finished her GED. "Detective Parker is with Sarah every step of the way," the mother wrote.

If anyone could help fill in the blanks of what happened on Greek Row that spring morning, it was Jerramy Stevens. On June 15, Parker went with another detective to Stevens's house—but no one was home. She tried reaching Stevens at Husky Stadium—but was told practice didn't start until August. She left a message on Stevens's phone—but he didn't call back. Marie's blackout and Stevens's silence made this anything but a typical investigation of alleged acquaintance rape. This was no case of he said, she said. She couldn't remember. He wouldn't talk.

Parker picked up the medical records at Harborview. The doctor's report said Marie's condition could be consistent with forcible rape. The report also said Marie's condition could be consistent with consensual sex. It was a push. Toxicology didn't help, either. For a date-rape drug to show up in someone's system, a urine sample must be collected within twelve hours. Too much time had passed before Marie went to the hospital. If she'd been slipped something, any trace was gone.

But Parker experienced breakthroughs along with the setbacks. Where did Marie go after being dropped off at her sorority? Parker ran a search of 911 calls for the early morning hours of June 4. One jumped out—the call received at 3:14 a.m. from the freshman named Chris. The freshman saw a black man and a white woman, dazed, near the alley connecting Sigma Chi and Marie's sorority. All the details fit—the description, the time, the place. Parker tracked down the caller and took his statement. An actual eyewitness? Parker couldn't think of one other case where her unit had been so fortunate.

Parker interviewed Marie's friends, who described how Marie's condition had changed suddenly that night, how she had trouble standing and talking, how she appeared to be drugged or exceptionally drunk. Parker knew that if Marie was physically helpless or mentally incapable of consent, the law calls it rape, whether or not Marie said no.

The case also offered forensic evidence—the vaginal and anal swabs, ready to be tested. Of course, Parker needed someone to test the samples against, for a possible DNA match. But she had a suspect: Jerramy Stevens. Parker checked Stevens's background. She already knew he had a felony charge in his past. Now, she wanted to know more. She requested law enforcement records from Thurston County, where Stevens went to high school and had gotten into trouble. She reviewed police reports, court records, newspaper accounts. Evidence of character won't always be admissible in court, but Parker wanted to know: What kind of person is he?

Unlike some of his teammates, Jerramy Stevens did not have what you'd call a rough background. No broken home, no absent father, no time spent on the streets. He was born in Boise, Idaho, in 1979, the third of four kids. When he was in elementary school, his family moved to Washington. He went to high school at River Ridge—Ridge, for short—a new school in a suburb of Olympia, Washington's capital city on the south end of Puget Sound, in the shadow of Mount Rainier, near the lakes and pine trees of the Nisqually Valley.

Stevens's father taught and coached at Ridge. His mother was a middle school teacher and later a vice-principal. The family belonged to the Mormon church, and Jerramy, for years, attended Sunday school. He also worked part-time at a gym, earning $5.50 an hour as a trainer. At Ridge, Stevens was a solid B student. The school was diverse, with blocs of students who were white, black, Hispanic, Asian. Because it was close to Fort Lewis, Ridge drew students from Army families passing through. A standout athlete, Stevens lettered in football, basketball, and track.

Even as a sophomore, Stevens towered over other students. In a picture of the 1995–96 basketball team, he's the guy your eyes are drawn to, the tall player in the middle, with other players falling off to the sides. In his senior photo, he's got this great smile, the one sportswriters would be so taken with in years to come. Another shot pictures him with four friends around a weight bench, their eyes hard and mouths tight, the epitome of suburban high school tough.

Ridge's football team lost more than it won, even with Stevens. His personal numbers didn't dazzle, either. He played quarterback (fifteen touchdowns and eleven interceptions his senior year), but what attracted recruiters was his blend of size and speed. He was already six foot seven, 230 pounds. Recruiters figured he would move to tight end or even defense in college. In January 1998—halfway through his senior year—Stevens committed to the UW, picking the Huskies over BYU and Hawaii.

That spring, just before Stevens's senior year ended, several friends of his showed up to a party uninvited and were turned away. One of the friends, a football player named Van Buckingham, kicked the front door and broke it. He also threw a bowl at a bedroom window, cracking it. This was on a Friday night. Word got around, and the following Monday a fight was arranged, to take place after school in a neighborhood park. Some "punk-ass bitches" want to fight us, Buckingham told one of his friends.

About fifty people showed up. Some arrived thinking fistfight; others expected guns, knives, and clubs. Stevens came with his girlfriend and Buckingham. Stevens hadn't even been at the party. Neither had James Hoover, a seventeen-year-old friend of the girl who threw it. But at the park Stevens and Hoover went front and center, jawing at each other and doing the will-we-or-won't-we routine. Hoover had a baseball bat. So did Brian Flowers, another of Stevens's friends.

Drop the bat, Stevens told Hoover. Fight like a man.

Hoover flinched at Flowers—that's what Flowers would later tell police. So Flowers took his metal bat and, with one swing, knocked Hoover to the ground, unconscious.

After Hoover fell, Stevens jumped up and stomped on him, bringing 230 pounds and the sole of his Nike shoe down on Hoover's face. A fifteen-year-old freshman, a friend of Hoover's, ran up. Stevens punched him in the face, kneed him in the head, and kicked him after he hit the ground. With Hoover down, two of Stevens's other friends joined in. One hit Hoover in the stomach with a stick, another kicked Hoover in the chest. A friend of Hoover's pulled out a gun and waved it around. The gun fired only pellets—but nobody else there knew that. Both groups fled the park.

When police arrived, Hoover was bleeding from his mouth and holding his head. He was saying something, but the words came out funny, like a baby talking. Two bats lay nearby. One was a Louisville Slugger, black and red. Hoover's jaw was broken and his gum line split. For six weeks, he ate through a straw.

Soon after the fight, officers pulled over a car with several teenagers inside, including Stevens. A sheriff's detective asked Stevens about the brawl. Stevens said he'd been at the park, but he denied seeing the assault or having anything to do with it. It didn't take police long to learn otherwise. They rounded up other students who put Stevens square in the middle of the fight.

Some witnesses said Flowers's bat hit Hoover in the head. Flowers said the bat hit Hoover in the chest.

What happened after you hit him? a detective asked Flowers.

"He looked at me, and his eyes rolled back in his head. He dropped the bat and fell."

Did he appear unconscious?

"Yeah."

His eyes were closed when he hit the ground?

"Yeah."

Stevens's girlfriend told police that Hoover "like blanked out and just fell right down . . . straight back."

Did his arms try to catch his fall? a detective asked.

"No."

He fell like dead weight?

"Yeah."

Police arrested Stevens on June 2, 1998, the day after the fight. The same detective questioned Stevens, and this time Stevens admitted stomping on Hoover's face.

"I didn't know he was knocked out," Stevens said.

Why did you lie to me yesterday? the detective asked.

"Well, 'cause I had done something wrong, and I didn't want to get in trouble for it," Stevens said. "I didn't want to go to jail. I don't know."

Stevens was charged with second-degree assault, a felony that carried a prison term of up to ten years. Eighteen years old, Stevens would be tried as an adult. On June 3 a prosecutor asked a judge to release Stevens and Flowers—who also was charged with second-degree assault—on nothing more than their word that they would show up for the next court hearing. The judge refused. With a charge like this, bail would normally be $10,000, the judge told the prosecutor. The judge set the amount at $2,500— and said if either defendant made bail, he must then be kept under house arrest.

Stevens did make bail. He returned home, tethered to an electronic monitoring device. A month later, in July, he tested positive for marijuana—a violation of his home-confinement conditions. As a result, he spent three weeks in the Thurston County jail.

The lead detective wrote two reports—one of them eleven pages long—summarizing the evidence. In each, he concluded that it was Stevens, not Flowers, who had caused the greatest injury. Stevens "jumped up and used his full body weight to stomp on James' face," the detective wrote. "James Hoover received a broken jaw as a result of that assault."

Some newspapers speculated that Stevens's arrest on a felony charge would lead the UW to pull its scholarship offer. But the UW's top three coaches wrote the judge to say that wasn't so. Scott Linehan, the offensive coordinator, wrote: "Our background checks on this young man show nothing but high marks. We believe this to be an isolated incident. Under our discipline and supervision I believe Jerramy will show this to be true." Washington's defensive coordinator at the time, Randy Hart, wrote that the UW had "recruited a good student and excellent athlete with high character recommendations." The assault charge had "hoisted a red flag," Hart wrote, so now, the team would pay special attention to Stevens's off-field behavior. The UW's head coach, Jim Lambright, wrote of the team's faith in Stevens's background, and how it would be in Stevens's "best interest to continue his college plans." "We do believe in Jerramy," Lambright wrote.

Stevens was hardly the first player with a criminal record to be recruited by Lambright. Sometimes, a recruit's criminal history escaped the notice of reporters. Other times, the record could not be missed. In 1997, the year before Stevens came to campus, the UW recruited Toalei Mulitauaopele, a 325-pound defensive tackle. At age sixteen, Mulitauaopele helped three other people break into the apartment of a reputed drug dealer in Tacoma. Armed, the four lay in wait. When the alleged dealer and a friend showed up, Mulitauaopele helped gag and bind them. When Mulitauaopele stepped outside to move a car, the others slit one man's throat and shot the other man in the back of the head. Both were killed. Mulitauaopele was convicted of two counts of manslaughter and served three years in the Washington penitentiary.

He played two years for Washington. The *Seattle Post-Intelligencer* wrote a profile on how he was one of the team's most liked players, how he gave of himself to set young people straight. A teammate called him "a big, giant teddy bear." Lambright's successor, Rick Neuheisel, spoke of "what a neat guy he is." After leaving the UW, Mulitauaopele was arrested time and again on charges that included illegal possession of a firearm, burglary, automobile theft, criminal trespass, and assault with a deadly weapon.

With Stevens, the UW coaches wanted more than to express their commitment. They wanted the judge to release Stevens from house arrest so that he could practice with the team before trial. In August, Stevens went to court in a white dress shirt and tie. Before the hearing, he sat with a family friend, who told a newspaper reporter: "He's a sweet, kind, gentle soul." The judge reviewed the itinerary for the team's upcoming football camp, and, with the prosecutor's blessing, agreed to the coaches' request.

"Don't let yourself or your family or your program down," the judge told Stevens, releasing him to go play.

"I won't, sir," Stevens said.

On this same day, the *Post-Intelligencer* ran a story on Stevens's troubles: "Stevens says he became involved in a fight in which his adversaries outnumbered his supporters and wielded baseball bats. 'I feel it's definitely political,' Stevens said. 'I feel it's a little bit of a witch hunt.'"

A witch hunt. As beginnings go, this was hardly auspicious. Before setting foot on Washington's practice field, Stevens was awaiting trial for felony assault. He was playing damage control in the papers. He was impugning the motives of police and prosecutors. At the UW football camp, the players had two-a-day practices, lunch with the media, picture day with the public. Fitness tests measured their vertical jump, power clean, bench press, incline press, and body fat. The freshmen put on skits for the other players. Lambright met with reporters. He talked up Stevens's 3.5 GPA and said: "We don't give up on a player because he makes one mistake."

Before Stevens's trial, at least a half-dozen people wrote the county's elected prosecutor, urging leniency. A "caring, conscientious and noble person," one teacher called Stevens. When Stevens overheard other kids making fun of a student with a speech impediment, Stevens "appropriately and promptly reminded those students that it was unkind to treat a person . . . in a mean and harsh way."

A Mormon bishop wrote on Stevens's behalf. So did two Sunday school teachers. Stevens "often voiced his faith in God. His Sunday school discussions always showed respectful reverence for deity and thoughtful consideration for others," one of the teachers wrote. Stevens "set a good example for the rest of my class by encouraging others not to get involved in drugs and drinking," wrote the other. This teacher hoped Stevens's "years of hard work" would not be "destroyed by an unforgiving legal system. . . . With all the truly terrible things that come into your office, it is a shame that court time has to be taken up with youthful errors in judgment. [Stevens] has a great future ahead of him and in speaking with him he has assured me he has learned his lesson about selecting friends and making choices. . . . I believe he will represent Olympia and our state well in the future and we will be proud to call him one of our own."

In the southeast corner of the state, seventy-two-year-old Wyoma White read about Stevens in her local paper. She typed a two-page letter to Richard McCormick, the UW's president, describing how her three children went to college, and how her grandchildren were now going, too. She bristled at Stevens getting a full scholarship. "All this," she wrote, "because the University of Washington feels the Football Team must win at all costs." What would Stevens learn at the UW? "That anything goes if you are good enough in sports." She closed her letter with: "You sure aren't helping Jerramy Stevens by showing him he does not have to follow the rules if he is good enough at football, and you sure are sending the wrong message to the other students who are in school for an education."

Mrs. White wasn't the only skeptic. A sheriff's captain did a background report on Stevens and summarized four prior incidents suggesting "a propensity towards violence." Stevens and another football player "allegedly were involved in punching holes" in classroom walls at River Ridge, the captain wrote. "We are told the school learned of the vandalism and quietly permitted payment of the damage." The sheriff's office also heard that Stevens had a habit of kicking at his teammates; once, while playing quarterback, he had allegedly booted his center in the testicles—"due to perhaps missing the snap of the ball." Stevens violated school rules on alcohol and marijuana, the captain's report said. And, playing basketball, Stevens was ejected from a game for being "overly physically aggressive." When the referees left the court, Stevens and other students tried to block them from the locker room, with Stevens threatening "to kick the refs' asses."

Months after Stevens stomped on Hoover's face, prosecutors cut a plea deal with him. Stevens was convicted in November 1998 of fourth-degree assault, a misdemeanor, and sentenced to time served. Flowers, meanwhile, was convicted in a plea deal of second-degree assault, a felony.

"Cowards," Hoover's father called them, talking to the judge.

"These guys tried to kill my son," Hoover's mother said.

"I want them to be in jail for a long time," Hoover said.

The outcome didn't sit well with sheriff's detective Cliff Ziesemer, the case's lead investigator. He was convinced that Stevens, not Flowers, broke Hoover's jaw. To his mind, Stevens should have been convicted of a felony. "Absolutely," he says. "I think it was deserving. That's what I arrested him for, and that's what I recommended the prosecutor charge him with. Because it fit the crime." Ziesemer was unmoved by the prosecutors' contention that they couldn't say, with absolute certainty, who broke Hoover's jaw. "Me? I was like, let's let the jury decide," he says.

Stevens's sentence required him to perform forty hours of community service. On a questionnaire to determine what he was suited for, Stevens said he worked well with people and added: "I would prefer not to do manual labor." He wound up doing custodial work at a community college, taking apart old office chairs and sorting recyclable metals. As punishment, Stevens also received a letter from his lawyer. His lawyer notified the court: "This writer, at the request of the Prosecuting Attorney, has given a written admonition to Mr. Stevens about the legal consequences of getting into fighting confrontations."

At the UW, Stevens didn't play his first year, allowing him to preserve all four years of his eligibility. The next year, in 1999, he caught four touchdown passes in his first nine games. Sportswriters took notice. A November 1999 profile in the *Seattle Post-Intelligencer* called Stevens a "soft-spoken, good-natured giant who is quick to laugh" and recited how he had graduated from high school with a 3.5 GPA. That number kept getting recycled—even though Stevens actually graduated with a 3.1, according to court records. Respectable? Yes. But he wouldn't have been admitted to the UW without football, the university later acknowledged.

Stevens's teammates nicknamed him "Louisville Slugger," the *Post-Intelligencer* wrote, an allusion to what happened in the park. Stevens called the assault conviction a "big-time kick in the pants," saying: "I'm more conscious of the choices I make now because I know there are consequences." The *Post-Intelligencer* wrote: "Learning doesn't figure to be a problem. Stevens has learned from his past. Because of that, he plans to have the last laugh."

A month later, in December 1999, the *Seattle Times* wrote its own profile of Stevens, remarking on his good grades and "gregarious, happy personality." The story provides this account of what happened in the park: "A friend served time for second-degree assault for breaking the jaw of another youth with a base-ball bat. Stevens agreed to a lesser charge of misdemeanor fourth-degree assault for kicking a victim." In this article, the prosecutor describes Stevens as less culpable than Flowers, and says of Stevens's plea deal: "I've felt good about that decision over time. I'm glad he was able to go on and have a good career. I haven't regretted whatever leniency he was shown by our office." In the story, Stevens accepts blame for putting himself "in that situation," but adds: "I do think they tried to make an example out of me." The story closes with Stevens saying: "I know I made a mistake. I learned from it. Hopefully, people can get to know me before they judge me."

Six months after that story ran, Stevens received an e-mail from a fellow UW student. The date was May 8, 2000—a month before the close of spring semester and all the parties that go with school's end. The e-mail was from a young woman. Not long before, Stevens had slept with her—one night, that was all. Stevens read the woman's message and, at 10 p.m., wrote back. His e-mail said:

> i know that you are not going to beliewhat i have to say especially after satterday night but when i got your e-mail today i laughed a first but then it started to sink in and my heart started to break as i read over your words. i realize that i have fucked up and I want to talk to you about being with you and how i can make it up to you. this is not a joke i want to have you in my arms and know that you are mine and ythat nothing that i have done or spence has said caould ever change the way that i feel about you. when i think back to the night that i spent with you by ourselves i wish that i would have done one thing and that is, i wish i would have put all nine inches of my cock in you little pink ass you whore dont ever utter my name again . . . . dis dick

Stevens was so proud of the e-mail he showed it off. So of course word spread. Some students read the e-mail, others heard about it. Some students laughed about the e-mail, others were repulsed.

The woman who received the e-mail read it while studying in Odegaard Library. She was so stunned, so taken aback, that she left straight away, and went home to her sorority in a daze. She doesn't remember if the tears came then, or if they came later. That summer, she heard about Stevens and Marie, the rumors going around. She didn't know Marie, but one of her sorority sisters did. The woman passed the e-mail to her sister, and the sister forwarded it to police. "It was because of the coincidence of the anal thing, that's why my sister sent it," the woman says. "The aggressiveness of the insinuation in the e-mail."

In time, the e-mail made its way to Detective Parker. She noticed the date—four weeks before the Jacked Up party. "It was very disturbing to read," she says. Parker placed the e-mail into her investigative file and called the woman who received it.

The woman, crying, told Parker she was afraid.

Why? Parker asked.

The woman knew what Parker was investigating, she knew what Stevens was accused of. She felt awful about what happened to that freshman, she told Parker. But she was afraid to be involved in this case.

Stevens's e-mail had shocked her. It was out of the blue, she told Parker. Stevens had never said a harsh word to her before. She had considered him a friend. The night she'd had sex with him, in April, nothing unusual happened. He wasn't aggressive or intimidating. That night, he told her that he had always dreamed of being with her.

The next time she saw Stevens was three days later.

Everything was fine, the woman told Parker. He was just being Jerramy.

What do you mean? Parker asked.

Jerramy is very moody, the woman said. He can really be aloof, off in his own world. When he doesn't want to have anything to do with you, you know it. He is either friendly or not.

Seven weeks after receiving the case, Parker had enough evidence to request a warrant that would allow police to search Stevens's house and draw his blood. The blood sample would allow forensic examiners to extract Stevens's genetic profile and see if it matched any sperm on the vaginal and anal swabs. Parker had already received one result from the state crime lab. Tests revealed the presence of semen on the black pants Marie had been wearing that night.

Stevens and Marie had once been friends. The two also had friends in common—football players and sorority sisters, mostly. But after Marie went to the police, one of Stevens's teammates called Marie's roommate at the sorority. He left a voice-mail message, saying: "Your friend is a liar, that dumb fucking slut." Another of Marie's friends—a sorority sister who had tried to help Marie figure out what happened—had left the UW, electing not to return in the fall. Her mother told Parker that her daughter had changed, that she hadn't been the same all summer. She used to be outgoing, the mother said. Now, she stayed close to home.

On July 24, Parker took her search-warrant request to a deputy prosecutor for review. A half hour later they went before a judge, who signed it. In addition to searching Stevens's house, Parker planned to have Stevens arrested. She had probable cause—and maybe, in custody, he would talk.

Nothing but Ashes

Detective Mudd suspected he had the wrong address.

It was April 25, 2000, six weeks after Kerry Sullivan had been robbed and shot. A judge had already signed a warrant allowing detectives to search Jeremiah Pharms's home. Getting her to approve was easy. So much evidence had rolled in during the investigation's first two days that Mudd had plenty to carry into court. And the faster a warrant was served, the better. The two gunmen had stolen a quarter pound of marijuana. With a stash like that, you smoke it, sell it, or share it. What you don't do is sit on it. Marijuana isn't wine. It doesn't improve with age. The faster police searched Pharms's home, the more likely they were to find the stolen marijuana—or maybe the guns, or maybe some other evidence. Besides, police needed Pharms's DNA and fingerprints, to see if they matched the bloody print left on the getaway car. The warrant would allow Mudd to collect comparison samples.

But now Mudd wondered if his suspect really lived at the address listed on the warrant he'd secured. It was evening, 6:30 or so, and Mudd was eyeballing the place from a discreet distance. The address was an apartment, in family housing at the UW. But Pharms was nowhere to be seen. Instead, Mudd saw a white guy inside the apartment. He was washing the apartment windows. He was watching TV. Mudd decided to call the search off.

A week later, Mudd found another possible address in some computer database. It was an apartment number, on 106th Street in Seattle. But when Mudd drove there and looked around, the address didn't exist. So Mudd went to the UW police and got another address for Pharms—this one in Lynnwood, a suburb north of Seattle.

By now, seven weeks had passed since Sullivan was shot. And more weeks yet would pass—one after the other—before that warrant would be served. In the Jerramy Stevens case, Parker started with little and moved fast. With Pharms, Mudd started with a lot and moved slow. If there was any sense of urgency—expediency, even—it's not reflected in the investigative file.

Mudd had been on the force for twelve years now, the last three in Gang Crimes. Mike Magan, the robbery detective who'd made Pharms for a suspect in the case's first hour, was a rarity—a cop with flair, constantly in the news, friendly with reporters and comfortable with the spotlight. Mudd was more the norm—a grinder, nothing flashy, thinning hair, thick mustache. He'd appeared in the newspaper only a couple of times—once for being caught up in one of those awful Candid Camera spoofs. A TV crew had set Mudd and his partner up, having them rescue some buxom window washer who'd gotten trapped in her harness. To free her, they needed to read directions that happened to be written across her chest, just below all that cleavage.

In mid-May, Mudd learned that the police department's Media Relations folks had mistakenly released the incident report from the robbery to a local television reporter. The report included names and phone numbers for Sullivan and other witnesses. The reporter was from KIRO-TV, an affiliate of CBS. She called Mudd, and each tried to figure out what the other knew. The reporter said she had information on the case. She said she wanted to work with Mudd. She said she didn't want to jeopardize the investigation, but she was working the story. Mudd said he didn't want a trial by media, that he wanted to protect the rights of any suspects who might prove innocent.

Are you doing this because the suspects are high profile? the reporter asked.

I'm doing this because I need more information, Mudd said. And I'd take whatever time is necessary, whether the suspects were high profile or not.

Are you under any political pressure in this case?

No, he told her. But that might change now that you have information on the case.

Whatever the reporter knew, whatever she had heard, she didn't go on the air with it. Mudd turned his attention back to the search warrant.

Without a doubt, Pharms was suspect No. 1 for the shooter. But other suspects also emerged, for both the shooter and the accomplice.

Police knew what car the robbers had used. The woman who owned the Chrysler reported it stolen the next day. She knew Pharms, yes. Pharms had been cheating on his wife with her. But when police questioned her, she said another guy, an ex-boyfriend, knew where she hid a spare key. The ex-boyfriend became a suspect.

Meanwhile, Sullivan told police that another football player—Sam Blanche, a linebacker—had hooked Pharms up with him. It was Blanche who had called ahead of time and asked Sullivan to sell to "J.P.," the dealer told police.

A couple of weeks after the shooting, Blanche again called Sullivan. Their conversation was not a pleasant one, according to Sullivan's account to police. He said he told Blanche of his suspicions—that he believed Blanche's friends shot him. To which Blanche responded: *You leave my name out of this. I've got a family, I'm on scholarship. If you fuck that up, you are wasted.* Even if Blanche had nothing to do with the robbery—and really, he didn't fit for the shooter or the fellow gunman—now he was being investigated on suspicion of intimidating a witness. Within two months of the shooting, all three of Sullivan's roommates had moved out, afraid that the robbers might return.

Sullivan told police that another football player, Curtis Williams, had also been a customer of his. Pharms and Williams were good friends. Williams was too small to be the shooter. But could he have been the other gunman? Mudd showed Banchero a photo montage—three mugs on top, three on the bottom, with Williams in the lower left. Banchero didn't pick Williams out. For that matter, Banchero never identified any player—and Mudd showed him the whole team, using the 1999 Husky football media guide. Besides, why would Williams, a guy known to Sullivan, show up at his door with a gun and no mask?

As it turned out, the ex-boyfriend of the car's owner had an alibi, and never panned out as a suspect.

No. For the shooter, the evidence pointed to Pharms.

On June 29, 2000, at 9:20 p.m., three cars pulled up to Pharms's house in Lynnwood, each with two detectives inside. One car parked across the street, the others north and south. This time, Mudd knew Pharms lived there. Six weeks ago he'd watched videotape from a surveillance camera that had captured Pharms coming and going. Mudd had a new search warrant, with the right address.

At 10:25 p.m., four men left Pharms's house. They split into two cars and drove off. Two detectives followed a gray car and pulled it over. The driver was Curtis Williams, the passenger a former Husky football player. Once the detectives confirmed that neither man was Pharms, they let the two go.

Another pair of detectives stopped the second car—a 1971 Chevy Chevelle, black and red, owned by Pharms. Pharms was sitting in the passenger seat. A detective radioed Mudd to let him know. Mudd picked Pharms up and, with another detective, took him to the police station. The other cops stayed behind and searched the house.

By now, three and a half months had passed since Sullivan was shot and robbed. The house reeked of burned marijuana. Police found a couple of marijuana pipes, but no drugs. The detectives rounded up a pair of gray Nike football gloves, some parking tickets that Pharms had failed to pay, and what appeared to be a roach, found in the ashtray of Pharms's car.

At the police station, Mudd used a cotton swab to collect a saliva sample from Pharms, to be used for DNA tests. A technician fingerprinted Pharms, recording all the arches, ridges, and whorls.

Mudd read Pharms his rights. Pharms said he understood them and would talk. He had yet to ask what was going on, why he had been taken in, what it was that police were investigating.

Mudd told Pharms they were investigating an assault from March.

You remember buying marijuana from an apartment house on Greek Row? Mudd asked.

Yes, Pharms said. He'd been unable to locate his usual supplier, so he'd asked some teammates if they knew where he could buy some pot. One of his teammates had hooked him up. It was either Sam Blanche or Curtis Williams, he couldn't remember which. Pharms said he'd gone there alone, driving his Chevelle. The dealer was a white guy. Pharms had bought $20 worth, or maybe $40. He left and never went back. If something happened later that night, he wasn't there.

You ever borrowed your girlfriend's car? Mudd asked.

Yes, Pharms said. That's because my Chevelle eats gas.

Another detective was there for the interview. He asked Pharms: You sure you weren't there when the assault happened?

Pharms hesitated. Then he said: I'm not sure what to do. I got so much going on. I think I need to talk to my mother for advice.

The detectives stopped the interview. Two officers drove Pharms home, dropping him off at 1:45 a.m.

One of the UW's best players had just been arrested and his house searched. But the public didn't know it. The public had no idea Pharms was suspected of shooting and nearly killing someone.

The day before the warrant was executed, Mudd convinced a judge to seal all records pertaining to the search. He signed an affidavit saying: "At this stage in the investigation, a great body of circumstantial evidence now links Jeremiah Pharms to the robbery and assault of Kerry Sullivan." But, Mudd wrote, police wouldn't have forensic or fingerprint evidence until sample comparisons were collected.

Pharms is a UW football player, Mudd wrote. Release of the

records would likely "create significant media coverage" of his arrest, alerting potential accomplices and complicating an unfinished investigation. If Pharms was innocent, Mudd wrote, coverage could subject him to "unwanted notoriety" and cause the real shooter to flee. Mudd asked for all records to be sealed until August 3, 2000, "at which time this investigation should be complete." That date was only five weeks out—an estimate that proved hopelessly optimistic.

On July 14 the fingerprint results came back. The print left on the car—in the blood smear, above the handle on the driver's side door—matched the second joint on Pharms's right pinky. It was four months to the day since Sullivan had been shot. Now, to go with all the other evidence against Pharms, police also had a fingerprint match—for a print left in blood.

The UW's football season would begin in seven weeks. The Huskies were scheduled to open against Idaho on September 2. Would Pharms play?

The one item of evidence yet to be tested was the DNA. Would the blood on the car door match the saliva sample taken from Pharms? Mudd had submitted the lab request at the end of June. He had no idea when to expect the results back.

Face-off 7

On July 27, 2000, a six-member SWAT team made its way into a north Seattle neighborhood and approached the house where Jerramy Stevens lived. It was early morning, making it more likely that Stevens would be home and sleeping. The players' house faced the neighborhood's main street, which drew traffic from a nearby shopping mall.

Parker's sergeant had made this call—a show of force, with the officers armored up—based on surveillance. Police had seen the half-dozen football players living there. They'd seen lots of other people coming and going. They'd seen the house's garbage, overflowing with empty beer cans and bottles. To the sergeant, this was a house full of big guys who liked to party. So a SWAT team it was. Police knew Stevens's bedroom was downstairs, second door on the left. One of Marie's friends had told Parker that.

Just before 7 a.m., the officers busted in the front door. Stevens didn't resist. Neither did anyone else in the house. And who knows? Maybe Stevens had been expecting this all along. He'd known for a month or more that he was under investigation. The rumor swirling about—that he had raped a Pi Phi—had made its way back to him. Plus, he had received that telephone message from Parker, asking him to call.

Once the SWAT team secured the house, Parker and other detectives went inside. In Stevens's bedroom, in a dresser, police found three items of women's clothing—a pair of thong underwear and two other undergarments, one with a leopard print, the other blue and gold. Stevens seemed to have a collection—but Marie's underwear wasn't part of it. Police never did find her underwear, not that day or any other.

Parker found Stevens downstairs, sitting on a couch, hand-cuffed. She walked up and introduced herself. She saw worry in his face. But was there surprise there, too? She couldn't tell. He didn't say much of anything. No questions. No protestations. He just sat there, waiting for whatever was next.

Parker and another detective, Tim Fields, escorted Stevens in a marked police car to the Special Assault Unit. There, Parker let Stevens read the search-warrant papers. She advised him of his rights, using a standard form. Then she asked if he would waive those rights—if he would sign a form acknowledging his willing-ness to talk and answer questions.

Stevens balked. I want to think about it, he said. I don't want to say anything incriminating. Can you give me more informa-tion about the case?

You're in custody as part of a rape investigation, Fields told Stevens. I can't tell you more unless you waive your rights. If you talk, you can always decide to stop. Nothing says you have to keep going once you start.

Stevens signed the waiver. Afterward, Parker itemized the top-ics that she wanted to ask him about. Hearing the list, Stevens did an about-face. I don't want to talk, he told the detectives.

Parker and Fields left the room. Later, a phlebotomist arrived and drew two vials of blood from Stevens, to be used for DNA test-ing. At a few minutes after 9 a.m., Stevens was taken to the King County Jail and booked, on suspicion of rape.

Spencer Marona came to the UW from Lake Oswego, a suburb of Portland, Oregon. In college he was a hard guy to peg. His build, his hair, his playing position—they were all subject to change. First he grew his hair so long that his locks reached his mouth. That was to win a $20 bet with Stevens, who didn't think he'd do it. Then he shaved his scalp so close he could have been a West Point cadet. Before college, Marona had been a state swimming champion in the butterfly and freestyle. He came to Washington as a lineback-er but had since bulked up, putting 270 pounds on his six-foot-two frame. For the 2000 season he was slotted to play nose tackle, putting him in the middle of the defensive line. Later he'd shed the pounds and move to fullback. But no matter which side of the ball he played, or which position, Marona's career never took off at Washington. He suffered one injury after another, with at least four surgeries on his shoulders by the time he was twenty-one.

While Parker tried to get Stevens to talk, another detective questioned Marona, first at the house, then at the department's north precinct. Marona had no problem talking. His interview at the police station was taped—and the transcript runs forty-three pages.

Marona walked Detective Rob Howard through all he had seen at the fraternity party and in the afternoon that followed. He talked about Jerramy and Marie in general, and of earlier times she'd visited the players' house. Marona said Marie had "fooled around" with some players, but not to the point of intercourse.

"She's a horny girl, really horny," Marona told Howard.

"But yet she's a virgin?"

"Yeah."

"With lots of opportunities to have sex when she had not had sex?"

"Well, we always saw her as a tease," Marona said.

The night of the party, Marona went to Sigma Chi first, having been invited. Once there, he called Stevens and said, come on over, I can get you in. At the party, Marie was hanging on Jerramy's arm, rubbing up on him.

"When you say rubbing up on Jerramy, what do you mean?" Howard asked.

"She was just holding onto his arm, kind of, you know, kind of just leaning on to him probably so she wouldn't sway."

How drunk was she, if she needed to support herself like that? Howard asked. On a scale of zero to ten, ten being flat-out wasted drunk?

"Probably like a seven," Marona said.

"About a seven."

"Six and a half, seven, yeah. She was pretty drunk."

Around 12:30 or 12:45, Marona and Stevens left the party to go get their own beer instead of the "crap" being served at Sigma Chi. On the way to a Texaco station, Marie "pulls up with her friends, hanging out the window, acting silly, you know."

"Jerramy looked at her like, she's kind of drunk tonight," Marona said.

After heading to the Texaco, Marona and Stevens returned to the party. Marie returned, too, Marona told the detective.

Marie began flirting with him, Marona said. "She was just giving me the eyes . . . she goes I love you . . . it wasn't like I'm in love with you, but it's like, you know, you're a really good friend I love you. . . . I was like, whatever."

Marie asked Marona if he'd walk her home. "Usually it's a guy's duty," Marona told Howard. "When a girl asks to walk her home, we walk her home, cause there's sick fucks out there." But he had a girlfriend, Marona told the detective. He was afraid that if he walked Marie home, he'd end up fooling around with her. So he told Marie: "I'll get Jerramy to walk you home. And she goes, 'Okay.'"

Marona went back into Sigma Chi, and that was the last he saw of them that night.

Howard asked about the following afternoon and night.

Was Stevens worried that Marie might be pregnant?

"No," Marona said.

"Okay. Or any concern about any kind of sexually transmitted diseases?"

"No. Cause she's a virgin," Marona said.

What about *Marie* getting some kind of disease? Was Stevens worried about that?

"No," Marona said.

Marona said he was sure Stevens didn't rape Marie.

"Cause I know Jerramy wouldn't do that shit."

"Why not?" Howard asked. "What's he like?"

"Well . . . he's my best friend. I hang out with champions,

that's my fucking thing. I mean, he's one of the most loyal guys in the world. . . . Jerramy is the type of guy where usually when he fools around he ends up having sex cause he's a charming guy, chicks dig him."

Howard asked Marona if he believed Marie when she called and said she didn't remember what had happened.

"No," Marona said.

You think she was lying?

"Uh-huh."

Toward the end of the interview, Howard asked about the e-mail Stevens had sent a month before the Sigma Chi party to a woman he'd slept with. Marona said he'd seen the e-mail, that Stevens had shared it with him. Marona described it as a "funny ass e-mail saying leave me the hell alone."

"Have you read the e-mail?" Howard asked.

"Yeah."

"And you considered it, I mean, it's funny?"

"Do you remember the e-mail talking about basically anally raping her?" the detective asked.

"No."

"That he had wished he put his full nine inches into her little pink ass?"

"No."

"You didn't read that in the e-mail?"

"It was, it was a long e-mail."

"You didn't read the whole thing?"

"No, no," Marona said.

Marona told the detective that he had also slept with the woman once. "She's what you would call like a typical football groupie," he said.

Howard finished the interview and turned off the tape recorder at 9:30 a.m.

Rick Neuheisel played a lot of golf. His contract with the UW included a membership to the exclusive Broadmoor Golf Club, one of Seattle's finest courses, played by the likes of Ben Hogan, Byron Nelson, Jack Nicklaus, and Arnold Palmer. If Neuheisel wasn't on the football field, or on the lake, or in some recruit's home, chances are he was swinging a club. His favorite vacation spot? "Anywhere with a golf course." His favorite way to spend a day off in June? "Playing golf." Neuheisel had a 3 handicap, thanks to a smooth swing and a light touch around the greens. He played celebrity tournaments, charity tournaments, booster tournaments, alumni tournaments. In years to come he would even use golf as an alibi to cover up a secret job interview. I was in California playing golf, he would claim. It was a lie, but what could be easier to believe?

On the day the SWAT team stormed Stevens's house, Neuheisel was playing golf. Someone pulled up in a cart and handed him a cell phone. On the other end was the university's sports-information director; he told Neuheisel that Stevens had just been arrested on suspicion of rape.

Neuheisel checked in with Barbara Hedges—his boss and the UW's athletic director—to see what she wanted to do. The football team had a system, of sorts, for situations like this. Randy Hart, the defensive-line coach, had police contacts who would alert him if some player was in trouble or heading that way. Maybe the player had been caught on some surveillance camera, hanging with the wrong people. Hart had contacts with the university and Seattle police, in an arrangement that preceded Neuheisel and was simply carried on, from one head coach to another. And then there was Mike Hunsinger, a Seattle lawyer whose name routinely popped up when Huskies were charged. "The tradition of Hunsinger as player counsel seems to be passed down from class to class, like freshmen singing for juniors and seniors at training-camp dinner," a *Seattle Times* sportswriter wrote.

At 1:30 p.m.—less than five hours after Stevens was booked into the King County Jail—a fax arrived at the police station, addressed to Detective Parker. The message was from an associate in Hunsinger's small law firm. "This law office represents Jerramy Stevens," the fax said. "Please contact me immediately."

On July 28, the day after Stevens's arrest, a meeting was held at the King County prosecuting attorney's office. The office, in the county courthouse, was connected by a sky bridge to the jail holding Stevens. The courthouse sits just north of Seattle's Pioneer Square district, a historic neighborhood that seems to attract and threaten in equal measure, with cobblestone streets, art galleries, bookstores, street drug sales, homeless men and women, and occasional outbreaks of violence.

The county's elected prosecutor, Norm Maleng, and his top deputies were livid that Stevens had been arrested. They called this meeting, Parker says, "for me to explain my actions."

If there was any doubt of the importance attached to this case, the meeting's lineup dispelled it.

Dan Satterberg showed up. He was Maleng's chief deputy. Mark Larson showed up. He was chief of the criminal division. Four other prosecutors also sat around the table, for an even half dozen. The police countered with five officers—Parker, and a lot of brass. Two sergeants. A lieutenant. An assistant police chief, who was one of the department's top commanders.

Satterberg sat across from Parker.

Why did you arrest him? he asked the detective.

One of Parker's bosses answered for her.

We don't need your permission to arrest someone. All we need is probable cause.

Even though a deputy prosecutor had helped Parker secure the search warrant, word of Stevens's impending arrest had not made it to the upper reaches of Maleng's office. "They were mad that we had arrested him, because they had to deal with the media fallout. After all, he was going to be a superstar," Parker says.

Maleng had been the county's elected prosecutor for more than twenty years. For the last ten, Satterberg had been his No. 2. Satterberg saw Maleng, a generation older than him, as a father figure. Both men had received their undergraduate and law degrees from the UW. Satterberg wrote Maleng's speeches and letters, and, over time, the two came to think and sound alike. "We were true partners" is how Satterberg described it.

Prosecutors challenged not only the matter of the arrest but the manner. Why a SWAT team? they wanted to know, to which the police responded: This was a house full of football players.

The use of a SWAT team had made one thing certain: Stevens's arrest did not escape public notice. Both of Seattle's daily newspapers had stories on it, with the *Post-Intelligencer* calling Stevens "a rising sophomore star." Barbara Hedges said the university would conduct its own investigation of Stevens's actions. "We don't have all the facts," she told the *Post-Intelligencer*. "Obviously we are very concerned. We take this kind of thing very seriously. We expect student-athletes to conduct themselves in a proper manner."

The media coverage meant that whatever happened next, the prosecutors would be scrutinized. Would they charge Stevens? Or would they let him go? This attention didn't sit well, Parker says. The Stevens case even triggered a change in how future investigations of sex crimes were to be handled, she says. If some suspect was likely to attract media attention—a school principal, say, or a priest or an athlete—the Special Assault Unit was to hold off on making an arrest until prosecutors had already decided that charges were in order.

Once Stevens was arrested, prosecutors had seventy-two hours to file charges or let him go. Parker gave prosecutors her investigative file. At 2:15 p.m., not long after the meeting with Satterberg and the other prosecutors, she received a call from one of Maleng's deputies. The deputy said Stevens would not be charged—not yet, anyway. The office needed more time to review the case, the deputy said.

That same afternoon, Stevens was scheduled to appear in court for a bail hearing. About a dozen of his teammates arrived in a show of support. When they heard that the hearing was canceled—that Stevens was going to be released—some of the players cheered.

It was late afternoon when Stevens left jail. He headed for campus and the offices of the football coaches. First he spoke with Keith Gilbertson, the offensive coordinator. Then he met with Neuheisel. The head coach told Stevens: I'm hoping for the best here. But you have to understand. If you're charged with rape, I'm going to have to suspend you from the team—indefinitely. I'm hoping the truth will exonerate you.

Stevens's arrest came five weeks before the season opener against Idaho. Would Stevens play?

Newspapers in Washington tried to anticipate the prosecutors' decision. Would Maleng's office charge Stevens? If so, when? The initial stories had some details about the case. The 911 caller. The freshman thinking maybe she'd been drugged. The blood sample drawn from Stevens. But then the coverage moved onto the sports pages.

A week after Stevens's arrest, *Seattle Times* sports columnist Blaine Newnham wrote about Neuheisel playing in the Fred Couples Wells Fargo Invitational, a pro-am tournament. On a 205-yard par 3, Neuheisel hit an 8 iron five feet from the cup. He reached a 509-yard par 5 in two shots with a driver and a 5 iron. But Neuheisel was troubled, Newnham wrote. His game showed "some lapses of concentration." The coach admitted he was "very concerned" about Stevens's arrest. "We've had such a productive summer, the kids are really working hard, and to have this kind of distraction just before we open our camp is not good." Newnham wrote: "A case can be made that Stevens is the second-best player on the team behind quarterback Marques Tuiasosopo." Neuheisel added: "Not having him would change who we are. His loss really hurts on third-down situations. He is so versatile."

Two days later, a *Seattle Times* story quoted Neuheisel saying: "I hope this is the biggest non-story in the history of University of Washington football." If Stevens isn't charged, Neuheisel said, "the assumption could be made" that the team wouldn't discipline him. The story talked about how thin the Huskies' receiving corps was. Chris Juergens, the team's leading receiver the previous year, was in jeopardy of missing the 2000 season with a bad knee. Another receiver had been lost to the Olympics. "With Stevens' situation clouded . . . the Husky receiver picture could potentially be ghastly," the *Times* wrote.

Other papers and news services hit the same themes. The *Seattle Post-Intelligencer*: "An ongoing investigation has cast a dark cloud over a talented player expected to be an All-America candidate." The Vancouver newspaper: "The recent losses pale to what would happen if Stevens goes out for an extended period." The Spokane newspaper: "Washington will have trouble finding someone to throw the ball to."

One *Seattle Times* sportswriter did a story in Q&A format.

Q: Can this team win a league title without Chris Juergens and Jerramy Stevens?

A: Flat-out, no.

The worry about Stevens was mixed with high hopes for the season to come. Sportswriters who covered the Pac-10 picked Washington to win the conference and go to the Rose Bowl. Other pre-season polls predicted good things nationally. The Associated Press had Washington at No. 13, the ESPN/USA Today poll at No. 14.

In August, the UW had two-a-day practices in Everett, north of Seattle. In the team scrimmage, Stevens caught two passes for 57 yards and one touchdown. Neuheisel said: "He's a big part of our offense. It just so happens we don't have a bunch of them behind him."

Sportswriters kept asking Dan Donohoe, Maleng's spokesman, when a charging decision might be expected. In late July, right after Stevens's arrest, Donohoe said there would be no decision for a week. A week later, he said not to expect a decision for "a couple of weeks." A couple of weeks later, he said: "It's still under review. It will probably be toward the end of August." Toward the end of August, Donohoe said it wouldn't be until September.

Barbara Hedges received updates on the case from Dan Satterberg, Maleng's chief deputy. Whatever Hedges learned from Satterberg, she passed on to Neuheisel. "Okay, here's the latest," she would tell him. Neuheisel received these updates "biweekly, maybe weekly," he says. Although Hedges had told reporters that the athletic department would conduct its own investigation of Stevens, the department never did.

With reporters pressing them—and with coaches, boosters, and fans also wanting to know Stevens's status—police and prosecutors couldn't afford to take their time. They needed answers, and quick. On August 3, a week after Stevens's arrest, Parker and a deputy prosecutor, Jim Rogers, went over the case with Marie and her parents. Rogers said the DNA evidence was being shipped to a lab out of state. A filing decision would be made shortly after the results came back, he told the family.

Ordinarily, the DNA would have been tested by the Washington State Patrol's crime lab. But the lab had a horrendous backlog that undermined the chances of a quick turnaround. So the evidence—the blood samples, the vaginal and anal swabs, Marie's stained pants, and Stevens's stained jacket—were sent to Cellmark Diagnostics, a private lab in Maryland. Parker used Federal Express and enclosed a letter, written by Rogers, asking the lab to expedite the tests. "We are asking that you RUSH these samples in TEN business days or as early as possible, understanding that there will be an additional fee as noted in your schedule."

Two weeks later, on August 17, Rogers handed the detective a long list of items that prosecutors wanted her to pursue. They were looking for some other independent witness, someone who might have seen something. Well, here we go, Parker thought. *Here we go.* It was the political powers that be. They wanted more information before making a decision. Parker had never before had a case involving a UW football player. But she'd heard stories of other cops with such cases, stories of cops butting heads with the prosecutors' office.

A half hour after that meeting with Rogers, Parker received a fax of the DNA results. It was a match. The genetic profile in Stevens's blood was consistent with the sperm on the vaginal and anal swabs. So prosecutors now knew what the DNA had to say. They'd asked for answers fast, and gotten them fast. But a filing decision? That would be slow in coming.

Days later, Parker returned to Greek Row. She canvassed fraternities and sororities that backed up to the alley between Seventeenth and Eighteenth avenues. Sigma Chi, Pi Beta Phi, Kappa Sigma, Delta Zeta. Did anybody see anything?

For its party, Sigma Chi had hired a firm, Titan Security, to keep things under control. The firm's president, Niko Jones, had worked that night, along with a crew of five or six. Jones told Parker that he had seen Stevens at the party. Jones remembered how one member of Sigma Chi was drunk and giving Stevens a hard time, "talking out his ass." But Stevens wasn't drunk, Jones said. He appeared to be levelheaded.

Parker interviewed Sigma Chi's vice-president. He said that after the party shut down, police showed up in the alley. An officer told him there had been a possible rape in the area, and that police were looking for a tall African American male. After the police left, he saw Stevens walking through the alley, from the direction of the Pi Beta Phi house. The fraternity brother told Parker that he should have called 911 and told police what he saw. But at the time, he just didn't put it all together.

Some witnesses turned Parker away. Spencer Marona's girlfriend had been in the football players' house when Stevens had emerged from his bedroom and pulled Marie's underpants out of his pocket. Parker wanted to know what she had seen and heard. But after agreeing to meet with Parker, the girlfriend canceled, saying she didn't feel comfortable giving a statement, that she didn't think she had anything to add to the investigation. She refused to come in to the police station.

As for Marona, he was expected to be a starter when the 2000 season opened. But in August, he left the team's football camp after one day of practice and drove home. He missed the next eight practices. Neither Neuheisel nor Marona would tell reporters what was up. "A personal issue" is all Neuheisel would offer. The *Post-Intelligencer* wrote that Marona "reportedly" was feeling "overwhelmed by a number of issues." When Marona returned to the team, he told reporters that his leave had nothing to do with football. "My mind's all right now," he said. "I'm ready to go. I can't wait to get out here with my teammates. I'm a Dawg. As far as my issues go, they're all resolved." He never said what his issues were.

Taking the Field

8

September 2, 2000: Idaho at Washington, Game No. 1

A tuneup game is what most folks would call it. Schedule the patsy first, work out the kinks, then take on the big boys. On Washington's schedule for the 2000 season, the role of patsy was to be played by the University of Idaho, a school that had moved up to the ranks of Division I-A only four years before. But if Idaho was a pushover, no one told Wil Beck, a three-hundred-pound defensive lineman for the Vandals. The week before the game, Beck told a columnist for the *Seattle Post-Intelligencer*: "Washington has been on a giant pedestal my whole life. Every year they imagine themselves as national champions. That's just, I don't know, ridiculous to think you're better than everyone else. There are a lot of egos over there." Beck called the Huskies "cocky and arrogant" and said he wouldn't be surprised—not at all—if Idaho, a 22½-point underdog, pulled an upset. He'd seen film of the Huskies. Wasn't impressed. Nope, not at all.

Beck spoke for all kinds of players and fans around the Pacific Northwest. When it came to football, Washington *did* have an attitude. But maybe an Idaho player wasn't the best person to be questioning the whys of it, or to be throwing challenges Washington's way. The last time Idaho beat the Huskies was in 1905—a year so distant that Washington's other opponents that season included two Indian boarding schools and the crew of the USS *Chicago*, a Navy cruiser. Since then the two schools had played twenty-six times—and the best Idaho could manage was two ties. Washington dominated the region's other schools, too. Four Pac-10 schools reside in the Northwest, but historically, only Washington challenged the top California teams.

More than thirty players on Idaho's roster were from Washington. But the truth was, Idaho recruited players from the state of Washington that the University of Washington didn't want. Beck was from Spokane. The offensive lineman he'd be going against, Chad Ward, was from the small Washington town of Finley. But Ward had been a blue-chip recruit coming out of high school—and now, in his senior year, was a pre-season All-American, a six foot five, 335-pound guard who could squat a school-record 733 pounds and power clean 430. Washington's strength coach, Bill Gillespie, said: "When the pro scouts ask about Chad, and we tell them his power clean numbers, their eyes bulge out."

With the game looking like a mismatch, Idaho wanted to pop Washington fast and hard, to make a statement. On the season's first play from scrimmage, Idaho's second-string tailback, who was playing only because the starter had a broken wrist, burst through a massive hole up the gut, shaded right—eluding one of Washington's surest tacklers, safety Hakim Akbar—and sprinted 82 yards for a touchdown. Many of Washington's 70,000 fans hadn't even taken their seats yet, but just like that, the Huskies were down, wondering what the hell just happened.

On Washington's first offensive snap, the team drew a penalty for a false start. The Huskies went three and out on their first possession, and again on their second. On Washington's third drive, quarterback Marques Tuiasosopo broke a couple of long runs. The Huskies reached Idaho's 5-yard line, but on third down, Wil Beck, the Idaho lineman who had been so dismissive of Washington, dropped Tuiasosopo for a 4-yard loss. Washington missed a chip-shot field goal, and the first quarter ended with Idaho up 7–0. Maybe Beck wasn't so crazy after all.

But in the second quarter, Washington ripped off three touchdowns in four minutes, aided by two Idaho fumbles and an interception by Akbar. It was *bang, bang, bang*. Almost as fast as Idaho had gone up, now it was down, 20–7. All was right in Husky Nation. Order was restored.

In the third quarter, Washington kicked off, up two touchdowns. Curtis Williams, a starting safety who also starred on special teams, stripped the ball from Idaho's return man, and Washington recovered. One play later—a nifty reverse—and the Huskies were in the end zone.

The Vandals managed to hang in, closing back to within two touchdowns. Idaho quarterback John Welsh had been sharp all day, completing fourteen of sixteen passes through three quarters. But in the fourth quarter Jeremiah Pharms laced into Welsh as he released a pass, opening a cut on the quarterback's chin that required five stitches. Welsh left the field, and his backup overthrew an open receiver, forcing Idaho to punt. Washington blocked the kick, scooped the ball up, and scored on the next play, putting the game away.

The final score was 44–20. And for Washington, the good news didn't end there. The team's backup tight end, John Westra, missed the game to be with his wife. At the University of Washington Medical Center—across the street from Husky Stadium—she gave birth to their daughter Taylor. The season had started with a birth.

Pharms's stat line against Idaho was nothing special—one tackle, that was it—but he helped seal the win with the game's most memorable hit. He played knowing that at any time, the DNA results could come back, that at any time, he could be charged with robbery or aggravated assault or even attempted murder. The fans didn't know that, but Pharms did. What the fans knew was that Jerramy Stevens could be charged at any time with rape—a subject of continuing fret, what with powerhouse Miami up next. What if Stevens "should be suddenly charged?" a *Seattle Times* columnist wrote after the Idaho game. Stevens had a quiet opener, with three catches for 40 yards. But lots of folks figured that without Stevens—a matchup problem for any team—Washington's chances against Miami would fade away.

Even with Stevens, Washington looked vulnerable. The opener's score made the game appear more lopsided than it was. Washington didn't win so much as Idaho lost. The Vandals committed five turnovers and had a punt blocked. Otherwise, the teams' statistics lined up pretty evenly. Washington didn't push the small school around. And Wil Beck? He still wasn't impressed. He said he expected Tuiasosopo to be faster than he was and that defending Washington's option "wasn't as hard as I thought it was going to be." Idaho linebacker Chris Nofoaiga said of Washington's national ranking: "Obviously, more people think they deserve to be No. 14 than me." The pollsters appeared to be entertaining doubts, too. After the weekend's games were over, they dropped Washington to No. 15, despite the 24-point win.

For Idaho's coach, Tom Cable, the game proved that his team could compete with Washington, no mean feat for a school so small that its stadium seated only 16,000 people. This was Cable's first game as Idaho's head coach. This was his first game as any college's head coach. He was only thirty-five—younger, even, than Neuheisel. He had been an offensive lineman at Idaho years before. Offensive linemen tend to be students of the game, soaking up the intricacies while other players draw the attention. Sportswriters described Cable as "no nonsense" and a "straight shooter." A devotee of Vince Lombardi—likewise, a former offensive lineman—Cable read every book he could find on the legendary taskmaster, looking for the secrets to success—not the flash-fire sort, but the kind that burns for years.

For Cable, it was all about accountability. Players had to train, prepare, show up on time. They had to go to class. Stay out of trouble. Treat people with respect. With academics, there were NCAA standards, and there were Cable's standards. Cable's were higher. Fail his, and you didn't play. Cable instituted a three-strikes policy. Each year a player could commit no more than two violations of team rules—and a single violation could be something as minor as arriving late to a team meeting or missing a weight lifting workout. A third strike meant a year's suspension. Cable enforced this rule for freshmen and established starters alike. Before the 2000 season began, he showed two players the door. Others would follow.

If, for Cable, the Washington game offered reason for hope, it proved to be false hope. The Vandals finished 5-6 in 2000 and went downhill from there. When the team started its 2001 season with eight straight losses, Cable told an Idaho newspaper, "I feel like throwing up every day." He was hearing it from fans, who had become spoiled during a stretch of good years in the 1980s and '90s. "They say you don't know what you're doing, or you don't know how to do it. Or they say I have no guts or the team hates me. Are you kidding me? Why, because I discipline them and make them go to school?" Idaho's athletic director said: "We like everything about our program except the record. We like the way we recruit, our discipline, the academic performance of the team. Again, everything except the win-loss record." In the end, Cable's record did him in. After going 11-35 in four seasons, he was canned. Lots of schools would have fired him after his second or third season. Cable went on to become an assistant coach for the NFL's Oakland Raiders. Then he became head coach—putting him in charge of professional football's most notorious team, an outfit known for welcoming hard cases drummed out everywhere else. Cable's introduction to the NFL ranks proved inauspicious—his team awful, the headlines awful, with one assistant coach accusing Cable of fracturing his jaw (prosecutors declined to bring charges).

If the lines Cable drew for players were straight and black, Neuheisel's were the faded yellow dashes that divide a country two-lane, the markers a suggestion more than anything else. He occasionally talked of rules, but it was really just that, talk. In 1999, he told a Seattle TV station: "The rules are clear. If you get involved with the law and are convicted of a misdemeanor, you're going to miss at least one game." But if there was such a rule, Neuheisel applied it unevenly—sometimes yes, other times, not so much. If there was such a rule, Derrell Daniels, a UW linebacker and the team's leading tackler during the 1999 season, would not have played against Idaho. In February 2000 the Washington State Patrol arrested Daniels on a DUI charge. His blood-alcohol content was .18, more than twice the legal limit. Daniels pleaded guilty in April to a misdemeanor charge and was sentenced to two days in jail and two years' probation. But the arrest and conviction didn't make the newspapers. And when Washington played next, so did Daniels. In fact, he led the team in tackles against Idaho, racking up ten. Maybe Neuheisel didn't know. Maybe he knew and decided not to apply his rule. Either would be telling.

Years later, under oath, Neuheisel would be asked how he decided whether to discipline some player. He didn't have a three-strikes policy like Cable. Instead, Neuheisel said he assessed whether a player's conduct had embarrassed himself, his family, or his team. This, of course, was nothing like that rule about a misdemeanor conviction triggering an automatic suspension. This rule was all fuzzy, a lawyer's dream. People can disagree about what is embarrassing. But the opinion that counted was Neuheisel's.

For Daniels, the DUI conviction looked to be an isolated case. He wasn't a bad guy. He was a guy who made a bad mistake. But at Washington, even a string of convictions didn't mean a player would get the boot. Against Idaho, the player with the second-most tackles was Curtis Williams, a hard-hitting safety. When Williams took the field in front of those 70,000 fans, there was a warrant out for his arrest.

The warrant stemmed from something years before that never made the newspapers, and which had been artfully dodged by the team's media guide. Williams came to the UW in 1996, but his player profile, written by the university, started with 1998. It was like a résumé with two years missing—the kind of hole that would make any employer leery, the kind of hole that beckons the question: What happened here?

Happily Ever After

9

The Summer of 1996

Curtis Williams drove down the Alaska Highway—through the Yukon, through British Columbia, through the frost heaves that buckle the road each winter, through the fireweed that blooms in summer, through Watson Lake, Fort Nelson, Dawson Creek. He'd turned eighteen a couple of months earlier. Michelle sat next to him, in the passenger seat of the Toyota Tercel, all her belongings stuffed in the back, even a bed.

He was eighteen, and already he was a husband. Michelle was two years and four months older than him. They'd met in central California, when she was babysitting his nephew and niece. She was a cheerleader and swimmer at her high school, he was a football star at his. "We were introduced," Michelle says. "We liked each other. We were together from then on, I guess." To Michelle, Curtis was smart, thoughtful, romantic, good looking. "An ideal boyfriend." When Curtis was fifteen, he took Michelle to Magic Mountain for Valentine's Day. They went on all the rides, from Tidal Wave to Viper, a looping coaster with a double corkscrew and a 188-foot plunge. They drove home the long way, along the coast, taking time to stop at beaches and walk the sand. She had just turned eighteen. "We were young, we were sweethearts. Who knows what they are at eighteen?" she says. A month or two later, Michelle became pregnant.

He was eighteen, and already he was a father. Their daughter was in the backseat. She was a year and a half old now. Curtis had her name, in cursive, tattooed across his heart. *Kymberly*. He was sixteen when she was born. When they reached the end of this forever road, when they got to the University of Washington, he would pick his uniform number—25—to match the day of the month she was born.

He was eighteen, and already he was under contract. You can call it something else, but that's what it was, a contract. He'd get paid $665 a month, and he'd play football, and he'd also go to school because, oh yeah, he'd be a full-time student, too. He'd be a full-time student at a university where everybody else had a running start on him, with SAT scores that were 200 or 300 or 400 points higher than his 900, and GPAs that shamed his 2.95, and high school transcripts that glittered with physics and calculus.

After graduating, Michelle had moved to Anchorage, because that's where her family was from, and maybe it would have ended there, only Curtis had visited after he graduated and wound up staying the summer. A UW football coach made a call and landed him a job with a Budweiser distributorship, pulling weeds and doing other yard work. Her family wasn't thrilled about this relationship. His wasn't, either. To Curtis's older brother David, Curtis and Michelle had no business being together. They argued all the time, and about all they had in common was taking on too much, too soon. In Alaska, Michelle's mother saw the same thing, but she knew if you push too hard, you could push your child away. In Anchorage, Curtis and Michelle saw a flier, on a trash can, advertising the services of a minister. He charged $100 to marry a couple, but only half that if the couple came to his house. On July 15, 1996, Curtis and Michelle got married at the minister's house. Michelle wore a sun dress. Curtis wore dress pants and a nice shirt. Afterward, they ate at Denny's. Curtis kept the news from his family. "He didn't tell us anything," David says. "He didn't tell me, anyway."

Over the summer, they had saved. So now he had $3,800 and a family, and already that family had secrets, there was Michelle's broken arm and the story that went with it, how she had broken it falling down but Michelle's family thought it was something else, but how the hell do you even ask? They also had plans. While Curtis played football and studied, Michelle would work. Once he graduated, she'd go back to school and study physical therapy or sports medicine, and maybe become a team doctor for some NBA or NFL team. "I had big dreams," she says.

He was eighteen, and already there were expectations, written in newspaper ink. He wasn't just any recruit. At Bullard High School in Fresno, he had scored thirty-one touchdowns his senior year—eleven on runs of 50 yards or more. *Blue Chip Illustrated* named him a prep All-America and one of the five best running backs in the western United States. Curtis visited the UW; in a separate trip, so did Michelle and Kymberly. Curtis told Michelle that he had the feeling the Washington program cared about her and their daughter. In January 1996 he chose the UW over USC, UCLA, and Arizona State, becoming the Huskies' most heralded running back recruit since Napoleon Kaufman five years before. The Washington newspapers placed him among the UW's top recruits overall—a "potential star," one called him—putting him up there with Jeremiah Pharms, an electrifying linebacker from Sacramento.

His family didn't shy from expectations or challenges. Donnie Williams was a farmer in Avenal, a small town near Fresno. He and his wife, Viola, raised six boys and two girls. Curtis was their seventh-born. The family was close, the children talented and driven. All the boys played football. David would bring game balls home for Curtis, who was fourteen years younger. "He was my little buddy," David says. James, or J.D., was eleven years older than Curtis. When Curtis was seven, J.D. practiced baseball with him at a dirt field near home. Curtis gloved one grounder after another, so they moved on to pop-ups. Higher and higher J.D. threw them, until one conked Curtis on the forehead, leaving him with a big knot. Walking to get ice cream afterwards, Curtis told J.D., "I don't like those high ones." But after getting the ice cream, Curtis said, "Tomorrow I'll catch those high ones." And he did. In 1990 the Buffalo Bills made J.D. a first-round draft pick. When Curtis was twelve, he watched his brother play in the first of four straight Super Bowls.

Because of football, Curtis and Michelle had been able to jump a waiting list and get into married housing. They'd unpack right away, if ever this road ended. Fourteen hundred miles separate Anchorage and Seattle. Few roads offer more open space, but most of its travelers pack their cars so tight with stuff and worry, they may as well be on a crowded subway. Magazines romanticize the Alaska Highway. But travel it, and look for happy faces.

The *Seattle Times* profiled Williams in mid-August, soon after he arrived on campus. The story, written after two days of practice, talked of how versatile he was. Offense, defense, special teams—any role was possible. Washington's head coach, Jim Lambright, said: "He's an athlete. He's picking it all up. He's mature enough that he can handle what's being thrown at him, and he wants to play right away."

In the story, Williams talked of reuniting with Michelle and Kymberly over the summer: "I was away from my daughter for about three months, and that was kind of hard. When I would go visit her, she didn't know me. She didn't know who I was, and she was kind of shy to come to me, and that hurt a little bit. It's been good getting to know her and spending time with her. After I got off work, I baby-sat while my wife worked at night. We'd play games, go to the mall, eat pizza. It was really nice. . . . A lot of guys get homesick, but I'm not. My family is here. It's a whole lot more fun being with them than being away from them."

The story said of Curtis and Michelle: "In the storybooks, they might live happily ever after; in reality, Williams' story is just beginning."

Two weeks after that story ran, Jan Zientek heard a woman scream in pain, "No! No!" It was August 30, about 11:20 p.m. Zientek, a graduate student from New Jersey, lived in married student housing with his wife, a nurse who worked at Harborview Medical Center. Their building had four units, side by side, each with two stories. The Zienteks lived at one end. Next to them was a German family. Then Curtis and Michelle Williams. Then a mother with three children.

Zientek scrambled outside and discovered the noise was coming from apartment 183, two doors down. He could hear Michelle Williams upstairs, crying. He called 911, then heard another scream. Two police officers arrived. They, too, heard the crying, coupled with a man's voice. They knocked, and the crying stopped. The light, upstairs, went off. The police kept knocking, but for twenty-five minutes, no one answered.

Neighbors told the officers that Curtis and Michelle had moved in earlier that month. The arguments—loud, frequent—had begun right away. That night, one woman heard Michelle cry, "I can't take it anymore!" then, "That hurts."

Done with knocking, the officers threatened to force the door if no one opened it. A minute later, Curtis and Michelle answered. Michelle lit into the two officers.

You woke up our daughter, she said.

But we heard you crying.

That's a lie. We were sleeping.

One of the officers saw some redness in one of Michelle's eyes.

We argued earlier, Michelle said. And yes, I cried. But that's all. I didn't say, "That hurts." Why would I?

Curtis backed her up. We argued, he said. That's all.

The officers saw no upturned furniture, no bruises or welts. With nothing more to go on, they documented the call and left.

The yelling continued, week after week, rattling the children who lived on either side. One girl thought Curtis's name was motherfucker, she heard him called that so often. The three kids in apartment 184 would sometimes run to Zientek's unit and hide, placing one more wall between themselves and the screaming. To Zientek, Michelle seemed quiet, reclusive. "She looked like a punching bag a few times," he says. He saw her with bruises, a black eye, and marks on her arm. Zientek called Lambright, the head football coach, to let him know what was going on. "He thanked me for being concerned," Zientek says.

The police kept getting called back. But what did they have to go on? In September, a neighbor heard Curtis beating at the door, trying to get in, with Michelle inside, yelling. Police arrived to find the window on the back door shattered, allowing someone to reach through and turn the handle. But Michelle had nothing to say, no complaint to make. In October, Michelle called 911. But when the officers arrived, she said only that they had argued, that she had felt intimidated, but he hadn't hit her, they would go to sleep now, there would be no more problems.

In November, Michelle called police again. When the officers arrived, Michelle was alone. She seemed quiet, nervous. She said they had argued, that she had wanted to leave the house and visit relatives, and that Curtis said no. As she lay in bed, Curtis punched her in the head. Then he left, taking Kymberly with him. This time, police had something to go on. When Curtis returned, they handcuffed him and took him to jail. Now he faced a misdemeanor charge of assault. Michelle told police she'd be leaving for Alaska that night, but she'd be willing to return and testify.

She never left for Alaska. Instead, she and Curtis moved to a new place, thinking new neighbors might be the answer. In December, a neighbor heard shouting, thumps against a wall, and a woman crying. He called police. The police knocked once, twice, three times, with no answer. The fourth time, Curtis opened the door, wearing only gray sweatpants. Officers saw specks of blood on his stomach and arms. Upstairs, in the bedroom, they saw puddles of blood—one on the pillow, six inches across, and four around the bed. Droplets ran to the bathroom, where a pile of Michelle's clothes lay, stained with blood. When Michelle came out of the bathroom, her nose appeared broken.

Police interviewed Michelle and Curtis separately. Both said they had returned home from a sports banquet when the telephone rang. Both said Michelle had received bad news about her grandmother and, in a fit, banged her head against the wall. Both said

Michelle's bloody nose was her own doing—that she "went all crazy," in Curtis's words—and that Curtis hadn't hit her. But beyond that, their stories fell apart. Either Curtis answered the phone, or Michelle. Either Michelle's grandmother died, or she was just ill. A sergeant pressed Michelle, asking who he could contact to corroborate their story about the late-night call.

He didn't mean to hurt me, Michelle said.

What do you mean? the sergeant asked.

Michelle retreated.

He didn't hit me, she said.

In another room, an officer asked Curtis if police had ever been called to their home before. No, Curtis said. Later, through dispatch, the officer learned of the four prior calls and of Williams's recent arrest. Police handcuffed Williams and took him in. He now had two assault charges pending against him.

A couple of days later, a victim advocate in the prosecutor's office met with Michelle. One of Michelle's eyes was black. Her nose, bruised, trickled blood. Curtis didn't hit her, Michelle said. Why was he being charged with assault? Charges would ruin him as a football player. Charges would cost him his scholarship. Michelle's family told the advocate that they believed Curtis had broken Michelle's arm when she was pregnant with Kymberly. The advocate wrote a report, saying, "I feel victim in <u>serious</u> danger."

In January 1997 a no-contact order took effect, requiring Curtis to stay away from Michelle. But the couple ignored it. They moved to a third place. In May, a downstairs neighbor called police to complain of yelling from above. Police tried reaching someone in the apartment, but no one answered on the intercom. No one came to the door. Two days later, on Mother's Day, Curtis surprised Michelle with new car speakers. He picked her up from work with one of her favorite songs playing, a 1980s tune by Ready for the World. "There were times when all the bad stuff didn't matter," Michelle says. "Because when it was good, it was so good, it was wonderful."

In late May 1997, Williams appeared in King County District Court. Prosecutors were cutting him a break: If he completed domestic-violence treatment and stayed out of trouble, they'd drop the two assault charges. The judge, Douglas J. Smith, approved the deal and lifted the no-contact order. Then he and Williams talked football.

Smith had grown up in the Bay area, a fan of the University of California Golden Bears. Now he had a son who was a football manager at Notre Dame. The judge and Williams chatted about spring ball, weight lifting, and the Huskies' game the previous season against the Irish. Williams said he'd missed that trip, because he redshirted his freshman year. "Yeah, that is a good way to do it," Smith said. "Learn the system before it gets too complicated."

"Okay," Smith told Williams, "as long as you don't play the Irish anymore, we can root for you. Except against the Cal Bears, too, I have a problem with that."

When Williams left court that day, he'd managed to escape a conviction, much less jail time. His scholarship was safe. He could still play. All he had to do was sign up for batterers' counseling and steer clear of any more charges.

Three days after the hearing, on a Saturday, Curtis wanted to go out with teammates. Michelle wanted him to stay with his family. This was the one day of the week she could spend with him. Monday through Friday, she worked fourteen-hour days. From 7 a.m. until 12:30 p.m. she worked at Kymberly's day care. From 1 p.m. until 9:30 or 10, she worked at the mall, first at Footlocker, later at Gymboree. She also worked one day each weekend. Curtis's scholarship covered the rent, but they still needed money for clothes, food, everything else.

Michelle wanted Curtis to go shopping with her for a new bed. But Curtis went out with Jeremiah Pharms, and pawned Michelle off on Jeremiah's wife, Franquell. That night, late, the two wives hunted down their husbands on campus, at a dance contest.

What time are you coming home? Michelle asked Curtis.

Why can't I be with my friends? Curtis asked Michelle.

Twenty minutes after they got home, Curtis wanted to go out again.

Fine, Michelle said. Leave. But you're not taking our car.

To keep him from driving off, she had hidden the key that deactivated the car's alarm. Tell me where the key is, he told her. She refused, so he went looking, making a mess of their apartment, tossing clothes she'd folded and placed into bins in the closet. He hollered at her, demanding the key, saying he wanted to go out, he didn't want to be there, she couldn't keep him there.

If you don't want me to hurt you, you'd better give me the key, he said. She refused. He grabbed her by the throat and began squeezing, choking her. Why do you make me do this to you? he said. He kept squeezing until Michelle passed out. She awoke soon after, coughing and vomiting. Curtis put his forearm to her throat and applied pressure again. This time, she remained conscious. He took off for the car and drove away, the alarm sounding.

Michelle called 911. When police arrived, just after midnight, she was crying. Her face was red, her hair disheveled. An officer saw a mark on her throat, two inches across.

As Michelle talked to police that night, she described her history with Curtis. He had choked her before, she said. He had cut her face with a key. He had broken her arm while she was pregnant. He would warn her: Don't tell anyone what happens. But tonight she'd had enough. She said in her police statement: "I cannot take it anymore."

Police offered to take Michelle and Kymberly to a shelter, but Michelle refused.

The police arrested Curtis after he returned to the apartment in the early morning hours. Curtis, crying, said he'd had an argument with Michelle, but denied choking her. He was booked into the King County Jail—and remained there for the next seventy-four days, unable to make $25,000 bail. He was charged with second-degree assault, a felony.

In July, Michelle recanted. She claimed to have made the whole story up. But the police had seen her neck. They had read the earlier reports. Prosecutors were used to women, abused and scared, taking back their words. They decided to move forward, even without Michelle's cooperation. If needed, they would let jurors hear the 911 tape from that night, with Michelle, crying, saying how afraid she was to report any violence, how afraid she was the state might take Kymberly away.

In September 1997, Williams pleaded guilty to third-degree assault, a felony. A probation officer interviewed Lambright for the sentencing report; she came away thinking the coaching staff was oblivious to how many times Curtis had attacked Michelle, oblivious to how dangerous he could be. Williams was sentenced to ninety days in jail—a sentence he had already served, with credit for good behavior. The judge placed Williams on probation and ordered him to stay away from Michelle and Kymberly.

The felony conviction negated Williams's deal in the two other assault cases. He returned to District Court and Judge Smith. This time, Smith didn't talk about some game or the advantages of redshirting. He talked about what happens when a football program loses control of its players. He criticized Nebraska, whose players were getting in trouble but still suiting up. "Tom Osborne didn't help anybody," he said, referring to Nebraska's head coach.

Oklahoma in the 1970s and '80s under Barry Switzer. Miami in the 1980s and early '90s under Jimmy Johnson and Dennis Erickson. Nebraska in the mid-1990s under Tom Osborne. All won championships on the field while players found trouble off of it. All raised questions about a lack of discipline and the price of victory. The Washington Huskies weren't breaking new ground here.

At least two dozen players on Washington's 2000 football team were arrested or charged with some crime while at the UW. But rarely did they miss playing time. This has become the story of college football. Some players do serious damage. Some get used up. A city looks away, and the game goes on. Variations of this story—more about culture than sports, more about a community than a team—can be found in colleges across the country. Florida State. Ohio State. Texas A&M. Washington isn't an aberration. It is an example.

Sometimes, a school cracks down. In 1996 almost half the University of Rhode Island football team staged a ferocious, coordinated attack on a fraternity, with some players rushing in while others blocked the exits. Why? Because two players had been turned away from a party there.

In the attack, three fraternity members were severely beaten. The coach responded by kicking two players off the team and suspending twenty-nine others. The university president forfeited the team's next game. "This is not about football," the president said. "This is about community standards. This is about character."

But Rhode Island was the exception. Tom Osborne was the rule. In November 2000—nearly three years after he retired from coaching—Osborne was elected to Congress with more than 80 percent of the vote. That's what three national championships will do for you. Of course, some folks outside Nebraska were horrified at how Lawrence Phillips dragged his ex-girlfriend down three flights of stairs by her hair, and how Osborne had reinstated Phillips after a six-game suspension. Other members of Nebraska's 1995 championship team played despite being convicted of sexual assault, or after being charged with firing two bullets into an occupied car, or while awaiting trial for attempted second-degree murder.

After reviewing the police reports, Judge Smith convicted Williams of the two misdemeanor charges and moved straight to sentencing. Williams's lawyer, a public defender, asked for leniency. The UW would no longer let Williams play football, she said. But Fresno State would. Fresno State had stepped in and offered him a football scholarship. Put him on probation, she asked the judge. Order him to get treatment. But don't give him any more jail time. Let him go to Fresno State and get an education.

The judge said he'd yet to see Williams acknowledge any responsibility for his violence. So Williams addressed the court: "Well, I feel real bad because I do, on the felony, you know, I hurt Michelle and I'm real sorry about that. I know that I need to get into counseling and I need to get my life back together because I lost it. . . . I'm going to get the treatment because I still love Michelle and Kymberly. I want to be there for them one of these days. . . . I'm just lucky that Fresno is letting me go, being convicted."

The lawyer asked that Williams be sentenced to community service. But the judge said social services agencies don't want people who hit women. "They don't mind thieves, people with traffic tickets, stuff like that."

Smith sentenced Williams to six months in jail and two years' probation. He said Williams would also get an additional six months if he failed to meet certain conditions. Williams had to get domestic-violence treatment, commit no more crimes, stay away from Michelle and Kymberly, and abstain from alcohol and drugs. "If he doesn't want to do that he can serve out a year," the judge said. Williams appealed both convictions—and was allowed to stay free in the meantime. He never transferred to Fresno State, deciding to stay in Seattle instead.

In December 1997, Michelle's mother visited from Alaska. She discovered Curtis living with Michelle, despite the no-contact order. Michelle's mom tried calling 911, but Curtis grabbed her, bruising her arm. Later, she contacted a probation officer and related what she'd seen. She also said that Curtis had threatened to kill his wife and daughter if Michelle ever left him.

Prosecutors filed two more charges against Williams—pushing the total to five since he had arrived at the UW. He was arrested and spent fifteen days in jail, his second stretch within a year. He probably would have stayed longer were it not for the football team. Two UW coaches, Scott Linehan and Ron Milus, appeared in Superior Court and vouched for Williams, urging his release. The judge went along.

By the spring of 1998, Curtis and Michelle were broke. The university had stopped paying Curtis his married allowance, and instead provided a dorm bed and about a hundred dollars a month. But Curtis rarely slept on campus. He and Michelle continued to defy the no-contact order, living together in an apartment. Soon, their money gone, they gave thirty days' notice. Curtis bunked in his dorm, while Michelle and Kymberly moved in with some childhood friends of Michelle's from Alaska. It made for tight living quarters, all those women and a young girl in a small apartment. But the lack of privacy offered one benefit: Curtis couldn't visit and be alone with Michelle. Nor could Michelle be seen near Curtis at the university. "When I moved in with my girlfriends, I guess I came to my senses," Michelle says. "My girlfriends were telling me that I didn't deserve to be treated that way. Not with Kymberly around."

Then came an offer. Gymboree was opening a store in Alaska. Was Michelle interested in relocating to help get it started? She was unsure, but said yes. Two weeks before she was due to leave, Michelle called Curtis. She wanted to give him a chance to spend some time with his daughter. He didn't pick up the phone. She left a message, but he didn't call back. A week later, she called again. Again, no response. Curtis and Michelle had never even talked about breaking up. Now, without a word spoken, they were finished. "It was my sign the relationship was over," Michelle says. Michelle and Kymberly stepped onto the plane and left Seattle behind.

Jim Lambright had seen enough. By the summer of 1998 he wanted to pull Williams's scholarship, to give it to someone else. A football program only gets so many—and Williams was wasting his. Plus, he had yet to do a single thing to help the football team. He hadn't even played a down.

Lambright and other members of the athletic department wrote up three pages of history to support their case. Williams had been convicted of a felony and served time. He blew off classes and tutoring sessions. His GPA was 1.84; he was academically ineligible to play. The team had let Williams miss practices to attend counseling for domestic violence—only to discover that he'd skipped two-thirds of the sessions. He defied the court by violating no-contact orders. His wife and mother-in-law were stirring up trouble. They were calling coaches, threatening legal action if Williams wasn't held accountable. They were also calling the press. It was only a matter of time before this hit the newspapers, and given the program's recent history, who needed that?

But for all its sweep, the athletic department's case ran light on detail. The felony conviction was due to an "altercation." That's all the documents said. No mention of choking his wife until she passed out. No mention of the other assault charges, for punching his wife in the head, for breaking her nose.

Williams contested the move to lift his scholarship, so the matter went to hearing before the Athletic Financial Aid Committee. Because of student privacy laws, confidentiality applied. Eric Godfrey chaired the committee. He was the financial aid director and later vice-provost for student life. The other members consisted of a law professor, a financial aid counselor, and the executive director of admissions. Williams represented himself; a senior associate athletic director stated the football program's case.

No one bothered to pull the court files on Williams's criminal history. Pulling a file is easy. You ask, the clerk gives. But to Godfrey, this was a hearing committee, not an investigative committee. The task of finding and presenting evidence fell to the athletic department. The committee's job was to weigh it.

In early September, a week after the hearing, Godfrey wrote to apprise Williams of the committee's decision: He would get to keep his scholarship. Two reasons had been offered to take his scholarship—lack of academic progress and "domestic difficulties." But both problems had been resolved, Godfrey wrote. Williams had earned fifteen credits during the summer quarter to regain his eligibility. "Moreover," Godfrey wrote, "your personal difficulties appear to have been eliminated, largely because your wife has relocated to Alaska." Williams's marriage was "the principal source" of his problems, Godfrey wrote. But now Michelle was gone—so that was that.

When the university renewed his scholarship, Williams had three assault convictions, two on appeal. Two other charges were pending against him. But the committee didn't concern itself with such particulars. It was a hearing committee, not an investigative committee.

At the UW, athletes got to sign up for classes before regular students, an advantage they seized. Football and basketball players flocked to Swahili in such numbers that other students could wait three or four years to get into the class. Swahili was a win-win. It earned foreign-language credits, the thorniest requirement of some majors. And it was an easy grade. It doesn't sound easy, learning to say things like "poa kichizi kama ndizi" ("cool as a banana"), but it was.

Seyed Maulana, the UW's sole Swahili teacher for more than twenty years, accommodated athletes, who typically accounted for about half his students. During away games, he faxed the exams to coaches, and they faxed the answers back. After a year of study, students could voice some greetings, but not much else. "I tend to focus more on the structure of the language," Maulana says. Robert Aronson, the faculty representative to the athletic department, noticed how Swahili appealed to football players, particularly those who struggled academically. "It was awfully suspicious to me," he says.

The summer his scholarship was in jeopardy, Williams turned to Swahili. All fifteen of the credits that Godfrey cited in his letter came from just one course, "Intensive Swahili," in which Williams earned a 3.0. This was a whopping fifteen credits' worth of B, enough to lift Williams's GPA from 1.84 to 2.05, above the 2.0 cutoff line that allows students to play. Williams recognized a good thing. In semesters to come, he kept taking Swahili, earning a C, an A-, and a B+. He earned thirty Swahili credits in all, nearly a fifth of his total at the UW.

Williams wasn't the first player to discover the benefits of Maulana's course. Swahili had been the football team's academic lifeline for years. When Washington quarterback Billy Joe Hobert dropped out of school in 1992, he also regained his eligibility by taking Swahili over the summer for fifteen credits.

Williams, who majored in American Ethnic Studies, also took other classes popular among players: Geology 100 (Dinosaurs), Geology 101 ("Rocks for Jocks," as other students called it), and Independent Study. The B's and high C's he racked up in those kinds of classes helped compensate for the courses he flunked: Appreciation of Architecture, Psychology 101, Astronomy 101, Introduction to Sociological Methods, Principles of Biological Anthropology, and Air/Space Vehicles.

For Curtis and Michelle, there was no happily ever after. But what story there was, the newspapers missed or ignored. Or they did what falls in between, reporting what someone says without checking to see if it's true.

Williams didn't play the 1997 season because he had choked his wife and been forced to drop his classes while in jail. He missed the season because he had been convicted of three counts of assault. But when Williams didn't show up for the 1997 season, the newspapers didn't check court records. Or if they did check court records, they didn't report what they found. Instead, they quoted the coach. Lambright told the beat writer for the *Seattle Post-Intelligencer* that Williams was off the team with "personal problems. He'll be invited back as soon as he gets himself together." A sports columnist for the *Seattle Times* attributed Williams's absence to "academic difficulties." The Tacoma paper cited "academic and unspecified off-field problems."

Williams returned for the 1998 season because he withstood Lambright's efforts to pull his scholarship. The team didn't expect Williams back. He wasn't even listed in the pre-season media guide. But coaches described Williams's return as a simple matter of getting his academics in order—which was true as far as it went, and since no reporter took it further, it was true enough.

Unable to cut him, the team played him. Against Utah State, Williams forced a fumble on one kick and recovered a fumble on another. He became a special-teams star.

When Williams had been sentenced in the felony case in 1997, the judge ordered him to get two kinds of treatment. He needed batterers' counseling, that was obvious. But Williams also seemed to have no compassion for Michelle's suffering, no remorse for what he had put her through. So he was also ordered to get victim-awareness counseling. But time and again, he failed to enter the two programs, or missed individual sessions, or showed up late. He also skipped appointments with probation officers. He blamed these lapses on the demands of football practices, games, and school— and since the university's records showed he was missing a lot of school, it's safe to say his time was going to football.

The court system let him get away with it. In February 1998 a probation officer asked that Williams get 240 days in jail for blowing off the two treatment programs and for other probation violations. Her request went before Superior Court judge Charles Mertel, who graduated from the UW in 1957 and had held football season tickets ever since. Mertel lettered in tennis all four of his years at the UW; he later returned to the university to coach the sport. In Mertel's courtroom, Williams appeared with one of the football team's assistant coaches. "I remember him standing up in front of me," Mertel says of Williams. "He was articulate and handsome. I thought, 'This guy has got everything in the world going for him, if he would just put it together.'" Instead of eight months, Mertel gave Williams fifteen days—time he had already served, which meant Williams could leave court and go home. Afterward, Williams blew off treatment again. The probation officer asked for forty days in jail, saying Williams "shows an absolute blatant disregard" for his court-ordered obligations. "There needs to be a consequence," she wrote. But this time, Mertel didn't give Williams any jail time at all.

A year later, a different probation officer threatened Williams with some punishment. Williams told the officer: Hey, take me to court. The judge won't put me in jail.

In June 1999, this probation officer wrote of Williams: "Is extremely self-centered and still does not take responsibility for his anger and violence. Has been in therapy for well over a year, and while there has been some change, he is as narcissistic as ever. Does not feel the rules apply to him and decides which rules he will follow."

If Williams was beginning to feel that the rules didn't apply to him, the court system was doing nothing to dispel that notion. In July 1999, Williams received an extraordinary break. A District Court judge reversed Williams's two misdemeanor assault convictions—not because of any doubt about the evidence's merits, but because the evidence itself was missing. Police records crucial to the case were supposed to be in the court file. But they "were inexplicably removed or lost or destroyed," the judge wrote, throwing out the convictions and ordering a new trial. Prosecutors now had to start over with those two charges. The missing records allowed Williams to avoid six months in jail—and to keep playing football.

And the breaks just kept coming. After two years of off-and-on counseling, Williams finished batterers' treatment. On a scale of zero to nine—with zero the most dangerous, nine the least—he scored a two: "able to recognize his controlling behavior." But Williams never finished victim-awareness counseling. Twice, he entered the program. Twice, he dropped out. No matter. Judge Mertel released him from probation anyway.

Mertel says he did nothing special for Williams or any other Husky athlete who came before him. "No. I dealt with them like anybody else. They got no different treatment or breaks. They are like anyone else."

The 1999 season was Rick Neuheisel's first as Washington's

coach. Neuheisel put an end to moving Williams around—one day at running back, the next at defensive back. Neuheisel planted him at safety and turned him loose. Starting every game, Williams led the team in solo tackles and was named an honorable mention All-Pac-10. Godfrey, the UW vice-provost, would see Williams around campus and feel quiet pride in how Williams had turned his life around. His committee had made the right call, Godfrey would tell himself. At the year-end banquet, Williams received the Chuck Niemi Award for the team's biggest hitter.

The UW media guide for 2000—Williams's final season—recited all those honors and statistics from the 1999 season. But it made no mention of 1996. It made no mention of 1997. The media guide picked up Williams's college career at 1998.

With all the breaks he had received, Williams could have entered his final campaign with a sense of relief, a sense that the worst was behind him. But he just kept defying the system. He kept missing court hearings—and judges kept issuing arrest warrants. One warrant was discovered when police stopped him for more than $800 worth of unpaid parking tickets. In the spring of 2000, Williams missed a hearing on the two reinstated assault charges. A judge issued another warrant—one that was still outstanding when the Huskies' season began.

Just as there was no telling when Jerramy Stevens might be charged, if at all, just as there was no telling when Jeremiah Pharms might be charged, if at all, there was no telling when Curtis Williams might be arrested.

The Twelfth Man

10

September 9, 2000: Miami at Washington

There, on the Washington sidelines, sat the national championship trophy, a football made of Waterford Crystal—worth $30,000, easy—affixed to an ebony base. The trophy traveled—from Saturday to Saturday, from college to college—its arrival an announcement that *this one matters*, this game could determine the best team in the land. Corporations even vied to sponsor the glass football. Pepsi. McDonald's. This year it was Sears.

Lynn Swann, the Hall of Fame wide receiver, reported from the sidelines. Bob Griese, the Hall of Fame quarterback, provided color in the booth. ABC was televising the game nationally: the Miami Hurricanes, ranked No. 4 in the country, against the Washington Huskies, No. 15. In 1991 these two teams went undefeated and shared the national championship. Both programs had slipped since then, but now, each figured it was back. For the winner, this game would prove it.

This Miami team was loaded. The Hurricanes' roster included at least seven players who would become NFL Pro Bowlers: Clinton Portis, Santana Moss, Ed Reed, Jeremy Shockey, Dan Morgan, Andre Johnson, Reggie Wayne. Before the game, in the stadium tunnel, the Hurricanes taunted the Huskies. "Miami was talking crap . . . saying you guys are just puppy dogs. They were going woof, woof, woof," says Rock Nelson, one of the UW's offensive linemen.

"And here comes the pride of the Northwest," said Brad Nessler, ABC's play-by-play man, as the Huskies emerged from the tunnel. Husky Stadium was sold out, the crowd so loud that Miami's players would struggle to hear their quarterback. "It felt like an earthquake was going on, the place was just rocking and rolling," Nelson says.

A ship canal borders Husky Stadium to the south. Union Bay, part of Lake Washington, hugs to the east. Sit high in the stands, and you can see the snowcapped Olympic range to the west, beyond Puget Sound. Other seats provide views of the Cascades or the Seattle skyline and its Space Needle. Some fans sailed their forty-foot boats to the game, dropping anchor in the bay. Washington's celebrated crew team picked them up and paddled them to shore. Some fans walked across the bridge from their Tudor-style homes in Montlake, a lovely neighborhood both moneyed and liberal. How many places with a yacht club back the Democrat for president five to one? Some fans drove. In the stadium's south lot they partook in tablecloth tailgating, with champagne and brie alongside the chips and brats.

The stadium was built in 1920 for $600,000. To help pay, the people of Seattle pooled $50 and $100 donations. To minimize the glare for players, UW astronomers calculated the sun's rays to determine the stadium's ideal axis. As the university and city grew, so did Husky Stadium. Four remodels expanded the seating capacity from 30,000 to 72,500, making Washington's the largest stadium, college or pro, in the Pacific Northwest. Two of the additions—massive cantilevers on the north and south sides—provide the stadium a peculiar look, like it fell from space and the hatch got stuck while opening. In 1968, Washington became the first big college to install AstroTurf. In 2000, the stadium shifted to FieldTurf, which uses, as fill, sliced-up rubber from recycled running shoes to cushion the surface and reduce injuries. This state-of-the-art turf came courtesy of a $1 million donation from Paul Allen, co-founder of Microsoft.

In this game, the oddsmakers liked Miami, even on the road. Washington figured to have trouble throwing the ball. Miami's secondary was perhaps the country's best, while Washington's receiving corps was a question mark. But against Miami, Jerramy Stevens provided an answer.

Although ABC made no mention of how Stevens played while under suspicion of rape, this didn't escape the notice of the Seattle Police Department. Fellow officers would tell Detective Parker: *I see Stevens is still playing.*

In the first quarter, a defender grabbed Stevens in the end zone, drawing a pass-interference flag that led to Washington's first touchdown. The Huskies went up 7–0—and were just getting started. On defense, the Huskies rattled Ken Dorsey, Miami's young quarterback. "Jeremiah Pharms has brought the farm," Nessler said, as Pharms threw Dorsey to the ground. Cornerback Anthony Vontoure reached Dorsey on a blitz, forcing a fumble. When Dorsey did hit his receivers, Washington's safeties punished them. Curtis Williams cracked Miami's tight end after a 5-yard gain. "Man, was he met head up, Curtis Williams, helmet to helmet," Nessler said.

Two minutes before halftime, Stevens lined up in the slot— more like a wide receiver than a tight end—and went into motion. No one on Miami picked him up. Twenty-three yards later, Stevens was in the end zone, the ball in his hands. His touchdown put the Huskies up 21–3.

ABC's announcers talked up the challenges that confront any team visiting Husky Stadium. Swann noted how loud the crowd was. And how smart. Whenever Dorsey checked off—trying, under center, to change the play called in the huddle—the fans screamed even louder, so his teammates couldn't hear. When the Huskies left the field at halftime, up eighteen, Neuheisel told Swann: "We've got a twelfth man here. Hopefully they're going to be ready to rock and roll in the second half."

Seattle loves football. Home games for the Seahawks get so loud that some opponents accuse the team of pumping noise in. It's tempting to associate the sport with the South (Florida, Alabama, Louisiana, Texas), the plains (Oklahoma, Nebraska) and with frigid pockets up north (Green Bay, Buffalo). But football transcends geography, denomination (Notre Dame, Southern Methodist, Brigham Young), size (Chicago, Odessa), education, and political lean. Football isn't red state or blue state. Football is America. Seattle's as crazy about football as Tuscaloosa, Norman, or Miami, way down in the opposite corner of the country.

Of course, the people of Seattle might reject such a notion. Or they might embrace it. It's hard to tell: The crowd watching the Huskies and Hurricanes came from one of America's most inscrutable cities, a majestic land of contradiction where visitors must learn to interpret silences.

Seattle values civility. You can go days without hearing a horn, months without seeing a middle finger. Drivers let other cars merge. Pedestrians obey lights. A man's on one side of the street, a woman on the other. They're looking at each other, all googly-eyed. They're giddy. He's waving, she's jumping up and down. There are no cars coming. Either could cross—only the stoplight says no. So they wait. She shifts her weight from one leg to the other, like she's going to pee her pants. Finally, the light changes. The glowing stick figure says go. The woman runs across the street and into the guy's arms. They hadn't seen each other in—what— months? But they waited for the light, because this is Seattle, and that's what people in Seattle do.

But Seattle's not what you'd call friendly. Say hi to a stranger, and he stares at his shoes.

Old Seattle harvested the forests and seas, and built planes to fill the skies. New Seattle paints itself green, repelled by plastic grocery bags and bottled water. New Seattle is a world leader. The Gates Foundation tackles global health with a programmer's pragmatism, emphasizing idealism with results. Starbucks is the anti-Chiquita; it treats foreign growers with respect. Costco is the anti-Walmart; it treats employees with respect. At home, New Seattle believes a half-million people can reach consensus—a noble but silly sentiment that begs paralysis. Study, study, study, vote, vote, vote—repeat. While Seattle works to save the world, local projects wither and die.

In Seattle, you can go into work on Monday, ask the guy next to you about his weekend, and he'll say he climbed Mount Baker, like it's no big deal. The people are fit, literate, and artsy. Church isn't big, but books are. One librarian became a celebrity, with her own action-figure doll. Seattle is the country's most educated city: More than half the adults have bachelor's degrees. But a lot of those degree holders come from somewhere else. Seattle struggles to educate its own. School funding is a mess. Teacher salaries lag behind most of the country. A third of Seattle's students don't graduate from high school. Of those who do, only one in six meet the requirements to go to college.

Seattle's got Hempfest and HUMP!, the former a celebration of marijuana, the latter an amateur porn festival sponsored by *The Stranger*, a gloriously unrestrained alternative weekly. On First Avenue, the Seattle Art Museum faces The Lusty Lady, a peep-show emporium. Monet, Degas, Manet here, and over there a pink-and-black marquee specializing in blue puns: "Check Our Stimulus Package" . . . "Veni Vidi Veni" . . . "Wood Friday" . . . "Erin Go Braugh-less." At the Solstice Day Parade, families line the streets to watch naked people on bicycles. One participant built a massive rocket ship that emerged from his nether regions. Another put an empty picture frame around his naked ass and labeled the result George Bush. In Seattle, a first-grader can watch this parade and not mention it to his friends the next day. Because naked people don't rate. The kid's seen them before. His friends have, too. In Indianapolis, a naked cyclist with his dingus painted blue would be a talker. But not in Seattle.

At the same time, the city council passed a rule saying no customer of a strip joint could come within four feet of a dancer. And turn up those lights, make them bright, bright, bright. (After the four-foot rule made Seattle the butt of jokes, the measure was rescinded by popular vote. Seattle does not like being laughed at.) One Seattle mayor waged war on nightclubs, as if shocked to discover that bar-goers often drink and don't always behave. Seattle is easily scandalized. The *Seattle Times* ran a front-page exposé about a uniformed cop who "embraced and passionately kissed" a stripper in her club's parking lot. Think that would make the newspaper in New Orleans? Cleveland? Detroit?

Compared to most other cities, Seattle is not racially diverse; it's mostly white and Asian. But in other ways it is spectacularly diverse. In Seattle, it's okay to be different. Pierce your eyebrows, tattoo whatever, wherever. The neighborhood of Montlake is more the exception than the rule. Most of the city is gritty. The University District—or "U District," more commonly—brings together, in one Seattle neighborhood, junkies and sorority sisters, homeless kids and aspiring doctors, smoke shops and vegetarian restaurants. Its best-known bar is the Blue Moon Tavern, a dive built during the Depression. One regular in the 1950s and '60s was Theodore Roethke, a poet who struggled with alcoholism and mental illness, and who wrote often of despair. "Dark, dark my light, and darker my desire. / My soul, like some heat-maddened summer fly / Keeps buzzing at the sill." When Dylan Thomas visited Roethke, the two went to the Blue Moon.

The U District's main street is University Way, which locals call The Ave. The street offers just about anything you'd want to buy, see, or eat, or have done to your hair, body, or spirit. On The Ave you can find Bulgogi, BBQ short rib, stir-fried squid, Mongolian, Trinidadian, Brazilian, Pakistani, meth, marijuana, coffee, cocaine, Bento, falafel, gargoyles, bubble tea, green-tea frozen yogurt with granola on top, massage, a pregnancy clinic, Persian musical instruments, geochemical art, vintage clothing, body piercing, kabobs, sake, a sliver of an apartment with the address of 4736½, a street ministry, Tai Chi, healing and meditation, drumming and energy dance, and lots of books, used and new. One Web site, which offers the skinny on where to buy drugs worldwide, endorses The Ave if you're passing through Seattle. Street kids, called "Ave Rats," cluster on the sidewalks and in the alleys. Sometimes, they give the panhandlers a hard time.

Seattle is a long ways from Lincoln, Nebraska, or College Station, Texas. But when it comes to football, the differences disappear. Football is religion, and religion roams.

Miami made a run in the second half, thanks to two fourth-quarter turnovers by Washington and the dynamic play of Clinton Portis. With less than three minutes to go, Miami closed to within 5 points, at 34–29. But Miami, with no time-outs left, needed the ball back. The Hurricanes opted for an onside kick.

Miami's kicker hit a low line drive—straight into the gut of Jerramy Stevens. Stevens held on, sealing the Huskies' victory. "That might be his biggest catch in a career-high day," Nessler said. Stevens finished with seven catches for 89 yards and a touchdown. Afterward, he said of Miami: "They were yelping a bit in the tunnel. They found out who the real dogs were."

As the seconds ticked down, Griese said: "We mentioned earlier, there's a lot of optimism around this school, this campus, this football program. And it's because of Rick Neuheisel." After the game, Neuheisel had his players leave the locker room and return to the field to celebrate with the fans. The chant went up: "Whose House? Dawgs' House! Whose House? Dawgs' House!"

In Hiding

11

Marie didn't go to the Miami game. She didn't watch it on TV, either.

After going to the hospital for the rape exam, Marie didn't return to school. She didn't return to her sorority. Her father and brother went to Pi Beta Phi and picked up all her stuff. She waited on word of the HIV test. Finally, the results came back. Negative. For weeks, she spent most of the day in bed. "She just wanted to stay home and hide," her mother says. "She cried all the time. Her dad cried all the time, he couldn't stop crying. I tried to cry away from everybody else, because I thought out of the three of us, somebody's got to not cry." Marie didn't answer the phone. Having no other way to reach her, sorority sisters and other friends wrote her letters, thirty or forty of them. "It was sad, because some of them were not signed, but they said similar things had happened to them," Marie says.

That summer, Marie's mother worked temporarily in northern Washington, near the Canadian border. Marie went and stayed with her. "No one knew me up there, no one knew who I was. I didn't have to worry about all the questions. In Seattle, it was just so in your face. Everywhere. Some people knew, some people didn't know, but it was wondering if they did know, and are they looking at me, are they wondering why." Her biggest fear was that people would find out that she was the student in the newspapers, the student behind Jerramy Stevens's arrest. She worried: What are people going to think of me? Am I going to be tainted? Are other guys not going to want to date me? Are they going to think I have a disease? "She was kind of like a hollow shell," her brother says. "She was not the sister that I knew. She was empty, beside herself, frustrated, didn't know what was going on. And that's just not her. She was always in control of everything in her life. Always."

Normally, when someone leaves a sorority—packs up and leaves, without a word—the sorority says she has *dropped her pin*, meaning, she's no longer a member. But Pi Beta Phi kept a place for Marie. "It was just, kind of, we knew—that she wasn't going to come back to the sorority, that she couldn't come back to the U," Sunny Rockom says. "I was angry. I felt bad for her. I think it was just always in the back of everyone's minds. Everyone loved her. She was friends with everyone in the house, and everyone was just devastated. And they missed her."

Marie confided in some of her professors, who let her take her final exams later that summer. But the university's administration never reached out. "Nobody protected me at all," Marie says. "Nobody gave me a call, nothing. It was like it never happened." As summer faded, Marie made a decision. She would return to school. It wouldn't be the U, because she couldn't face the possibility of seeing Stevens or his friends on campus, she couldn't stomach how the university had taken no action against him, letting him continue to play football. But it would be school, it would be classes, getting back on track, a small step back. She enrolled at Bellevue Community College. She bought all her books. She woke up her first week of classes—and got dressed up, packed her things, and prepared to leave.

At the front door, she stopped. She dropped her purse. She started to cry.

"I can't do it, Mom," she said.

"It's okay, honey. You don't have to."

Marie went to work at Nordstrom, in women's hosiery. "It kept my mind off stuff. That was the whole purpose. And it was good work experience, and kept me busy, so I wouldn't be home all day, moping." Marie's mother didn't see her daughter smile, for weeks on end. "Just not my little girl," she says. "It was heart-breaking to look at her day in and day out. I thought, 'It's going to affect her for the rest of her life.'"

One day that summer, Marie's mother saw King County's elected prosecutor, Norm Maleng, on TV, saying something about how college girls who drink too much get in trouble. She believed Maleng's remark was a veiled reference to her daughter. Infuriated, she made an appointment to go see him. Marie's brother went, too.

Marie's mother told Maleng: Something you need to realize is that everybody's all worried about Jerramy, Jerramy is going to be this big Husky football star, and Jerramy's going to be this, and Jerramy's going to be that. Well, what about my star? What about my star who has had her heart ripped out?

Maleng had been the county's chief prosecutor for more years than Marie had been alive. The color had long since left his hair. "He comes up and puts his arm around me, and says, so fatherly, 'You know, you should be thankful you have your daughter.' And I looked at him, and I said, 'Well . . . I am.' And he said, 'Well, I lost my daughter. She was in a sledding accident. So you are very lucky that you have her.' And I said, 'I'm terribly, terribly sorry that you lost your daughter. But what does that have to do with what happened to my daughter?' And he goes, 'Well, it's time for you to go home now,' and scooted me out the door."

As the weeks turned to months, Marie's mother had had enough. "She wanted me to get angry, rather than be sad," Marie says. "She would say, 'Get angry. Be mad. Don't be sad. Don't let him take that from you. Don't give him that validation that you're not going to go places because he's there. That you are going to sit at home. Don't give that to him.'"

Taking a Pass   **12**

Washington's win over Miami impressed the voters who rank college football teams. When the Associated Press poll came out Sunday, Washington jumped six spots, to No. 9. The UW looked like a program on the rise. Sportswriters, potential recruits, other coaches—they all took notice. The usual obstacles appeared—one Husky broke his elbow against Miami, depleting the team's depth on the defensive line—but otherwise, good vibes rippled across the sports pages. "Washington's bandwagon is becoming crowded," the Associated Press wrote.

But unbeknownst to Washington's fans—unbeknownst even to its players—a forensic report threatened all the good cheer. Five days after the Miami game, Detective Mudd received word from the Washington State Patrol crime lab. DNA tests had linked the bloody fingerprint to Pharms. The blood on the car door—the blood left by one of the two men who robbed and shot Kerry Sullivan, the campus drug dealer—was consistent with Pharms's genetic profile. If this report became public, those good vibes would be replaced by ugly headlines.

The report reached Mudd's desk on September 14—six months to the day after Sullivan was shot. Half a year had passed, and now police had DNA to go with all the other evidence implicating Pharms: the fingerprint matching his right pinky; the Nike glove; his girlfriend's car; how he'd been there earlier the same night—how he knew where the stash was, how he and the shooter had the same build and thick neck.

Prosecutors often file charges on less. Juries often convict on less. But the problem in this case wasn't the evidence. The problem—to the mind of prosecutors, anyway—was the suspect.

The King County prosecuting attorney's office assigned two top deputies to the case: Mike Lang and Steve Fogg. In a normal case, they would have filed charges as soon as the DNA results came back. They might even have filed earlier, based on the other evidence. But the suspect was Jeremiah Pharms, a Husky standout ticketed for the NFL—and to Fogg and Lang, that signaled trouble. They had no doubt Pharms was their guy. But they looked at it this way. The media lionize sports figures. Jurors do, too. This case offered a drug dealer as victim—"unsympathetic" is the adjective prosecutors would use—and a football star as defendant. If the prosecutors weren't careful, they could wind up in a trial where the media would second-guess and the jury balk. "If you have a Husky or a Seahawk as a defendant, people will want to believe the best of their sports heroes," Fogg says. "That's true in somebody's living room, that's true in the jury room. If there's any doubt at all, that doubt will go in favor of the sports star."

The prosecutors decided they needed more evidence; they decided they needed to bulletproof their case. Instead of relying exclusively on the state crime lab, the prosecutors sent the blood evidence to Edward Blake in Richmond, California. In the world of forensics, Blake was a star, a DNA pioneer who had helped exonerate dozens of people falsely accused. His work figured in all kinds of high-profile cases: Gary Dotson in Illinois, Kirk Bloodsworth in Maryland, Earl Washington in Virginia. Here was a guy who could wow jurors. He had even advised the defense team when O. J. Simpson stood trial for double murder, and everyone knows how that turned out.

While Blake ran his tests, the prosecutors would hold off on charges. Pharms would suit up for game No. 3, at Colorado, and then he'd just keep suiting up, for however long it took to get the results back. No one would be the wiser. The fans would remain oblivious. The sportswriters would remain oblivious. So would most—but not all—of Pharms's teammates. The prosecutors had opted to go cautious. And nothing suited their boss more.

Norm Maleng was a prosecutor defense attorneys respected, a Republican Democrats liked. He was a politician, but with no taste for the demands of politics. Campaigning, he could drop into a Dairy Queen in some remote town and neglect to chat up even one person. None of this, "I'm Norm Maleng, and I'm running for governor, and I'd sure appreciate your vote." To him, a coffee shop was a place to drink coffee—not an opportunity to make the rounds and press the flesh. It's no wonder he ran for statewide office three times—and lost every time. He never came close.

Maleng may have lacked the charisma to be elected the state's governor or attorney general, but to the voters of King County, he was a civic treasure. As head of the prosecuting attorney's office, he was steady and sober, decent and kind. He didn't grandstand. He didn't play politics. The county, a Democratic stronghold, elected Maleng, a Republican, eight straight times. It was never even close.

The son of Norwegian immigrants, Maleng grew up on a small dairy farm in northern Washington. Rise early, milk the cows, attend school or church, milk the cows, study, go to bed. Maleng's résumé tracked as straight as the man. High school valedictorian. A bachelor's degree in economics from the University of Washington. Three years in the Army, in the quartermaster corps. A law degree from the University of Washington, where he graduated top of his class and was editor of the law review. He worked as a Senate aide in Washington DC, in a law firm in Seattle, and as a deputy King County prosecutor, running the civil division. In 1978, at the age of forty, Maleng won the election to run the whole show.

His voice came more from his nose than throat. He was a bit of a klutz, wore big glasses, and said things like "gosh." Staffers became familiar with Maleng's love of certain phrases: "Do good. Make a difference. . . . It's not a problem, it's an opportunity. . . . You're a blessing in my life." When his daughter Karen died at age twelve, in a sledding accident, Maleng believed she became an angel; simple delights, he attributed to her. He quoted the Bible, identified with the pain of others, volunteered countless hours at his alma mater, and found joy in sports. He took in Mariners, Sonics, and Husky games with his son, attended spring training in Arizona, and bedecked his office with sports memorabilia.

He was not the prosecutor of stereotype—a blunt instrument blind to life's grays. He established a special drug court that emphasized counseling more than jail. Faced with Gary Ridgway—the Green River killer, a man who murdered at least forty-eight women—Maleng abandoned a pledge never to plea-bargain with the death penalty. He spared Ridgway's life in exchange for information about all the women he killed and where he dumped the bodies; that way, every victim's family could know the truth.

The stereotype was Chuck Carroll, King County's elected prosecutor throughout the 1950s and '60s. *He* was a blunt instrument. A Husky football legend, he took a mediocre academic record and brilliant athletic career and cashed in. He stood for patronage and power and unspoken threat. He played footsie with the *Seattle Times* and was rewarded with one flattering story after another. One rumor had it that he secretly tape-recorded conversations; his successor found weird wiring in the desk. Another rumor had it that he went easy on Husky football players. He was called "Iron Man" for his football exploits and "Fair Catch" by critics who thought he dodged tough cases, particularly ones with no political payoff. Wave your hand in the air. Don't risk fumbling.

Maleng cared more about competence than party affiliation. He was New Seattle. He was civility and respect. But he had some of that old "Fair Catch" in him, too. When Maleng was a deputy prosecutor, more than a dozen current and former public officials stood trial on corruption charges; the lead defendant was none other than Chuck Carroll. Maleng personally tried the case—and lost. He never tried another criminal case again.

When Maleng ran the office, few doubted his integrity. But some staffers whispered how he didn't take on people with the means to fight back. He didn't charge a federal judge accused of cutting down trees on public land to improve his view. He took a pass on charging any number of cops. The rumors about Carroll's gentle treatment of UW athletes attached to Maleng. There were plenty of examples to choose from.

In 1999, Maleng declined to charge three football players accused of taking part in an attack on the Tau Kappa Epsilon fraternity—the scene that took place outside Kerry Sullivan's window. Maleng's spokesman cited "confusing and conflicting statements" and said "identification seemed to be a problem." But the Seattle City Attorney's Office seemed to have no trouble with the strength of the witness accounts. After Maleng's office turned the case down, the city attorney's office reviewed the same evidence and charged all three players. All three pleaded guilty to misdemeanors. One player, convicted of assault, was sentenced to ten days in jail.

Three years later, Maleng's office declined to charge another Husky, Eric Shyne, with either rape or indecent liberties. Shyne was represented by Mike Hunsinger, the lawyer who represented so many football players. Shyne had met an eighteen-year-old freshman at a fraternity party, where she was so drunk she fell on him and later vomited. She told police that she awoke with a "goobery" fluid in her vaginal area, semen on her panties, and a flash of memory—Shyne atop her, her legs spread, and her saying, "No, don't, I'm a virgin." The freshman took a shower before getting a rape exam, depriving investigators of a chance to test the "goobery" fluid. Still, police did find semen on her panties; DNA testing showed it was Shyne's. A Seattle police detective recommended a charge of second-degree rape, saying the freshman was so drunk she was incapable of consent.

In declining to charge Shyne, Maleng's office questioned whether prosecutors could prove that sexual contact occurred. "While the presence of Shyne's semen on [her] panties could be corroborative of sexual contact, it is not dispositive by itself," deputy prosecutors wrote. "Arguably, Shyne could have ejaculated on or into her panties without ever touching [her] vaginal area." The woman later filed a civil suit against Shyne, accusing him of rape. Shyne didn't show up in court to defend himself. A Superior Court judge reviewed the evidence and ordered him to pay $350,000.

Another example of Maleng's caution involved a case that had Jeremiah Pharms front and center. The robbery investigation wasn't the first time Pharms had faced possible charges while at the University of Washington. Nor would it be the last.

Jeremiah Pharms was not a guy to blend in. A player with his talent, his build, his tattoos, was going to attract notice. When he committed to the UW in 1996, Pharms was perhaps the school's top recruit. "Cream of the crop," one newspaper called him. "The head of this freshman class," wrote another. Jim Lambright, Washington's head coach, penciled Pharms in as a backup strong safety before practice even started, making him the only true freshman on the team's two-deep chart. "He's that good," Lambright said. "In the high-school films, he just jumps out at you. . . . He can flat lay you out."

Lambright wasn't exaggerating. Pharms played at Valley High School in Sacramento, and if you go to YouTube you'll find a highlight reel from his prep days that runs for nearly nine minutes. Watch No. 1, in blue and white. He flattens quarterbacks, stands up ball carriers, knocks balls loose, blocks kicks, grabs interceptions. A marching band—horns, drums, "Fight! Fight!"—accompanies the highlights. Pharms explodes on other players. Twice, the reel uses slow motion just to let you see. A runner with steam up hits a hole, only to be met by Pharms; he lowers his shoulders, launches, and drives the runner 5 yards back before planting him in the ground. Pharms jacks another player so hard the guy's feet shoot into the air, like he hit a patch of ice. In high school, Pharms also played fullback and tight end. On the reel, he makes an acrobatic catch in the back of the end zone. He takes a hitch pass and goes the distance; when he crosses the goal line, no other player is in the frame. He's Secretariat in the Belmont, leaving the field thirty-one lengths behind.

Pharms fielded scholarship offers from Texas, USC, Colorado, Nebraska. But in the end he chose Washington, saying he felt comfortable with the coaching staff. On the highlight reel, a narrator says: "Jeremiah Pharms could be the most exciting and versatile defensive player to sign with Washington in years. . . . Every Pac-10 school but Stanford wanted him. . . . A consensus All-America. . . . A vicious hitter. . . . Predicted, by his high school coach, to start for the Huskies as a freshman and to make the NFL."

Growing up in Sacramento, Pharms never knew his father. "He's the one who missed out," he told one newspaper. His mother worked as a program technical supervisor with the state's Department of Justice. Pharms recounted how she would get up early, ready her kids for school, then put in a fifteen-hour shift. "She is the most special lady to me in my whole life. Watching her when I was growing up, watching how hard she worked to raise me and my brothers, never giving up even when we had nothing—she's an inspiration. She gave me guidance and taught me the love I have about family."

Pharms went to one high school for two years, then another for his last two. In class, he struggled. On the basketball court and football field, he excelled. His junior year, Pharms played in a three-on-three basketball tournament in Sacramento's William Land Park. At game's end, a fight broke out. A player on the other team later filed suit, accusing Pharms and his teammates of kicking and hitting him. The court file describes a wild scene, with one player's mother in the middle of it all, swinging her purse. In all the confusion, the player's gym bag disappeared, with $5,026 inside. Tournament officials searched Pharms's team, but came up empty.

When Pharms arrived in Seattle, he discovered from the first whistle how much attention he could draw. In August 1996, both Seattle dailies ran stories about Pharms's first practice with the team on the front page of their sports sections. The *Seattle Times* headline trumpeted how Pharms had stolen the "limelight" in the Huskies' opening practice.

> Pharms wore a purple No. 4 jersey and on his helmet was a piece of white tape with his name scribbled in black ink, but no identification was needed. His reputation as a punishing tackler had

preceded him. "A lot of people wanted to get a look at him up close and personal, and no one was disappointed," defensive back coach Scott Pelluer said yesterday.

The *Post-Intelligencer* headline quoted an assistant coach who described Pharms as a "man among boys."

Blessed with an unusual package of size, speed and strength, he stands 6-foot-1, weighs 210 pounds and has the biceps of an arm wrestler. On the back of his right bicep, he has two tattoos—a Roman Gothic P, which stands for Pharms, and a pit bull, which stands for nightmare if you're a mail carrier or ball carrier.

Pharms told reporters after his first practice: "I knew I wouldn't be just another freshman wherever I went." But, he said: "I didn't expect all of this. . . . Everybody is talking about how good I am and everything. But to me it seems like I've got a long way to go." Reporters asked Pharms about his hometown, his expectations as a Husky, his approach to football. "I'm usually really quiet," Pharms said. "But when I'm on the field everything comes out and I'm really emotional."

A fractured thumb ended Pharms's first season after only three games. In late September—on a Sunday, before the season's fourth game—Pharms went to Nevada and married Franquell Moppins in the Heart of Reno Chapel. Pharms's mother and his brother Sean witnessed. The bride and groom were both eighteen. They had met three years before; Franquell had become pregnant in high school and had the couple's first child. Because Pharms missed so many games, he was declared a medical redshirt—a do-over, basically, allowing him to start anew, with all four years of his eligibility intact.

In college, long playing streaks tend to be rare. Coaches shy away from freshmen. Injuries crop up. A player can get knocked out by grades, or a new recruit, or a change in coaches. But Pharms played all twelve games in 1997. He started all twelve games in 1998, and all twelve games in 1999. A concussion once kept him from practice for a week, but that was it. When the whistle blew,

No. 4 was there. He didn't save his intensity for the games, either. "He was just an animal," says Rock Nelson, a three-hundred-pound offensive lineman who would square off with Pharms in practice. "I had never been laid out in my life. Once, he ran me over, put me on my back, and walked over my chest. After it happened, I slowly got up. I was angry, it was embarrassing. He just trucked me. I took a good day to get over it. I was fuming. But hey, what can you do?"

In the spring of 1998, the Husky Union Building—the UW's gathering place for students, with a cafeteria, barbershop, bowling alley, pool tables—held a special preview screening of Spike Lee's new movie, *He Got Game*. The movie explores the relationship of Jesus Shuttlesworth—the hottest high school basketball prospect in the country—and his estranged father. Lots of students showed up for the flick. The audience included a group of football players, decked out in shorts, athletic shoes, T-shirts, and sports jerseys.

The movie ended at a little before 10 p.m. When the students filtered out, Pharms and a fifteen-year-old bumped shoulders.

What's up? Pharms said.

What's up? the fifteen-year-old answered.

The fifteen-year-old's brother was a UW student named Kenneth Washington. Washington came up and asked Pharms what his problem was. The two exchanged words. Pharms threw a punch—and missed. Washington swung back, and the fight was on. Pharms's friends joined in. This group—it could have been four men, or six, or ten—punched and kicked Washington while he was on the ground. "We're football players!" someone screamed. "We can't do this!" A student building coordinator heard the commotion while moving some AV equipment. He ran over and saw four or five guys—big guys—pummeling someone. No way I'm taking those guys on, he said to himself. He ran behind a newsstand and called the UW police.

The beating lasted anywhere from ten seconds to three minutes, depending upon the witness. When it was over, Washington got up and yelled: Is that all you got? It takes all of you? I'm still standing. You can't hurt me.

At this, Washington was knocked back to the ground and punched and kicked again. This second beating ended when police sirens approached. Pharms fled, but identifying him proved easy. Standing in the student union after the fight, the fifteen-year-old looked at a large color poster of the UW football team. He told police: No. 4 is the guy.

Washington, his shirt torn, was treated at a hospital for scrapes and bruises. Police showed him a photo lineup of suspects, using the latest issue of *Husky Football* magazine, with the names stripped out. Washington identified Pharms and two other players.

A week after the fight, the university police stopped Pharms coming out of class. He waived his rights and provided a written statement. He said of the fifteen-year-old: "I tapped him on the arm and asked him what was the problem in a non-violent manner wanting to talk the situation out." He said the kid's brother raised his voice and balled a fist: "Out of a natural instinct I swung to defend myself." He didn't flee because he had done something wrong, Pharms told police. He fled because he knew the situation "didn't look good."

Police submitted the case to King County prosecutors for possible assault charges against Pharms and two other players. But in June, prosecutors took a pass. A spokesman for Maleng said: "In reviewing the case, we discovered some conflicting witness statements that presented some problems." A *Seattle Times* story said prosecutors were "unsure whether Washington accurately identified his assailants." No mention was made in this or any other story of the statement Pharms gave to police. Whether Pharms could argue self-defense was one matter. But there was no doubt that Washington and his brother had identified the right guy. When the 1998 season started, so did Pharms. And why not? No charges had been filed. To the football team, it was no harm, no foul.

Narrowly Honest

13

As he stepped onto the field where he had been head coach for four years, he knew he wouldn't be getting any love. The cheers came last week, in Seattle, when his team upset Miami. And he had soaked the cheers up, bringing the Huskies back out of the locker room to celebrate with the fans, storing up enough love to last the next two road games. This week it was Boulder, where the fans would chant "Ri-cky, Ri-cky" every time his team screwed up, and where they would hold up signs saying just what they thought of their old coach. After that it would be Eugene, where fans would throw duck shit at him.

The day had an ominous feel to it. It was hot, for one thing—ninety-one degrees, a record high for a Colorado home game. Burnt pine and aspen scented the air. A wildfire had burned west of Boulder that morning, smudging the sky and forcing a few subdivisions to evacuate.

The year before, when he had bolted Colorado for Washington, Neuheisel said it wasn't for the money. He said it over and over, like a proselytizer who's discovered the power of repetition. "I'm not about money." "This is not a monetary decision for me." "Salary is just not an issue with me." Maybe someone somewhere believed him. But not in Boulder. Boos hurled down as he emerged from the stadium's bowels. In the crowd, signs were held high: "All About Cash"; "Hey, Rick. Show me the money"; "Loyalty pays, but not as much as Washington."

With Rick Neuheisel, there was honest, and there was narrowly honest. A lawyer would ask him: Now, Mr. Neuheisel, when you said this, were you being honest? And Neuheisel would say: "Yes. Narrowly. These were honest answers, narrowly honest."

A lawyer would ask him: Mr. Neuheisel, when you were head coach at the University of Colorado, did you ever loan or give money to a student-athlete?

"No," Neuheisel says. But seconds later he reconsiders and says, "Define 'student-athlete.'"

"Pretty self-explanatory."

"Not really."

So the lawyer says: Someone who is a student and an athlete at the university.

"Okay. Then my answer stands."

Why did you seek clarification? the lawyer asks.

"Just making sure."

Richard Gerald Neuheisel Jr.

Born in Madison, Wisconsin, in 1961. Grows up in Tempe, Arizona. Blond hair, blue eyes, rosy cheeks. Parents: Dick and Jane. Three younger sisters. Dick, an attorney, teaches real-estate law at Arizona State University. He also has a general practice—"a Marcus Welby of law," Rick says—and serves on Tempe's City Council. The Neuheisels live on hole No. 3 at Shalimar Country Club, a nine-hole golf course. They later buy the place, and Jane manages the employees.

High School

Plays football, basketball, and baseball. "I was the most valuable player in all three sports, is my recollection," Neuheisel says. Top 10 percent of his class, with a 3.8 GPA. "I think I was a sophomore class president, is my recollection," Neuheisel says.

College

Considers going to Princeton. Opts instead for UCLA, where he's a walk-on quarterback and a Sigma Nu. His roommate and best friend is Jerry Nevin. One of Rick's sisters follows him to UCLA, joins a sorority, and introduces Rick to her roommate, Susan. Rick and Susan later marry. (Jerry is Rick's best man, and Rick is Jerry's.) Political science major with a 3.4 GPA. Plucky. Earns a scholarship. Works his way up to starter. As a senior, leads UCLA to a Rose Bowl upset of Illinois and is named MVP.

Employment History

Plays for two years in the USFL, with the San Antonio Gunslingers. Then goes to law school for two years at USC. "It had always been my plan to become an attorney," he says. The NFL goes on strike. "I was, for the first time in my life, recruited," he says. Plays three strike games for the San Diego Chargers. His contract is guaranteed for the whole season, but "it was very uncomfortable when the players returned to the team. I was made to feel unwanted." The head coach suggests mailing the checks to him. "So I went back and lived in a condominium in Marina Del Rey with my sisters." UCLA hires him as an assistant coach. He finishes law school. Flunks the Arizona bar on his first try, passes it on his second. Never practices law, but flirts with becoming an agent. Leigh Steinberg (agent to Troy Aikman, Steve Young, Oscar De La Hoya . . . possible inspiration for Jerry Maguire . . . *Show me the money*) makes overtures about bringing him on, but says: Be sure that coaching is out of your blood first.

After six years at UCLA, gets passed over for offensive coordinator. Takes a job at Colorado, coaching quarterbacks and wide receivers. Salary: $60,000. *The Miracle in Michigan.* It's 1994, Colorado at Michigan, and ABC's cameras become enraptured with Neuheisel. The broadcast keeps returning to him as he counsels quarterback Kordell Stewart. Colorado's down five, with time for one more desperate heave. The play: Rocket. Formation: Jets. The 64-yard tip play wins the game for Colorado and enters the college football pantheon alongside Flutie's Hail Mary and Cal crashing through the Stanford band, and there's Neuheisel afterward, in the locker room, capturing the essence of sport: "You become a little kid. You become euphoric. You're, like, elevated. You're exploding. You look over there, and those guys are absolutely devastated, and you're parading." *A star is born.*

The head coach, Bill McCartney, retires. The athletic director calls a meeting with the assistants and says: If you're interested in the job, let me know. He leaves the room. There's nine guys there, looking at each other. Three say they're interested: Assistant Head Coach Bob Simmons; Offensive Coordinator Elliot Uzelac; Defensive Coordinator Mike Hankwitz. "Elliot Uzelac then looked at me and said, 'Rick, are you going to throw your hat into the ring?' And I said, 'You know, I probably will . . . just for the experience of it.'" Neuheisel interviews with the athletic director, the chancellor, and the university president. (A Denver sportswriter later writes of the president: "Judith Albino was charmed by his twinkling eyes.") McCartney recommends Simmons. Boosters rally behind Neuheisel. And the job goes to . . . Neuheisel.

He's thirty-three, he's never even been a coordinator, and now he's head coach of a national powerhouse. Salary: $256,000 (or $300,000, or $350,000—it depends on who's calculating it, and how). Perks: All kinds. A membership to the Boulder Country Club. Free use of a private jet, thanks to Bradley Calkins, president of Bradley Petroleum. Calkins lets Neuheisel take the plane for recruiting trips to San Diego, Phoenix, Dallas, Virginia, Oklahoma, South Carolina, Baton Rouge. Neuheisel taps Jerry Nevin, his old Sigma Nu buddy, to be director of football operations. Nevin has never before worked in intercollegiate athletics, but he's already in Colorado, working in national sales for Bradley Petroleum.

In 1995, his first year, Colorado goes 10-2. (But loses to Nebraska.) His second year, Colorado goes 10-2. (But loses to Nebraska.) Before his third season, the *Sporting News* picks Colorado to be national champion. A few years before, UCLA wouldn't even make him offensive coordinator. Now, the school's athletic director offers him the job of head coach. "Yes, he did," Neuheisel says. "At least it was my understanding that he did. He subsequently has said he did not, but it was my understanding that he did." The offer, as he understood it, included a home in the Pacific Palisades (hello Steven Spielberg) and a membership to the Bel-Air Country Club (hello Jack Nicholson, Tom Cruise, Barron Hilton). But Neuheisel says no thank you. At least that's what he said he says. He has a meet-and-greet with the owner of the New Orleans Saints. What's the harm in looking around? He's having fun. His team is having fun. He takes the players inner tubing, he takes the players skiing. He plays the guitar on his weekly radio show. He plays the guitar on stage with Jimmy Buffet, strumming "Margaritaville" in front of 20,000 parrotheads.

But that third year, the team goes 5-6. (And loses to Nebraska.) Forget the national championship. The 1997 team doesn't even go to the Insight.com Bowl. Fans start to grumble. *His teams get penalized too much . . . they're soft . . . can't run . . . did he forget to recruit linemen? . . . why is he letting the players eat popsicles? . . . and why the hell can't he beat Nebraska?*

Trouble percolates. A few signs hit the newspapers now; others will surface years later. Recruiting, Neuheisel gets cute, or what he might call *creative*. In years to come, the NCAA will conclude that he committed fifty-one recruiting violations while at Colorado. None is particularly egregious, no under-the-table payments or anything like that. These are violations born of being too clever by half. He's recruiting a player in Houston, Andre Gurode. He's already had his one in-person visit, and he's not allowed another, so he pulls up to the curb of Andre's house, calls Andre on a cell phone, and says: Look outside, I'm here, let's talk. They're separated by maybe 15 yards. Later, Neuheisel disputes that this is a "contact" under NCAA rules: "It is important to note that it was dark out at the time, so I do not think Andre could see me." He's evaluating a player in Oklahoma, Matt Holliday. He's not allowed to talk to Holliday, but he talks to a coach *about* Holliday, with Holliday in earshot. He talks about what a sensational prospect Holliday is, about how high Holliday is on Colorado's wish list.

Neuheisel will later say of all these violations: "I was reading the rules as an attorney. I need to read the spirit of the rules."

After practice one day, Colorado's All-America offensive lineman, Chris Naeole, tells Neuheisel to shut up and lunges at him. An assistant coach grabs Naeole before he can reach the coach. For this, Neuheisel makes Naeole apologize to the team—and that's it. Some players sense a double standard: *You think some backup would have gotten off that easy?* They see a lack of discipline, a lack of accountability. Neuheisel keeps racking up the nicknames. It's not just Skippy and Coach Kumbaya and Slick Rick, Rookie and Sneus. There's also Golden Boy, Boy Wonder, Neuweasel, Boy Genius, and Surfer Rick.

His fourth season, Colorado bounces back, sort of. The team goes 8-4. (But loses to Nebraska.) By now he's making $625,000 or $630,000 or $650,000, depending on who's crunching the numbers. The 1998 season ends on Christmas Day, in Hawaii, with a win over Oregon in the Aloha Bowl. Right after, in the same stadium, Washington plays in the Oahu Bowl and gets thumped by Air Force. Washington's fans grumble. *Air Force? By 20?* In Hawaii, Neuheisel runs into Barbara Hedges, Washington's athletic director. They had met before—when Washington lost to Colorado in the 1996 Holiday Bowl, and when Neuheisel was at UCLA and Hedges at USC. Hedges likes Neuheisel. "Well, I knew Rick," she says. "And from everything that I had heard, Rick was an outstanding young man. Very bright. A very good football coach."

She'll be giving him a call.

While Neuheisel replaced one legend in Bill McCartney, Jim Lambright replaced another in Don James. Neuheisel went 33-14 at Colorado, Lambright 44-25-1 at Washington. But Washington went 6-6 in 1998—the school's first non-winning season in twenty-two years. (Of course, it wasn't a losing season, either. But Air Force? By 20?) Five days after the Oahu Bowl, Hedges fired Lambright. "I wanted to move in a new direction," she says.

Soon after, she called Colorado's athletic director, Dick Tharp, and asked for permission to talk to Neuheisel about the Washington job. The whole routine struck Tharp as funny. What was he going to say, no? Sure, he said, you can talk to Rick. Hedges didn't ask about Neuheisel's background. She didn't ask if there was anything she should be concerned about. "Dick Tharp and I were friends," she says. "If there were any issues at all, Dick Tharp would have said something to me." She felt the same about the folks at UCLA. "These people are all my friends," she says. "They would have said something to me if they felt there were any concerns at all." She didn't run checks with even one athletic director in Colorado's conference. Why bother? If there was smoke, her friends would have sounded the alarm.

After Hedges called Tharp, Tharp called Neuheisel. Neuheisel said he would have no interest in the Washington job. I've already got the best job in America, he told Tharp.

Tharp and Neuheisel weren't close. Tharp hadn't hired the coach. He had inherited him, from the athletic director who came before. In early 1998, not quite a year before Hedges's call, Tharp had picked up the Boulder newspaper and been rocked by a story about a police investigation. A couple of CU football players had been hosting recruits visiting the campus. They had been partying at some hotel with gin and Mickey's malt liquor, and some high school girls had come over, and one of the girls alleged that she was raped. *Damn.* But for Tharp, there was also this: Why was the athletic director learning about this investigation from the newspaper? Why hadn't the coach told him? DAMN. Now he had to call the chancellor, and explain what he knew, and explain why he didn't know more.

Tharp summoned Neuheisel, but the two men have different memories of their meeting. Tharp remembers Neuheisel saying he knew about the investigation but figured there was nothing worth sharing, since no rape charges were being filed. Neuheisel remembers learning of the investigation the same way as Tharp—from the newspaper. More clear is the thrust of a meeting held afterward— a come-to-Jesus meeting called by the Boulder district attorney. He and his staff met with Tharp and other university officials. The assistant prosecutor who ran the sexual assault unit criticized what she called Neuheisel's lax standards. She told Tharp: You're on notice. We're not filing charges this time, but whatever happened, happened on your watch. It better not happen again.

A few days after firing Lambright, Hedges called Neuheisel. She caught him in California, recruiting.

Would you be interested in the Washington job? she asked.

I've got a good job, Neuheisel said. For me to leave, there'd have to be an awfully good reason.

She called him again the next day and caught him in Houston, recruiting.

What would it take to make you interested? What if we could put together a big package?

Would it mean like a blockbuster deal? he asked.

What does blockbuster mean?

I don't know, he said. We'd have to figure that out.

Hedges asked when they could talk this over. Neuheisel told her that he happened to be flying in to Seattle tomorrow, to recruit a couple of kids. Why don't you call me tomorrow night when you're done? Hedges said. We'll get together then.

The next day, Neuheisel visited Paul Arnold, one of the nation's top running back prospects. Arnold would later remember how Neuheisel told him: "Everybody thinks I'm up here for the Washington job, but I'm not. I think you'd look good in black and gold." That night, Neuheisel attended another recruit's awards banquet, which went on and on. "Ad nauseam," Neuheisel says. Afterward, he visited the player and his parents in their home. By the time he got to his hotel it was after eleven, too late to meet with Hedges. But he called her, and they agreed to meet the next morning.

The way Neuheisel remembers it, he was supposed to meet only with Hedges. So he was taken aback when the university's sports information director escorted him to the forty-second floor of some downtown law office—the floor was vacant, for secrecy—and into a conference room, where all these people were gathered around. He wasn't meeting with Hedges. He was meeting with the university's search committee. The committee members were just as surprised to see him. Hedges had said only that she had a mystery candidate to offer. This committee included several boosters: Ron Crockett, owner of the Emerald Downs horse racing track (donations to the athletic department: $2.5 million); Rick Redman, former Husky All-American and now chairman of Sellen Construction (donations to the athletic department: $1.1 million); and Wayne Gittinger, a lawyer who had married into the Nordstrom family, owners of the department-store chain known for fabulous service and high-end wares (donations: $4.1 million).

Neuheisel was reluctant to interview with the search committee. But "they made it more comfortable by saying 'consult,' this is a consulting thing," he says. *Consult*. Such a nice, soft word—and narrowly honest. Neuheisel told the committee that Washington could recapture its standing as a national power. But it needed to make a statement. Whatever coach the UW hired, the contract needed to declare: This university is serious. Committed. Ready to compete with anyone. Committee member Robert Aronson, a law professor, asked about Neuheisel's recruiting style. Some other coaches had been heard to grumble, Aronson said. Neuheisel responded: I compete within the rules. I try to be creative. He provided an example. At Colorado, he wanted to take his players skiing, but skiing is expensive, so he needed a freebie. The hitch: The NCAA frowns upon student-athletes getting special privileges. The solution: He convinced a resort to offer a free ski day to *all* CU students, saying, hey, think of all the media play you'll get from my team hitting the slopes. And he was right. ESPN picked it up. The papers picked it up. Problem solved. Everybody won. The team got to ski, and for free. "He had answers for everything," Aronson says. "He's the kind of guy who walks into a room, and half an hour later everybody thinks he walks on water."

Neuheisel spent only forty-five minutes or so with the committee. He had a plane to catch. But after he left, the members turned to one another and said: We've got to get this guy. They had interviewed three other candidates: John Mackovic, Gary Pinkel, and Chris Tormey. "We were all asked to write the name on a piece of paper, our choice," Crockett says. "It was unanimous." The choice was Neuheisel.

Now, it was time to make a statement. That night, Hedges called Neuheisel at his home in Colorado. She offered him the job—for $1 million a year, for seven years. *Blockbuster*.

I'll have to think about it, he said.

The next night, he called her back. I'm leaning toward yes, he said. But let me sleep on it one more night.

The next day, he said yes. And just like that, Washington had a new coach. The search lasted all of nine days. Neuheisel alerted CU officials, and word got out—quick, sooner than he wanted, before he could tell his players—and the reaction in Boulder was swift and ugly. He was abandoning Colorado in the heat of recruiting season. He was breaking his contract. He was greedy. His word was no good.

Mark Kiszla, a sports columnist for the *Denver Post*, wrote:

> The Colorado Buffaloes have no football coach this morning, which is an improvement over their position 24 hours earlier.
>
> With his voice packed with the sincerity he always fakes so well, Rick Neuheisel said, "I'm going to have a hard time saying goodbye," then did the best thing he possibly could do for Colorado football.
>
> He took the money and ran off to Washington, where his guitar can gently weep in the rain.

He's thirty-seven, he's never won a conference championship, and now he's in seven figures, an exclusive club with three other members—Steve Spurrier of Florida, Bobby Bowden of Florida State, and Phil Fulmer of Tennessee. All three of those coaches had won a national championship. Colorado responded by throwing money at Northwestern's Gary Barnett, convincing him to ditch his long-term contract, leaving Northwestern with even less time to scramble than Colorado, prompting the Chicago papers to flay Barnett just like Colorado's were flaying Neuheisel. In Chicago, Barnett was a traitor. In Boulder, he was a savior. In Boulder, Neuheisel was a traitor. In Seattle, he was a savior. The hypocrisy was everywhere, and when Hedges said, "I don't get it—all coaches come from somewhere else, don't they?" she was right of course, but just wait until someone tried to take a coach from her.

Never, it seemed, had a university been so thrilled to spend so much money. The same weekend Washington hired Neuheisel, UCLA announced it was giving its football coach a raise to $578,000. "What does that say about us, when our deal is twice that?" said Aronson, the UW law professor. "We wanted it to be a splash," he said. Besides, the big number protected Neuheisel. Aronson quoted the coach as saying: "If I leave a job as good as Colorado and my reputation is attacked, the deal here has to be so much better that no one would question my decision." It wasn't about the money. It was about integrity. *Pay me more, lots more, so much more that no one could possibly blame me for saying yes.* Neuheisel told reporters that his decision was based on the "platform" at the University of Washington. He said he believed the UW could become "the beacon university in the West," or even, let us dare dream, "the beacon university for the whole United States."

People leave jobs all the time for more money. For more security. For enhanced opportunities and resources. There's no shame in that. In taking the Washington job, Neuheisel had nothing to apologize for. But coaches don't want to spook recruits by admitting they might someday take another job, so they shoo the very thought away. At Colorado, Neuheisel said: "I'm anxious to be on board for the long haul." In his first day at Washington, Neuheisel said: "I am hopeful this is my last stop." Uh-huh. He was thirty-seven. But forget Notre Dame. Don't bother me, Michigan. Florida? Go away. Same with the Dallas Cowboys, same with the San

Francisco 49ers. He was home, yes he was. Now, if only someone could tell him who to call for electric.

While Neuheisel would make $1 million, the university's president would make $228,000. The average faculty member would make $60,000. Not everyone was as thrilled as Aronson. "Sort of obscene," said the president of the uw chapter of the American Association of University Professors. Oregon's athletic director suggested a cap on coaching salaries. Other newspapers poked fun. "Hedges just hired a fair-haired fraud," the *Omaha World-Herald* said. Bob Kravitz of the *Rocky Mountain News* called Neuheisel "a phony from the get-go," and added: "Didn't anybody in Seattle get a tape of the Kansas game? The Fresno State game? How about Missouri?" Hedges had blonde hair with a coiffured swoop. A Spokane writer called Neuheisel "the perfect Ken doll for Athletic Director Barbie."

It took months to work out the contract, but in August 1999 the deal was done. It turned out to be for five years with an option for two more. With incentives, the contract came to $997,000 a year—assuming the team made a bowl game, and assuming enough players graduated. That total included base salary, compensation for TV and radio appearances, a housing allowance, and payments toward retirement. The small-ticket items included a membership to Broadmoor Country Club and the use of two courtesy cars.

But the deal was really worth more than $997,000. Had Neuheisel remained as Colorado's coach until June 2001, cu would have forgiven an $800,000 loan he had received to buy a house. The uw agreed to pick up the tab—adding, in effect, $160,000 a year to the five-year contract.

And as coach, there were all kinds of ways to pick up extra change. In 2000, Neuheisel received $15,000 from CoachPaterno.com for providing clinic articles and video clips of drills. Sony paid him $8,000 for consulting on a video game. Bank of America paid $2,500 for a half-hour talk on "building a winning team." Food Services of America paid the same for a talk on "overcoming adversity." GE, the same, for "facing challenges." Public-relations giant

Porter Novelli, the same, for "making the most with what you've got." U.S. Bank paid double—$5,000—for the same speech, a thirty-minute talk on "making the most with what you've got."

Sometimes, it's hard to reconcile ethics with college football. But that doesn't mean lawyers won't try.

One holdup to finalizing Neuheisel's financial package was a contract he had with Nike. Everyone knows about these contracts. Nike pays a coach an obscene amount of money, and in exchange, the coach wears Nike and his assistants wear Nike and his players wear Nike. The team appears on TV, and the swoosh is everywhere—jerseys, pants, shoes, sweaters, jackets, hats, whatever. At Colorado, Neuheisel had one of these contracts that didn't pretend to be anything other than what it was—an endorsement by the university's coach and his football team of all things Nike, for all the world to see. The five-year contract started at $60,000 and climbed to $100,000, and threw in an annual credit that allowed Neuheisel to buy $10,000 worth of Nike merchandise "for personal and family use."

But Washington isn't Colorado. Washington is a land of googoos, or good-government types. Washington hypes ethics and has an ethics commission that tends to do a lot of investigating and hand-wringing, followed by ineffectual fines of a thousand dollars or so.

When Neuheisel went to Washington, Nike agreed to pay him $125,000 a year. He would get an extra $10,000 for winning the Pac-10, or an extra $25,000 for winning the national championship. So he could receive, from Nike, up to $150,000 a year—or enough to buy two and a half professors at the UW.

But here was the rub. Washington law says state employees cannot receive outside compensation for performing official duties. In other words: If the state is already paying you to do something, some private company can't pay you extra for doing the same thing.

Now, a state employee can get extra income if (1) the work

falls outside official duties and (2) the contract is "bona fide and actually performed." That means the employee must actually do the non-official work, and the work must be worth the pay. This law would, for example, prohibit the governor from being a contractual shill on government time. Some lobbying group—say, the state's trial lawyers—could not pay the governor $150,000 for delivering the State of the State Address while wearing a baseball cap that said "Trial Lawyers Rock" and a sweater embroidered with "No Caps on Damages."

For the Nike contract, these rules meant trouble. After all, what did Nike want Neuheisel to do? Wear Nike, and have his team wear Nike, while doing football stuff—practices and games, particularly games, and particularly big games that would be televised. And what was the UW paying Neuheisel to do? Football stuff: Get his team prepared—and win games.

Enter the state's lawyers. First, the Nike contract was amended, with strike-throughs and italicized insertions, to try and make it comply with the state's ethics laws. Here's one of the reworked clauses: "NEUHEISEL shall wear and/or use exclusively NIKE Products while participating in ~~all~~ *non-official* athletic or athletic-related activities, including but not limited to football practices, clinics, exhibitions, games, sports camps and any other non-official occasions during which NEUHEISEL wears football or other athletic shoes."

Get it? Everything is fine now, because the games and practices are now "non-official."

A separate clause was reworked the same way, saying Neuheisel must now wear Nike while appearing "on any *non-official* television broadcast."

Because the UW is a state institution, it's represented by the state Attorney General's Office. An assistant AG assigned to the UW argued that this new contract was hunky-dory. But the Executive Ethics Board is also a state institution. It, too, is represented by the state AG's office. An assistant AG assigned to the board argued that this new contract was absurd. "We do not know what a '*non-official* game or football practice or telecast' is," he wrote.

This went on for months, with the state's taxpayers paying lawyers for both sides to argue back and forth. The assistant AG for the ethics board said: If Neuheisel isn't being paid to hawk Nike in his capacity as the UW football coach, how could his services under this contract conceivably be worth $125,000? And the assistant AG for the UW would write back: "The private market has established the value of Mr. Neuheisel's endorsement. NIKE is in the best position to determine this value. The University is reluctant to question the adequacy of this value."

For Neuheisel—"I was reading the rules as an attorney, I need to read the spirit of the rules"—the UW's pretzel logic could have made perfect sense. It was like finding an institutional soul mate.

In the end, the UW found a way around these ethics rules. The value of the contract was set at $60,000, and instead of having Nike pay Neuheisel, Nike paid the UW. The university, in turn, required Neuheisel to wear Nike products, and paid him the $60,000 as part of his contract with the university.

"It's a triangular thing," said a special assistant to the university president.

"That's nothing more than money laundering," said the president of Citizens for Leaders with Ethics and Accountability Now (CLEAN). "It's a distinction without a difference."

But apparently a distinction was good enough. The ethics board signed off on the deal.

The *Seattle Times* profiled Neuheisel in January 1999, the month he was hired. In the story, some Colorado players described Neuheisel as too lax, too slow to discipline. True enough, Neuheisel said. "I would say that there's been one or two times when kids should have been kicked off the team," he said. "There were kids that needed sterner discipline than I administered. My goal was to get them to the finish line, and maybe I shortchanged them and the team by doing that." When that All-American charged him in practice, he screwed up by settling for an apology. "There should have been more of a penalty," Neuheisel said. "I'm learning." The reporter wrote: "The lessons were costly for Colorado but priceless for Washington. The coach says the Huskies have a new and improved Neuheisel."

Neuheisel was a hit in his first meeting with the players. He knew Lambright had pissed off players by switching their helmets from gold to purple and their shoes from black to white. For years, those gold helmets had signified Husky football. The gold was a special mix ordered by Don James, who made sure the helmets were repainted before every game. The players hated the purple helmets. They hated the white shoes. "We're going back to gold!" Neuheisel yelled at that first meeting, and the players burst into cheers. What was $20,000—two hundred new helmets at $100 a pop—compared to that?

In his first month as Washington coach, Neuheisel ran afoul of NCAA rules. Five of his assistant coaches visited recruits during a quiet period, and Neuheisel called players at Colorado without first getting his old school's permission. Colorado accused Neuheisel of poaching. Neuheisel said he was just saying good-bye. He also blamed any confusion on the bustle of moving, saying the coaches had yet to unpack their NCAA manuals. Hedges issued Neuheisel a reprimand, and, as punishment, the UW agreed to cut the number of days he could recruit off campus that season from twenty-nine to nine.

Neuheisel brought Jerry Nevin with him from Colorado. Neuheisel and Nevin befriended Wayne Gittinger, the influential booster who had helped select Neuheisel as coach. Gittinger, along with two members of the Nordstrom family, owned a private jet, a twin-engine turbo Canadair that seated ten passengers. The three men took that jet to golf outings in California and Pennsylvania; at least three times, they flew to Pebble Beach.

Neuheisel's first season, Washington finished 7-5. Only an overtime loss to UCLA kept the Huskies from reaching the Rose Bowl. Hedges wrote in the coach's review: "Rick Neuheisel is an exceptional person and coach. His attention to every detail of the program results in success. He is a role model in every sense of the word." She wasn't thrilled with the players' GPAs, scoring that as "below expectation." And she sure wished Neuheisel would learn how to use a computer. (He was a cell phone guy, not an e-mail guy. In years to come his cell phone would go off during a deposition and even while testifying in court.) But the team "exceeded expectations," Hedges wrote, "due in part to the outstanding coaching."

As a recruiter at Washington, Neuheisel could dazzle. He would find out what music some recruit liked and have it playing when he picked him up at the airport. Or, better yet, have a recruit fly in by seaplane, set down in Lake Washington, and pull up to the coach's $4.2 million, three-level mansion with 130 feet of waterfront and sixteen sets of French doors, where Neuheisel's beautiful blonde wife would be waiting, on shore, with fresh baked cookies.

Who could say no?

To make sure the UW followed NCAA rules, the athletic department employed a small team of lawyers in its compliance office, headed by Dana Richardson. In Neuheisel's self-evaluation for the 1999 season, he wrote: "Dana Richardson is thorough and easy to work with. I would like for her to continue to be creative; continue to look for ways to be on the cutting edge." In time, Richardson would accumulate some thirty-five hundred written interpretations of NCAA rules on her computer.

As a fund-raiser, Neuheisel excelled. During one dinner at his house, he secured a pledge to the athletic department of $500,000.

To the players, the coaching switch was dramatic. Lambright had mystique. He kept a distance, sometimes watching practice from a cherry picker. He was old school, a guy who liked his players tough and mean, and who had little time for complaints or screwups. "Lambright, he didn't give a damn about having fun," Hakim Akbar says. "Throw a bone, work your ass." Neuheisel learned everyone's name. He picked up their lingo, and invited players to his house to jet-ski, and found ways to motivate that sounded corny but somehow worked, like lumping the games against WSU and the Oregon schools into what he called the Northwest Championship.

Under Lambright, fighting in practice was almost a rite of passage. But Neuheisel wouldn't allow it—a crackdown some players chafed at. "You've got to play this game a little angry," Rock Nelson says. "If you don't play angry, you get your butt kicked." Neuheisel convinced the university to spend more on the players. "Under Lambright, you couldn't get a pair of socks," Nelson says. "With Neuheisel, you got a whole package." Now, the players stayed at the Crowne Plaza before each home game. They dined at McCormick and Schmick's. On Sundays they watched game film and ate prime rib and lobster.

Washington was 2-0. Colorado was 0-2. But coming into the game, Colorado was a three-point favorite. Go figure.

After three quarters, Washington trailed 7–3. But in the fourth quarter the Huskies scored two quick touchdowns, to take control. Washington's wide receivers caught only three passes the whole game, but once again, Jerramy Stevens picked the offense up, with seven catches for 102 yards. He "must have NFL scouts drooling already," the *Denver Post* wrote. In the final minute, Colorado drove to midfield, trailing 17–14. But Anthony Vontoure—a Huskies cornerback known for big plays at big moments—stripped a Colorado receiver of the ball, and Washington recovered to put the game away.

Afterward, the fans who had traveled to Boulder from Washington chanted: "Neuheisel Rules, Neuheisel Rules." Neuheisel found Hedges and gave her a hug.

14

Scoreboard, Baby

It was now two months since Jerramy Stevens's arrest, but in the newspapers it was the same old same old. The wait continued. Maybe, just maybe, this would be the week that prosecutors would announce whether Stevens would be charged. Then again, maybe not.

By now, no one doubted Stevens's importance to the team. Against Miami and Colorado he had recorded back-to-back career days, with more catches for more yards than the team's entire corps of wide receivers. "Jerramy Stevens is a go-to guy," Neuheisel told reporters. "He's a weapon." Sometimes, the Huskies would move their six-foot-seven weapon off the line and isolate him on some undersized cornerback. Stevens looked in one corner's eyes—the guy was five foot nine—and knew exactly what he was thinking: *Oh, shit.* No one doubted that Stevens was ticketed for the NFL. Teammates liked to joke with him, I'll be your limo driver, I'll be your agent.

On September 18 the *Seattle Times* wrote about Washington's 3-0 start and its upcoming game against Oregon: "There is one storm cloud on the horizon. . . . A long-awaited decision on Stevens's legal status could come down this week. . . . Any sort of prolonged absence of Stevens could be fatal to the Huskies' Rose Bowl chances." The next day, the newspaper followed up with the *maybe not.* "More of the same," the paper said. A spokesman for Norm Maleng "said no determination is likely this week." The storm cloud drifted off.

The Huskies had a bye week before the Oregon game, scheduled for September 30. That gave them two weeks to prepare—

and given how dangerous the Ducks had become, the Huskies could use every day.

While the Huskies prepared, prosecutors fretted. In private meetings with police, they expressed misgivings about the evidence against Stevens. The case was still being managed from on high, with Maleng's top deputies calling the shots. On September 21, Dan Satterberg and Mark Larson met with an assistant police chief, a captain, and a sergeant. The prosecutors said they saw "potential proof problems" with the case—those are the words that appear in police reports—and that they considered it crucial that Stevens be interviewed. The meeting also dealt with media fallout. The assistant chief asked that whatever prosecutors decided, the two agencies work together on the press release.

At the time, 1.7 million people lived in King County. There were 100,000 crimes reported each year; about 7,500 were violent. To handle criminal and civil matters, Maleng's office employed hundreds of lawyers and support staff. It was a busy place—but never too busy to let some football player's case get lost in the shuffle. A system alerted the front office to particular investigations that demanded attention. A deputy would fill out a form, saying why some case transcended the run-of-the-mill. Investigations involving UW football players—even ones with lower profiles than Stevens—could trigger these alerts. Over several months, the Stevens case received attention not only from Maleng, his chief deputy, and the head of the criminal division, but from all kinds of other deputies: Scott O'Toole, Mindy Young, Jim Rogers, Lisa Johnson, Nelson Lee. That's a lot of prosecutors for a single rape case. These prosecutors gave Parker one directive after another. Interview that player's girlfriend. Interview that roommate. Canvass the fraternities and sororities again. Parker went along, feeling like she'd interviewed the whole of Greek Row, saying to herself: *I've had other cases that went forward with not even half as much evidence.*

The day after Satterberg met with the police brass, O'Toole went to the police department's Special Assault Unit to update

Parker's sergeant, Rose McMahon. He told her an interview with Stevens had been scheduled for September 27—five days out. That was the good news. The bad news—from the police department's perspective, anyway—was that the prosecutors' front office had agreed to certain conditions while negotiating with Stevens's attorney, Mike Hunsinger. No. 1: The interview would take place in Hunsinger's office. No. 2: Parker could not ask any questions. Only O'Toole would be allowed to do that.

A few hours later, McMahon filled Parker in on the deal. Parker didn't care for it. Not at all. She steamed at condition No. 2. This was her case. She knew the evidence best. Sure, O'Toole could review her reports. But that's not the same as doing all the work that went into those reports—recording impressions, testing hunches, knocking around theories for days on end. Parker had been living with this case for more than three months; now, come time to question the suspect, the prosecutors were cutting her out. "If he agreed to talk, we should have done the questioning," she says. "That was our job."

McMahon didn't like the deal either. But she told Parker that if Maleng's office considered this interview a must, so be it. She would go along. Call O'Toole, she told Parker. Schedule a time to meet. Go over the evidence with him. Make him as knowledgeable about the case as you are.

So Parker called O'Toole. And when she did, she learned there was now a condition No. 3. O'Toole said his front office had made yet another concession. And if condition No. 2 made Parker steam, No. 3 put her on boil. The prosecutors had agreed to let Stevens and Hunsinger see all of the victim and witness statements before the interview. They had agreed to hand over the evidence. This meant that Stevens—before being questioned—would get to know just what Marie had said. Just what Chris, the 911 caller, had said. Just what the people at the fraternity party had said. Stevens would know the times, the details, the whole sequence of events as revealed by Parker's investigation.

You've got to be kidding me, Parker told O'Toole.

Parker knew what every cop knows. Police turn over evidence after charges have been filed, not before. Disclosing statements before an interview allows a smart suspect to tailor his story to the facts already gathered. Parker called her sergeant at home—this news couldn't wait for the office. McMahon had the same reaction as Parker: This was going too far.

The day after Stevens's arrest, police and prosecutors had one showdown. Now, a second one loomed.

Some tension between the two agencies is a constant. Police don't work for prosecutors. Prosecutors don't work for police. Prosecutors complain of police shorting investigations. Police complain of prosecutors afraid to try tough cases. Reporters who cover crime learn early: You want the word on prosecutors, ask police. You want the word on police, ask prosecutors. But the Stevens case was replacing tension with something more raw, something akin to hostility or mistrust.

The weekend passed. On September 25, a Monday, McMahon and her lieutenant consulted the police department's legal adviser, Leo Poort. In all his years in the job—and he'd started in the 1970s—Poort had never heard of such a deal. Handing over the statements would violate the department's standard operating procedures, he told the officers. But his objection went beyond some recitation of policy. This policy served a purpose. "In general, if you're going to allow someone to study the case of the police department before an interview, you can't really test the independent recollection of someone from their point of view," Poort says. "Doing interviews strategically and effectively means you get to hold back a little of what you know—if not everything you know—to test the credibility of the person you're questioning."

"To this day I don't know why they would have agreed to that," Poort says of prosecutors.

While police mulled their response, the papers performed their weekly ritual. On September 26 the *Post-Intelligencer* reported: "The King County Prosecutor's Office said that no action will be taken on the Jerramy Stevens sexual assault investigation this week." That meant Stevens would play against Oregon, no matter what. That afternoon, Parker sat in on a conference call. An assistant police chief, John Pirak, told Satterberg and Larson that the Seattle Police Department had made its decision: No go. The department was drawing the line; it refused to suspend its procedures just to secure an interview with Stevens. The prosecutors could take their deal and stuff it.

The next day, there was no interview. Stevens never would answer questions about what happened in the early morning hours of June 4—not to police, not to prosecutors, not to lawyers handling civil suits against him or the university or other football players. The case would remain what it was at the start. She couldn't remember. He wouldn't talk.

It's hard to say how Hunsinger came to represent Stevens. The way Hunsinger remembers it, he got a call from Stevens in jail. Or maybe the call came from Stevens's parents. Stevens would later stipulate in a legal document that Keith Gilbertson, the team's offensive coordinator, had referred him to Hunsinger. Gilbertson, in a deposition, would deny this. It hardly mattered. It's not like Hunsinger's name dropped from the blue. The football team had passed his name down from class to class, in the same way freshmen players learned to take Swahili if they needed to bump up their grades.

Hunsinger received his bachelor's degree from the UW, his law degree from the University of Pennsylvania. He began representing Husky players in 1993. That's when he helped sue the Pac-10, and later the NCAA, on behalf of the team, claiming the university had been improperly hit with a two-year bowl ban for violating NCAA rules. A year or two later he received a call saying some player was in trouble on a misdemeanor charge. Could he help out? Sure, Hunsinger said. He assigned an associate to the case, and the charge was dismissed.

On the 2000 team, Hunsinger represented at least fourteen players. DUI. Hit-and-run. Punching a security guard. Punching windows out of cars. Unpaid child support. Animal cruelty. Hunsinger handled them all. He also represented at least five coaches, plus the director of football operations, in the face of ethics investigations. A *Post-Intelligencer* columnist once profiled Hunsinger under the headline "Dawg in Distress? This Lawyer Answers the Call." Hunsinger, the column said, "could get a hurricane downgraded to a breeze."

Hunsinger's work for the Huskies represented a departure from his typical practice as a civil litigator. He handled medical-malpractice cases, real-estate disputes, product-liability claims, lawsuits against car dealerships, the occasional divorce. Defending football players wasn't a lucrative departure, either. Hunsinger suspended his hourly rate of $330 and instead fashioned a retainer to fit each player's case. He says he did the same in all criminal cases, whether his client was a football player or not. For every player, the total bill was hundreds of dollars, not thousands. Not even Stevens's tab topped $1,000. "I charge them, and they pay me," Hunsinger says. "Some of them take a hell of a long time to pay me—and I'm fine with that." Hunsinger liked the kids—and that's what he called them, *kids*. "These are 19-year-old kids, being asked to act like adults," he says.

Hunsinger found Stevens to be intelligent, likable, compassionate. Stevens insisted he was innocent—and Hunsinger believed him. Most defense attorneys would swear off any thought of offering up a client for questioning. If the interview breaks bad, the lawyer looks a fool. But Hunsinger didn't want prosecutors to make their charging decision without hearing Stevens out. To Hunsinger's mind, if Stevens was charged, he was toast. His season would be over, and even if acquitted, he would always be tagged as a guy charged with rape. Some things stay with you forever.

Hunsinger figured a quid pro quo was in order. One unconventional gesture was good for another. For starters, he wanted a lawyer asking the questions, not a cop. He felt more comfortable that way. The word from prosecutors: *Agreed*. So he pushed for more. He insisted on getting the police's evidence. "I just thought, well, hell, I might as well get something out of it. If you're getting my witness, I should get yours." *Agreed*. Larson, the head of the prosecutors' criminal division, says the deal wasn't customary—but it wasn't unprecedented, either. "This office is always interested in hearing both sides." But then the deal fell apart. Hunsinger, wanting to patch it back up, had made one last offer: Put the witness statements in a sealed envelope, and we'll read them after the interview. But it was too late. Police had scotched the deal.

The bye week was good to Washington. Without playing, the Huskies moved up in the national rankings from No. 8 to No. 6. There was talk of a national championship for the team, talk of a Heisman for Tuiasosopo. Of course, Washington would need to beat Oregon.

The Huskies used to dominate the Ducks, but no more. Oregon had won four of the last six games between the two.

Under normal circumstances, Oregon despised Washington. But this game offered something more, because Oregon's fans also despised Washington's coach, even before he came to Washington. In Neuheisel's four years at Colorado, his team faced Oregon twice in bowl games, and won both times. In the Cotton Bowl, he called a fake punt in the closing minutes, with his team up 25. Piling on, is how Oregon saw it. After losing the Oahu Bowl, Oregon coach Mike Bellotti had complained that Colorado's defensive backs should have been flagged for grabbing onto Oregon's wide receivers. Bellotti also said he believed Oregon was still the better team. When Neuheisel learned of Bellotti's comments, he offered a simple rebuttal: "Scoreboard, baby." Two words to end all arguments, two words to silence any complaint.

Scoreboard, baby.

The Ducks, god-awful uniforms and all, had become monsters at home, winning seventeen straight. On September 30, 46,000 fans packed Autzen Stadium, determined to see that streak run to eighteen. Close to half banged plastic tubes together whenever Washington had the ball and needed to hear. Some fans wore stickers that said "Neuter Neuheisel."

Oregon was known for flash and dash, not muscle. But in this game, the Ducks pushed the Huskies all over the field. By halftime, Oregon was up 17–3. On offense, Washington couldn't run. On defense, it couldn't stop the run. By the end of the third quarter it was 23–3, and it would have been worse had Oregon's kicker not missed two field goals and an extra point. Washington still couldn't run. It couldn't pass, either. The Ducks shut down Stevens, with a linebacker short and a safety deep. Through three quarters, he had only two catches for 8 yards.

In the fourth quarter, Washington made a run. With four minutes to go, Stevens broke free for 59 yards, the game's longest catch. The Huskies scored on the next play, to close within a touchdown. But on Washington's next possession, Tuiasosopo threw four straight incompletions, dooming the comeback. The final score was 23–16, Oregon. Just like that, the wins against Miami and Colorado faded. The Huskies had started Pac-10 play 0-1. The talk of a national championship? Done. Talk of a Heisman? Done.

After the game, Oregon defensive end Saul Patu accused Washington of playing dirty, in particular Stevens. "He's not a good blocker," Patu said. "He tries to do a lot of cheap things to block, hold you, grab your throat. When you do that stuff, I've got no respect for a guy like that."

The next week, Detective Parker checked off the final items on the prosecutors' to-do list. She closed the investigation and sent her file to prosecutors on October 5, two days before Washington's next game, against Oregon State. She had done what she could do. Whatever happened next was up to Maleng's office. The *Seattle Times*, citing Maleng's spokesman, wrote: "A determination on whether to file sexual-assault charges against UW tight end Jerramy Stevens might not be made this week . . ."

We will carve their names
In the Hall of Fame
To preserve the memory of our devotion.

From "Bow Down to Washington"

Carving Their Names

15

In some ways, Rick Neuheisel broke from Washington's past. He wasn't some taskmaster who confused a football field for a military parade ground. He wasn't one of those coaches forever quoting Patton or MacArthur or Robert E. Lee. Neuheisel liked bouncy songs about beaches and girls. He liked movies with happy endings. But in the most critical sense, Neuheisel fit the program's history. Three legends have coached football at Washington: Gil Dobie, Jim Owens, and Don James. All three posted winning records that brought glory to the university. At the same time, each coach's program tested the values of a community, forcing it to weigh what would be tolerated in order to win.

For overlooked parts of the country, football has always had the power to attract notice. That's true now. It was true a hundred years ago. In 1907 the University of Washington, tucked away in a remote corner of the United States, craved national attention. Football could deliver it. But the team that year went 4-4-2, with one of those losses to the crew of the uss *Nebraska*. A .500 record would never entice some marquee opponent from the East. Washington's coach had a great name, no doubt. *Victor Place*. But a more fitting label for his team was, Win Some, Lose Some.

In 1908, Victor Place stepped down and a new coach came stomping and glowering onto Washington's campus. Gilmour Dobie arrived off back-to-back unbeaten seasons at North Dakota State. To lure him, Washington had dangled a dramatic offer: $3,000 a year. You can bet the professors talked about that. A thousand dollars a month in the fall to teach *football*?

Dobie cut a striking figure. He was tall and thin, wore a long black overcoat, and kept a cigar or straw jammed in his mouth. But it was his manner that everyone remembered. "No smile, no handshake, no slap on the back," recalled one freshman. "Nothing but a pair of eyes peering coldly out of a dark face." Dobie's nicknames gave him away: Gloomy Gil. The Sad Scot. The Apostle of Grief. Talk up the speed of his running backs, and he'd say: "This means they only get to the tacklers all the sooner."

Dobie had learned to intimidate at North Dakota State. There, the story went, the players weren't much impressed when their new coach arrived. With a frame like that—the man could be mistaken for Ichabod Crane—how could he know anything about smashing down an opponent? Dobie heard the snickering, and knew it was time to act.

You fellows have got it into your heads that I'm not a fighter, he told them. I'm going to show every one of you that you've made a big mistake.

With that, he peeled off his coat and sweater, tossed his cap onto the ground, and marched into the center of the football field.

I'll take you all on. I'll fight every last one of you.

The players? They walked away. Dobie never heard another crack.

When Dobie got to Washington, he took intimidation to a new level. He would call his star quarterback, Wee Coyle, into his home each week and berate him: Kid, you're a rotten quarterback. If I didn't have so many cripples, you'd be sitting on the bench. The opponents this week are great big monsters and we're going to get licked. We haven't got a prayer, but we'll do the best we can.

If anybody questioned Dobie's tactics, nobody doubted his results. Year after year, his team racked up win after win. Sure, some of the games were against Queen Anne High School or the Washington Park Athletic Club. But the team also tattooed Washington State, 45–0. Oregon State, 47–0. California, 72–0.

By 1916, Dobie had turned Washington into a recognized power. But everything fell to pieces in November of that year when Bill Grimm, the team's star tackle, was caught cheating on a history exam. It was a serious breach, and the faculty wanted Grimm banned from competition at once. The players had a different idea. They wanted his punishment to begin after the Thanksgiving Day finale against California. After all, the Pacific Coast Conference championship was on the line.

Meetings about Grimm's fate went until midnight. The faculty held firm. So did Grimm's teammates. The players declared a strike. They vowed to stop practicing. They vowed not to play California. "Our objection," team captain Louis Seagrave told a Seattle newspaper, "is that after we've overcome everything, and have a fighting chance to finish the season as champions, the faculty should wreak its wrath on the entire team for the supposed irregularity of one of its members." Dobie told the newspapers he sympathized with his striking players. He bemoaned the team's unforgiving academic workload and the lack of "faculty mercy." He called Grimm the team's best defensive player ever; he labeled Grimm's cheating an "indiscretion." Dobie even spoke of the good that could come from this standoff: "I think a start has been made that will make it possible for a football coach hereafter to develop a team without too many stifling restrictions."

Henry Suzzallo, the university's president, heard about the strike while traveling in Kansas City. The news incensed him. "Do not permit Grimm to play under any circumstances," he wrote in a telegram. "The team is not a bunch of individuals, but a set of representatives. It must keep the university honor by complete fulfillment of the agreement [to play] California."

After two days, the players backed down. Playing without Grimm, Washington beat California, 14–7, to wrap up the latest in a string of undefeated seasons. But in the days afterward, tensions continued to escalate between the president and the coach. Suzzallo held Dobie responsible for the mutiny, saying the coach exerted control over his team and could have stopped the strike at any time. With Dobie's future in doubt, boosters urged Washington to keep him. "Dobie's loss would be a loss to Seattle as well as to the university," said C. B. Yandell, secretary of the Seattle

Chamber of Commerce. "With a big game in the East probable, it would seem unwise to change coaches at this time."

But on the evening of December 8, it was official: Dobie was fired. "He has not accepted in practice the obligation to be a vigorous moral force as well as an excellent technical instructor," Suzzallo said. "Every part of the university organization must cooperate toward one end, character building." Word of the firing raced through the Greek houses. Fraternity brothers poured into the streets. By 2:30 a.m., three hundred students, maybe more, tramped down Greek Row. One of Seattle's papers described the scene with the language of medieval romance: "The fair maids of the sororities, as did the ladies fair of old, sent their knights to the 'fray' provisioned and with more than words of encouragement. For as the long lines serpentined through the sorority houses, dainty bits of food were pressed on them, apples in one place, cakes in another."

After covering the four blocks to Dobie's house, the students gathered and began to chant. *We want Dobie. We want Dobie.*

"But he's asleep and very, very tired," his landlady told them.

The students refused to leave. Eventually, Dobie stepped out his front door wrapped in a bathrobe. "This is the happiest moment of my life; this expression of your loyalty to me," he said. "Coming in this manner, at this time, it is more than a man could ever have dreamed of." Dobie held court for fifteen minutes. He told the crowd how he had battled faculty meddling at every turn, how he had produced the best football team possible, how his only real loyalty lay with the students and the team. When he finished, the students broke into Washington songs. "Fight 'em," they yelled, as the coach disappeared inside. "Fight 'em Dobie."

Three weeks later, BeVan Presley, a former player under Dobie, was in Alaska when the Seattle newspapers reached him with the news. He wrote to Suzzallo, saying the president's comments were unfair and that Dobie built character in his players. Suzzallo's executive secretary wrote back. He said Dobie's "cold-blood-ed and determined defense of insubordination" broke the spirit of team play, which carries weight beyond football. Cheating, in the end, is a test of morals, he wrote.

Dobie's final record at Washington was a thing to behold: fifty-eight wins, three ties, no losses. His teams outscored opponents 1,930 to 118. To this day, no other team in college football has matched the nine-year unbeaten streak that Dobie produced in Seattle. Dobie later coached at Cornell, where his teams won eighty-two games, lost thirty-six, and tied seven. He was fired there, too. He left with a quote for the ages: "You can't win games with Phi Beta Kappas."

Jim Owens was not a man to roll with the changes. He didn't like changes to the game he coached, bemoaning the passing of one-platoon football, and he didn't like changes to his campus. In 1966, a tumultuous year in a tumultuous decade, Owens stood for the old guard, although he was only thirty-nine. That year, the track coach at Stanford suspended a sprinter for refusing to cut his hair. The coach even accused the runner of being part of some Communist conspiracy. Owens thought this was great. He wrote the coach's boss: "I certainly concur in the action you took in the 'Goldilocks Case' and compliment you on your stand. Our university students competing in intercollegiate athletics have a fine image which is at the extreme opposite pole from the beatnik type, who fortunately are in the minority on our campus today."

Owens was introduced as the new Husky football coach in 1957, looking like a man who had drifted north on his way to Hollywood. Six foot four, handsome, with a square jaw and close-cropped hair, he could have been mistaken for John Wayne. He grew up in Oklahoma; starred on his championship high school football team; joined the Navy for two years; and married his high school sweetheart. He played football for Oklahoma and later became an assistant coach at Kentucky and Texas A&M under the fabled Bear Bryant.

When he arrived in Seattle, Owens was introduced as thirty

years old. In fact, he was twenty-nine. But thirty carried more gravity somehow, and Owens feared coming across as too young or inexperienced. Washington played along. At the time, the university was on probation, banned by the league for two years from sharing in any Rose Bowl money or competing in any athletic championships. An investigation eight months earlier had revealed twenty-seven football players were on the payroll of boosters, who had set up a secret slush fund. Some seventy-five boosters were said to be involved, including the publishers of both daily newspapers.

Owens, like Dobie five decades before, imposed his mark from Day 1. In one practice he instituted a drill that came to be called the "Death March," in which players ran endless sprints without water breaks. Memories differ over how long it lasted. It may have been one hour. It may have been two. One player remembers losing nearly fifteen pounds. Some players passed out, or finished in tears. At least six went to the hospital.

Under Owens, players learned to dismiss their pain. Put tape on an injury, and the coaches mocked you. You didn't call an injury time-out unless a player was unconscious. If hurt, you crawled off the field. Owens's players aimed to inflict pain on others. One Husky who joined the team in 1959 said: "I remember one game . . . it was the greatest thing we ever did . . . we had three guys down at once. We had injured three guys. We thought that was neat."

In 1960, Washington crushed favored Wisconsin to win the Rose Bowl, its first victory in five trips to Pasadena. When the players arrived home in near-freezing conditions, 2,500 fans awaited them at the airport. The celebration lasted days. The squad received the keys to the city. The next year, Washington repeated with a Rose Bowl victory over Minnesota.

But as the decade lengthened, Owens and his cadre of white assistants from Texas and Oklahoma struggled to adjust to a changing nation. Black players said Owens harassed them for dating white women. That he stacked black players at the same positions, to limit their playing time. That he punished black players more severely than white players for the same transgressions. The team's trainer used the word "nigger." In 1968, *Life* magazine described how thirteen black players had met in secret and then presented Owens with four demands. Owens and the university met two by firing the trainer and hiring an African American assistant coach. But Owens made out like it was all a big misunderstanding.

A month after that article ran, a union president at the university wrote Owens to complain that four gymnasts had been honored at the Lake City Elks lodge, which didn't allow African Americans to become members. At the time, Owens also served as Washington's athletic director. Owens wrote back: "The fact that this is one of the 'private clubs' practicing discrimination in their membership didn't enter [the gymnasts'] minds, and I must confess it would not have occurred to me. I respect you for your stand and thank you for your interest and concern."

The next year, Owens demoted a black halfback. Black teammates talked of refusing to play, in protest. Owens got word and summoned the whole squad. He took players aside, one by one, and insisted they pledge an oath of loyalty to him and the program. Afterward he suspended four black players, apparently because they didn't say what he wanted to hear.

Washington's next game was at UCLA. When the Huskies left for the airport, the team's eight remaining black players elected to stay behind to boycott the game. That evening, Owens's seventeen-year-old daughter was driving her car when she was forced off the road and hit in the face by an unknown attacker. The turmoil deepened divisions on the team and in the community—but also created a backlash of support for Owens. At Washington's next home game, Owens received thunderous applause and a standing ovation—an unexpected greeting for a coach with a season record of 0-7.

Owens reinstated three of the black players. But the distrust continued, and at the end of the 1970 season, four black players resigned from the team. After a long investigation, the university's Human Rights Commission said Owens and the athletic director, Joe Kearney, should be fired. When the Faculty Council on Student Affairs concurred, Seattle's best-known sportswriter, Royal Brougham, took offense: "Why don't the nine UW faculty members who are throwing karate chops at Jim Owens and Joe Kearney attend to their teaching duties, for which they are paid handsome salaries, instead of trying to dynamite the athletic department, which isn't their bag? . . . If the pettifogging profs aren't happy here, why not encourage them to transfer to Berkeley, or Wisconsin U where their talents would be more appreciated?"

Some fans wrote university president Charles Odegaard in defense of Owens. "For over a year now, a small group of domineering negro fucks have been attempting to take over the athletic programs at the University of Wash," a Spokane man wrote. "What's the matter Odegaard, can't you say go to hell and mean it?" The owner of an insurance company threatened to pull his financial support: "I can't believe that you or your Board of Regents will tolerate any sort of boycott situation, or the elimination of the athletic program at the university, but just in case I should decide to do something with my Tyee contribution, I wonder if you would be good enough to let me know what to expect?"

A few expressed support for the players. "I feel that you would agree that a healthy, productively dissident black community is essential to the health of the whole city and state," wrote Roberta Barr, vice-principal at Franklin High. "I don't expect a great many people would agree."

In the end, the university regents voted to keep Owens. He retired in 1974, after eighteen years as coach. His teams went 99-82-6. In 2003 the university placed a statue of Owens outside Husky Stadium, reigniting anger in the African American community. James Kelly, president of the Urban League of Metropolitan Seattle, said: "Now is not the time to be erecting statues of false gods that symbolize a dark part of our university's and city's history."

A month after Owens retired, the university announced his replacement—Don James, the coach at Kent State University. If Dobie was sour, James was stoic. He ran marathons in his spare time and took pride in his organizational skills. "A tidy ship is a happy ship," he liked to say. James wrote detailed plans for every month of the year, whether he was recruiting, scouting, or coaching. He ran practices from a wooden tower high above the field—"alone, imperial, impassive," one sportswriter wrote. After two middling years, the Huskies gained traction. The 1977 squad won the Rose Bowl—the start of a stirring run under James, one that included no fewer than six trips to Pasadena. In 1984, *Sports Illustrated* named the top three coaches in college football: 1. Don James. 2. Don James. 3. Don James. Fans dubbed him "The Dawgfather."

The program peaked with the new decade. The 1990 Huskies beat Iowa in the Rose Bowl, to finish 10-2. The 1991 Huskies returned to Pasadena and thumped Michigan, to finish 12-0. No other Washington team had gone undefeated since Dobie's final victory over California, seventy-five years earlier. Billy Joe Hobert, the uw's sandy-haired quarterback, earned Rose Bowl co-mvp honors. Washington won a share of the national championship. Voters named James the national coach of the year.

The next year, Washington picked up where it had left off. But midway through the season, with Washington riding a twenty-two-game winning streak, a banner headline in the *Seattle Times* changed everything: "Huskies' Hobert Got $50,000 Loan." As newspaper stories go, this was a blockbuster.

Hobert had been a homegrown hero—a handsome, rugged, blue-collar kid who spoke his mind and won and won and won. The story said Charles Rice, a nuclear scientist in Idaho, had lent the fifty grand to Hobert, a friend of Rice's son-in-law. Hobert burned through the money in three months, spending it on guns, cars, stereo equipment, golf clubs, and wild weekends with his buddies. He bought a 1991 Chevrolet Camaro and then, a few weeks later, traded it in for a 1992 model. If he didn't like some golf clubs, he'd hand the set to a friend and buy another. As his spending spiraled, he hit up Rice for more money, pitching himself as a young guy just trying to get his life on track: "Chuck, I can honestly say that you have saved our marriage and gotten us, for the most part, out of debt. . . . Thanks a Million," he wrote in one letter. Rice complained that he had given Hobert nearly four times as much money as any of his eight children: "It appears I have befriended a bottomless pit," he wrote the quarterback. But Rice kept saying yes—and Hobert kept borrowing, with so little care that he signed one promissory note without even reading it. "He claimed he was still in an alcohol haze after a drinking binge and reading anything gave him a headache," a Pac-10 investigative report says.

The money from Rice violated NCAA rules, but James brushed it aside, saying he couldn't be held responsible: "There's a lot of things that players do. I let them walk around with cellular phones, wear earrings, which I don't particularly enjoy. But I don't run their lives."

The news kept getting worse for the team. Soon after the Hobert story broke, prosecutors charged linebacker Danianke Smith with dealing crack cocaine. One place he sold it, according to charging papers, was the campus crew house where the players would hang out. Later, these charges were dropped because the prosecutors screwed up, failing to turn over all their records to the linebacker's lawyers.

In December, a month after the story broke about the $50,000 loan, someone stole Hobert's 1992 Camaro. When police found the car, it had been stripped, shot full of holes, and spray-painted with the message: "You can't afford this, B.J." Hobert split town, fearing for his safety. That same month, a Los Angeles Times investigation revealed that some Washington football players had received paychecks for summer jobs that required little or no work. Some players described playing dominoes or cards, or sleeping, or leaving work to lift weights. This, too, violated NCAA rules. Outsiders suggested the UW had lost control. But James argued the opposite. "We run too clean a program," he told the Los Angeles Times. "It's frustrating to me when we've got a program that has worked so hard to abide by all the rules."

In the summer of 1993, after a six-month investigation, the

Pac-10 conference hammered Washington, suspending the team from bowl play for two years and docking scholarship spots and television revenue. James resigned in protest. "It's like hearing that the pope quit," one booster said. "The whole deal was a conspiracy to get the University of Washington," another booster said.

While the university debated whether to fight or accept the Pac-10 penalties—ultimately, it gave in—UW president William Gerberding wrote letters that left no doubt of football's importance to the institution. "This situation has been more carefully monitored by the Board of Regents than any set of decisions I have made in my fifteen years here," he wrote to one booster. To a couple of regents, Gerberding emphasized the need to consider public relations. "Fighting all the way," he wrote, might appease the "rabid football fans." But there was the faculty to consider: "There is no doubt whatsoever in my mind that a failure on our part to accept these penalties, and to do so at once, would be regarded by nearly all of them as an embarrassment to the University of Washington, a manifestation of petulance and skewed priorities."

Many fans blamed university leaders for not doing more to defend the school against Pac-10 sanctions. "After sitting in the rain for thirty years and watching our university be embarrassed many times, we finally were able to hold our heads high," one fan wrote to the board of regents. "Now your great president has really screwed that one up. Maybe for thirty more years we sit in the rain and be embarrassed."

Washington cut ties with four boosters caught up in the investigation. One was Jim Kenyon, who funded a professorship at the university. "I still love the school but cancel the professorship," he wrote to Gerberding. "Cut me a check for $150,000 and I'll find a better place to put my charitable support." Another was Clint Mead, a booster with powerful friends. Five members of the Nordstrom family wrote and urged Gerberding to rescind Mead's "disassociation." When Gerberding replied, he emphasized the university's indebtedness to the Nordstroms and how distressed he was to be at odds with them. But, he wrote, he needed to protect Washington's good name and send a message to boosters who broke the rules. Gerberding also met in private with the wealthy family. His handwritten notes say: "Cordial, friendly throughout. I said that I *was* willing to consider rescinding the disassoc., but not now . . . that I wanted to get the NCAA matter behind us . . . that I expected that to be done by Feb."

Another letter to Gerberding came from Jerry Woodman, an alumnus and small-town pastor. "Every time an athlete receives a tainted degree from the University of Washington solely because of athletic ability, my degree is cheapened. It also sets up an ugly attitude in the mind of the athlete that the rules are for everyone else but the athlete is above all that because he has some salable physical ability. I am very proud of our football team. I would be even prouder if this institution and others like it would once and for all address this issue honestly without dollar signs to cloud their thinking; without the attitude of winning at any cost."

In his eighteen years as Washington's coach, James racked up 153 wins against 57 losses and 2 ties. In 1997 he was inducted into the College Football Hall of Fame—joining Jim Owens and Gil Dobie.

Heaven help the foes of Washington;
They're trembling at the feet
Of mighty Washington.

From "Bow Down to Washington"

Body and Soul

16

October 7, 2000: Oregon State at Washington, the Season's Fifth Game

It was a night game—no rain, no wind, sixty-five degrees—and Husky Stadium was sold out as usual, with an announced attendance of 73,145. In a normal year, Washington fans would have marked this game down as an automatic "W." But this was not the Oregon State of old. This OSU team had one of the best defenses in the country. This OSU team had one of the country's best tandems of wide receivers in Chad Johnson and T. J. Houshmandzadeh. This OSU team was 4-0 and nationally ranked for the first time in more than thirty years.

The explosiveness of the Beavers' wideouts—both would become NFL standouts—put added pressure on Washington's secondary. That made the cover of the game-day program all the more fitting. The program featured a long profile of Curtis Williams, Washington's strong safety. The headline was: "Designated HITTER."

> On the football field, Curtis Williams just likes to hit.
>
> There is not much about which you can ask Williams that will get him to open up. That is, until you mention laying a hit on an opposing player from the safety position. Then his eyes light up.
>
> "It's just a good feeling," the 5-foot-10, 200-pound senior says. "You can get all your frustrations out on that guy. Hitting a guy real hard like that, that's what the game is all about."
>
> If this is what football is all about—stopping an opposing player dead in his tracks and sending his body crashing down towards the turf with a vicious thud—then Curtis Williams has mastered the game.

The story said Williams "has earned his reputation as one of the nation's most devastating hitters." Bobby Hauck, the team's safeties coach, talked at length about Williams and his style of play: "Curtis loves everything about the game of football, which is probably why he's a good player, and a really good guy to be around. . . . It's definitely an attitude. Some of the biggest, fastest guys don't want to stick their nose in there and put a hit on somebody. At that position, you get a chance to make some big hits and he doesn't miss too many of those opportunities. He seems to really enjoy that part of it, which makes him one of my favorite guys to be around because that is a big deal to me."

The story made no mention of Williams's criminal history. It referred to his 1997 season—missed because of jail time—as "a redshirt year," which wasn't true; his redshirt year had been the year before. Nor did the story delve into Williams's playing style, aside from his love of hitting.

Williams liked to play without a mouth guard, a standard piece of protective gear. He wanted to intimidate, his teammates say. Protective gear whispered fear. A mouth guard also garbled his words, and he wanted to be understood while taunting an opposing player. He would go for the ball carrier's mouth—hitting him, face to face—and then get into his ear. "Curtis would run up, hit you in your mouth, take your lunch money and tell you you ain't nothing," says Hakim Akbar, the team's free safety.

Mouth guards protect teeth and jaws. Some research suggests they protect against concussion. As for hitting another player in the mouth, football has worked since the 1970s to reduce or eliminate helmet-to-helmet contact, the sport's leading cause of brain or spinal-cord injuries. Keep your head up and tackle with your shoulder, coaches typically tell players. Don't lead with your helmet. A hit becomes particularly dangerous if a player leads with his helmet and dips his head.

Like Williams, Akbar preferred playing without a mouth guard. He also shared Williams's approach to striking fear in opponents. "We made sure they would feel us and know us by the end of the game. . . . We would hit their face with our masks, with the tip of our heads, just to make it a bigger blast."

Before taking the field against Oregon State, Rock Nelson, one of the UW's offensive linemen, iced his back. He stretched it and applied heat. The lower segments—L3–L4, specifically—had caused him pain for so long now. The lower back carries the torso's weight, and Nelson, six foot five, weighed more than three hundred pounds. But on this night, he would let adrenaline take over. Unless he was lying on the field, unable to walk, he was going to play.

Nelson and his teammates played a game to remember. Washington's safeties excelled. Akbar recorded a team-high nineteen tackles. Williams had the second most, with nine. But tonight it was Washington's offense that dominated. The Beavers came in with the country's fourth-best run defense, giving up only 58 rushing yards a game. The Huskies blew holes in that defensive front, racking up 281 rushing yards. Nelson and the rest of the offensive line wore the Beavers down, allowing the Huskies to pull out a 33–30 win.

Afterward, Nelson's teammates went out to celebrate. Nelson drove home, to the Lake City house he rented with two other players. His back was tensing up. He slept in bed, but painful spasms jolted him awake. So he took a blanket and moved to the floor, with his feet propped up. The next morning, he could barely move. Nelson crawled to the bathroom and hoisted himself onto the toilet with his arms. He crawled back to his room. When he heard his roommates getting ready to leave for a team meeting, he knew he couldn't join them. He opened his door a crack. With his head on the floor, he looked up at his roommates and said: Hey, man, I'm not going. Tell the coaches. Have 'em call me.

On the verge of tears, Nelson knew this was bad. "That was the worst morning, because I knew I was going to miss a lot more games. And that was my biggest concern at the time. That's what was killing me."

Washington football has long prided itself on toughness: work harder than the other team, gut it out, play through pain. You want to insult a Husky, call him soft. To some, the UW's work ethic explains its success. To others, the football program pushes too hard.

While the Huskies took the field in 2000, a former quarterback challenged the UW in court. Shane Fortney accused Jim Lambright, the coach from 1993 to 1998, of pushing him to play while hurt, leading to a severe knee injury. Fortney also blamed the medical staff for clearing him to play without a brace—allowing Fortney greater mobility, at the risk of greater injury. The lawsuit settled in 2000 for $150,000. The UW paid $50,000; a team doctor paid $100,000. The doctor was Steven Bramwell, an orthopedic surgeon who had played football for Washington in the 1960s, under Jim Owens.

A year earlier, the university paid $59,000 to settle another ex-player's lawsuit. Chad Wright complained of being treated "like a piece of meat," saying he had been forced to take part in dangerous weight-training exercises that injured his back. When Wright got hurt, Lambright accused him of exaggerating his pain and told him he "would be nothing without football," the lawsuit said. The coaching staff mocked Wright's masculinity, questioned his commitment to the team, and revoked his scholarship. Wright eventually needed spinal surgery.

The *Seattle Post-Intelligencer* had published a story in 1998 about all the team's back injuries, listing Wright among fifteen injured players in six years. The same year that story ran, Rock Nelson hurt his back. The list grew one name longer.

At the UW, Nelson was just another guy who challenged his body's limits and played hurt, pounding away until his body quit, leaving him to wonder, years later, if it was all worth it. Lots of players say yes. Nelson isn't so sure.

Playing high school ball, north of Seattle, Nelson weighed between 235 and 265 pounds. At the UW he bulked up to 314. His body wasn't built for that weight or the resulting impact. He knows that now. But every practice, every snap, he lined up and traded blows with some other lineman, also big and strong.

In his second year, Nelson injured his back in the weight room while doing a power clean. The lift stresses explosion and technique; the lifter pulls a bar from the ground to his shoulders in one fluid motion. "I kind of whipped my back right out of joint," Nelson says. "I remember being in massive pain." One of the team's strength coaches was Bill Gillespie, a world-class weight lifter who, in competition, once ripped his shirt in half while bench-pressing more than six hundred pounds. "Bill didn't have time for complaints," Nelson says. "He was one of those real gung-ho tough guys. It was like, 'Hey, you hurt your back, go rest. See you later. Get out of the weight room.' He didn't seem too concerned."

Nelson went through a cycle of rehabilitation and re-injury. To him, classes didn't matter: "I was a football major." What mattered was playing. When he was injured, he didn't feel like part of the team. He seemed to live in the training room—stretching, receiving massage or electrical stimulation therapy—and took whatever painkillers the team gave him. He managed to start seven games in 1999, but his injuries mounted.

In the 2000 season, two bulging disks in his lower back limited Nelson's playing time. His first full-contact practice came just four days before the UW played Colorado, in game No. 3. Nelson went with the team to Boulder as an emergency backup. But in the first half, another lineman got hurt. Nelson played forty snaps, in ninety-one-degree heat, 5,000 feet high. On the plane trip home, his back started acting up. He played again in games four and five, but the morning after the Oregon State game, Nelson couldn't twist his frame. He could hardly turn his neck.

He stayed in bed the next three or four days. His mother and friends brought him food. Later, he received six or seven shots, needle to spine, to kill the pain. His mother, who didn't weigh half what he did, would help him to the car. She had never wanted him to play football. He would get her tickets to the games, and she would go, but she would hang by the concessions or stand in the stadium corridors, refusing to watch.

Nelson had played football since he was eight. He was now twenty-two. Football is who he was. But after the Oregon State game, with the season not halfway over, a doctor told Nelson to get fusion surgery, or give the game up.

Big as he was, Nelson didn't stand out around his teammates. Elliot Silvers weighed 320, Chad Ward, 335. They also played on the offensive line, opening those holes that turned the game against Oregon State. So did Dominic Daste, a fifth-year senior from California.

Daste's ankle problems rivaled Nelson's back. Four years before—against Oregon State—Daste was leading the way through a hole when two players landed on his right leg, shearing the cartilage that connected his leg and ankle. Doctors put a fourteen-inch plate in his leg and ten screws in his ankle. Daste decided to keep playing. He sat out a year, rehabbing, then took the field. He couldn't run as fast or jump as high, but he could still play. Before the 2000 season began, Daste explained his decision this way: "I love football, I love the guys. In some ways, it was no more complicated than that."

Other players on the team also worked their way back from injuries. One had four shoulder surgeries by the age of twenty-one. Three tailbacks went down—a fractured vertebra, a separated shoulder, a broken collarbone—but the fourth tailback stepped up. One receiver played with a torn knee ligament. Another played with a shoulder injury that required off-season surgery. A third played after missing two seasons, recovering from surgery to remove cysts from his knees.

Nelson elected not to have back surgery. After Oregon State, he never played another game. "It's kind of hard to let it go," he says. "It's like your first love or something." Deprived of his identity, with no plan for his future, Nelson went into a funk. He felt expendable: "Once you're not playing, it's kind of like, 'Okay, we've got to move on to the next kid.'" After the 2000 season, Nelson dropped out, abandoning his sociology degree. "I was so close to graduating," he says. "It was just stupid."

In years to come, Nelson would read the newspaper and see all these stories about football players and concussions. A study released in 2007 said players who have had three or more concussions run three times the risk of clinical depression or mental impairment. "I didn't realize what a concussion was," Nelson says. "Now, looking back on it, I think I had a lot of concussions playing football. If I saw a few stars, as I call them, I wouldn't think anything of it. But really, that's a mild concussion. That happened like a dozen times." He would worry about his future, and about the abuse he endured. "I completely trusted the uw. I gave them my body and soul." Back then, he never thought about getting a second opinion.

He would remember how football was everything, and how he drove himself to play through pain, to be tough. "I look back and think about how dumb I was really." These days, Nelson's back acts up maybe once a year. Sometimes, he'll lift a heavy box and be fine. Other times, he'll break down tying his shoe.

While Nelson worries about concussions, some teammates worry about weight. Mortality studies provide grim news for all those linemen who weigh three hundred pounds or more, finding an increased chance of heart disease, among other risks. In 2006 one study found that, compared to their teammates, football's heaviest players are more than twice as likely to die before their fiftieth birthday. Nelson has lost about fifty pounds since leaving the uw. One teammate has lost about a hundred. But some players have kept the weight. One former lineman, who still tops three hundred, says losing weight is on his list of things to do.

Up, Down, In, Out

17

October 14, 2000: Washington at Arizona State

On a warm night in the desert, Anthony Vontoure could only sit and sweat while a freshman took his place against Arizona State. Vontoure had been suspended, sort of. Sometimes it was hard to tell. Coaches would announce that their star cornerback was being punished, then say, no, no, it isn't really punishment, it's this or that. Sportswriters tried counting his disciplinary episodes, but how do you count something that is, then isn't? This time, Vontoure had been late to a team meeting. But his suspension came with an asterisk. "We decided we'd put him in if it was necessary," Neuheisel told a reporter after the game. "We decided it wasn't necessary."

With his talent and personal struggles, Vontoure seemed always to be creating problems—for other teams, or for his own team. Against Miami, he sacked the quarterback on a corner blitz, forcing a fumble that he recovered. Against Colorado, he stripped the ball to kill a last-minute drive. But tonight, he sat. After trailing early, Washington rebounded to beat the Sun Devils 21–15 in what one newspaper called "the ugliest football game in history." The teams combined for twelve turnovers, eighteen penalties, and two blocked kicks. But a win is a win, and this win moved Washington to 5-1. The Huskies were now 2-1 in conference play. The Rose Bowl remained within reach.

After the team flew home, Vontoure returned to the studio apartment where he lived alone, with nothing but an air mattress and his crippling self-doubts.

Vontoure's position coach at the UW, Chuck Heater, has a résumé that includes stops at Notre Dame, Ohio State, and Florida. He's coached for more than thirty years, working mostly with defensive backs. More than twenty of his players have made the NFL; at least four were first-round picks. So when Heater calls Anthony Vontoure "the most talented kid I've ever had," the words mean something.

Neuheisel saw it too. "An unbelievably gifted athlete," he said of Vontoure. Kyle Benn, a teammate, called Vontoure the best athlete he ever saw, "hands down." "I watched him in a dunk contest, him and Tuiasosopo going at it. I was in awe. He was doing 360s; tomahawk dunks. His head was up by the rim. If he was 100 percent, he could have been one of best—*the* best defensive back to come out of the UW."

Vontoure came to Washington in the fall of 1997, the year after Curtis Williams. Like Williams, Vontoure was a high school star in California. He impressed the scouts—"He could be an All-American," *SuperPrep* said—and chose Washington over USC. He was the best player at the best high school program in the country. But unlike Williams, Vontoure arrived at Washington without fanfare. He was lumped in with the other recruits, with little attention cast by coaches and little paid by reporters.

It may have been different, were it not for what happened in January 1997, three weeks after Vontoure's high school team wrapped up another perfect season.

Vontoure grew up in California, the youngest of three sons. His parents moved to the Bay Area when he was two, but divorced soon after. When he was seven, Anthony moved in with his dad. At eight, he begged to play organized football. When he was nine, his father relented.

Anthony's oldest brother, Mike, went to De La Salle, an all-boys Catholic school in Concord, east of San Francisco. The motto of the school, run by the Christian Brothers, is "Enter to learn, leave to serve." Ninety-eight percent of its graduates go on to college. Mike starred in basketball and track. Chris, the family's middle brother, also attended De La Salle. In 1992 he starred in football; that year the Spartans went 13-0, starting the longest winning streak in football history. In a book on the streak, sportswriter Neil Hayes wrote of Chris: "He was a gifted athlete who struggled in other areas. He was kind-hearted, soft-spoken, and always made his teammates laugh. But Chris could also be volatile and temperamental."

Mike Blasquez, an athletic trainer at the school, worked with Chris. The two cut a deal: If Chris committed himself in the weight room, Blasquez would take him rafting. Chris followed through. Rafting that summer, the two hit white water. Their raft capsized, and Chris went under. His body turned up five days later, nine miles downriver. He was just shy of seventeen.

Anthony was thirteen when his brother died—a loss he would replay and recount for years to come. He entered De La Salle a few months later and traced his brother's steps. Anthony starred in football—playing both ways, at cornerback and receiver. The school had retired Chris's number, 23, but made an exception for Anthony, letting him wear it. Like Chris, Anthony had a temper. When he would erupt in practice, an assistant coach would make him walk across the field to the head coach. The walk seemed to calm him.

"He was a talented kid, young and immature," says Terry Eidson, the defensive coordinator at De La Salle. "He was no different than a lot of high school kids. He had trouble keeping his mouth closed, and knowing when to talk and when not to talk. . . . He was his own worst enemy." Vontoure also found trouble away from football. On his fifteenth birthday he was arrested for burglary, accused of stealing a car stereo.

At De La Salle, the football team stresses humility, discipline, and respect for one another. Bonds are tight, the rules and expectations clear. The head coach, Bob Ladouceur, turns "selfish teens into selfless teammates," Hayes wrote. "He has created a culture, a community, based on timeless values where teenagers hold themselves and each other accountable." Each player fills out a commitment card—listing goals for weight lifting, practices, games,

1. Linebacker Jeremiah Pharms started
the 2000 season needing a standout
year to catch the eyes of NFL scouts.
Photo by Bryan Patrick, courtesy of the
Sacramento Bee/ZUMA Press.

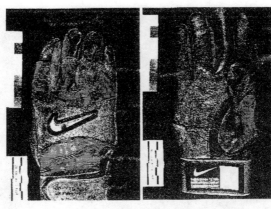

FIGURE 11
ITEM 2
RIGHT HAND GLOVE #12
OUTSIDE BACKHAND
SURFACE

FIGURE 12
ITEM 2
RIGHT HAND GLOVE #12
OUTSIDE PALM
SURFACE

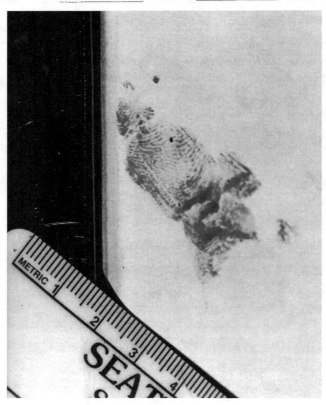

2. (*Opposite top*) Seattle police found a type of Nike
glove worn only by the Washington football team inside
a car that was connected to a robbery and shooting.
Photo by the Seattle Police Department.

3. (*Opposite bottom*) Seattle police also found this
bloody fingerprint on the car door.
Photo by the Seattle Police Department.

4. (*Above*) Tight end Jerramy Stevens (*left*) and
quarterback Marques Tuiasosopo proved an explosive
combination for Washington's offense.
Photo by Jim Bates, courtesy of the *Seattle Times*.

5. Freshman Marie ran into Jerramy Stevens at a party held in the Sigma Chi fraternity on Greek Row.
Photo by Ken Armstrong.

6. (*Opposite top*) Marie couldn't remember how she got back to her sorority, Pi Beta Phi, after leaving the party.
Photo by Ken Armstrong.

7. (*Opposite bottom*) Seattle police detective Maryann Parker, who investigated Marie's case, talks to a troubled teenager and her mother outside juvenile court.
Photo courtesy of Maryann Parker.

8. Linebacker Anthony Kelley with his family in 2002. *From left*: Devan, Dominec, Anthony, Tonya, Diamond, and Siya. Photo by Steve Ringman, courtesy of the *Seattle Times*.

9. This photo of Curtis Williams ran with a *Seattle Times* story heralding his arrival on campus. Two weeks later, police responded to a domestic-violence call at his apartment. Photo by Jimi Lott, courtesy of the *Seattle Times*.

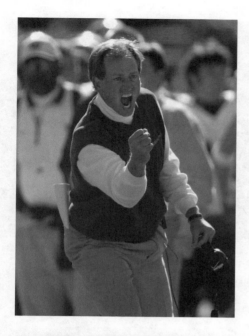

10. Coach Rick Neuheisel's enthusiasm helped charge the Huskies. Photo by Dean Rutz, courtesy of the *Seattle Times*.

11. Washington's athletic director, Barbara Hedges, lured Neuheisel to the UW with a blockbuster salary. Photo by Rod Mar, courtesy of the *Seattle Times*.

12. (*Above*) Husky Stadium was completed just hours before this inaugural game against Dartmouth College in 1920. Dartmouth won, 28–7. Photo by Chapin Bowen, courtesy of Paul Dorpat.

13. (*Below*) Giant additions have given Husky Stadium an imposing appearance. This panoramic shot was created by stitching six photos together using Photoshop. Image courtesy of Jean Sherrard.

14. This statue of former coach Jim Owens was erected at the UW in 2003, igniting protests over his treatment of black players in the 1960s.

Photo by Ken Armstrong.

15. Don James, the "Dawgfather," turned Washington into a national power in the 1980s and '90s. Later, the UW attached his name to its luxury-seating area.

Photo by Ken Armstrong.

16. Cornerback Anthony Vontoure was as electrifying on the field as he was troubled off of it. Photo by Mark Harrison, courtesy of the *Seattle Times*.

17. Arizona police took this mug shot of Jerramy Stevens in 2007 after he was arrested on suspicion of DUI. Photo by the Scottsdale Police Department.

and life—and hands the card to a teammate or coach, who makes sure those goals are met. Vontoure, on his card, dedicated himself to being the best person he could be.

By the time he was a senior, Vontoure "got it," Eidson says. He understood his role and responsibilities. A high school team has forty-some players, not a hundred or more, as in college. Vontoure felt loved and supported, Eidson says. Football was fun, the pressure manageable. In the locker room, he became a leader. On the field, his play drew scouts from all over. In 1996, Vontoure returned eight kickoffs—four for touchdowns. De La Salle finished 14-0 and extended its winning streak to sixty-six games.

In January 1997, soon after De La Salle's final game of the season, Vontoure accepted a scholarship to Washington.

That same month, Mathew Clark, a nineteen-year-old Chico State freshman, was at a birthday party in Danville, California, celebrating his friend Darcy's seventeenth. It was a family party, with pizza, M&Ms, turns at the piano. Clark played Nintendo with Darcy's thirteen-year-old brother, chatted with her seven-year-old sister. Then, after dark, a black Jeep Cherokee, its lights off, pulled up with several other cars, and twenty to thirty people piled out. The group approached the house, hooting, and someone in front said, "Hey, hey, any of you got a problem with Mike Stadelhofer?"

Stadelhofer was looking for a guy named Trevor, to settle some ill-defined score. Clark's friend Gavin was out front, alone. He said Trevor wasn't there, that there were parents inside, no drinking, nothing worth crashing. Stadelhofer's friends called Gavin four-eyes. They called him pussy. Eight, maybe ten, guys circled Gavin and began throwing punches. Clark rushed outside. Vontoure, who was with Stadelhofer's group, jumped in front of him. Clark didn't know Vontoure, Vontoure didn't know Clark. "Don't step, don't step, you're going to get your ass kicked, don't step," said Vontoure, who had been drinking for hours now. Clark pushed past and grabbed Gavin. But when Clark turned for the house,

Vontoure punched him, once, twice—"What are you doing? Don't do this," Clark said—and the two wrestled to the ground. Clark regained his feet, but the group closed on him. Someone hit him from the side, someone else knocked him down. Then they began kicking.

Clark heard someone yell, "Hey, watch this." The kicking stopped. Clark, on his hands and knees, felt a crack on the back of his head, a bright flash, everything went white, and as he collapsed, he heard it, he remembers it to this day, the sound of a brick hitting the ground, bouncing off the concrete. They kept kicking him, in the eye, in the nose, he felt his nose break, he remembers the left side of his head becoming wedged against a fire hydrant and a black boot slamming his head into steel that had no give. They dragged him through rosebushes, ripping his clothes, cutting his back. His friend Jeremy ran over, and Clark looked up, tried to say "help," and Jeremy saw blood pour from his mouth like water. Blood soaked Clark's shirt and pooled on the concrete. "I thought I was watching someone die," Darcy's dad says. The beating stopped only when Clark's friend Josh ran up, and the crowd turned on Josh.

The attackers split before police arrived. Clark's right eye swelled to the size of a softball. To examine the damage, doctors pried it open. Doctors reconstructed his nose—putting a metal rod up his nostril, to break it clean—and stitched up his head. His skull was fractured, hairlines radiating from his eye socket. "My head was a mess," he says. "There were little splinters going off in all different directions." For a month his right eye registered nothing but fuzzy light, and he suffered headaches, sharp and relentless.

For Clark, the emotional injuries were ten times worse. Posttraumatic stress. Nightmares, waking up screaming, dripping sweat. Anger, humiliation, the endless questions and doubts. Clark's mother drove him home from the hospital. When they pulled up, a black car was in the driveway. They didn't recognize it, and Clark got scared, thought it was them again, back to finish up. He begged his mom to drive away. But your brother's in the house, she told him. Fear seized Clark, fear they might be inside, attacking his younger brother. He was desperate to help, but the fear was greater. Paralyzed, he did nothing. The car backed out of the driveway. It was his brother's friend. The friend stared at Clark's face, which was unrecognizable. Clark cried the whole night. The shame stayed with him for years.

Witnesses identified Vontoure as the person who hit Clark with a brick. Police arrested Vontoure an hour or two after the fight. He was wearing a Dallas Cowboys jersey, No. 22. He was still drunk. He staggered a bit and spit a lot. He denied throwing the brick, then admitted it, he said the guy he hit was "some fat fuck," he said he only "lobbed" the brick, that he only "tossed" it, and even then it was self-defense. "I was just saving my ass," he said. To the cop, Vontoure seemed excited, erratic, a fount of obscenities. Vontoure told the cop how he had been hitting on some girl that night, he even got graphic about it, describing just what he wanted to do to her. Calm down, the cop told Vontoure, and Vontoure calmed.

Vontoure was arrested on suspicion of assault with a deadly weapon. He was seventeen, an age at which he could be tried as a juvenile or adult. One of the area's top lawyers, Bill Gagen, defended him. "He had great potential as a person and as an athlete," Gagen says. "The goal is not to ruin his life." Gagen managed to keep the case in juvenile court. A De La Salle coach spoke on Vontoure's behalf. So did a priest. Clark remembers how determined everyone seemed to be to preserve Vontoure's playing career, to make sure he could still suit up for Washington. "I can't remember if the judge or lawyer said it, but they said he needs to be up in Seattle by this date," Clark says.

Vontoure served two months in a juvenile facility, doing time with "a serious bunch of guys," Eidson says. Washington's coaches knew of the attack, but elected to stand by their scholarship offer. Vontoure went from being in custody in California to walking onto the practice fields at the UW—and without a word of the assault being reported in the Seattle newspapers.

Vontoure wrote the UW an essay, saying he would seize all that Washington had to offer: "I'm very excited about the opportunity that I have to receive a first class education from a premier school in the nation. . . . I plan to take full advantage of this opportunity to become the student I'm capable of. I hope to graduate one day and say I'm a Washington Husky and I love what I've become."

Before Vontoure left for Seattle, Eidson took him aside and issued a warning: "With your personality, you really can't be involved in drugs and alcohol. It's really not good for you."

In his first year at the UW, Vontoure shared a dorm room with J. K. Scott, a backup quarterback from suburban Los Angeles. "I've tried to make sense of that time living with him," Scott says. "Honestly, a lot of it was very difficult. He was very depressed. He drank a lot. He had some sort of malt liquor in his drawer, and every day, he would start the day off with that. He often missed classes. . . . In fact, I don't remember him going to many. . . . And he slept more than anyone I've ever met. He often talked about how he didn't like it there, and loved home."

Vontoure and Scott lived in McMahon Hall, one floor above Marques Tuiasosopo and Pat Conniff—two players who had gone to high school together and were tight friends. "Whenever we would go out to a party or something, we'd invite Anthony," Scott says. "It was a coin toss if he would come or not, and how he would act. You would never know if he was going to be mad, pissed off, quiet, or jovial, joking Anthony.

"I've been trying to recall our conversations. It's interesting, because a lot of them had to do with, 'Do the guys on the team like me? What do they say about me?' He would ask about that all the time. He had this one shirt he always wore, it said, 'Chicks hate me.' He was proud to wear it. But he really wished it wasn't the case. . . . Every night, all the time, he'd be, 'Why can't I get a girl?'"

Vontoure talked often of his brother who had died. He talked of messages in the music of Common Sense, a rapper. He embraced philosophical conversations, venturing into religion, economic inequality, social injustice. "He was not a shallow guy," Scott says. "I enjoyed that about him."

His freshman year, Vontoure and two friends walked into a party in some dormitory lounge and walked off with a keg of root beer. Police tracked the three to another dorm, where Vontoure tried holding the lobby door shut to keep the officers out. Once police got through, Vontoure mounted a struggle before being handcuffed. A silly stunt turned into charges of third-degree theft and obstructing a police officer. Vontoure later told police he was too drunk to know what had happened. Prosecutors dropped the obstruction charge in exchange for a guilty plea to the theft count. Vontoure received a deferred sentence and was fined $150.

On campus, Vontoure tooled around on a BMX bike, wearing Chuck Taylor All Stars and a De La Salle sweatshirt. In the locker room he held court, offering his opinion on anything and everything. There, he seemed brash—cocky, even. Vontoure talked football as war. *If we are not successful, let no man come back alive.* But in private, his self-doubts surfaced.

At the UW, Vontoure found a father figure in Abner Thomas, "Big Ab," a Vietnam veteran and football operations assistant. Some days, Vontoure talked five, maybe six times with Thomas. "I've never dealt with a student like Anthony," Thomas says. "He needed mentoring. If you could be around him, he'd just about depend on it for daily activity." One time, Vontoure dressed up to attend the team's kickoff luncheon. When he discovered that other players had dressed down, he was so mortified that Thomas had to console him. From then on, Vontoure left his nice clothes in the closet.

Maybe because of his high school days, Vontoure expected never to lose. As Vontoure kept track of De La Salle's streak—watching it stretch to 78 games, to 90, to 102, to 115—Thomas would tell him, nothing lasts forever.

Looking back, Thomas sees now that he missed some signs. "To this day I wish I had an opportunity to see if I could save him. . . . I could have helped him more really, but I didn't, I didn't know."

Vontoure came to the UW with a high school GPA of 2.5. His ACT score was 19, a little below the national average. In his first quarter at Washington he took only two classes for credit: Introduction to Anthropology and Introduction to Composition. In the anthropology class, Vontoure blew off the first exam, which was worth a quarter of the class grade. But the professor didn't dock him. Instead, he conceived an alternative. "Since you missed the first exam and made little effort to complete this work, we have a new assignment for you that parallels the value of that exam," the professor wrote to Vontoure. "We think you will enjoy this assignment."

Vontoure was asked to write a four-page paper about Latrell Sprewell, an NBA player who had been kicked off the Golden State Warriors for choking his coach, P. J. Carlesimo. "What is the public conflict here? Is it really about race? Or is there another, more private conflict?" Vontoure was instructed to "expose the hidden societal problem. Is Sprewell guilty? Carlesimo? The Warriors? The NBA? Since American society glorifies professional sports and athletes, what is Sprewell really guilty of? Is American society not also guilty?"

The professor gave Vontoure four weeks to do the paper—and sent a copy of the assignment to Ron Milus, an assistant UW football coach. The university's file on Vontoure doesn't show how he fared on this paper. But for the course he received a B-.

Like Curtis Williams, Vontoure struggled with grades. Heading into the 2000 season, he had completed twelve quarters; six times, he fell below the 2.0 line, threatening his eligibility. But each time he recovered. Vontoure took five Swahili classes, good for twenty-five credits. He took two Paper Science classes, good for seven credits. The bulk of his classes were in sociology, the most common major among the football players on the 2000 team. But he also took History of Jazz, Introduction to Dance, and Dinosaurs. His highest grade, a B+, was in "Sexuality in Scandinavia," a class that hundreds of students pack every year.

On the field, Vontoure emerged as one of the most exciting, most unpredictable players the UW had ever seen. He redshirted his first year, and broke a finger his second. Before Vontoure's third year, Neuheisel became coach, replacing Jim Lambright. Neuheisel shifted Vontoure from safety to cornerback, saying he could be "sensational" in that role. "He's got moxie," Neuheisel said. "You better have some confidence at that position, and he's got that." The cornerback position can isolate players, leaving them to cover some wide receiver one-on-one. Pressure magnifies. If a corner gets beat, everyone knows it.

From the get-go, Vontoure put on a show—up, down, in, out, hero, goat. In 1999 the Huskies opened at BYU. Washington rallied late from 13 down—a comeback made possible by Vontoure, whose interception set up the Huskies' go-ahead score. Then, with a minute left, Vontoure got beat. His man hauled in a long touchdown pass, and the Cougars pulled the game out.

Two games later, Vontoure, with a minute left, made a game-saving interception in the end zone. The game after that, he sat—suspended. Neuheisel didn't detail why, but reporters learned that Vontoure had erupted in practice, screaming at his position coach, Chuck Heater. The week after that, Vontoure returned an interception 44 yards for a touchdown, and forced one fumble and recovered another. "We welcome him back with open arms," Neuheisel said.

Against Stanford, Vontoure made two acrobatic interceptions—a one-handed tip job and a diving grab—that had Husky fans buzzing. "Both of those catches, I guarantee you, are as fine of catches as you'll see any offensive or defensive player make," Neuheisel said.

Despite missing two games—one to suspension, the other to

injury—Vontoure finished the season with six interceptions, the most by a Husky in eight years.

His spectacular play in 1999 fueled expectations for 2000. One publication predicted he would be a first-team All-American.

From afar, Mathew Clark kept up with Vontoure's career. A year after he was beaten, Clark developed a tumor behind his right ear. Doctors told him he had bone cancer. Clark went through three surgeries, chemotherapy, radiation. For Clark, the beating faded in importance. He let the anger go. At Chico State he became a resident adviser in the dorms and met students who had known Vontoure in high school. "It was hard for them to believe that Anthony could have been involved in that. They said he was a really good guy. . . . I didn't know him. It was one night, and he could have made a huge mistake. My parents had much more of a hard time with it. The newspapers, every day, in the *San Ramon Valley Times*, there would be a huge write-up about Vontoure, playing for Washington, and how great he was. My parents felt like they had no justice. I remember my dad being very angry for a long, long time."

In Seattle, Vontoure's erratic behavior threatened to spoil his football prospects. Sometimes, his coaches at the UW would sit him down and get his former coaches from De La Salle on the phone. "The coaches there were like parents to him. He really was like a little kid with those guys. He wanted them to pat him on the head all the time," says Wayne Moses, the UW's running backs coach. "It was when he was down, not feeling real good, feeling homesick and stuff. He had a lot of respect for those guys down there. . . . They knew all the buttons to push."

By Neuheisel's second year at Washington, the coaching staff started to understand the depth of Vontoure's problems. The team had arranged for counselors, who reported back that Vontoure likely had bipolar disorder. Trainers can deal with muscle strains, coaches with lousy fundamentals, but how does a football team deal with mental illness? "Any person with that kind of chemical imbalance, they can't function in the structure of the team. It's an awful situation," Heater says. "It's an issue, it's a disease, a sickness. First off, they have to admit they have a problem, and they need to admit they need to do what needs to be done. It's a major deal, to deal with someone who is up and down. You are asking him to be consistent every day. It's impossible."

When Heater learned of Vontoure's disorder, he backed off on his demands. He just hoped Vontoure would show up to practice each day—with some energy, and a good attitude. "He was a beautiful kid," Heater says. "I loved that kid." Vontoure had been prescribed medication, but he wasn't taking it. Heater doesn't know why. "We never really did get that together. I know it didn't happen. It was a learning experience for all of us. . . . We were dealing with something we didn't really have a grasp of. And by the time we got our hands on it, it was probably a little late."

As the 2000 season approached, Vontoure seemed more scattered than ever. On the way to football camp in Olympia, he was pulled off the team bus because he hadn't finished a sociology assignment. He missed two days of camp. When he arrived, he overslept and missed another practice. Neuheisel demoted him—temporarily.

The following week, Vontoure took an open-ended leave of absence. He considered leaving the team, citing "the pressure of what was expected." "It was about what it takes to finish one of these seasons," Vontoure told the *Post-Intelligencer*. "I had some doubts I was going to be able to have the energy it takes."

In 2000, Vontoure moved into a studio apartment, where he lived alone, sleeping on his air mattress. Friends couldn't call. Vontoure didn't have a phone. If friends visited, they'd find no place to sit. Some teammates offered help. They'd buy Vontoure sandwiches to make sure he was eating, or drive him to a pay phone so he could call home.

Back in California, Vontoure's old coaches worried about what was happening to him. He seemed to be withdrawing from his team. He was getting harder to reach. "He needs to see someone, have someone to talk to," Eidson says. The coaches urged Vontoure not to become isolated. Neuheisel worried, too. He even arranged for Bob Ladouceur, Vontoure's old coach at De La Salle, to visit Vontoure in Seattle. "He was good to Anthony," Ladouceur says of Neuheisel. "He was searching for a way to reach him." In Seattle, Ladouceur told Vontoure: Get a phone, so I can talk to you. "He said he would, but he never did," Ladouceur says. "He just seemed to drift out."

After hearing of Vontoure's disciplinary problems, an old high school teammate went and saw Ladouceur. This was the teammate Vontoure had entrusted with his commitment card. The teammate told Ladouceur that he now planned to mail it to Vontoure, to remind him of his pledge to be the best person he could be. But despite all the efforts of his old coaches and teammates to reach out, Vontoure would continue to slip away from everyone, an enigmatic figure desperate for help, unable to find his way.

Taking a Shot

18

Anthony Kelley didn't lunge. He didn't waver, either. His mentor, Tom Williams, had told Kelley that if he wanted to study abroad, he would have to work for it. Kelley was doing just that.

With his academic adviser, Sarah Winter, Kelley scrutinized a host of university programs before hitting upon one in the Comparative History of Ideas department. It involved spending an academic quarter in South Africa, studying the effects of apartheid and how the country had fared since being freed from its rule. Nelson Mandela, the first South African president chosen in open elections, had retired the previous year. The blush of goodwill that had accompanied his ascension, and the subsequent airing of grievances in front of the Truth and Reconciliation Commission, were already in the past. Old animosities festered, and the country's long-term direction remained a question mark.

South Africa was a far cry from the frescoes and cafés of Old Europe that Williams had come across while studying in Italy. If Europe was sedate and cultured, South Africa was raw and violent. A visitor to South Africa needed to keep his wits. Yet something about the country appealed to Kelley. Its history of black oppression and struggle reminded him of the United States' troubled past.

Kelley wondered if he could get credit for the program, given that he was a sociology major. Winter checked it out—no problem. He just needed to register for some different classes. Winter helped Kelley prepare. She guided him through the paperwork needed to get his first driver's license. She helped him open a checking account. She helped him fill out forms for a passport.

One problem remained. Kelley needed a plane ticket to South

Africa, but he didn't have any money. His parents were in no position to help. So Kelley and Winter came up with an idea—apply for a Mary Gates scholarship.

Long before Bill Gates became a household name, his mother, Mary, was a force at the university. An alum, she became one of the UW's most respected regents, serving on the board for eighteen years. "She was a woman of such dignity and stature that people didn't become petty and air small grievances" around her, said former UW president William Gerberding. She took a particular interest in the welfare of undergraduates, wanting to ensure they didn't get slighted at the big research institution.

After Mary died in 1994, Bill and Melinda Gates established a scholarship in her name, putting up $10 million, a figure they later doubled. The money goes exclusively to undergraduates, who are chosen for their potential as researchers or leaders. The student who wanted to design a telecommunications network to bridge five Asian economies? Mary Gates Scholar. The student who wanted to study genetic mechanisms and their relationship to Alzheimer's disease? Mary Gates Scholar. But a linebacker? No football player—in fact, no athlete that anyone could remember—had ever won a Mary Gates scholarship. It just didn't happen.

Kelley gave it a shot anyway. He wrote a personal essay, mining his past, pondering his future. He described how his project might help him blossom as a leader. At the last possible moment, Kelley handed in his application. He had kept the whole thing low-key, especially with his teammates and coaches. He hadn't lied about what he was doing. But he hadn't broadcast it, either. "When they tell us as an athlete that we get to choose our own classes, I figure, you know, if it was in the off-season and I was working out, it would be fine. I really didn't know what I was getting myself into."

A Week in the Life

19

Thursday, October 19, 2000

A hard rain fell as Donald Preston drove south on Interstate 5, cutting through Seattle on the start of a long drive home. In Seattle the rain is usually soft, settling, like a showerhead set to fine mist. But tonight, the rain slashed. Preston's ten-year-old daughter, Kelsey, sat next to him in the passenger seat. She was a bright kid—a child correspondent for Radio Disney, a gig that had allowed her to interview Christina Aguilera at a concert a couple of weeks before.

The Prestons lived near Olympia, an hour and a half south of Seattle. They had just left the Ronald McDonald House, where they stayed while visiting Preston's son, a six-year-old who was being treated for cancer at Children's Hospital. They'd been making this trip for months now. To save on gas, Preston had traded in his construction van for a Dodge Daytona, a little two-door he had picked up for $2,500.

It was a few minutes past eleven. Preston used the carpool lane, skimming over the painted diamonds with a narrow shoulder and concrete divider to his left. In the distance, right of the interstate, he saw a twelve-foot-high "T," neon green, shimmering in the night. The "T" marked the headquarters and roasting plant for Tully's Coffee, a chain with stores all over Seattle, each one typically next to a Starbucks. The plant used to be the Rainier Brewery—with a landmark "R," big, red, and loopy—but hops had given way to beans.

Ahead, in the road, Preston saw orange flashes—emergency lights, or maybe brake lights. There was some kind of accident, blocking traffic. Preston applied his brakes. But as he slowed, the night exploded. Something smashed his car, punching in his door, popping metal.

A red Toyota pickup had barreled up from behind. Unable to stop, the driver had tried to swing around Preston, to squeeze between the carpool lane and divider. Instead, the truck had slammed into the Dodge's side, from the rear quarter panel to the driver's door. After hitting the Dodge, the pickup careened into the barrier, smacking the truck's front end. The pickup skidded, then stopped, some twenty feet away from the Dodge.

The pickup driver was alone. Despite the nasty weather, he had been cranking it down the highway, using the carpool lane to pass more cautious drivers. One witness, a thirty-one-year-old woman, said he had been driving "like a maniac."

Preston's daughter was shaken up. To steady her, Preston gave Kelsey something to do. Memorize the truck's license plate, he said. Kelsey looked ahead. One letter, five numbers, another letter. Preston tried to get out, but his door was stuck. He had to kick it open.

The other driver had stepped out, too, and was leaning against the truck. To Preston, the guy looked like a college student. A college student who was trashed. Or maybe he was just tired. He was tall, young, and black, with a mustache and goatee. He was wearing a red and white shirt. The other driver said something, but Preston struggled to make it out. "Is everybody okay," or something like that. Then the guy climbed back into his truck—and took off.

About ten minutes later, a state trooper arrived and took down a report. "Unit 1 fled the scene," she wrote. Now she had to figure out who the driver of Unit 1 was. Kelsey gave the trooper the plate—the letter, five numbers, another letter. The truck belonged to Robert and Francine Stevens, a couple with an Olympia address. The trooper's work just got a whole lot easier.

Jerramy Stevens was having a lousy game. It was October 21—two days after the accident on I-5—and Saturday afternoon had turned into evening. The Cal Bears were in town, meaning this one should have been easy. Oddsmakers had made the Huskies a 16-point favorite. The Bears had only two wins this year. Washington owned the Bears, having beaten them seventeen straight.

But for three quarters, Cal had dominated. Its linebackers and safeties had grabbed and clawed at Stevens, doing whatever they could to keep him from breaking loose. Opponents knew how thin Washington's receiving corps was. Washington's wide receivers didn't scare anybody; they lacked the speed to stretch a defense. Stevens was the threat. Stop him, and you could shut down Washington's passing game.

Through three quarters, Stevens had managed only one catch. Cal led, 24–13. The crowd, 70,000 strong, had quieted, stupefied. Fans couldn't believe it—Washington's Rose Bowl hopes were being dashed by the gimmes from Berkeley.

Even though Washington trailed by two scores—and Cal looked great, Washington miserable—a sense of the inevitable hung over this game. Already this season, Washington had won four times coming from behind. And with Cal, there was history. In 1988, Washington trailed Cal by 24 points before scoring the final 25. In 1993, Washington came from 20 back. Last year, the hole was 14—but the result, the same. Washington won.

With eleven minutes to go, Cal collapsed. Fumble, interception, fumble, blocked punt. "It must be a gypsy's curse. Bad stuff just kept happening," Cal's punter said afterward. In six minutes Washington scored 23 points, to put the game away, 36–24. The Huskies won despite drawing thirteen penalties, a season high. They won despite giving up five quarterback sacks. Stevens broke out with three catches in the fourth quarter, including a 10-yard touchdown reception. The team named him an offensive MVP. "When you win, and you don't ever lose, you don't know how to lose, so you don't give up," Stevens told reporters after the game. "When you lose all the time, you get used to it."

For Stevens, this game, like every game, offered escape from his worries. Football demands adrenaline, focus, commitment. Even in fall practices, Neuheisel had talked up how Stevens seemed able to shelve any thoughts of trial or prison. With all his troubles, Stevens continued to excel on the field. He continued to talk off the field, too. Here was a guy staring at a possible rape charge—not to mention any other charges he might face—taking reporters' questions. The sportswriters who covered the Huskies saw Stevens as a good quote. They would ask specifically for him after games—can we get a few minutes with Jerramy?—knowing that he would give them something better than the canned stuff other guys served up. Stevens accommodated them, comfortable that the rape investigation would remain off limits, comfortable that their questions would keep to football.

Against California, Curtis Williams tied for the team lead in tackles, with eight. Anthony Kelley sacked Cal quarterback Kyle Boller twice in the fourth quarter, once causing a crucial fumble. Jeremiah Pharms had a quiet game, with three tackles. Anthony Vontoure didn't play, because of a foot injury.

Washington moved to 6-1. The Huskies would next play at Stanford, in what would be the 1,000th game of Washington's storied football program. Stanford, the Pac-10's defending champion, was having a down year, but, like Washington, thrived on dramatic comebacks. The same day Washington beat Cal, Stanford beat USC with a touchdown pass on the final play.

Three days after the Cal game—three days after Washington's latest can-you-believe-this escape, three days after Stevens's latest MVP performance—Norm Maleng, the King County prosecuting attorney, held a news conference to announce whether Stevens would be charged with rape. The day had arrived—at last. Fans had been waiting for this. Sportswriters had been waiting for this. Stevens's teammates had been waiting for this. They knew their Rose Bowl run might ride on Maleng's decision. Stevens knew his freedom and his future could. Everyone appreciated the stakes—Stevens's coaches, family, and friends, the university's boosters, administrators, and faculty. As for Marie, she already knew what Maleng would say. The chief of the office's criminal division had met with her the night before.

By now, three months had passed since Stevens's arrest. An investigation that had been expected to take days or weeks had dragged on as prosecutors kept adding to Detective Parker's to-do list. Each time, Parker followed through. And each time, her doubts about the prosecutors grew.

With his prepared statement, Maleng played it straight. No dramatic buildup, no memorable phrases, no tug at the emotions. He looked into a wall of microphones and television cameras and said: "We have reviewed a very thorough investigation conducted by the Seattle Police Department. We have concluded that there is insufficient evidence to support the filing of criminal charges."

So that was it. Maleng said more, of course, but to many fans, his explanation hardly mattered. What mattered was the result. Stevens would not be charged with rape. Maleng offered no apology to Stevens for his arrest. Nor did Maleng condemn him for his conduct. There was no moral judgment, only a legal one, and the way Maleng viewed the law and the evidence, Stevens was in the clear. Was Stevens's behavior right or wrong? That discussion had no place here. When questioned by reporters, all Maleng would offer was: "I think what this case demonstrates is what we've always known. . . . Excessive drinking can lead to poor choices."

Parker, like Marie, had been notified of Maleng's decision before the news conference. "I was very upset. I was very upset. I was shocked. I was really shocked at first—and then I felt, I should have known it was coming." She had an eyewitness. She had DNA evidence. She had witnesses to Marie's condition. But she didn't have enough.

After Maleng's announcement, reporters scrambled for reaction. Stevens begged off interviews and instead offered a written statement: "From the beginning, I was assured this case would be handled appropriately through the legal system. I want to thank my friends and teammates for the support I have received the past three months. I am relieved this matter has been resolved and I can continue to focus on being a student at Washington and a member of the football team."

Neuheisel told reporters: "It has been a difficult time for everyone involved. I'm glad this has been resolved. My general feeling is one of relief."

In the news conference, Maleng's legal analysis ran short on detail. He said that because the freshman couldn't remember what happened—whether she said yes, whether she said no—prosecutors needed to prove that she was either physically helpless or mentally incapable of consent. The evidence, he said, was insufficient either way.

The details came a week later, in a confidential memorandum written by two of Maleng's deputies. Called a decline letter, the memo went to police to explain why charges weren't filed. But if the prosecutors hoped to win over the detectives, they failed.

The memo said witnesses "universally" described Marie as "very intoxicated." But to the prosecutors, that wasn't enough. "Our standards," they wrote, required Marie to be so out of it that she was "unconscious or nearly so."

But Washington law doesn't require that. It doesn't suggest it, either. Under the state's statute for second-degree rape, being "unconscious or nearly so" goes to the issue of physical helplessness. Mental incapacity stands as a separate issue. To be incapacitated, someone need not pass out, or even verge on it. In this case, a jury could have convicted if it found Marie was so intoxicated that she couldn't understand the consequences of sexual intercourse—and that her condition was obvious to Stevens.

The prosecutors' reading of the statute defied logic. It's as though they misread the conjunction, as though they believed the law says physically helpless *and* mentally incapacitated, not *or*. The King County prosecutors acted as if there was some walk-and-talk test out there. If you can walk and talk, you can consent. But the law imposes no such standard. If it did, any woman, no matter how drunk or drugged, would be deemed capable of consent, provided she could keep her feet and mutter a few words. A year later, in a different case, a Washington appellate court chided a King County prosecutor who likewise equated "unconsciousness" with mental incapacity. "Inexplicable," the appellate judges wrote, saying the law treats them as different. In this other case, a medical expert had testified that someone with a blood-alcohol content of .15 or higher would be mentally incapacitated—and the appellate judges had no quibble with that. One of Parker's fellow detectives in the Special Assault Unit pointed King County prosecutors to this appellate opinion while urging a rape charge against another UW football player, but the prosecutors took a pass.

To compound matters, the prosecutors' description of the evidence understated what Parker and other police officers had written up. The decline letter says the 911 caller—the eyewitness who reported a possible rape in progress—described Marie as "conscious and standing." But, according to police reports, he also described her as "half passed out against a building . . . like she was drugged or drunk." The decline letter says Marie's friends "describe her as standing, making limited conversation, and making decisions." But, according to police reports, her friends described her as "unable to keep her balance," having "slurred speech" and "acting like she was drugged." One friend told police: "She couldn't really talk or stand." The decline letter says none of Marie's friends "appeared afraid for her welfare." But, according to police reports, one friend tried to take away her keys. Two others drove her home. Marie's sorority was nearby, but Marie was unfit to walk, one friend told police.

When it came to passing judgment, the confidential memorandum used stronger language than Maleng's public statement. "It seems highly unlikely that the victim would have consented to anal intercourse with the suspect in a fraternity alley," the deputy prosecutors wrote. "However, the character of the victim and the character of the suspect is generally inadmissible at trial."

The decline letter closed by saying that with the holes in the evidence, "a jury could find reasonable doubt." Of course, the same could be said in any case. And that's not the standard anyway. In Washington, the legislature has adopted guidelines for prosecutors to use in making charging decisions. For property crimes, prosecutors need evidence "of such convincing force" that conviction is "probable." But for violent crimes—including rape—the guidelines tell prosecutors to be more aggressive; after all, the potential threat to the public is greater. For these crimes, prosecutors should file charges if the evidence "would justify conviction."

Had Stevens been charged, proving guilt would not have been easy. Maybe he committed a crime—and maybe he didn't. But what rankled Parker was that prosecutors didn't let a jury make that call. "I thought he should have been charged," Parker says. "I think most people in the police department thought he should have been charged. From the police perspective, I think there was overwhelming evidence that a crime had occurred. And then I think we should have left it to a jury to decide. Why didn't we let it go all the way through the system? There's no reason why it shouldn't have. I think we just felt, in our unit and in the police department as a whole, that this case was handled differently. And we felt it was because he was a University of Washington football star."

Mark Larson, the chief of the criminal division under Maleng, says: "I will tell you that in a prosecutors' office there is one opinion that counts. And in this case it was Norm Maleng's." Even so, Larson says he agrees with Maleng's call. "We have no doubt she was pretty drunk that night. Real drunk." But, Larson says, that wasn't enough. He calls any suggestion that Stevens received preferential treatment "outrageous and untrue."

Maleng's decision devastated Marie. "It was humiliating for me. I know it's not supposed to be, but it was. They took hope away from me." Marie worried that the decision—receiving as much attention as it did—would deter other women from coming forward.

The day after Maleng's press conference, Parker received a thank-you card from Marie. Flower petals graced the cover, with a lace ribbon running down the side.

"I don't know where to begin. You helped me through the toughest obstacle I have ever encountered. . . . There were times throughout the past 4 months where I just wanted to give up. . . . It meant the world to me that you believed in me and did everything you could do to get all the evidence. I have to say going through all of this and sticking with it to the end and finding out that nothing was going to be done broke my heart. It made me feel as though the prosecuting attorneys were on his side. But then I realized that I didn't care what they thought and that people like you & my family and friends were the ones on my side, and who cares about the others. . . . I can't thank you enough for the compassion you showed me. . . . You were the only one I trusted and could depend on through this whole process."

On October 25, the news of Maleng's decision was all over the newspapers. "No Charges in Stevens Case," the *Seattle Times* headline said.

That same day, the state trooper working the I-5 accident wrapped up her investigation. She now knew the identity of the pickup's driver. The driver of Unit 1 was Jerramy Stevens.

Under Washington law, a driver involved in an accident must remain at the scene; provide his name, address, and insurance information; and, if someone's hurt, try to help. Failure to do so amounts to hit-and-run. If the accident results in death or injury, fleeing is a felony. If only damage results, it's a gross misdemeanor, punishable by up to a year in jail.

But Stevens wasn't charged with any crime. Instead, the trooper wrote him a ticket, a citation for driving too fast for conditions. Stevens paid a $119 fine. "I thought it was pretty typical," Donald Preston says. Flip it around, he says. Make him the driver who split: "I would have been put in jail."

Stevens had hit a car and fled. Led a stirring comeback on the football field. Learned he would not be charged with rape. Learned he would not be charged with hit-and-run. All within six days.

The accident totaled Preston's car. It took him six months to get the insurance company to pay. Still, Preston counts himself lucky. He figures that if the truck—big as it was, as fast as it was going—had plowed straight into the back of the Dodge, he and his daughter could have been seriously hurt, maybe even killed.

Love, Love, Love   20

Few events appeal to nostalgia more than homecoming. Just the word and it's the 1950s all over again, with Fred MacMurray in a scarf and letter sweater, leading on the boys. For a university, homecoming is a time to shine. Parents visit. Alumni return. Students discover cleaning supplies. The leaves turn gold, and grunge gets wiped away. At the University of Washington, students gather in Red Square, a campus plaza paved in red brick. The marching band plays, the cheerleaders cheer, the head coach gives a pep talk. Which is not to say that every tradition remains trapped in time. In recent years the UW abandoned the rite of homecoming king and queen, opting instead to crown the two most deserving students. Could be two men, could be two women. "I think it's great the UW has chosen to have a nongender-specific homecoming royalty," said one winner, a communications major.

For Washington, the game against California had been homecoming. That stood to reason; schools pick homecoming opponents they figure to beat. Lose the game, and you lose a little of that luster. Some 70,000 fans had attended the game. As they streamed into Husky Stadium, many had picked up a game program, produced by the athletic department's Media Relations office. This program featured a long profile of Jeremiah Pharms, the Husky linebacker in his fifth and final year. The headline was: "Putting Phamily Phirst."

The profile celebrated Pharms the player, student, and man, Pharms the son, father, and husband. What school wouldn't be proud? He takes advantage of the university "to make himself into the most well-rounded player—and person—he can be," committing himself to the weight room *and* the classroom. He loves his mother: "She was so much mother, that I needed no father." He loves football: played thirty-seven straight games, racked up 128 tackles, gave 110 percent. He loves his teammates—tells them that every day.

Love, love, love. The word appears a dozen times in the story. Pharms's love for his wife and three kids is "overwhelming." He keeps "his family foremost in his mind in everything that he does." A picture shows Pharms knocking helmets with an Idaho player, his left hand, in a gray Nike glove, near the guy's throat. The caption says: "When not leveling opponents on the football field, Pharms is a devoted husband and father, dedicated to raising his children in a loving environment."

The profile notes that Pharms's last game as a Husky is approaching.

When the game ends, Pharms will change his clothes and exit the locker room, into the smiling faces and open arms of his wife, Franquell, and his children. Win or lose, the game is only secondary to Pharms, who understands the value of family, of the love a mother—or father—can share with their children, and pass on to future generations. "There is no more important thing in life than family," he says.

The story ends with Jeremiah Jr. smiling up at his dad.

Pharms smiles, too, echoing a gift of love from a child to his father, from a mother to her son, a love that knows no bounds, and—like the Husky senior in whom it overflows—can never be contained.

The story's writer was Brian Beaky, a senior studying journalism. Working part-time in the sports information office, he and other student assistants churned these stories out, week after week. The idea was simple. Promote. Write positive. Make the players and families feel good about the story. The writers weren't supposed to dig. They didn't ask around, or check police reports or court records. They would talk to the player, write up what he said, and maybe round out the story with some statistics and career highlights.

Once the profile was published, Beaky presented Pharms with a couple of copies. Pharms liked the story.

Twelve Months before "Putting Phamily Phirst"

One police officer shot a roll of thirty-five-millimeter film taking pictures of the damage. Another officer wrote up a list and attached estimates of the costs.

Bathroom door kicked in with broken frame: $150.
Broken glass coffee table: $100.
Broken sliding screen: $50.
Dent in drywall: $75.

It was October 1, 1999—a year before Washington hosted Cal, a year before "Putting Phamily Phirst." Just before noon, Franquell Pharms had called Seattle police and said her husband had attacked her and was high on marijuana. Officers arrived to find Franquell on the street outside her apartment, holding a kitchen knife. An officer named Sjon Stevens took the knife away and asked Franquell to get in his car, to go look for Jeremiah. Soon after, another officer spotted Jeremiah on a street corner. Stevens drove up with Franquell, Franquell said that's him, and Jeremiah was arrested. Police took him to the north precinct on suspicion of assault.

Stevens returned Franquell to the apartment. She told him this story:

> This morning, I flew up from Sacramento. That's where I live, although my name's also on the lease for this apartment. I knew Jeremiah's cousin, Calvin, had just brought up a child from California. Jeremiah had this child with another woman, named Cassandra. I figured something was going on behind my back, so I decided to confront Jeremiah.
>
> I heard him in the bathroom, talking on the phone. He's talking to Cassandra, and I hear him say, I love you. The door's

locked, so I kicked it in. I kicked it in and I yelled at him about fooling around behind my back.

I went into the living room. Calvin was there, playing video games. I grabbed a bowl and threw it against the wall. Jeremiah came at me. I grabbed some scissors, from on top of the stereo, to defend myself. Jeremiah grabbed me, and I dropped the scissors, and we hit the floor, near the fireplace. Calvin pulled me away from Jeremiah. We got back on our feet. Jeremiah held me against the fireplace wall, his hand around my neck, his arm straight out. I grabbed him by the neck and kicked him in the testicles. He let me go. I left, and on the way out, kicked the screen door. I went to a neighbor's and called police.

After taking Franquell's statement, Officer Stevens left for the police station. He had one side of the story. Now he wanted the other. To Stevens's eye, Jeremiah didn't appear to be high. Jeremiah told Stevens:

Franquell and I are separated. She flew up, to pack up her things in the apartment. She heard me on the phone with Cassandra and kicked in the door. In the living room, she picked up scissors and stabbed at me. I grabbed her hand, to defend myself. My cousin grabbed Franquell and they fell to the ground. Franquell got up and stomped the glass coffee table. Then she kicked out the screen door and left. I called my mother, and she advised me to leave the apartment.

Calvin, the cousin, also gave police a statement, supporting Jeremiah's version. He said that before leaving the apartment, Franquell told Jeremiah: *You ain't shit. Never will be shit. You're not playing this weekend. I hate you.*

Stevens went to his sergeant to screen the case. Here they were, with conflicting accounts, Franquell saying Jeremiah attacked her, Jeremiah saying she attacked him. The police decided to let everyone go. Late that afternoon, they released Jeremiah without charges.

Rick Neuheisel wasn't sure how to handle this. He knew Pharms had been arrested. He knew Pharms had been released. He knew the Huskies were scheduled to play the next day. Neuheisel reached out to Mike Magan, the Seattle police detective who spent so much time with the team, consulting the coaches, chatting up the players. Neuheisel summoned the detective to a hotel that the team used before home games. The domestic-violence case wasn't Magan's, but he had conferred with the investigating officers.

What do you say? Neuheisel asked. Should I play him tomorrow?

I can't tell you what to do, Rick, Magan said. But in my opinion, Jeremiah is the victim.

With that, Neuheisel heard what he needed to hear.

The next day, on October 2, 1999, the Huskies hosted Oregon. It was a night game. Before kickoff, a group of six people took seats in the student bleachers, around the 20-yard line. This group included Pharms's mother, his cousin Calvin, and Cassandra. As they watched the Huskies warm up, Franquell walked by. She said something like, "I'm getting him out of the game." Then she walked down to the field.

Pharms's mother knew this was trouble. She asked a friend of Jeremiah's to go and intercept Franquell. On the sidelines, Franquell found Ralph Bayard, a senior associate athletic director, and told him about Cassandra being in the stands. Bayard was a distinguished figure, with oversight of NCAA compliance, student-athlete academic services, community relations. He had played under Jim Owens—and was one of the four players suspended for refusing obeisance to Owens's misguided loyalty oath. Now he was faced with an upset wife. Franquell pointed Bayard to the stands and said Jeremiah's girlfriend wasn't supposed to be there, that Neuheisel didn't want Jeremiah to have any distractions. As they talked, Jeremiah's friend caught up. He started talking to Bayard, too. Franquell headed back toward the stands.

Pharms's mother saw her coming. Get ready, she told Cassandra.

As Franquell approached, she took off her coat.

Don't do this here, Jeremiah's mom told her.

Franquell pulled Cassandra's sweatshirt over her head and began punching. Cassandra couldn't see the blows, but she could feel them. She was getting punched in the back. She was getting punched in the head.

Jeremiah's mom tried to get between the two. Franquell pushed her away.

Calvin stepped in. "You don't fuck with my auntie blood," he said. Franquell jumped on Calvin from behind, wrapping herself around his shoulders. She grabbed his gold chain and broke it. Calvin spun around and pinned Franquell to the ground.

Nearby, a cop was working security. He heard whistling and looked up. People were pointing him to section 21, near the 20-yard line. He ran up to Calvin and Franquell. The cop had no idea what started all this, all he saw was a guy on top of a woman, with a crowd gathered around. He told Calvin to let Franquell up. Calvin refused. Calvin was screaming, and he just kept screaming. The officer saw blood on the woman's lip. He told Calvin again: Let her go. Calvin refused. After a third round of this, the officer pulled out a canister of pepper spray and blasted Calvin in the face.

The pepper spray did the job. The fighting stopped, and everyone was separated. Afterward, the university police took statements—from Franquell, Cassandra, Calvin, Jeremiah's mom, Jeremiah's friend, even from a vendor selling hot chocolate. "I believe Franquell is acting like a woman scorned," Jeremiah's mother told police. Franquell said she'd had enough. While giving her statement to police, she got on the phone and made airplane reservations to go back to California.

Later, she would return to Washington and live with Pharms again. Authorities elected to charge Franquell with fourth-degree assault, a misdemeanor. But the case lingered in the courts for years, with nothing much happening. In the end, prosecutors dropped the charge.

The one person who didn't give police a statement was Jeremiah. He was too busy playing. That night, he scooped up a fumble in the fourth quarter and returned it 22 yards. Before a packed house of 72,000 fans, Washington beat Oregon, 34–20.

The fight in the stands didn't make the newspapers. Nor did the fight the day before. Some details of the domestic-violence investigation made it into a court filing, but a King County judge sealed the entire record, in an order that violated state laws designed to discourage such secrecy.

Six Days after "Putting Phamily Phirst"

Cassandra wasn't Pharms's only girlfriend. On October 27, 2000—six days after the homecoming game against Cal, and one day before Washington would play Stanford—a twenty-year-old woman named Tarah arrived at the King County courthouse. She had no choice. Prosecutors had subpoenaed her. Tarah was with her mother. Her mother had been subpoenaed, too. They made their way to the courthouse's seventh floor, to the courtroom of Judge William Downing.

Inside the courtroom was Mike Lang, a King County prosecutor, and Jeff Mudd, the police detective investigating the shooting of Kerry Sullivan. That investigation was now in its seventh month—and the public still didn't know a thing. Today's hearing would keep it that way.

Called an Inquiry Judge Proceeding, the hearing would allow Lang to question witnesses under oath. Doing it this way provided two advantages. First, the hearing was hush-hush. Each witness would be sworn to secrecy. Second, the trappings of a courtroom—the judge in his robes, the swearing of an oath, the threat of perjury—can sometimes loosen up a reluctant witness.

Today, Lang had also subpoenaed Nick Banchero, the roommate of Sullivan's who had been held at gunpoint by the second robber. Judge Downing explained the proceeding to the three witnesses, then had his bailiff and clerk leave the courtroom. Afterward, the door was locked.

It was late morning when Tarah took the stand. The Chrysler LeBaron that the two gunmen had abandoned after the robbery belonged to Tarah's family. This was the car with the Nike glove, the bloody fingerprint, the empty gun holster. The day after the robbery, Tarah had reported the car stolen. Today, under questioning by Lang, she held to that account. Maybe Lang hoped she would change her story, that she would say Pharms had borrowed the car that night. If so, he didn't get his wish.

By now, this case had begun to rankle Lang. He was one of King County's top prosecutors, a guy so respected he would later move on to the U.S. Attorney's Office and lead a racketeering case against the Hell's Angels. He would be sent to Baghdad to investigate whether a Blackwater security operator had killed the Iraqi vice-president's bodyguard. What bothered Lang was how Pharms had yet to pay for what he'd done. Lang had no doubt Pharms was the shooter, no doubt Pharms had almost killed a man. But each Saturday, Pharms suited up and played in front of sold-out crowds. Each Saturday, he took in the applause. To Lang, it wasn't right. Still, he didn't want to push. He figured delay comes with crime-lab work. His thinking was: Let's keep everything quiet until we know what we've got.

Tarah told Lang that she had seen Pharms on the afternoon of March 14, hours before the robbery occurred. She had driven to the house that Pharms rented in the suburb of Lynnwood, and stayed for maybe a half hour, forty-five minutes. Afterward, Pharms gave her a kiss, and she drove away.

Did you have sex? Lang asked.

"Probably."

Were the two of you in a romantic relationship at the time?

"It was kind of dying off. I was getting more and more upset."

"What do you mean by that?"

"Because he is married."

"When you say you were getting upset by that, what do you mean?"

"Just that it's not right to be with a married man, and he is talking to his wife on the phone and I have to keep quiet, you know. And I've helped him so much. I've helped him a lot. I'm the one who found the house for him. So I was expecting too much, so I had to push myself away."

Tarah told Lang how she had met Pharms. In June 1999 she was driving through Seattle's Central District when Pharms pulled up next to her at a stoplight and smiled. At the next stoplight, they stopped together again. Pharms asked if she would pull over. She agreed, and he came over to talk.

They dated for more than a year. Tarah found the house Pharms was renting. Hooked up his phone. Brought him food from Wendy's. She would even go and buy marijuana for him.

"He smoked a lot," she said.

"He smoked marijuana pretty much every day?" Lang asked.

"Uh-huh."

Tarah said Pharms was hopeless with finances.

"He doesn't know how to pay his bills."

Even before he met Tarah, Pharms had a way of letting responsibilities slip. In 1998 he was caught driving with an expired license, in a car with expired plates. Charged with a misdemeanor, he failed to show for a pretrial hearing. So a judge ordered his arrest. That fall, a cop discovered the warrant, and Pharms spent a night in jail. Three days later, he started the season's second game. The charge was later knocked down to a ticket, and Pharms paid a small fine.

While dating Pharms, Tarah would drive him around just about every day, she told Lang.

"Didn't he have his own car?"

"Yeah, but he doesn't like to drive."

"Why not?"

"That's J.P."

"When you say he doesn't like to drive, what do you mean?"

"He doesn't like to be by himself, he doesn't like driving, he doesn't like a lot of things."

Their relationship took a turn in recent months, Tarah told Lang.

Franquell moved up from Sacramento and into Pharms's house in August, along with their two kids. The next month, in September, Tarah and Jeremiah broke up.

Still, she had visited him just yesterday, Tarah told Lang. Pharms had called and said his wife was out of town, and that he wanted to see her. She came over, and they talked about sex—whether they would keep having it or not. She didn't say what they had decided.

"Do you plan on seeing Jeremiah Pharms in the near future?" Lang asked.

"Probably."

"Now, you are not engaged in a romantic relationship with him, he has a wife and kids. Why do you keep seeing him?"

"Because I'm his friend."

"You consider yourself his friend even today?"

"Yeah, I'm trying to get him to realize he is married."

"What do you mean by that?"

"He doesn't even acknowledge what marriage is. It's frustrating for me."

Tarah said she spent maybe an hour and a half with Pharms the previous day.

"I told him I have to go to court tomorrow," she told Lang.

"Did you tell him why?"

"No, but he pretty much knows why."

Of course he did. Pharms knew he was still under investigation. He knew he might be charged any day. He may not have known why the investigation was taking so long, but he knew he wasn't in the clear yet.

After forty-five minutes of questioning, Tarah was excused.

The next witness was ushered in. The hearing continued. The investigation continued. The season continued. Tomorrow, Washington would play at Stanford, and Pharms would suit up again. For Pharms, football was simple. Life was complicated. "He doesn't like to be by himself," Tarah had said. By his final year of college, that was no problem. He had a wife, two girlfriends, three kids, and at least four dogs.

I Can't Breathe

October 28, 2000: Washington at Stanford

For the Washington Huskies, this was football game No. 1,000.

One thousand games. Of the first 999, they won 612. Tied 50 others. Went unbeaten for nine years—the longest streak in college football. Reached thirteen Rose Bowls. Had forty-seven first-team All-Americans, from George Wilson to Hugh McElhenny to Steve Emtman. And don't forget those quarterbacks. Don Heinrich, Sonny Sixkiller, Warren Moon, the Huard brothers, Damon and Brock. And that 1991 team? One of history's very best.

This was a milestone game for a storied program. And yet, and yet . . . the game seemed like such a letdown. The Huskies were playing in a dump—Stanford Stadium, a great place to pick up a splinter or two on the rotting bleachers, or maybe wave at the next fan fifteen feet over. This place hadn't seen a real crowd in years, and it was in such bad shape that some Stanford officials feared the county would condemn it.

The Huskies were playing in the rain—a downpour, really. It was fifty-seven degrees, gray and wet. They may as well have stayed in Seattle. The stadium could hold 85,000 people. On this day, the crowd was announced at 31,300—and that was a lie. There may have been 25,000. Maybe. Half were Husky fans, crammed into a corner, wearing purple ponchos. A few fans wore yellow. With their hoods up, they looked like ducks on a purple pond.

The Huskies were playing the Stanford Cardinal—a team they owned, a team they had beaten all but once the last fourteen times out. And this wasn't one of Stanford's better editions. The Cardinal were 3-4. Stanford's quarterback, Randy Fasani, was playing with a bad knee.

Gulls flocked overhead. The rain flattened the cheerleaders' hair. The game wasn't even televised live—the only Pac-10 game that weekend to go dark. It was just as well. Mist settled on the lenses of cameras taping the game. It was like looking through gauze, or glass smeared with Vaseline.

Stanford could beat you with the pass, but the football was slick. Washington could beat you with the option, but the footing was treacherous. Runners struggled for traction. Balls squirted through receivers' hands. During one play, Marques Tuiasosopo flew out of bounds and landed on a tarp. He didn't stop for a good twenty feet, like a kid on a giant Slip 'N Slide.

For Washington, the first quarter was a dismal affair. Tuiasosopo hit freshman receiver Justin Robbins in stride, but Robbins muffed it and the ball was intercepted. Stanford kicked two field goals, while Washington managed only two first downs. But in the second quarter, Washington mounted a fourteen-play drive. Todd Elstrom, the team's most reliable wideout, made two catches for first downs. Willie Hurst, the third-string tailback, sliced through holes. Washington covered 79 yards to go up 7–6.

Stanford's offense sputtered, thanks in no small part to Curtis Williams, Washington's senior safety. Williams dominated the first half, with one big play after another. During one stretch he made six tackles in seven downs, throwing his body around the field. With a couple of minutes left in the half, he crowded the line, knifed through, and exploded on Stanford's tailback, dropping him for a loss. But while he was punishing Stanford's offense, Williams was also drawing warnings for his style of play. Cardinal tailback Kerry Carter heard a referee warn Williams: *Keep your head up. Don't hit with your helmet's crown.* Other players heard similar warnings.

Husky freshman Greg Carothers watched Williams, fixated, determined to learn. Carothers was a backup safety from Helena, Montana. In high school he had doubted any big-time college would want him. When Washington offered, he jumped. In the Stanford game, he kept his eyes on No. 25. "He was not the most in-shape guy," Carothers says. "But when it came to game time, you would think he could run a marathon. . . . The things he could do on the football field were amazing."

Williams had emerged as a leader on this team. What Tuia-sosopo was to the offense, Williams was to the defense. He set the tone. He could be goofy as hell in the locker room, joking, wrestling, teasing. "He was a happy spirit," says Hakim Akbar, the team's other starting safety. "People were drawn to him. He had the biggest smiles, man." But blow the whistle and he was nasty. "No fear was in his eyes," Akbar says. Blow the whistle and he was committed. His motor never dropped a gear. "As competitive as the day is long," says Wayne Moses, an assistant coach. Williams and Akbar roomed together on road trips. They would pop some chew, watch a movie, talk about making it to the NFL. Williams would tell Akbar: "I want to get a shot, man. I want to take care of my daughter." Williams hadn't seen his daughter for a year now. But he called her every Tuesday and Thursday, at seven at night. Kymberly was now five years old, closing in on six.

Bobby Hauck coached Washington's safeties. He told his players: "Get a piece on every play." Hit someone. Don't just run around for exercise. Watching the starters, Carothers learned how to intimidate. "It was really just disregarding any feeling or warning about what might happen to your body, as I had seen Curtis and Akbar do so many times. . . . You want to catch them in the face, catch them in the mouth, and set the tone: This isn't going to be easy. . . . It takes a special person to go out there and want to beat up on people. It was something special about our safety group." Going for the mouth can be dangerous, Carothers says. What you have to do is, don't duck your head.

Carothers wasn't the only person keying in on No. 25. Two of Williams's brothers, David and Paul, were in the stands. David was older than Curtis, Paul younger. David had played football at Fresno State. Paul would do the same in years to come.

With three seconds left in the first half, the Huskies called a time-out and summoned their kicker for a 34-yard field goal. Afterward, the teams could retire to their locker rooms. The fans could find shelter. But this day wouldn't allow something so simple as that. The kicker, John Anderson, measured his steps, three back, two to the left. But before the snap, the whistle blew. Stanford had called a time-out. So the teams waited, the rain fell, the fans murmured. A minute later, the teams lined up again. The whistle blew. Stanford had called another time-out. Fans booed. The rain fell. The holder toweled off his hands. The Cardinal still had one more time-out, and sure enough, when the teams lined up, Stanford used it. Anderson threw up his arms in disgust. Stanford coach Tyrone Willingham kept his arms folded, his face impassive. More fans booed. The rain fell.

In all, five minutes passed before Anderson's kick. Maybe Willingham hoped more rain would muck up Anderson's footing, or maybe he wanted to play with Anderson's mind. Whatever he hoped for, he didn't get. Anderson nailed the kick; the ball split the uprights. Running off the field, he looked to the Stanford sidelines and shook his head.

Could a half of football be any drearier? Usually, a Stanford game is at least entertaining, with balls flying all over the field. But in the first half the Cardinal completed only one pass, for all of 4 yards. This was no aerial circus. It was more like watching the circus elephant get whipped.

The second half, the rain continued. So did the sloppy play. Washington threw another interception when wide receiver Wondame Davis let the ball bounce off his hands. Washington had more luck staying on the ground. Following a shanked punt by Stanford, the Huskies went 56 yards for a touchdown, to go up 17–6. The teams settled into a routine as dull and gray as the stadium and the sky. Stanford got the ball and went: stuffed run, incomplete pass, incomplete pass, punt. Washington got the ball and went: stuffed run, incomplete pass, incomplete pass, punt.

Washington's punter wanted to pin Stanford deep. But the ball hit at the 12 and took off, four quick jumps, bounding for the end zone. Curtis Williams was a gunner on the punt team, one of the first players downfield. He caught up to the ball at the 1-yard line and swatted it back into play, to prevent a touchback. Williams was doing it all, sparkling not only at safety but on special teams.

Stanford took over at its 4-yard line. On first down, Fasani, the quarterback, handed the ball to Kerry Carter, the tailback. Carter took the ball at the goal line. This year, Stanford had struggled to run. But last week Carter had a breakout game, scoring four touchdowns against USC. He was a power back, six foot two, 235 pounds.

From his safety position, Williams inched up, watching the play develop. When he saw the handoff, he took off from the 10-yard line. Carter cut into the right side of the line. Williams charged up to fill the hole. Carter saw Williams coming and tried to lower his shoulders. Williams's head dipped. They crashed at the 6-yard line, helmet to helmet. To a cameraman on the sidelines, it sounded like a train hitting a wall.

Off the field, Curtis Williams's past was catching up to him. The state was coming after him for unpaid child support. Two years earlier, Michelle had obtained a judgment requiring Curtis to pay $283 a month. Curtis hadn't paid anything. He wrote in court documents that he couldn't afford to, being in school. "When I was living with Michelle she supported all three of us. So why does she need money from me for just her and Kym at this point?"

Williams hired Mike Hunsinger to help out. Hunsinger discovered that Williams also had an outstanding arrest warrant, for missing a hearing in a pending assault case. Nine days before the Stanford game, Hunsinger helped Williams get an appearance bond so the warrant would be dropped. Then the two went to lunch. Hunsinger found he liked Williams. He seemed like a guy who was twenty-two going on thirty. "He'd been a terrible father," Hunsinger says. But Williams knew he had been a terrible father—and was looking forward to turning that around.

Anthony Kelley was at outside linebacker. He knew it was a bad hit, knew it right away. He saw Williams bounce off—his body already rigid, like it was frozen in air. Williams landed on his side. Then he rolled onto his back.

Jeremiah Pharms ran up. "Good hit, good hit," he said. Pharms and Williams were about as close as two players can be. Same class. Both married. Each a father. They partied together, talked NFL together. As Williams lay there, in the mud, the rain still falling, Pharms said: Shake it off, shake it off, hop up.

Kelley saw Williams's body start to shake. He saw his eyes start to roll toward the back of his head. Williams looked like he was trying to say something, but there was no sound. Then Kelley got it: *I can't breathe*. Williams was mouthing the words: *I can't breathe*. The cameraman, on the sidelines, heard Kelley yell: "Curtis! Don't you stop. Curtis! Don't give up. Curtis! Keep fighting."

Other players gathered around. Can you hear us? they asked. Move your hands if you can hear us. Nothing. Dave Burton, the team's head of sports medicine, ran onto the field. Williams's breathing was labored. He couldn't speak, he couldn't move his feet. But he was conscious. Burton looked into Williams's eyes and saw awareness and panic.

As Williams lay there, Pharms cried. Larry Tripplett, the team's nose tackle, watched from the sidelines. He hadn't been on the field for the play. He heard players saying, "He ain't moving, man, he ain't moving." He waited for Williams to get up. He knew that he would get up. The longer Tripplett waited, the harder the realization hit.

Rock Nelson, the offensive lineman, lay in bed in Seattle, in the dark, listening on the radio. He was in a bad place, depressed, feeling his identity slip away. His back injury was taking football away from him. Listening, he knew this was bad. Curtis, he would drag himself off the field if he could. As time passed, Nelson began to think: That could have been me.

For fifteen minutes, doctors tended to Williams. They placed his neck in a brace and moved him onto a stretcher. Kelley went to the sideline. He gathered the other players around and asked them to kneel. Kelley led a prayer. He lifted Williams up to God, and told God to heal him, to take care of him, to look over him, to bring him back to his family. He asked that Williams be healed in Jesus's name. An ambulance took Williams off the field.

The clock showed 2:01. That's how much time was left in the third quarter. To Tuiasosopo, it seemed that time had stopped. His thoughts went every which way. *How are we going to continue this game? Curtis may be fighting for his life. And this, this is just a game. But it's a game we love. And Curtis would want us to win.* Tuiasosopo made up his mind. *Let's win . . . and get it over with.*

When play resumed, Kelley struggled to keep it together. Crying, he almost jumped offside, he was so desperate to hit someone. Akbar, one of the team's surest hitters, began missing tackles. "I was really upset, man," he says. "I couldn't see how something that freakish could happen." Derrell Daniels, a linebacker known to his teammates as "The Silent Assassin," worried he might be next. A couple of times he was supposed to blitz, but he just stood there, afraid to go.

In the fourth quarter, Kerry Carter, Stanford's big back, fumbled at midfield. Kelley recovered. Washington started a drive that figured to put the game away. The Huskies kept feeding the ball to running back Willie Hurst—3 yards, 6 yards, then 22 yards, for the score. Washington was up, 24–6. Only 5:57 remained. *Let's win . . . and get it over with.*

Stanford returned the kickoff to its 36. Some folks called Stanford the Cardiac Cardinal, because of their propensity for comebacks. But against Washington, Stanford had yet to show even a spark. With the game almost over, Fasani had only six completions for 47 yards.

On first down, Fasani's pass sailed out of bounds. On second down, the center flubbed the snap. Fasani picked the ball off the turf and threw to a receiver in the flat. Akbar had an open shot at him, but missed. The receiver spun and raced 60 yards down the sideline, reaching the 4-yard line.

With that play—a broken play—the game shifted. What happened next, Washington's offense could only watch—powerless to stop, unable to believe. Stanford scored a touchdown and two-point conversion, to close to 24–14. Five minutes remained. Stanford gambled with an onside kick—and recovered. Fasani took Stanford down the field, to score another touchdown. It was 24–21. Two and a half minutes remained. Stanford tried another onside kick—and recovered again.

Bad knee and all, Fasani barreled down the left side of the field, breaking tackles. After 30 yards, three Huskies dragged him down. From the 2-yard line, Fasani faked a handoff up the middle. Akbar bit, leaving the left side of the field open. Fasani ran into the end zone, untouched.

The Stanford crowd would have gone crazy—had there been one. It was 28–24, Stanford. And only fifty-three seconds remained. Cardiac Cardinal, indeed.

All season, the Huskies had come from behind. Now, they had just watched an opponent do the same number on them—and not just any number, but a comeback for the ages. When Tuiasosopo last took a snap, Stanford had only 6 points. The Cardinal had scored three touchdowns without letting Washington's offense back onto the field.

On the sidelines, Tuiasosopo huddled with the offensive linemen. They told each other: Let's do this. We are not losing this game. The Huskies returned the kickoff to the 20, burning six seconds. They had 80 yards to go, and forty-seven seconds to get there. They had one time-out. A wet ball. And a young receiving corps that had vexed coaches and fans all season long.

Tuiasosopo threw a bullet to Elstrom, over the middle, good for 27 yards. Elstrom, a junior, had been terrific all day. He wasn't the question mark. The clock ticked down to thirty-seven seconds.

Wilbur Hooks, a sophomore from Alaska, had caught only one pass in the last five games. But Tuiasosopo threw to him over the middle, and Hooks skied to take it down. The play covered 31 yards. Ten more seconds ticked off.

Tuiasosopo took the snap. He scrambled out of the pocket, rolling to his right. In the end zone, Justin Robbins shadowed him. Robbins, a freshman, had dropped a first-quarter pass that turned into an interception. Now he put his hand up, to help his quarterback see him, to show he was open. Tuiasosopo, nearing the sideline, threw across his body. The wet ball hit Robbins in the hands. Robbins bobbled the ball—slightly, so slightly it took a replay to see it—then hauled the pass in.

Tuiasosopo fell to his knees. He leaned back and pointed two fingers to the sky. Then he began throwing punches—right, left, right, left, right. Other players ran to the end zone, to celebrate. They fell into a heap, three players, then four, five, six. On the Washington sidelines, teammates bumped helmets, hugged, threw their arms up in victory.

Then they remembered.

For the Washington Huskies, this was football game No. 1,000. And it may have been the most extraordinary game of the whole bunch. The two teams scored five touchdowns in the last six minutes. Washington won with a monumental drive that took three plays and thirty seconds. "Three perfect throws," Neuheisel said afterward. But leaving the field, tears smeared Anthony Kelley's face. Wilbur Hooks cried so hard he had trouble breathing. The locker room was quiet. "It's a bittersweet taste," Willie Hurst told reporters. "We won. But we lost one of our soldiers." Tuiasosopo said: "He's a warrior. Look up the definition of a Husky and you'd find the name Curtis Williams. He'd want us to win the game."

Neuheisel and assistant coach Bobby Hauck stayed in California Saturday night. On Sunday they visited Williams in Stanford Medical Center, where he was in intensive care, on a respirator, sedated. Neuheisel later recounted the meeting for reporters. Williams, he said, could respond only with his eyes. When Neuheisel talked about Washington's upcoming game with Arizona—and the need to finish what the team had started—Williams blinked twice as fast.

The same day Washington beat Stanford, Oregon defeated Arizona State in double overtime, 56–55, to remain unbeaten in the Pac-10. To have any shot at the Rose Bowl, Washington needed to keep winning.

Neuheisel told reporters that the team needed to play with the same passion that Williams displayed. The team needed to press on. "I don't think there's any question it's going to be difficult," he said. "We've got to find a way to get up and play. I know for a fact old No. 25 would want it that way."

The day after the game, Kymberly Williams sat in her grandmother's house in Alaska, watching Washington play Stanford on tape delay. Michelle, Kymberly's mother, was at work. No one from the University of Washington had called to tell her what had happened to her husband.

In the third quarter, Kymberly found her grandmother and said: "Grandma, Grandma, Daddy fell down and he's not getting up."

The day after the Stanford game, Bud Withers received a tip. Usually, when a reporter gets tipped to something, he can't wait to tell someone else. He hangs up the phone and says, *This is good, you're not going to believe this, but . . .* A good tip snaps you to. Pumps you up. Lets you beat the other paper. It makes the beer taste better after work.

It was Sunday. Withers was a sportswriter, and sportswriters work Sundays. On weekends, football players play and sportswriters write. A sportswriter's day of rest is Tuesday, unless, of course, something's happening Tuesday, and something often is.

Withers covered Husky football for the *Seattle Times*, the city's largest newspaper. By now, he had been writing sports for thirty years. Although his byline was sports-page perfect, he was not so easy to peg. Here was a guy named Lawrence, who went by Bud, who used words like "capacious" and made it work.

On his beat, Withers was wired. He received lots of tips. But this tip was different. This tip generated no feelings of excitement or satisfaction. It came tinged with dread—that, and the question: *What the hell do I do now?*

People think they know sportswriters, because they see them in movies and on television. There's Dickie Dunn, the sportswriter in *Slap Shot*, the classic flick about a minor-league hockey team. The coach wants to spread a rumor? Float a lie? He tells Dickie, and Dickie runs with it. Dickie doesn't check it out. He takes the coach's word. Now it's in the newspaper—now, it's gospel. Dickie and the coach, Reggie Dunlop, sit in a bar. The hometown Chiefs got lit up the night before, but you wouldn't know it from Dickie's account. Dunlop reads from the newspaper: *To see the three*

Chiefs make a scoring rush, the bright colors of their jerseys flashing against the milky ice, was to see a work of art in motion.

"Hey, that's good writing, Dickie."

"I was trying to capture the spirit of the thing, Reg."

"Oh, you did."

Reg passes the newspaper around, and the players grab at it, delighting in Dickie's fawning words. Dickie is a homer and a dupe, and a bit of a dope.

On TV, sportswriters often scream. They talk too much and talk too loud, and the more they talk, the less they report, until they don't know what they're talking about. When Jay Mariotti worked at the *Chicago Sun-Times*, he did an ESPN show from his newsroom. He screamed so much, the newspaper soundproofed the walls around him. Mariotti seemed forever angry—at players, coaches, owners, beat writers, fellow columnists, you name it. When Mariotti resigned from the newspaper, the editor wrote: "We wish Jay well and will miss him—not personally, of course—but in the sense of noticing he is no longer here, at least for a few days."

But most sportswriters fit neither stereotype. In most newsrooms, sportswriters earn respect by virtue of their work ethic. They work crazy long hours cranking out ridiculous amounts of copy. They thrive on pressure. On deadline, they write puns. Sportswriters drive revenue; the sports section draws huge readership numbers. Editors make exorbitant demands of sportswriters—the travel, the nights, all the game stories, features, and beat items. Those demands come with a price.

Withers used to work at the *Post-Intelligencer*, Seattle's other daily, and before that, the *Register-Guard* in Eugene, Oregon. He also covered Husky basketball and pitched in on other sports, be it hydroplanes or track and field. He covered Summer Olympics and Final Fours. Twice his peers had named him Oregon's sportswriter of the year. In Washington he had won the honor three times in four years.

In a typical year he was good for 250 to 300 stories. He would go on these long tears. Take the Huskies' 2000 season. From the practices in August through the bowl season in January, Withers wrote about 180,000 words—the length of two novels. At the *Post-Intelligencer* he worked for a week with a fever. Diagnosed with pneumonia, he worked from bed, knocking off a feature on Jason Kidd. "That's not recommended, but is appreciated," his performance evaluation said. One afternoon the newspaper dispatched him to Pullman, 250 miles east, to write about a Washington State football player killed by a pipe bomb. Withers filed his story at 9 p.m. The next day, he was back in Seattle, writing two stories about a Mariners no-hitter.

Withers could take a stand on principle and refuse to give. When the *Post-Intelligencer* passed him over and hired a woman to be sports columnist, he sued, alleging gender discrimination. After five years, the lawsuit settled. Withers bristled at prissiness. In a self-evaluation at the *Post-Intelligencer*, he wrote: "We bend over backwards not to offend anybody; sometimes it seems as though we're overly concerned with being politically correct. Is the test of a story whether we're going to get 15 phone calls protesting it, or whether the story is accurate and well done? . . . In an NCAA-tournament story recently, I used the phrase 'high-tech nerds on the Eastside' . . . I didn't say all high-tech people were nerds. And it's common knowledge that a lot of computer types refer to themselves as computer nerds. Why doesn't that fly? Instead, the phrase gets changed to 'office workers.' Gee, what a dynamic alteration."

"I take things like this seriously," Withers wrote.

When Withers received the tip that Sunday, he was writing about Curtis Williams. So were the AP, the *Post-Intelligencer*, and other newspapers. Washington's season was being redefined. Before, it was all about this remarkable string of late rallies, about a team that seemed able to surmount any deficit. Now, tragedy interrupted. An MRI showed blood at Williams's C2 vertebra, high on the spine. The higher the damage, the worse the prospects. Williams remained in intensive care—conscious, but unable to speak.

The tipster told Withers that Williams had an ugly past, that he had served time on a felony assault conviction. No word of that had ever appeared in any paper. But what was Withers to do with this information now? Williams might never walk again. For all anyone knew, he might die from this injury. His teammates and coaches were devastated. Lots of fans were reeling, too. But this was news . . . right? Williams could become the focal point of this season—a symbol of sacrifice, a martyr, maybe an example of grace, depending on how things played out. Writing this now seemed like piling on. But not writing it seemed like withholding an important truth—sanding the edges off history, for fear the edges could cut. *Is the test of a story whether we're going to get 15 phone calls protesting it, or whether the story is accurate and well done?* Newspaper deadlines don't allow for deep reflection. Withers would deal with this on the fly.

Covering the Huskies was never easy. Fun, yes, but never easy. It was like being embedded with a military unit: access, at a cost. Some coaches expected you to be Dickie Dunn. At Washington, head coach Don James allowed reporters into practice. Most colleges did the same—only with ground rules. If the team was working on a trick play, you didn't put it in the paper. What good is a surprise play without surprise? But sometimes the coaches and reporters disagreed on where these lines were drawn. In 1988 three reporters saw Washington's quarterback hurt his thumb. James demanded they not report it. Two reporters defied him. The next day, James banned them from practice. The third reporter—he was allowed in. A day later, the third reporter wrote about the injury. James banned him, too. Practices were now closed.

James's successor, Jim Lambright, announced in 1996 that Rashaan Shehee, the starting tailback, had hurt his foot in practice. Reporters still couldn't watch practice, so who was to say different? Withers, then with the *Post-Intelligencer*, heard whispers that the story was a lie. He confronted Lambright, and Lambright fessed up. Shehee and some teammates had been at a party. Someone with a gun showed up and opened fire. In the scramble,

Shehee jumped off a second-floor balcony, hurting his heel. Lambright told Withers that he had lied to protect the team, to avoid negative publicity. He had asked Shehee to back him up. Afterward, UW president Richard McCormick lectured Lambright on the need to tell the truth. Lambright told reporters: "I made a mistake." To make amends, he reopened practices.

Neuheisel, too, would on occasion lie to the media. Once asked by a lawyer if the UW was obliged to be truthful, Neuheisel said: "The university had a policy of trying to be very careful with what the press needed to know and what the press got to know." The lawyer asked Neuheisel: "Well, in general terms, did you consider it important that you always be honest?" Neuheisel answered: "In general terms, yes."

For reporters, scrutinizing the Huskies took fortitude. In the late 1960s, the *Post-Intelligencer*'s Shelby Scates wrote about racial discrimination under football coach Jim Owens. "It seems incredible now, but it was almost like we had attacked the church and cast racial aspersions on the pope," Scates later told a radio station. "The phones came off the hook at the P-I, and the mail poured in. I thought I was going to have to leave town." In the 1990s, sportswriter Tom Farrey and investigative reporter Eric Nalder broke the story about Billy Joe Hobert's $50,000 loan in the *Seattle Times*. When the Huskies landed on probation, many fans blamed the newspaper, and held a grudge for years. A more recent exposé in the *Times* drew thousands of reader responses, with the reporters called "garbage," "slime," and "whores." "I hope you go to hell for writing this." "A newspaper should contribute to its community with some level of boosterism and local pride." "If this were the SEC, you would have to change your name." "Husky alums, pull your ads." "Subscription cancelled."

Some columnists were tougher than others. The *Post-Intelligencer* featured Art Thiel, nobody's fool, and Jim Moore, a bit of a goofball, but a goofball who knew how to round up police reports. The *Times* countered with Blaine Newnham, a columnist the Huskies could count on for gentle treatment. When Neuheisel got caught in a lie and had to come clean, the first sportswriter he called was Newnham. There was a reason for that.

Two sportswriters could hear the same words and reach different conclusions. Take Neuheisel's account of his hospital visit with Williams—the one where Williams blinked twice as fast when the subject turned to how much the Huskies needed to win their next game. Lee Jenkins, a writer with the *Orange County Register* in California, recoiled. He wrote, "Are we supposed to cheer now? Or should we cry? Another athlete has fallen and another ugly motivational tool has been brandished. In Seattle, Williams is representing all the reasons the 7-1 Huskies should go out Saturday and beat those Wildcats."

But Newnham liked what he heard. "Imagine its impact," he wrote of Neuheisel sharing this story with the team. Newnham noted for readers how Neuheisel had been careful not to use the exact words "Let's win one for Curtis."

Covering the Huskies, the *Times* and the *Post-Intelligencer* both missed a lot of off-field troubles. More often than not, player arrests didn't make the newspapers. When they did, the coverage tended to be forgiving. The sportswriters weren't crime reporters. They knew the football field, not the courthouse. Their workweeks included press conferences, teleconferences, injury reports, recruiting updates, coaching changes, player features, analysis of upcoming opponents, league developments, and, of course, game coverage. Who had time to background the roster? For beat writers, unvarnished coverage could also diminish access. Write up everyone's rap sheet—and good luck with that next interview request.

In 2000 the *Post-Intelligencer* had Ted Miller on the Husky beat. Miller, a sportswriter since 1993, had established himself at the *Mobile Register* in Alabama, covering Auburn and getting named the state's sportswriter of the year. During the football season he worked sixty-plus hours a week; like all sportswriters, he woke up each day worried about what he might find in the rival sports pages.

Two days before the Stanford game, Miller profiled Elliot Silvers, a six-foot-seven, 320-pound offensive tackle and future NFL draft pick. In practices, Silvers fought with teammates. In games, he drew personal fouls. The headline of the story—a funny Jekyll-and-Hyde piece—called Silvers "a handful on field, exact opposite off it." The story recounted memorable incidents of Silvers's bad-boy behavior. Ripping a teammate's helmet off and trying to hit him with it. Grabbing another player's face mask and trying to poke him in the eye. But Silvers's aggressiveness "isn't a part of who he is off the field," Miller wrote. The story quoted teammate Anthony Kelley: "People make fun of him and say he needs anger management classes. But it's funny how he turns it on and turns it off. Off the field, he doesn't get mad at anything."

The problem was, Silvers *did* need anger management, at least in the eyes of the courts. The year before, a judge had ordered him into just such a program. In 1999, Silvers pleaded guilty to misdemeanor assault. Police reports say a campus parking attendant was putting down traffic cones when Silvers, in a pickup, starting running the cones over. The attendant—five foot ten, 170 pounds— told Silvers he was going to call police. Silvers responded with: "What the fuck are you grinning at?" Then Silvers shoved the attendant, twice.

This incident hardly made Silvers a menace. The attendant wasn't hurt, and when police located the truck, parked elsewhere, Silvers walked up and said: I'm the guy you're looking for. But the case did show that Silvers's temper flared off the field, too. What's more, when Miller wrote the story, Silvers was on probation. And he was wanted—for failing to show up in court for a review hearing. He had been playing the whole season with a warrant over his head. The misdemeanor conviction was later tossed out— after Silvers provided proof that he had completed anger management treatment.

As deadline approached, Withers had to make a decision. He elected to split the difference. He reported Williams's felony conviction, but rejected the idea of billboard treatment. He didn't put it in the lead. Instead, he layered it in, relying on what little he could get from the research library's review of electronic dockets and other online records. The conviction appeared in the sixteenth paragraph of a twenty-eight-paragraph story. Even then, Withers gave it only one sentence: "In 1997, he served a 90-day jail term in King County for second-degree assault, sitting out that season." The sentence didn't say who Williams had assaulted, or how. It got the degree wrong—Williams had been convicted of third-degree assault, not second. And it didn't account for all the other criminal charges that Williams had faced, or continued to face. Still. Withers had done it. He had put it in the newspaper. And in the days to come, he would be the only one.

Before Washington's next game against Arizona, more than a dozen other reporters wrote about Williams and his injury. But not one wrote about Williams's criminal record. Not one picked up that sixteenth paragraph in Withers's story and went deeper, exploring what Williams had been doing on the field to begin with. Blaine Newnham didn't. Ted Miller didn't. Nor did any other paper that covered the Huskies—Tacoma, Vancouver, Everett. The subject of Williams's past may as well have been radioactive.

When the courthouse opened Monday, Withers didn't show up to read the voluminous files on Williams's history of domestic violence. Nor did anybody else from his newsroom. Withers went back to Husky Stadium, back to cranking the stories out. The newspapers and their editors looked away—unable, or unwilling, to bend the story line of a remarkable season interrupted by a tragic injury, and a team's determination to soldier on.

November 4, 2000: Arizona at Washington

His nickname, his number, his initials. Everywhere you looked— at the fans, at the band, at the stitching of the players' uniforms— Curtis Williams was there. His injury had united the team and the city. People wanted Williams to hear their words of hope; they wanted Williams to see how much they cared.

Before the game, the school had passed out 25,000 stickers

with the number 25 to fans streaming through Husky Stadium's five main gates. Many fans stopped to sign banners or message boards for Williams. Minutes before kickoff, a formal tribute took place, televised by ABC. The players from both teams lined up and prayed. The marching band formed Williams's nickname on the field while the crowd chanted it above, call-response, one side the first part, the other the second.

C!

Dub!

C!

Dub!

C!

Dub!

All of this, Williams saw. All of this, he heard. The folks at Stanford Medical Center had put a TV above his bed in intensive care so he could watch the game. Williams was still on a ventilator, still unable to talk, still unable to feel his arms or legs.

Days before, Neuheisel had asked the fans for help. He wanted energy, passion, devotion. He wanted *volume*. Bring it Saturday, he told the Husky faithful. From his players, Neuheisel wanted urgency. "Number 25 wants us to carry out our assignments," he said.

The outpouring of support had begun even before this day. More than a thousand fans wrote to Williams on a university Web site. The team embroidered "CW" on each player's jersey. Players at Washington State University sent Williams a letter with words of encouragement. USC sent a helmet with the exhortation "Fight on." Stanford players put Williams's number on the back of their helmets. A Husky booster offered up his jet so that Neuheisel and six others could visit Williams in the hospital.

In Alaska, Michelle watched from a distance, devastated by her husband's injury, and wondering if his past would ever come out. Jan Zientek, the former neighbor who had called police and the Husky coaching staff, kept track too. "It was nauseating to see how he was made such a hero," he says.

The weather was cool, the sky November gray. But inside Husky Stadium, the mood was electric. Then the game began. On its first play, Arizona threw for 43 yards, covering half the field, easy as that. Its next play, a run, ripped off 11 more. It was happening again. Just like Idaho. Just like Colorado. Just like Oregon, Oregon State, Arizona State, Cal. Washington was starting ugly. In the first half Arizona flattened the Huskies, running through, around and over them. Arizona had nineteen first downs, Washington, four. Arizona held the ball twenty-three minutes, Washington, seven. With numbers like that, the score should have been ugly. But somehow the Huskies managed to trail only 16–10.

No matter. The third quarter took care of that. Unable to get a first down, Washington punted. Sean Sweat, a freshman from Southern California, had replaced Williams on the punt team, assuming the role of gunner. Sweat had a clean shot at Arizona's return man—and missed. The return man went 60 yards for a touchdown. On its next possession, Washington fumbled. Arizona capitalized, driving 41 yards for a field goal. Now the score was 25–10. Now, the score fit the game.

Washington didn't panic. It still had Marques Tuiasosopo at quarterback, and that meant more than any stat sheet. Tui's teammates understood. His opponents did, too. "You can't shake him," Arizona's Keoni Fraser said after the game. "We hit him and we stopped him, and he just gets back up there. When he comes to the line, he's all happy like they're winning or something. That's what a true quarterback is, I guess."

And on Washington's defense, a new leader had emerged. With Williams out, the new starting safety was Greg Carothers, the freshman from Montana. Williams's injury had made the defense tentative. Some players shied from contact. They reached with their arms, hesitant to throw their bodies into a ball carrier. Carothers wasn't big, he wasn't fast, but he could hit. He figured it was now his job to set the tone. Arizona handed the ball to Larry Croom on a draw. Carothers laced into Croom. He just crushed him, landing the kind of hit that Williams used to make. And both players . . . got up. The Husky defense found itself again.

In the fourth quarter, Willie Hurst, the Washington tailback who had fallen as low as fourth on the team's depth chart, broke one touchdown run for 65 yards and another for 23. Jerramy Stevens made a critical third-down reception to keep a drive alive. For the game Stevens had eight catches, a school record for tight ends. And Tuiasosopo? With a minute left, he burst over the left guard and into the end zone, to win the game.

The final score was Washington 35, Arizona 32. Neuheisel sent a game ball to Curtis Williams. Jerramy Stevens said afterward: "We just knew we had to win for Curtis. . . . All through the game, we said, 'We've got to do this for him.' We knew he was watching." With eight tackles—including a quarterback sack—Jeremiah Pharms was named a defensive MVP, for the second game in a row.

Two days after the game, the UW announced that it was creating a fund for Williams. Money donated by fans would be used for long-term expenses not covered by NCAA and university insurance policies. Also on Monday, the new BCS rankings came out. Washington moved up two spots, to No. 6 in the country.

California Fun

November 17, 2000: King County Superior Court

Samuel Adonis Blanche, a reserve linebacker for the UW, showed up at the King County courthouse at a little before 10 a.m. He was accompanied by a lawyer, Mike Hunsinger. Blanche had called Hunsinger beforehand and asked for help, saying he had been subpoenaed to testify.

Tomorrow, the Huskies would play in the Apple Cup, their regular-season finale. If they beat Washington State—and Oregon State beat Oregon—the Huskies would be going to the Rose Bowl.

Blanche had been summoned as part of the Inquiry Judge Proceeding into whether Jeremiah Pharms had shot Kerry Sullivan. The same people were present: Judge William Downing, prosecutor Mike Lang, detective Jeff Mudd. All season, Lang had smoldered at Pharms taking in the cheers. Now it was only worse. Pharms was playing his best ball of the year down the stretch. A week earlier, Washington had beaten UCLA, 35–28, to run its record to 9-1. Pharms had forced a fumble on a quarterback sack and been named a defensive MVP—for the third straight week.

The judge swore Blanche to secrecy. He couldn't tell his teammates or anyone else about this hearing. Under questioning by Lang, Blanche sketched his history. He was in his fourth year at the UW, twenty-one, married, with a two-year-old daughter. He had met the woman who would become his wife during his senior year of high school, in Rialto, California. He saw her again during his freshman year of college, while visiting home.

"Relations happened and a baby happened," Blanche told Lang. "I'm a true believer, I told myself when I was young that the first woman that I impregnated or had sex with without a condom, with no protection, that if she had a baby, she was worthy enough to be my wife and that's what I stuck with."

Blanche said he met Pharms his freshman year, and considered him "a big role model."

"He had family, and being a newcomer to the world of being married and having a daughter and, you know, more responsibility, I consider him a very good person in the way of how he carried himself around other people. As being married, as males, we can get into a lot of locker room talk about other women and stuff. And I never saw him do that. I never saw him go to clubs and get outrageous and do wild things or anything. He was pretty much mellow and kept to himself."

Players liked to hang out at Jeremiah's house, Blanche testified. "We tend on certain nights just to get together and just be together as gentlemen and talk as gentlemen."

"You smoke marijuana?" Lang asked Blanche.

"On occasions, on occasions, on occasions. The occasion could just be on Thanksgiving, you know?"

"Ever smoked it with J.P.?"

"I have."

"Have you ever met his girlfriend, Tarah?"

"I've seen her before."

"What kind of gloves does the football team use?"

"Nike."

"What color?"

"Gray."

Can players take the gloves home?

"Once they issue the gear to you, the gear is yours. . . . You can do what you feel with it."

Lang turned the subject to Kerry Sullivan.

Blanche said he began buying marijuana from Sullivan the year before. He couldn't remember for sure, but he may have met Sullivan through another football player. He had gone to Sullivan's apartment maybe ten times, but hadn't been there since about March. Sometimes he would buy from other people.

Did you set up the deal for Pharms to buy marijuana from Sullivan? Lang asked.

"I didn't set up any deal for anybody," Blanche said.

Two people have identified you as the go-between, Lang told Blanche. He reminded Blanche that he was under oath, and asked again if he had set up the deal.

"No, I didn't, sir," Blanche said.

Did you threaten Sullivan after the shooting? Lang asked. Tell him that if he fucked up your scholarship, he was wasted? That you would send some people after him if he reported your name to police?

"I never said any of that to Kerry," Blanche said.

Two days earlier, Lang and Mudd had interviewed Blanche at the police station. They told Blanche they didn't believe him when he denied hooking Pharms up with Sullivan. What if we granted you immunity? Lang asked. Would that make you more forthcoming? Blanche said he might have heard Pharms or Pharms's cousin complaining about being shorted by Sullivan in a marijuana deal. He might have heard them saying they were going to "get him."

Now, on the stand, Blanche denied saying any such thing. There must have been a "mix-up," he told Lang. *I said that I had been shorted by Sullivan. I didn't say Jeremiah had.*

Blanche finished testifying at a few minutes after eleven. That gave him time to make the team's afternoon workout at Husky Stadium. The team was scheduled to hop a 4 p.m. plane for Pullman, the home of wsu.

A few hours after Blanche left the stand, Pharms's girlfriend Tarah was sworn in, to testify a second time. The police still didn't know who the second robber was. Lang showed Tarah some pictures of Pharms's friends and asked if she could identify any. One picture was of Curtis Williams. "Yeah," she said, "Dub." She had met him maybe twenty times. But being Pharms's friend didn't make Williams a robber. To make him for the robber, you'd have to believe he showed up at the home of a drug dealer he knew—with a gun, and without a mask.

Another hearing also took place this day, in another court-room. This other hearing wasn't secret, but it may as well have been. It was a pretrial matter for Curtis Williams. He was still on the hook for those two assault charges that had been reinstated—one accusing him of punching Michelle in the head, the other accusing him of breaking her nose. Williams's lawyer appeared on his behalf and agreed to have the trial date pushed back. Nothing about the hearing or charges appeared in the newspapers.

November 18, 2000

For once, it was easy.

For the Huskies, every Pac-10 victory this season had come down to the final few minutes. But against Washington State, the drama evaporated. Word made it to the Washington sidelines in the first quarter that Oregon State had beaten Oregon, clearing the Huskies' path to the Rose Bowl. By then, Washington was already up 13–0. By halftime the score was 27–0. In the locker room, Neuheisel told the players how he had visited Curtis Williams two days earlier, and how Curtis had whispered to him: "Coach, make sure those guys know I really want a ring." Washington's offense was clicking. The defense was clicking. Jeremiah Pharms sacked Wazzu's quarterback—earning, yet again, defensive MVP honors. By the fourth quarter, Neuheisel had inserted the second string. By the final minutes, he had gone deeper into the bench than that.

J. K. Scott, Washington's third-string quarterback, came from the suburbs of Los Angeles, a blond-haired kid who had finished high school with sparkling statistics and a near-perfect GPA. But in four years at the UW he had never managed to break through. Always, it seemed, there was one quarterback ahead of him, or two. He had yet to play a down this season. But in the regular-season finale, he made it onto the field in the game's final minutes. By then, the score was 51–3. The call came in from the Washington side-lines: Run out the clock. On first down, Scott took the snap, then touched his knee to the ground. On second down, he took another knee. On third down, yet another. Three plays, three knees. The clock ran out. Scott finished the season with a stat line that read: three rushes, minus 4 yards.

The 48-point victory was the biggest thumping in the hundred-year history of this rivalry. For Neuheisel, it was career win No. 50. And he was still only thirty-nine years old. To celebrate, his wife gave him a bottle of champagne. Rose Bowl officials presented the team with a bouquet of roses and an invitation to Pasadena.

About the only off note was Anthony Vontoure, who missed the trip to Pullman. At first the team said he was being disciplined for missing practices. But then Neuheisel backtracked. Vontoure had surgery pending on his hand and thumb, and Neuheisel blamed that for Vontoure's absences. "I'm not calling it a suspension," Neuheisel said. "The surgery was weighing heavily on his mind."

November 20

Two days after the Apple Cup, the Washington football team held its annual awards banquet. Curtis Williams won the Guy Flaherty Award, given to the team's most inspirational player. Jeremiah Pharms won the Chuck Niemi Award, presented to the team's biggest hitter. Jerramy Stevens was named co-winner of KOMO Newstalk 1000's Most Outstanding Offensive Player.

Anthony Vontoure didn't pick up any awards. He had surgery earlier in the day, and his hand was put in a cast. The question loomed of whether he would play in the Rose Bowl. The coaches certainly wanted him to. He was Washington's best cover man, and in Purdue's Drew Brees, Washington would be facing one of the country's best quarterbacks.

For Jerramy Stevens, the honors rolled in during the post-season. CollegeFootballNews.com named him first-team All-Pac-10. Gannett News Service and *Football News* named him second-team All-America. He was one of eight semifinalists for the John Mackey Award, given to the nation's top tight end.

Sports Illustrated had named Washington the country's best college for tight ends. In 2000, four tight ends from the UW were playing in the NFL: Mark Bruener, Cam Cleeland, Ernie Conwell, and Aaron Pierce. But Stevens had just posted the best season of any tight end in school history, with forty-three catches for 600 yards. And he was only a sophomore.

November 21

Six weeks separated the Apple Cup and the Rose Bowl. For the sports pages, that's a lot of space to fill with incremental developments about injuries, practices, curfews, BCS rankings, and speculation about players leaving school early for the NFL. The same profiles and feature stories pop up in one paper after another.

On November 21, Bud Withers wrote a piece in the *Seattle Times* headlined "Neuheisel Doubters Get Lost in Roses." The Rose Bowl berth validated Neuheisel, Withers wrote. "I've always felt great about hiring Rick Neuheisel," athletic director Barbara Hedges said in the story. "I've never spent one minute thinking it was not the right decision." And it wasn't just the wins, she said. It was "the atmosphere of the program."

That same day, the *Post-Intelligencer*'s Ted Miller wrote about Curtis Williams. Neuheisel said Williams hoped that Washington would get a shot at the national title. "Curtis wants the big prize," Neuheisel said. Washington was ranked No. 4. Two teams ranked higher still had a game to play—and if one or both should lose, maybe the Huskies would be elevated into the title game. And why was Miami ranked above Washington anyway? Hadn't the Huskies beaten Miami? In Miller's story, Neuheisel emphasized that he wasn't saying *Let's win for Curtis*. "I never want to use Curtis' injury as a motivating factor," Neuheisel said.

December 1

Rick Neuheisel's mind was on football. His team was about to resume practicing after a thirteen-day break. He was also focused on recruiting, racking up players to build on this season's success. Neuheisel was meeting with other coaches when an assistant walked in and said: "You're in that class in twenty minutes." *That class*. He had forgotten all about it. He had agreed earlier to talk to Professor Al Black's lecture class, "Social Problems in American Society," an undergraduate course that covered racism, drugs, guns, gangs, sexism, poverty, teenage pregnancy. About four hundred students took the course, including a number of football players. Neuheisel hadn't prepared a lecture. But he could always wing it.

He decided to talk about the stereotypes of football players, how some folks think they're just big and dumb—and how nothing could be further from the truth. To show how complicated football is, he would demonstrate a play. He opted for a counter, a running play where offensive linemen pull. The play requires an appreciation of angles and exquisite timing and synchronization.

Neuheisel asked for volunteers. He selected twenty-two—all of them women. They came up to the stage, and he assigned each a position. When the women on offense crouched, their rear ends were to the audience. Neuheisel told one woman she would be the center. Then he drew some laughs by turning to the crowd and saying: "No, you can't be the quarterback." He asked another woman if she had ever been "double-teamed" before. Laughter again. "You guys are terrible," Neuheisel said. The coach said football players get scrutinized more than other students and should take care who they flirt with. Neuheisel, according to some students, told the class that football players must avoid "the wrong kind of girl."

Neuheisel's presentation—and the reaction to it—made the student newspaper. Several teaching assistants found Neuheisel's conduct to be sexist and juvenile. "I'd expect it from my freshmen students, but not from him," one assistant said. Some students were offended, others not. One said the "wrong kind of girl" phrase sounded like blaming the victim in a date-rape situation. This student wanted to speak up, but felt intimidated by the football players in class. Another student said it was "probably the best class I've attended at the UW in terms of fun." She thought critics were being too sensitive.

Neuheisel met with eight teaching assistants and apologized. Hedges went with him. To reporters and—in years to come—lawyers, Neuheisel offered this explanation: He had picked women because they don't normally play football. He meant "double-teamed" only in the football sense. He didn't use the words "wrong kind of girl," and what he meant anyway was that football players should avoid girls with jealous boyfriends.

This was the second year in a row that Neuheisel had stepped in it. The year before, Washington went to San Diego to play in the Holiday Bowl. Art Thiel, a *Post-Intelligencer* columnist, described the scene aboard the USS *Constellation*, an aircraft carrier.

> After issuing the standard thanks to the hosts for their hospitality, the Huskies football coach told more than a thousand guests how excited his players were to "board the Connie," as he described it.
>
> Then, in mock horror, Neuheisel said, "No! No! It's a ship!"
>
> There was some laughter, a few nervous titters, and a lot of darting eyes. Having been around the male jock culture for a day or two, I had heard far worse—and far better.
>
> Then I caught the look on the face of the female fighter pilot two seats away. No smile, no movement. Just a cold stare at the podium.

By early December it was official: Anthony Kelley had won a Mary Gates scholarship, the first football player ever to achieve the honor. He was getting $3,000. He would be leaving for South Africa just a few days after the Rose Bowl. The news thrilled the academic staffers who had quietly encouraged him. Kelley was so happy he cried. Neuheisel seemed caught off guard by the news. "I'm all for it," he told one newspaper, but added, "I don't know that it's something that we could have happen widespread."

"I'm pretty sure he didn't want me to go," Kelley says. "And my defensive coordinator at the time wasn't too fired up about it.

But Tom Williams was like, 'Go ahead, do your thing.'" As sports-writers looked for nuggets in the buildup to the Rose Bowl, Kelley's scholarship became a story line they couldn't resist. "Kelley's Tale: From 'Hood to U District," read one headline. "His Bed of Roses; Academics, Not Game, Bowl Highlight for Kelley," read another.

December 4

Al Black liked Neuheisel. He respected Neuheisel. But, Black told his sociology class, Neuheisel's comments the previous Friday were sexually offensive. The professor said he planned to approach Hedges with a request: Make the coaching staff take a course on preventing sexual harassment. Black also passed the microphone around so students could offer their thoughts. But as some students talked of being offended by Neuheisel's presentation, others in the class booed and jeered. "Sit down! Sit the fuck down! You are gay!" one heckler screamed at another student, adding: "I'm going to fuck him up."

December 7

To get the publicity rolling, Rose Bowl officials held a press conference in Pasadena, offering up Neuheisel and Purdue coach Joe Tiller. The two joked with each other. Neither said anything to offend.

In 1984, Neuheisel appeared in this game as a player. He quarterbacked UCLA to one of the biggest upsets in Rose Bowl history—and he did it while suffering from food poisoning. At this press conference, Neuheisel relived the day for reporters, recounting how his dad had told him: *This is no time to get sick! This is the most important game of your life!* Before the game, Neuheisel had sat in the tunnel, wrapped in cold compresses, struggling to get his bearings. Then came the signal to take the field. "I ran onto the field and everybody was in their seats and it was beautiful out. It was the most magical experience of my life. It was like I was floating—and I never felt sick again the rest of the game." He threw four touchdown passes and was named the game's MVP.

December 9

Anthony Vontoure kept going to the equipment room, day after day, to get a new jock strap. For a week this had been going on, and Josh Dabbs was sick of it. Dabbs, a senior at the UW, was a student equipment manager. From behind his glassed enclosure, he had been telling Vontoure: Do your laundry. Wash the jocks you already have. Stop asking for new ones. The day before, he had given Vontoure a final warning. *Ask again, and you'll be turned away.* But here was Vontoure, back at the equipment window, demanding another jock.

I'm not giving you anything, Dabbs told Vontoure. You should have done your laundry.

Vontoure had a cast on his right hand from his surgery a month earlier. He cocked that hand back and let fly, smashing the safety glass separating him and Dabbs. Shards flew everywhere, spraying the equipment manager, showering the counter and floor. Vontoure jumped onto the counter, reached in, and grabbed a jock. Then he took off into the locker room.

The head equipment manager heard the explosion. He looked over and saw Dabbs with a face cast in disbelief. Hey, you're bleeding, someone told Dabbs. The glass had cut Dabbs's face and arms. The wounds were small, but there were lots of them. Dabbs was taken to the training room, where the cuts were disinfected and bandaged up. Neuheisel, alerted by the head equipment manager, came by to check on Dabbs.

You all right? the coach asked.

Good enough, Dabbs said.

Neuheisel told Dabbs that he would make sure Vontoure was punished, that he would make sure there were consequences. Neuheisel dismissed Vontoure from that day's practice. Without providing details, he told reporters that Vontoure had done something "not acceptable" to a staff member. He didn't know if Vontoure would be allowed to play in the Rose Bowl. He would have to think about it.

December 13

Charles Frederick, one of the nation's most highly touted prep wide receivers, said he would be committing to Washington. Frederick was from Boca Raton, Florida. Neuheisel was now landing stars from the opposite corner of the country. In college football, winning begets winning. Flashy records and marquee bowl games attract top recruits. During this recruiting season, Neuheisel landed a class that made the scouting services gush; they called Washington's one of the country's very best.

December 15

Neuheisel announced his decision: Vontoure would be allowed to play in the Rose Bowl. But, as punishment, he would be excluded from the team's off-field fun once they arrived in California. Up until Christmas anyway. "He will just be practicing and staying at the hotel," Neuheisel said. The coach said he had reflected on his own Rose Bowl experience, and decided that taking that away from Vontoure "would really be difficult."

December 20

The team arrived in California and, first thing, went to Magic Mountain. At the amusement park, Vontoure showed up with the rest of the team. When reporters asked about this, Neuheisel said the team meal was part of the trip, and Vontoure couldn't miss the meal.

December 21

On its second day in California, the team visited the Playboy Mansion. Criticism followed. To which Neuheisel responded:
"We have a lot of architectural majors on our team."

"It's a tourist attraction and the players voted that they wanted to see it."

"There's always going to be criticism. Vegetarians could criticize us for going to Lawry's Prime Rib."

Years later, in a deposition, Neuheisel said he probably didn't think through this trip's ramifications. Asked what Hedges had to say about it, Neuheisel testified: "She didn't seem to be bothered by it. Matter of fact, she said she'd been there herself."

December 24

On Christmas Eve, the *Seattle Times* ran a story on how Jerramy Stevens had found sanctuary in football this season. Stevens said he might not have made it through without the game: "I wouldn't know how to act without it." The *Tacoma News Tribune* and the *Seattle Post-Intelligencer* published similar stories. Stevens told the *Post-Intelligencer*: "I know what happened and I know what the truth is. I didn't let it get to me." The Tacoma paper said Stevens had been "cleared" of sexual assault. It quoted Stevens: "It was unfortunate that I had to go through it and that there was a situation at all." And it quoted Washington's offensive coordinator, Keith Gilbertson: "I would defend him in all terms to the *n*th degree. . . . As strong as I can say it, I will say it—he is a nice kid." The reporters didn't pull the investigative file, even though the case was now closed—and therefore a public record. They treated Maleng's press conference as the final word.

December 27: Southern California

Two days after Christmas, Rick Neuheisel spent the morning at the City of Hope, a cancer hospital in Duarte. Six players accompanied him, including Sam Blanche. Six players from Purdue also showed up, along with Joe Tiller. Each team brought souvenirs, including pins, banners, posters, and T-shirts. Upon arriving, the players met with the media in the lobby while the head coaches presented the chief physician with an autographed ball. Some players visited patients in their rooms. Others remained in the lobby, signing autographs. Television cameras captured it all, while newspaper reporters scribbled notes.

This was all per the "University Participation Manual," ninety-five pages long, that each school received before coming to Pasadena. This manual said who should be where and when, in increments of time that, come game day, could be as short as fifteen seconds. If either school failed to comply, a penalty could be imposed: $1,000 for each minute out of step. Gestures of grace were scripted and publicized. Cues were arranged, music approved, exclusive contracts signed. Even clichés became the subject of suggestion or dictate. The Tournament of Roses sent the University of Washington's president a letter, saying he should "perhaps issue an informal challenge to the opposing president on the outcome of the game with something at stake such as a quantity of a product from your region of the country."

For the players, the days before the Rose Bowl were crammed with California fun. On Christmas, they went to a Lakers game. Yesterday, it was Disneyland; tonight, Lawry's Prime Rib; tomorrow, the *Tonight Show with Jay Leno*.

Anthony Vontoure struggled to keep up. While some players visited the City of Hope, the rest went to practice. Vontoure, however, missed the team bus. After hopping a ride with a producer from a sports radio station, he arrived forty-five minutes late. In sports, being late to practice is a big deal. Vontoure's earlier punishment had extended only until Christmas, so Neuheisel came up with a new punishment. Vontoure would be confined to his hotel room for a night—right after the Lawry's all-you-can-eat prime rib dinner.

December 27: Lynnwood, Washington

Jeremiah Pharms, who was with the team in California, rented a two-bedroom house north of campus, in the town of Lynnwood. The landlord, a uw alum, hadn't checked references before handing over the keys. He figured he would take a chance on a fellow

Husky. "A mistake," he says now. A three-foot fence hemmed the backyard. There and in the house, Pharms kept pit bulls, adults and puppies, all kinds at once, some with heavy, galvanized chains around their necks, with padlocks dangling. Their excrement piled up, fouling the neighborhood air in warm weather.

Grace Lundeen lived next door. In her fifties, she used to work at the VA, but now she stayed home to care for her disabled husband. She couldn't help but notice how Pharms had friends over all the time. They partied night and day—*loud*. But it wasn't noise that bothered Lundeen now. Pharms had left a week ago for the Rose Bowl. What bothered her now were the dogs he left behind.

There were four of them, all pit bull terriers. Lundeen could see their ribs, and worried they were starving. She had been throwing ham bones over the fence and spraying water from a hose, hoping some would land in the hollow of a plastic toy or in some other receptacle.

The dogs scared Lundeen. But she felt bad for them, too. She was sure Pharms was breeding them and selling the puppies. She had seen him with friends, sticking bloody rags under the dogs' noses. The men would tie the rags to a wooden cross, used for growing raspberries. "Good dog, good dog," they'd say, as the dogs lunged for the rags and shredded them. A little boy across the street was all excited about Pharms being a football player. He would tell Lundeen: Oh, he gave me tickets. But Lundeen would say: You should see how he's treating those dogs. One time, a dog got into her backyard and chased her inside. Lundeen began placing rocks along her yard's edge, to block any holes. And she stopped weeding that one flowerbed next to the chain-link fence.

This morning Lundeen had called Lynnwood police. One of the dogs had jumped the fence and was running loose in a nearby apartment complex. At a little before noon, Paul Coleman, an animal control officer, arrived. He had been there before. Twice he had warned Pharms about not licensing his dogs; once he had issued a criminal citation for having too many.

Two days before the Miami game, Pharms had appeared in

court and pleaded guilty to the misdemeanor charge. He was sentenced to ninety days in jail—all suspended—and placed on probation for two years. If Neuheisel's rule on misdemeanor convictions had applied, Pharms would have missed at least one game. But against Miami, he played. Afterward, he returned to doing what he had done before, blowing off the municipality's demands about his dogs. They still weren't licensed. He still had too many.

The dog that had escaped ran up to Coleman. She was gray and maybe a year and a half old. "Very friendly" is how Coleman described her—that and "very scared." After he leashed her, she lay and began to shake. He tried comforting her, then placed her in his patrol van. A second dog jumped the fence and ran up to Coleman. Seeing how the fence couldn't hold her, Coleman impounded this dog, too.

Coleman went into Pharms's yard. There was so much dog shit, he couldn't help but step in it. The two remaining dogs craved attention. In some bowls and in the dirt, Coleman found bits of soggy dog food. With no water bowl in sight, the dogs lapped from a gutter drain. Coleman filled a food bowl with fresh water, and both dogs drank for about five minutes. Because these dogs hadn't left the yard, Coleman couldn't impound them.

After leaving a note saying he'd taken away two of the dogs, Coleman drove both female terriers to a veterinarian. The vet's notes described one as thin, with a bloated abdomen, and the other as malnourished. "Very underweight," the vet wrote. "All bony prominences." This dog was nursing and in heat, with blood coming from her vulva, scabs on her tail, and sutures still in her ears, from an old crop job.

In the days to come, Coleman would keep returning to Pharms's house, to check on the two other dogs. Lundeen would keep tossing food over the fence.

December 27: Seattle

Detective Mudd arrived at the prosecutors' offices at 3 p.m. He was there to meet with Steve Fogg, to go over DNA evidence to be mailed to California. It had now been nine and a half months since Kerry Sullivan was shot. It had been three and a half months since the DNA results had come back from the state lab, implicating Pharms. But the authorities had yet to forward the evidence to Ed Blake, the renowned forensic scientist. Fogg's paralegal wasn't available. So the prosecutor and detective decided to meet again next week and take care of it then. First they would mail the holster and glove. Some time later—a month, maybe two—they would send the sample from the bloody fingerprint.

December 28

The Associated Press ran a flattering profile of Barbara Hedges, saying she "might always be known by University of Washington football fans as the athletic director who hired Rick Neuheisel away from Colorado." UW president Richard McCormick called Hedges's hiring of Neuheisel "a stroke of genius on her part." The UW women's basketball coach said: "It seems that everything she touches turns to gold."

This same day, Hedges announced that Neuheisel would be getting a contract extension after the Rose Bowl. When the UW hired Neuheisel in 1999, his $1 million-plus contract trailed only that of Florida's Steve Spurrier. But since then, five other coaches had signed bigger deals. "Naturally, he's getting an automatic raise," Hedges said. "I'd certainly be remiss if we didn't do that."

December 29

Peggy Watson died in a hospice of breast cancer, at the age of fifty-two. She had been the secretary for Washington's last three football coaches, including Neuheisel.

Neuheisel told reporters: "She'd go to chemotherapy in the afternoon, then come back and finish what we were doing. She will long be remembered in Husky lore as a real soldier. I went to her before we left and said, 'So, what do you want us to run for the first play?' She perked right up. So the first play we call will either be Peg Left or Peg Right, depending on what hash mark we're on. . . . We feel she'll be watching us from her special sideline seat at the 50-yard line."

December 30

Curtis Williams will attend the Rose Bowl and watch from the press box, Neuheisel told reporters. "Our team will know he's watching," the coach said, "and they'll want to give him their best effort."

A Mystical, Magical Day **24**

If you watched the 2001 Rose Bowl on TV—and millions did—you may have seen a large gray billboard atop the stadium's east stands, anchored with four black posts. Five corporate sponsors had their logos on the billboard: one per corner, and in the center AT&T's, that blue ball with a white ribbon running around it. But if you looked close—your eyes on the gray rectangle and nothing else—you may have become suspicious of this particular advertisement.

The billboard appeared whenever ABC provided a wide-angle view of the stadium—a signature shot with the San Gabriel Mountains as backdrop, the kind that inspired Keith Jackson to wax about *the magical panorama of New Year's Day in Pasadena.* In the first quarter, ABC offered up this shot, the camera panning right to left. As the camera swivels, the billboard is there, there, there—then it's gone. Poof. It disappears. The space where the billboard was remains in the picture frame, but the billboard is gone.

In the second quarter, things get weirder. Of course, you'd notice only if you watched the billboard. Stay fixed on the field, and you'd miss it. ABC gives us the same shot, but this time, the camera remains still. And this time—the billboard isn't there. Then it is. Then it isn't. Now you see it, now you don't. A few minutes later, the camera pans. In the upper-left corner of your TV screen there's a graphic with the score. As the camera sweeps, the score passes *behind* the billboard. How can a computer-generated graphic pass behind matter? This would be like having the graphic pass behind the moon in the sky, or behind some player's helmet on the field.

The billboard wasn't there. It was virtual. It existed only in the ether—summoned by a computer program, connected to a sensor, rigged into the camera. The technology behind this billboard was in its infancy—hence, the poor execution. But the ability to snooker us would only improve. At the opening ceremony for the 2008 Olympics, the Chinese produced a thrilling fireworks show that proved to be a digital fabrication. In the same Olympics, the Chinese had a girl with angelic features lip-synch for a child with crooked teeth. "It was for the national interest," the ceremony's music director said. "The child on camera should be flawless." Hearing this, many Americans shuddered. Meanwhile, in the 4 × 100 freestyle relay—the most treasured moment of the Olympics for many Americans—the anchorman for the U.S. team put tape over his swimsuit's Speedo logo. After all, he was sponsored by Nike.

If you watched the 2001 Rose Bowl on TV, you saw what ABC wanted you to see, what the NCAA and the universities wanted you to see, what AT&T and Nike and other corporate giants wanted you to see. You saw a glitzy, profitable production built upon an array of scripts, contracts, and manuals.

You saw one sideline shot after another of Rick Neuheisel, in a purple shirt, with a small swoosh on his left sleeve. The swoosh was small, but it popped. Nike made sure of that, encompassing the play of colors in its contractual language, saying there must be "contrast" between the swoosh and its background.

You saw all these drinking cups on the Washington sideline, each cup emblazoned with Charles Schwab. You couldn't help but notice. The camera lingered on the cups, as though they were interesting. This was per the "University Participation Manual." Don't bring your own cups, the manual told each school. Your own towels, either. These will be provided by a sponsor. The manual also says that absent pre-game approval, neither team can use sideline equipment—a coach's headset, say—that displays its manufacturer's name. The camera might pick that up, resulting in an accidental, uncompensated promotional benefit for some non-participating company. Bring your own headsets, sure. But unless the Rose Bowl committee signs off, the name of the maker must be covered up.

The Rose Bowl is college football's oldest bowl game, dating to 1902. Is there a lovelier, more evocative name in all of sport? *The Rose Bowl*. For so long, the Tournament of Roses officials refused to give in, refused to go the way of the Chick-fil-A Peach Bowl or the Poulan Weed-Eater Independence Bowl. But in 1998, they finally agreed to a title sponsor. Only they refused to call it that. AT&T would be a presenter, as in: The Rose Bowl presented by AT&T. When the deal was announced, a bowl representative named Harriman Cronk said: "It's not going to be AT&T all over the field, AT&T in every nook and cranny." But watching the 2001 Rose Bowl, you see AT&T on the 50-yard line and around the stadium. You hear it mentioned over and over. It's not enough that AT&T is bringing you the game; according to the announcers, it is also bringing you the starting lineups, the aerial coverage, the highlights of a previous Rose Bowl, and the replays from this Rose Bowl.

If yours was among the 13 million households that tuned in to the 2001 Rose Bowl, you listened to the sound of profit killing language. ABC had paid $525 million to televise the Rose Bowl and three other major bowl games for seven years. The network, in turn, sold naming rights to whatever you could slap a name on. The New Ford Escape Pregame Show. The Nokia Player Comparison. The AFLAC Trivia Question. Some announcers sailed through the corporate adjectives. Here's John Saunders, at halftime: "This is the National Car Rental Halftime Report—South Beach, in Miami, Florida, the site of the FedEx Orange Bowl for the national championship, and there's the Sears trophy." That's three plugs in under thirty words—smooth as can be. But Keith Jackson? He was seventy-two now, and about to hang it up. For decades he had graced college football with his Georgia drawl, his signature pause midsentence ("Let's play . . . some football"), his folksy way of enlivening the mundane. He wouldn't bore you by saying some player had jumped offside. "The left tackle is dancing," he'd say.

"Matt Light is gone to the prom right there." Now, Jackson was saddled with scripted gibberish. "Well, the Dean Witter Morgan Stanley Well Connected, uh, halftime, stature . . . " Jackson gave up and said, "The numbers on the ballgame at this point."

Watching the game, you saw an anti-gambling spot, sponsored by the NCAA, that would become ironic only in retrospect. A number of athletes—including Michael Vick, Virginia Tech's spectacular quarterback—say what a crazy time college is, and would you really want to bet money on that? "Fool," Vick says.

You listened to banter—queued up, waiting for the right moment—about the wonderful opportunities available to student-athletes. Here's what you heard in the third quarter, when Washington's Anthony Kelley stuffed Purdue's tailback for a short gain.

"Isn't Anthony Kelley the one who's going off to South Africa for advanced studies?" Keith Jackson asks.

"Yes he is," says Tim Brant, the color commentator.

"He's excited about that," Jackson says. "He was a young man that didn't care much about all the class work, but along the way . . . some teacher lit his candle and he is absorbed with it."

For more, Jackson kicks this story to a sideline reporter. The reporter says Kelley will leave for South Africa in four days, having won a special scholarship to study abroad. "And get this," the reporter says. "He was a partial qualifier out of high school."

"Give a kid a chance," Brant says. "He can succeed."

If you watched the 2001 Rose Bowl on TV, you saw a wonderful advertisement for college football in general, for Washington football in particular, and for the ideal of the student-athlete. You saw the resurrection of Washington as a national power—a statement game, the kind that can draw top recruits for years to come and even lead to national championships.

But what you saw—was it really there? Or was this game, this production, more a testament to stagecraft—ephemeral and ethereal, curious and clever—with a foundation as illusory as the four posts anchoring that massive billboard?

The day began with a parade. Up to a million people lined the streets and watched an explosion of flowers go by—carnations, chrysanthemums, and roses in bursts of red, bronze, white, and golden yellow. The petals were glued to frames of steel and chicken wire. In Los Angeles, the Tournament of Roses parade appeared on CBS, NBC, ABC, the WB, Univision, Telemundo, and Home and Garden Television. Organizers claimed that 350 million people tuned in worldwide. Navy jets buzzed the crowd. Army paratroopers landed on Colorado Boulevard, on an emblem of a rose. The Marine Corps Mounted Color Guard stepped off first, and the Freemasons last, and in between were mules, marching bands, Spanish horses, clowns, and a couple of newlyweds, real ones, emerging from a fake chapel. The procession was five and a half miles long. Hundreds of volunteers in white suits kept the parade moving. If some tuba player fell ill, he was to seek out the nearest white suit and be ushered away. Each band's music had been approved beforehand, and no counter-marching was allowed. The parade's theme this year was Fabric of America. Floats sponsored by pancake houses, department stores, mortgage lenders, and sprinkler manufacturers turned flowers shipped from around the world into butterflies, waterfalls, the Statue of Liberty, and a bald eagle, fifty feet tall, wing tips to the sky, a rippling American flag clutched in its talons, the float's sound system playing "God Bless the USA."

The parade ended before noon. Attention then shifted to the game, which was scheduled to kick off at just after two.

Rick Neuheisel was in a chauffeured car, on his way from the Beverly Hills Hilton to the Rose Bowl Stadium, when his cell phone rang. The caller said Curtis Williams wanted to go off script.

Williams had arrived that morning from a rehabilitation center in San Jose. One medical transport company had flown him into Burbank. Another had taken him by ambulance from the airport to Pasadena. Both companies had donated their services, making it possible for Williams to reunite with his teammates at college football's most celebrated stage. The plan had been for Williams to watch the game from the press box, then meet with the team after the game. But now Williams wanted to see his teammates before they took the field. Neuheisel's assistant coaches didn't like the idea. This could backfire on us, they told Neuheisel. It could drain the team's emotion.

Another fear also loomed. When Williams had been injured, some teammates started playing scared. Derrell Daniels said as much. So did Hakim Akbar, who missed six tackles in the team's next game. In time, the team's fog lifted. But if Neuheisel let the players see Williams—a guy once so vital, now vulnerable and frail—didn't he risk having all those doubts resurface? Did he really want them to take in those five medical attendants accompanying Williams, checking on his respirator, making sure the strap around his chest held firm?

For so long, Neuheisel had been hopeful. He'd flown to California week after week, to see Williams and to report back anything that suggested improvement—some hint of feeling in the shoulders, or the brightness in Williams's eyes. Neuheisel and his wife had visited Williams on Thanksgiving Day. The coach had also reached out to colleagues in other programs, to find stories of other players who had recovered from severe injuries. But in the past week, Neuheisel had told reporters he wasn't seeing much change in Williams's condition.

Neuheisel decided to give Williams his wish. Williams was wheeled into his team's locker room, under the south end of the old stadium. Medical attendants moved him from a gurney into a wheelchair, and he was changed into a special Rose Bowl jersey with his number, 25. His teammates, meanwhile, set out from their hotel. They had no idea Williams would be there when they piled off the bus and walked in, ready to suit up for the biggest game they would probably ever play.

Paralyzed from the neck down, Williams could now twitch his chest muscles, but that was about it. He was a quadriplegic. His weight had dropped from 200 pounds to about 160. His legs were atrophied, his voice a whisper. A brace secured his neck. A tube helped him to breathe.

Seeing Williams, many players cried. Some backed off, retreating to a corner, wanting to steady their nerves before approaching. Eventually, a line formed, and one by one, the players made their feelings known, kissing Williams on the forehead, patting him on the shoulder, whispering in his ear. Williams smiled and cried and whispered back. Carothers, the freshman who had taken Williams's place, approached and told Williams he loved him. Williams told Carothers: It's your job now. Play like it was yours from the beginning. Akbar hugged Williams and said he was going to play hard for him. He would play without fear, the way Williams would have played. One player after another told Williams that the team would win today—that the team would win for him.

And there, in the locker room, an ABC camera crew hit the record button, filming the scene to show to millions of viewers a couple of hours later.

As the morning deepened, the temperature climbed from the forties into the seventies—sunny, balmy, and blue, postcard perfect. For players from the Midwest and the West Coast, no game in college football meant more than this one. This was America's oldest bowl game, "The Granddaddy of Them All." George Halas played in the Rose Bowl. So did Bubba Smith, Dick Butkus, and the Four Horsemen of Notre Dame. Knute Rockne coached in the Rose Bowl. So did Bo Schembechler, John McKay, and Woody Hayes. O. J. Simpson broke loose for an 80-yard run. Jim Plunkett threw for two touchdowns in the fourth quarter. Charles White, his nose gashed, his body consumed by fever, finished off Ohio State. Even the game's gaffes could become legend. In 1929, a California lineman picked up a fumble and ran 65 yards—the wrong way, claiming one of football's most enduring nicknames, "Wrong Way Riegels."

For whatever reason, oddsmakers doubted this Washington team. The Huskies had a better record—10-1, to Purdue's 8-3—and were ranked No. 4 in the country, compared to Purdue at No.

14. Still, Las Vegas had made Purdue a slight favorite. Maybe it had to do with their conferences. The Big Ten had won seven of the last eight Rose Bowls, leading some folks to wonder if the Pac-10 was soft. Purdue's tailback, Montrell Lowe, had even made a comment that some Huskies interpreted as a slight to the Pac-10's ability to play smash-mouth. The players on Washington's defense talked among themselves of proving Lowe wrong.

ABC promoted the matchup of marquee quarterbacks: Purdue's Drew Brees versus Washington's Marques Tuiasosopo. "The Texas gunslinger from Indiana against the Samoan prince from the Pacific Northwest," Keith Jackson called it. The network also highlighted the reunion between Williams and his team. ABC showed Tuiasosopo bending down and kissing Williams on the forehead. "We join football fans across the country in wishing our very best to number 25, C.W., Curtis Williams," an ABC reporter said.

Before the game, ABC showed clips from a Washington practice, with Neuheisel being one of the boys. "Coaches finding ways to motivate their team—Rick Neuheisel will do anything that needs to be done," the ABC announcer says. Encouraging the team's kicker, Neuheisel doesn't say "good." He says "sweet." He says "money." He doesn't shake hands. He bumps fists.

"Give me some," he says.

"Don't leave me hanging," he says.

Neuheisel invited Washington's last two head coaches, Jim Lambright and Don James, to share the sidelines with him at the Rose Bowl. Fired two years before, Lambright had recruited half the team. "To be on the sidelines, close to kids I recruited, makes me see this is still one big family," Lambright told reporters. Neuheisel talked up Washington's proud history and told reporters how Huskies were all in this together: "The Huskies are one, one deal. They're just letting me steer the wheel a little bit now."

A Rose Bowl, like every football game, hungers for a story. Today, and in days before, Neuheisel had obliged, sketching one story line after another. *A hero returns.* That was Neuheisel, returning to Rose Bowl Stadium. *We are family*—Lambright and

James, home again. *The special play*—Peggy Watson, watching from above. *A promise kept.* That was Curtis Williams. Neuheisel had promised Williams a Rose Bowl ring—and now the team was determined to keep that promise. When the Huskies took the field, they were playing for C.W. and Peg, for school, for conference, for each other and for themselves—for personal pride. More than a third of Washington's players were from California. For them, the Rose Bowl amounted to a sort of homecoming.

Tom Brokaw, news anchor and Tournament of Roses Grand Marshal, joined the captains at midfield and flipped the ceremonial coin. Each Husky player wore Williams's initials on the front of his purple jersey and on the back of his gold helmet. Washington won the flip and said you take it. We'll defend.

Purdue began its drive at the 20. All season, its offensive line had excelled at protecting Brees, a Heisman finalist. But on third and 1, Anthony Kelley sacked the Purdue quarterback. For the Boilermakers, it was three and out.

Washington's first play—Peg Left—was a quarterback option, with Tuiasosopo able to pitch or keep. He elected to run the ball himself, but was dropped for a 1-yard loss. No matter. The Huskies were off and running. A carry up the gut. A catch by Stevens. "He's a problem maker for the Boilermakers," Tim Brant said. A long reception by a Husky wideout. Another catch by Stevens. An option pitch, for the score. The Huskies went 64 yards in ten plays to go up 7–0.

Purdue's second drive stalled, with Derrell Daniels making three tackles, including a quarterback sack. Fear? Hesitation? There was no evidence of that now.

When Washington got the ball a second time, the Huskies scored again, in just three plays. The first quarter ended with Washington up 14–0, threatening to make it a blowout.

Purdue, wearing black on gold, steadied in the second quarter. Brees took his team 90 yards for a touchdown, and by halftime the Boilermakers closed to within 14–10. But whatever the score, the game's tone had been set. Akbar, who would lead the Huskies in tackles this day, hit Lowe so hard in the second quarter that the running back fumbled. Carothers, the freshman replacing Williams, landed an even bigger blow that sent Lowe's helmet flying. "They're getting serious now," Keith Jackson said. Carothers's hit split Lowe's lip, a cut that would require stitches at halftime.

To start the second half, Washington received. On the first play from scrimmage, Tuiasosopo pitched the ball to Rich Alexis, a freshman running back. Washington had been reluctant to play Alexis, because he had an injured shoulder. Alexis took the ball and raced 50 yards down the sideline. At the end of the play, he went down hard, separating his bad shoulder. The team popped it back in, and he played on.

All kinds of Huskies were banged up, but playing. There was a receiver with a torn ligament in his knee, a running back coming off a broken collarbone, an offensive lineman with ten screws in his ankle. But if there was one given on this team, it was that Tuiasosopo would take the field. Not once in college had he missed a play due to injury. In 1999 he hurt his hip and buttocks in the first quarter against Stanford, suffering a bruise so severe he would be on crutches the next day. All he did that day was pass for 300 yards and run for 200—the first time that had been done in NCAA Division I history. Teammates revered Tuiasosopo. They called him Superman, a warrior, a god.

As the third quarter wound down, Washington clung to a 20–17 lead. Then the unthinkable happened. A Purdue linebacker pulled Tuiasosopo to the ground, injuring his right shoulder and forcing him to the sidelines.

On Washington's next series, Tuiasosopo's inexperienced backup—a rodeo star from Idaho named Cody Pickett—took the Huskies 9 yards in three downs, leaving them with a crucial fourth and 1 as the third quarter expired. Tuiasosopo sat in the locker room, getting X-rayed. Keith Gilbertson, Washington's offensive coordinator, worried that Tuiasosopo wouldn't return in time for the next snap. Neuheisel knew better. The break before the fourth quarter is when new inductees to the Rose Bowl Hall of Fame get introduced to the crowd. Neuheisel had been in this ceremony just two years earlier and knew how inductees were in no hurry to leave the field. Don't worry, Neuheisel told Gilbertson. Marques will be back.

ABC went to a commercial break between quarters, allowing Washington Mutual to tout its home loans. Before Washington's first play of the fourth quarter, Tuiasosopo emerged from the locker room. "He went in to see Dr. Feelgood," Tim Brant said. "He looks pretty good."

Just having Tuiasosopo under center was huge, because he posed so many threats. He planted so many thoughts in a defensive player's mind. Would he throw? Sneak? Option? This time, he simply handed the ball to Alexis, who went 3 yards for the first down. Washington was now at Purdue's 35-yard line.

ABC's cameras panned across the Husky fans in the crowd, some with faces painted purple and gold. One fan held up a sign: "Neuheisel Let the Dawgs Out." The game was a sellout, with the official attendance pegged at 94,392. The fans in Rose Bowl Stadium included Washington's governor, top state legislators, university regents, and famed Huskies from glory years past, like Warren Moon and Steve Emtman. Mike Hunsinger was also in the stands, watching the game with his son.

Washington's drive reached Purdue's 8-yard line. With Tuiasosopo injured, Washington's coaches wanted to take it easy on his throwing arm. But on first and goal, Tuiasosopo changed the play at the line of scrimmage. Instead of a run, he lofted a perfect fade pass to Todd Elstrom—an 8-yard touchdown, from a quarterback with a bum shoulder to a wide receiver with a bad knee.

Washington was now up 27–17. Purdue tried to rebound, but Carothers hammered Lowe again, forcing a fumble that all but sealed the game. Each team tacked on another touchdown, and Washington ran out the clock. The scoreboard said Washington 34, Purdue 24.

And what more need be said?

On Washington's sideline, two risers were set up for the awards presentation. The Tournament of Roses president, a gentleman in a red jacket, handed Neuheisel the trophy. Neuheisel held it high, wanting everyone to see, wanting everyone to be part of this. "Coach," an ABC announcer said, "it's been a long season for you. I know this means a lot to you and your Huskies. But let's talk about C.W., number 25. You made a promise to him—and you delivered."

Neuheisel looked up to the press box, his eyes glassy. "Well, Curtis, I know you're sitting up there, partner. This one's for you, baby!" The announcer was done—"Thanks, coach"—but Neuheisel wasn't, he kept talking, he'd keep talking for days, there'd be so many stories spilling out of him that one columnist would suggest he be tranquilized. "The entire state of Washington is honored," Neuheisel said. "We're back where we belong—back in Pasadena!" Band members threw their heads back and thrust cymbals and drumsticks to the sky. The Washington fans whooped and whistled. Hundreds hung over the rails, wanting to shake the players' hands or pat them on the shoulder.

Neuheisel, a long-stem rose in hand, climbed a ladder facing the UW marching band and yelled, "On three!" Band members laughed. It's on four, they called back. Neuheisel counted it off—"One, two, three, four"—and, using the rose as baton, transformed from coach to conductor, his hips swaying, the band playing, the crowd dancing along. To Neuheisel, enjoying the moment mattered. He believed celebration was lost on too many coaches. Can you imagine Woody Hayes—dour, stomping, glaring Woody—swinging his hips, high-fiving the fans, kissing his mother, hugging the athletic director, leading the horns and woodwinds and drums in a rousing rendition of "Tequila"? On this day, Washington's fans couldn't get enough. "We love Rick! We love Rick!" they chanted. As Neuheisel grooved, the ladder teetered, threatening to fall.

Jerramy Stevens ran around the field with a rose clenched in his teeth. He had led the Huskies with five catches, wrapping up the best season of any tight end in school history. He draped his arm around Tuiasosopo, and with both hands signed a "W"—three fingers up, two down. *Flash*. A photographer caught the moment, the players' smiles brilliant, the rose a dazzling red.

The Husky players gathered at the rose painted at midfield. Jumping, they pointed skyward and chanted, "C-Dub, C-Dub." Williams, high in a press box, watched the celebration below. During the game, ABC's cameras had checked in on him from time to time. He used to be Curtis Williams, football player. It's hard to say what he was now. Hero? Martyr? Rallying cry? So many stories had been written about him. So much money had been raised. Now everybody knew his number. Down on the field, Neuheisel was wearing it on the chest of his purple sweater.

After the game, Neuheisel told reporters how he had asked Brokaw to give the game's commemorative coin to Williams, and how Brokaw had said he would be honored to. Neuheisel told reporters: "This win is for Curtis. . . . We had a dream to give our buddy a chance to get a Rose Bowl ring, and we achieved it. I promised him after [he was injured] that we'd try to get it done. It was an absolute thrill to have him here. It's an unbelievable story line."

Once the celebration on the field ended, reporters began filing their stories. The Huskies "kept a promise to a fallen comrade," *USA Today* wrote. Reporters praised Neuheisel's selflessness. What did he do with the spotlight? He shared it with Husky coaches from years gone by. Reporters also quoted Neuheisel's summation of the season: "A magic carpet ride." "It's not about the trophy," Neuheisel said. "It's about the climb to the trophy."

Sportswriters searched for their own words to describe the Rose Bowl and all the events leading up to it. "A mystical, magical season," the *Seattle Times* wrote. "The Washington Huskies are back," the Associated Press wrote. "They're No. 1, with a finger as long as a rose," the *Los Angeles Times* wrote. When the sportswriters filed their stories, they were flush with the game, flush with the day's drama. They wrote the kinds of stories that attract so many people to sports, stories full of wonder and will. On the field, there was romance. On the green green grass, between the clean white lines, you could find magic, and honor, and resurrection.

For Jeremiah Pharms, the game had been uneventful. He had a couple of tackles in the first quarter, and that was it. Anthony Vontoure started the game but then played sparingly, recording only one tackle. Afterward, he blew up at Chuck Heater, the assistant coach. Vontoure had another year of eligibility left, but who knew if he would be coming back now.

Marques Tuiasosopo and his brother Zach, a redshirt freshman on the team, were celebrating in the locker room when their dad appeared. "We have to go," he said. The two brothers had a lot of relatives at the game, including their father's cousin Aima Amituanai. Marques and Zach called her "Auntie." After the final whistle, Aima had come down to the field's edge and congratulated both of them, a big smile on her face. We'll see you outside, she said. Afterward, she walked through a tunnel and, mere steps outside the stadium, collapsed and died of heart failure.

After the Rose Bowl, Neuheisel stayed in California—to recruit, and to tape a show on ESPN's "Up Close." Hedges and the team climbed aboard a chartered 737. Walking off the plane—home, in Washington—Hedges was radiant, her smile wide and white. She carried red roses in one arm and newspapers in the other. A reporter asked her about luring Neuheisel to Washington with that splashy salary of $1 million. "It was a great investment," Hedges said. "It paid off, didn't it?"

The next season, the team's ticket sales would jump $1 million. Contributions to the football program would jump $1.5 million. And who knows how many other donations—ones not specifically marked for football—could be attributed to all this good cheer? When they're raising money, university presidents like to talk football, at least they do when the football team is winning.

To Anthony Kelley, the season was a testament to togetherness. "The fact that we might have had people with criminal charges against them, or had bad moral standards with their family, or just made some bad mistakes, one thing they can't take away from us is the fact that we were all champions at one point in our lives. We all worked together, and we all sacrificed for one another, and we were all the best. And that's kind of the ultimate thing, where you put aside whatever habits you have in the outside world and sacrifice for your partner next to you. And I think all of us were willing to do that. We were willing to do our best for each other."

25

Climbing the Hill

On a crisp, sunny morning four days after the Rose Bowl, Sarah Winter drove her old Saturn to pick up Anthony Kelley from his student housing near the university. Kelley looked serious, maybe a little nervous. He didn't say much, just tossed his backpack into the car and kept his eyes focused on the road ahead. He wasn't at all like the guy Winter had worked with the previous few months, the guy so full of energy he could liven any room. Winter drove away from Husky Stadium and onto the highway, heading south, toward the airport.

The whole team had been there three days earlier, arriving back from Pasadena. The players had been relaxed, laughing. The team had kept its return quiet, and only a handful of diehard fans knew where to be and when. But that hadn't stopped random passengers from breaking out in applause when they saw the players picking up their luggage, or the pleas for autographs. All the hugs from proud girlfriends and parents weren't bad, either.

Today, Kelley had headphones clamped over his ears. He was wearing his sweatpants and windbreaker, along with a skull cap that kept his unruly hair in check. Nobody at the airport recognized him. There was no family, no fans, no roses. Just two young people from different worlds striding across the terminal. *He's really going*, Winter thought. Even though she and Kelley were close in age, Winter felt like she was putting her kindergartner on the school bus for the first time. Kelley took out the ticket to South Africa that his Mary Gates scholarship had paid for. He handed over the passport he had secured after gathering all that documentation. Then, he walked through security. *Wow*, Winter thought. *He really made it. Nobody is getting him off that plane.*

District Six was once one of Cape Town's most vibrant neighbor-hoods. It was freewheeling and raucous, with jazz clubs, cinemas, and curry houses. On the docks you'd find stevedores looking for work, and in the bathhouses you'd find outlaws. Black families lived in modest brick homes and worked the menial jobs afford-ed them under apartheid laws. Then, in 1966, District Six was de-clared whites only. Bulldozers rumbled into town, flattening hous-es and destroying a community. Tens of thousands of black people were evicted. They moved to shacks in nearby marshy townships, which, in turn, grew into small cities.

Guguletu, a fifteen-minute drive from Cape Town, wasn't the worst of these settlements. Some pockets were comparatively af-fluent. But vast slums dominated. The *New York Times* called Guguletu an "unexceptional black settlement foundering in the ocean of destitution that laps at the edge of idyllic Cape Town." In 1986 the township became the site of a massacre that epitomized the country's rule and the era. A police squad hid and waited four hours before gunning down seven black activists, who, the police claimed, were plotting some kind of attack. The officers involved were cleared of any wrongdoing. Years later, the truth came out. It had been a planned hit all along—the police never intended to take any prisoners, and kept on shooting even after some of the men raised their arms in surrender.

Three years after the massacre, police tear-gassed Archbishop Desmond Tutu and five hundred children in a Guguletu church. Tutu had just finished convincing the children to end a protest against apartheid.

In 1993, with apartheid finally crumbling, Amy Biehl, a white, twenty-six-year-old Stanford graduate and Fulbright scholar, was in Guguletu working on a voter education program and doing re-search on the creation of a new constitution. One day, she encoun-tered a group of fired-up black youths. "One settler, one bullet!" they yelled, throwing stones and bricks at her car. When Biehl got out and ran, she was stabbed to death.

The killing of a young American brought worldwide attention

to the problems of Guguletu. Biehl's parents, who would later forgive the killers, launched the Amy Biehl Foundation to improve conditions in Guguletu and other townships. They started literacy, health, and music programs, even a community bakery. One of the programs was for after-school care. Tutors would teach arithmetic, dance, and sports for a couple of hours to educate children and to keep them safe from the violence all around them. They would also supply the kids with a nutritious meal.

It was this after-school program that tapped Kelley, assigning him to tutor at Intshinga Primary in Guguletu, working with the girls from Room 7. Amy Biehl's parents and sister Kim had visited Intshinga the year before. Kim noted that just getting to the school involved navigating a maze of streets cluttered with children, dogs, and goats. She said the after-school program, with all those bubbly kids wanting to put on a show just for them, was her pick of all the foundation's work.

After Kelley arrived in South Africa, Winter e-mailed him all the time—making sure he had remembered this, taken care of that. A week into his trip, Kelley e-mailed back: "Sarah, I paid for that already. It's okay that I'm ahead of you. I'm becoming a grown man. I'm learning to take care of things on my own now!!" Winter realized it was time to let go. She had done everything she could to put Kelley on that plane. Whatever happened next was up to him.

Kelley would be one of the last football players Winter would guide through the university. She would quit a few months later, seeing only hype surrounding the team's "special admits," a misplaced belief they were rising above. To Winter, Kelley's educational ambition was the exception, not the rule. "They are running a business at the expense of the kids," she says. "I felt like I was feeding the business, rather than helping."

Because Intshinga was on summer break, Kelley spent his first few weeks traveling. He had thought that as an African American, being in Africa would be a way to reconnect with his ancestors, that it would be a type of homecoming. But he soon realized he'd been naive. So much separated him from the people of the townships, down to the way he spoke—the English of the privileged, not the Xhosa of the poor, with its guttural clicks. "I was associated with America and the way America is perceived by them: As the land of the free. Money. And white."

When classes resumed at Intshinga, one girl who showed up every day, dressed in a neat uniform, was Siya Manyakanyaka. She was eleven years old. She lived with her brother, sister, and parents in a one-room shack that her dad had built from scraps of wood and tin. They had done their best to make the place a home, dividing off the cooking area and making a little space for each of them to sleep. But there was no running water and no electricity. After dark, the family used candles and kerosene lamps.

Each day, Siya's mom would tend to the house while her dad left to find work as a laborer. He had built a reputation as a hard worker, but jobs could be scarce. When there was work, there was plenty of food for dinner. When there wasn't, the family sometimes went hungry. Paying for the school uniforms and fees took just about everything they had. Still, Siya's parents were determined to do at least that much for their children.

Introduced to Kelley, the first thing Siya and her classmates noticed was his size. "He was huge," Siya says. "I don't think I'd seen anyone as big as him before in my life." Then they saw his tattoos and thought: "Americans. Oh my gosh."

Kelley decided to teach the stretches and drills he used in training, and the basics of football. But the structure and routine of organized sport surrendered to chaos and laughter. He would taunt the children—*catch me if you can*—and they'd give chase. He would sprint ahead, leap into a tree, and leap out again before they could reach him. When he tried to teach football, it would turn into rugby, the South African version of the sport. It didn't matter. What mattered was that Kelley was forming a bond. He felt like he didn't have a whole lot to offer these kids. But every day, they turned up. Every day, they took whatever he had to give. Their commitment amazed Kelley—and forced him to reflect. "I looked at myself, and here I am at this great university, even a good high school, and they made my projects look like a cakewalk. It was really unfortunate I didn't have the same attitude."

Kelley realized that no matter how smart these kids were, their circumstances meant they would probably end up with nothing. On the other hand, back in the United States, he was squandering his education and opportunities.

One day he showed up to school early. He could hear a beat thumping as he walked toward the classroom. He opened the door to find Siya leading the girls in glorious flight, drumming on their desks, pounding out rhythms. Some girls danced. Others sang. There was not an instrument in sight, but it was the most beautiful music Kelley had ever heard. Whatever I was teaching you, we need to stop immediately, Kelley told them. I need to learn this.

Kelley bought the girls some drums from the market and threw himself into their music. The girls laughed at the sight of it, this huge man, who couldn't dance, jumping around to their rhythms. But they delighted in his energy. Siya, in particular, developed a connection with Kelley.

When it came time to leave South Africa, Kelley made the girls a promise: One day, he would return. He would even try to bring them back to visit America. "I was really just speaking from the heart, and didn't know how it would happen." How could it happen? He was a student. He didn't have any money. Yet he was determined to find a way.

Back in Seattle, Kelley came to appreciate what his trip had meant. "I had a chance to engage," he says. "To feel, touch, and smell what I was reading in these books. That's when I had the big idea of education as an engaged experience."

At the uw he approached his professors and began asking for lists of books—not for class study, but simply to learn. He read up on civil rights leaders like W. E. B. Du Bois and Martin Luther King Jr. He read up on South Africa. He tackled dense academic treatises. As his library expanded, so did his vocabulary and his

confidence. He grew bolder. He toyed with ideas and experiment-
ed with forms of expression. He found joy in writing essays. He
started a journal and began writing poems. "I was opening up to
a whole new world," Kelley says. With that came a realization:
"I actually can write. I actually can read. I actually can have in-
tellectual conversations and actually forge some ideas that can be
very productive. I didn't realize I had that type of potential. It was
kind of like being reborn into a new world that had been closed
off for so long."

A couple of years earlier, Kelley had spotted a woman named Tonya
Britt in a San Jose nightclub. She had been stunning in a black
dress, but Kelley had brushed past, without saying a word. Later
that night, he pried Tonya's number from one of her friends, and
called after they both left the club, at maybe two in the morning.
Tonya, furious, told him never to call that late again.

Kelley called Tonya the next day, and the day after that, and
they started a friendship that lasted for months. They lived in different cities, but kept in touch by phone and e-mail. Tonya had
two boys from a previous relationship, but Kelley didn't mind.
"You can't help what happens in life," he says.

Maybe eight months after they first talked, they got to spend
some time together when Kelley booked a hotel room in San Jose.
Tonya came over with her kids, who wanted to see the pool. Her
older son, DeVan, was splashing around with Anthony in the deep
end. She had told her younger son, Dominec, to stay on the side
with his cousin. But without anyone noticing, Dominec had walked
down the steps into the pool, until only his hand was above the
surface. "All I could do was scream," Tonya says. "By the time I
had run around, Anthony was there. Dominec was throwing up,
and stuff was coming out of his nose. But he was okay. . . . That
was the icing on my cake. He was the man of my dreams at that
point."

But the coaches didn't like this budding love affair. "They
were so against it," Tonya says, "so against it. It was unbelievable.

I knew they had a problem. Why? I was self-sufficient. I had my own place, my own car, my own job. I took good care of my children. They felt I would be a hindrance, somehow. But I was a big support system." The coaches feared Kelley would become consumed by this relationship. Kelley struggled to focus, to narrow his choices, to appreciate moderation. He wanted it all—in life, as in football—but no one gets it all, and the more you try for everything, the greater the risk you get nothing. To the demands of football and school, Kelley was adding a family. Even Tom Williams, the coach who had encouraged Kelley to study abroad, feared it wouldn't work out.

As the 2001 season got under way, the coaches had an even bigger problem with Kelley. He'd informed them that after football wrapped up, he wanted to travel, just like the year before. He wanted to return to South Africa. The coaches didn't like hearing that. "My credibility and my commitment to the team started to be questioned," Kelley says. "And it was ironic in the fact that you wanted me to be a student-athlete." Kelley felt like he was breaking a code. "There are these unwritten rules that you have to follow to make sure that the coaches are okay. And I really just looked at it as an issue of control. They didn't have immediate control over me."

College football programs know how players become entranced by the prospect of reaching the NFL. Coaches use that to motivate. But through academics, Kelley had discovered he could be successful even without professional football. "And so they couldn't use that to manipulate me. And so I did what I had to do. And whatever they did was fine with me, because I had a class to get to, you know what I mean?"

That season, Kelley recorded nineteen tackles, down from thirty the year before. He lost his starting linebacker job to Sam Blanche, the player who had become entangled in the police investigation of the Sullivan shooting. Kelley also won a second Mary Gates scholarship. He was going back to South Africa, and this time he was taking his family. Just before they left, Anthony and Tonya got married. Earlier, they had also taken in Tonya's goddaughter, Diamond, whose family was having problems with drugs. All five of them—Anthony, Tonya, DeVan, Dominec, and Diamond—got on that plane.

In South Africa, Siya was resigned to her fate. A year earlier, this big American had walked into her life, bringing excitement and hope. He'd talked a big game. After he'd left, she had waited to hear from him. Sure, she didn't have a phone number or an e-mail address, but he would send a letter, right? But he hadn't. Not once. Siya had thought they'd formed a bond. But, as the months slipped by, she wondered if it had all been an illusion. *Okay, forget about it. Move on*, she told herself. *I'm going back to my normal life. I'm going to make everything work the best that I can.*

Siya was in high school now, but every day after school she went back to Intshinga Primary, to lead the other girls in music and dance. One day she was in Room 7, playing the drums, when Anthony Kelley and his family walked through the door. Tonya had never seen a photo of this girl Anthony had talked so much about, but somehow she knew right away. Siya was the girl with the big smile, her face radiating joy. Then Siya looked over. She was in shock. She was in tears. Siya ran over and hugged Diamond, this girl she had never met. "It was a done deal," Tonya says. "It was done at that moment. I knew that, okay, she's in our lives, and it's going to be that way forever."

Once the Kelleys got settled into their apartment, Siya came over to visit. She ended up staying with them for almost the entire three months. One day, Siya's dad took Anthony aside and told him: My daughter won't be able to make anything of herself here. And so, if there's anything she can do with you, I give you permission to take her. Anthony vowed to do all he could to help.

When the Kelleys returned to Seattle, they told their friends: There's this group of South African girls who dance like nothing you've ever seen. We're trying to raise money to bring them over here, to perform in Seattle. Can you help out? The Kelleys hosted a '70s party, a spaghetti dinner, and an auction. Diamond sold lemonade for fifty cents a cup. The money began to add up. By the spring of 2002, leaders on the upper campus had heard about this football player and what he was trying to do for these South African children. They decided Kelley would be the perfect student to speak at a ceremony marking the first honorary degree the university had awarded in more than eighty years. It was being given to Archbishop Desmond Tutu.

Kelley sat behind the stage, nervous, knowing he was about to address hundreds of students. He had just met the university regents, including Bill Gates Sr., father of the world's richest man. Kelley held notes of his speech, which he and Tonya had written together. But now he watched as Ron Sims, the political head of King County, a man who would later join the Obama administration, got up and spoke with power and emotion, and without any notes at all. How can I compete with that? Kelley thought. Then it was his turn. "I just remember walking up to the stage, and I didn't look out into the crowd. I really wasn't looking at anybody's eyes or anything. I just really tried to focus on finishing."

Kelley tripped over his words at first. Then he picked up momentum. He talked about how, growing up, he and his mother had been forced to live in a car for months. How he had taken his life for granted at a great university, before getting a rude awakening in South Africa. How he had found such inspiration from these girls he was now trying to bring to the United States. How education, no matter where you live in the world, is the key to a better life.

By the end of his speech, the crowd was on its feet, cheering. One woman yelled, "That's what I'm talkin' 'bout!" Tutu, who was seventy years old, leaped from his seat, strode across the stage, and intercepted Kelley before he could sit down. The two men hugged.

By now, the media were all over the story, and the UW was hailing Kelley as the ideal student-athlete. Bill Gates Sr. donated $5,000 to help bring the girls over. So did Rick Neuheisel. "He, for whatever reason, has found his passion," Neuheisel said of Kelley.

The next month, the Kelleys paid for eleven girls and three teachers to travel from Guguletu to Seattle for a six-week tour. "I could always see planes flying, flying, flying," Siya says. "I never thought that, one day, I would be on one." The girls, calling themselves the Ipintombi dancers, performed at the Paramount Theatre and at the Mount Zion Baptist Church. A *Seattle Times* reporter who watched was captivated: "Wearing green, orange and black and with their faces outlined with paint, the girls stomped, chanted and flung their arms and legs in every possible direction, like a tornado of energy ripping across the stage." When it came time for the group to return to South Africa, only ten girls got on the plane. Kelley was keeping his promise to Siya's dad. Siya was staying.

That summer, Kelley graduated with a bachelor's degree in the comparative history of ideas. He had arrived four years earlier academically ineligible to play and with a high school GPA of about 2.0. Unlike most students, whose GPA peaks in high school and falls away under the rigors of college, Kelley's grades had been climbing. He finished his degree with a GPA of 2.83. And because he graduated within four years, he earned back his lost year of football, making him eligible to play the 2002 season.

That year, he recorded just eleven tackles in thirteen games. His football career had all but faded away. At the same time, he became the first UW player to be named to the Good Works Team, chosen by the American Football Coaches Association. Kelley's teammates wondered about his focus on academics, and how he seemed to shrug off the promise of an NFL career. "The thing was, amongst my peers, it was really like, 'A.K., you're crazy.' But at the same time, they would say 'A.K., I wish I could do what you did.'" Assistant coach Tom Williams says Kelley's approach stood out: "Guys generally pursue the dream of playing in the NFL until it completely dies. Then they say, 'Now what do I do?' Anthony made that decision before all that came up."

Kelley's family was growing up. Then, in the spring of 2004, Siya got the news. Her five-year-old sister, Sesethu, who the family called "chocolate" after her favorite snack, had died. She'd been traveling in the back of an overcrowded van, a cheap form of public transportation in Guguletu, when a fire erupted. She stood no chance of escaping. In the aftermath, Siya thought about her own life. In Seattle, she was thriving at Roosevelt High School and had opportunities no one else from her township could hope for. Now, she felt an added responsibility to seize them. She had an American family, after all, who would do everything possible to help her achieve her goals.

One day at Roosevelt, Kelley offered to help raise money for a student-exchange program. He wanted to give back, to help all these teenagers discover new worlds. For the school auction, he donated a football helmet. It was the one he had worn in the Rose Bowl.

Kelley didn't stop with a bachelor's degree. He went after a master's degree in education at the UW, and his GPA rose to 3.65. After that? It's hard to say. Even with his academic awakening, Kelley sometimes struggles to hold it together. He has ups and downs, good days and bad. He struggles to stay on track, to follow through. His marriage has had rough patches. At heart, he's still that young recruit who wanted to play wide receiver, and tight end, and safety, and linebacker. Some days he talks of becoming a lawyer. Other days he talks of getting a PhD. Maybe he'd like to teach. Or maybe coach. Or maybe return to South Africa and open an academic, sports, and arts complex. It's hard to say. But because he has discovered the depth and reach of his capabilities, anything remains possible.

For years, Kelley nurtured this vision of helping other athletes reach beyond sports, just as he had. In 2008 his persistence paid off. The UW gave him a stipend to help organize a group of twenty students on a study-abroad trip to South Africa. To blunt the kind of criticism he had faced from coaches years earlier, Kelley made sure the students would get access to workout facilities while away.

Kelley was particularly eager for football players to come. He took his idea to Washington's coach, Tyrone Willingham. "He was actually agreeing with it," Kelley says. "He didn't have any qualms about it at all. I think he assumed that no student-athletes would want to take part in it. I think he underestimated my gift for the gab." Kelley helped recruit ten student-athletes for the trip, including three football players. There would have been more, he says, but Willingham did an about-face: He soured on the venture. Not many players were willing to buck their coach. The players who did go spent their afternoons working with children, teaching English and sports. They also kept to their off-season workout regimen, lifting weights and running. Because the meals were smaller, one player lost more than five pounds and felt better for it. When they got back, the players described the trip as "intense" and "life-altering."

That spring, Willingham released his depth chart. All three players who'd gone to South Africa had been dropped to the bottom rung. "The truth of the matter is they have two responsibilities: their education and their football," Willingham told reporters. "In most cases, it is the football that brought all of our group to this university. They all have different majors, but they all share football. That is the unifier. That is the single factor that has them here, so they have a responsibility to that."

To Kelley's mind, the coach was creating a false divide. A student can play football *and* discover the world beyond. Sure, the players share sports. But they also share school. Kelley now realized that football wasn't his life's calling. But there's only one reason he knew that: He had dared to wonder and wander. He had ventured off the lower campus and walked up that hill.

Always Hated, Never Faded

26

Blaine Newnham saw something special in Jerramy Stevens. Three months after the Rose Bowl, the *Seattle Times* columnist wrote up how Stevens was "so good" last season. And this season? "He should be everybody's All-American." He was bigger. He was stronger. The rape investigation was behind him. "People don't know you," Stevens told Newnham. "They don't know what really happened." He was on track to graduate. And, well . . . "Stevens has a 2.9 grade-point average. His parents are teachers. He is amiable and articulate."

Three weeks later, at about a quarter till one in the morning, Stevens's pickup truck rolled through shrubs, bounced over large landscaping rocks, and smashed into the side of the Merrill Gardens retirement center in Seattle, ripping a hole in the wall and shattering the window to unit 101. This was the same red pickup Stevens had plowed into Donald Preston's Dodge some six months earlier. Sleeping in unit 101 was Myrla Crawford, ninety-two years old. The impact knocked a dresser onto her bed, but she escaped getting hurt.

Richard Stephens lived above Myrla, in unit 203. Seventy-two years old, Stephens had gotten up to use the bathroom when he heard a loud thump and looked outside. He saw a tall man—six foot five maybe, in blue jeans and a sleeveless white T-shirt—stumbling around. The driver was trying to free his truck, but the front end was damaged, one tire was flat, and the guy kept falling down. Stephens called 911 and said the driver appeared to be hurt or drunk. Back at the window, Stephens saw the man get some books out of the truck—university textbooks, it turned out—and put them under the tires, for traction. The driver backed away from the wall and took off, leaving the books behind.

Stephens got a good look at the driver and caught some of the plate. An hour and a half later, police found the truck a quarter mile away, parked in front of a rental home on Roosevelt Way, its front end damaged, the right front tire flat. A check showed the truck belonged to Robert Stevens, of Olympia. The officers knew the Roosevelt Way house. One wrote in his report: We "are very familiar with the residents . . . from previous contacts." They knew Jerramy Stevens lived there. They knew Stevens matched the description of the driver. The police knocked. Todd Elstrom, a Husky wide receiver, answered.

Whose truck is that? police asked.

That's Jerramy's, Elstrom said.

Stevens came out of the house.

Yeah, he said. That's my truck. But I don't know who's been driving it.

With Stevens refusing to come clean, an officer drove to the retirement home and picked up Stephens, the elderly witness. Between three and four in the morning, the officer escorted him to the house on Roosevelt Way.

Is that the driver?

That's the driver, Stephens said.

Hunsinger, called at home in the wee hours, agreed to defend Stevens. Neuheisel, in San Diego playing golf, issued a statement saying he would call a team meeting "to discuss the importance of behavior, making good decisions and citizenship." Stevens, he said, "will be dealt with according to my policies that I set forth for our student-athletes." He didn't say what those policies were.

Five days after Stevens rammed the retirement home, the university's student newspaper ran an editorial: "How can the UW justify keeping Stevens on the roster? Whether he played a part in bringing the Huskies a Rose Bowl trophy or not, there is absolutely no legitimate reason why someone who has had Stevens's history should be allowed to continue to play football. He is an utter disgrace to the football program and this university."

In June, Stevens pleaded guilty to hit-and-run, a misdemeanor. His parents took the truck's keys away. The judge gave Stevens a ninety-day jail sentence, suspended on condition that he stay out of trouble.

In August, Stevens addressed a contingent of reporters and said: "I'm not a bad person. I'm not a bad guy." His comments blended remorse and denial. "I've made some decisions I wish I wouldn't have made. . . . I was in situations where I felt I wasn't at fault." "It breaks my heart if I feel like there's someone out there that doesn't like me." Stevens told the reporters he was going to quit drinking. Not that he had a problem with alcohol. It was just that drinking and trouble seemed to be traveling partners.

That same day, Neuheisel told reporters: "I think Jerramy has made great strides in correcting some of his mistakes. Unfortunately, that's not as well documented as the transgressions. Discipline will accompany the transgressions." He didn't say what that discipline would be.

A month later, Washington hosted Michigan in the 2001 season's first game. Neuheisel made Stevens sit out the first half. That was Stevens's punishment—being benched for thirty minutes. It was the only suspension he would receive in all his time at Washington. The Huskies won the game, 23–18.

Afterward, Neuheisel said: "I think that was a worthy punishment."

Stevens said: "It was hard sitting the first half."

Neuheisel said: "It's behind him now."

After his junior season, Stevens announced that he would leave school early and enter the NFL draft. "If dreams come true, I'd go to the Oakland Raiders," he said. But unlike most players who go pro before their eligibility expires, Stevens planned to finish what he started. He "promised himself, his family and Neuheisel that he will earn his degree in American Ethnic Studies, hopefully in June," the AP reported.

In April 2002, the Seattle Seahawks drafted Stevens in the first round. The coach, Mike Holmgren, tended to avoid players with off-field troubles. But for Stevens, he made an exception. Before the draft, Holmgren had a long sit-down with Stevens. He talked to Stevens's parents. He talked to Neuheisel. Holmgren consulted his own wife. His own children. And, well . . . "People make mistakes," Holmgren said. "We all do. This is the first time I have ever done this, and it wasn't just the fact that I saw a good football player. Something in our conversation, something that day clicked for me. I felt I understood as best I could the situation and the young man."

On a "Meet the Seahawks" Q&A, Stevens said the best day of his life was when he graduated from the UW. "I graduated from college, got my new Range Rover and moved into my new house. All in the same day." Year after year, the Seahawks media guide said the same thing, that Stevens had graduated. But it wasn't true. Stevens left school without his degree, no matter what promises he had made.

In July, the month after Stevens got his new Range Rover, a state trooper ticketed him for speeding down the interstate at ninety-eight miles per hour. Stevens would get pulled over again in August, September, October, November.

In his first NFL practices, Stevens wowed teammates and sportswriters. Quarterback Trent Dilfer: "He's huge. And he can run. And he can catch." Plus: "He's so smart." The *Seattle Times*' Steve Kelley: "Stevens is looking good. Real good. Tony Gonzalez good. Shannon Sharpe good. Tight-end-of-the-future good."

Stevens signed a five-year, $6.2 million contract that required him to repay $300,000 if he got into any trouble. No problem, Stevens said. He had quit drinking. Three months later, a trooper pulled Stevens over after his Range Rover veered into oncoming traffic. Stevens, who had alcohol on his breath, blew a .051, below the legal limit. He was cited for negligent driving and paid a $490 fine.

Medina, east of Seattle, is a small town with big money. Only 3,000 people live there, but they include Ichiro Suzuki and Bill Gates.

On April 3, 2003, at about 2:15 a.m., a Medina police officer followed a Range Rover heading south. The Range Rover drifted right, then left, toward the fog line, the center line, the fog line, the center line. When the Range Rover rolled through a stop sign, the officer pulled the SUV over. The driver was Jerramy Stevens. His eyes were watery, sleepy, bloodshot. His breath reeked of alcohol. Inside the car were two open bottles of champagne—Moet & Chandon White Star, both cold, both half full.

You been drinking the champagne?

No, Stevens said.

He told the officer he hadn't been drinking anything at all.

Stevens agreed to do field-sobriety tests. On the walk-and-turn, he lost his balance—while listening to the instructions. He flunked the one-leg stand three times. "This isn't good," he told the officer. At the police station, Stevens admitted drinking the champagne and running the stop sign. He said he had been preoccupied, talking on a cell phone. He blew a .172 and .148—about twice the legal limit—and was charged with DUI.

Two weeks later, Stevens was pulled over again. A trooper clocked him doing ninety in a sixty.

For the Medina stop, Stevens hired Jon S. Fox, one of Washington's leading DUI attorneys. Fox and his partners have defended all kinds of professional athletes against DUI charges, including such football players as Warren Moon and Lofa Tatupu. In this case Stevens cut a deal, pleading guilty to reckless driving in exchange for the DUI charge being dropped. At sentencing, Fox told the judge: "I believe that I've come to understand the character of Jerramy Stevens. He is an individual, your honor, who is growing up. He is at a place, at age twenty-three, where the spotlight of the media is constantly on him, where his life is going to be watched from many different angles. He's accepting that, he's willing and able, eager in fact, to move forward. I'm willing to wager, your honor, that you're not going to see any more speeding tickets."

Stevens told the judge, Albert Raines, that he didn't have a drinking problem. Raines wasn't convinced. "You know who Reggie Rogers is? He could play football like nobody's business. He was an All-American at the University of Washington. First-round draft pick, just like you. Got into some trouble with alcohol behind the wheel. First time, no significant problem. Second time, he ended his career with a broken neck." The "especially tragic part," Raines said, was that three teenagers in Michigan were killed in that accident.

"I don't want that to be you," the judge said. "Let this be a mantra to you: If you do what you've always done, you will be what you've always been."

At the sentencing hearing, a woman sat toward the front of the courtroom—just behind Stevens, and in front of the media. It was Marie's mom. No one knew who she was. "I wanted to see him," she says. "I wanted to look at him." She didn't say a thing. She just looked. "I was shocked," she says. "I think I expected to see this terrible person, and he was actually a nice-looking guy. He didn't look like the kind of person I thought he should look like." She watched as Stevens's mom addressed the court and said, "Whatever happens to Jerramy, we're going to love and support him." Stevens's mom talked about how her son had visited the students at her school and was such "a positive force for them." She recounted how her son would say, *Wouldn't it be nice if people could just see me as Jerramy?* Marie's mother rolled her eyes at all of this, but she understood: "Of course a mother is going to believe in her child." She stared a hole in the back of Stevens's head. "I wanted very badly to say something to him, but I didn't."

The conviction for reckless driving violated Stevens's probation in the hit-and-run case involving the retirement home. Stevens served seven days in jail—five for the probation violation, two for the conviction. Each judge also ordered community service. The court in Seattle let Stevens work at a weeklong youth camp. Raines made Stevens pick up trash on the highway.

The NFL ordered Stevens into a substance-abuse program. The Seahawks forced him to repay $300,000 for violating the good-conduct clause. But the team didn't suspend Stevens. He lost no playing time.

When Raines had sentenced Stevens, he ordered him to attend AA meetings twice a week. A month later, Fox asked the judge to reconsider. There was no way Stevens could attend the AA meetings during training camp, Fox argued. And during the season? Impossible. Fox proposed some alternatives. One was to have Stevens watch *My Name is Bill W.*, a made-for-TV movie with James Wood and James Garner. Fox called it "an excellent portrayal of the original development of AA as a resource for alcoholics."

Raines said no to *My Name is Bill W.* But he did knock the meeting requirement down to once a week.

Fox would have lost his wager. Stevens continued racking up speeding tickets: 90 in a 70, 74 in a 60, 50-plus in a 35.

In 2003, Marie sued Stevens, accusing him of rape. She also sued Sigma Chi and the University of Washington. Marie was represented by Becky Roe, a lawyer who used to prosecute sex crimes in Norm Maleng's office. Roe also represented three other women accusing UW football players of rape. Two sued Roc Alexander, a cornerback on the Rose Bowl team who went on to the NFL. Another sued Eric Shyne, a defensive back who later transferred to Utah. To Roe, her clients' cases were linked. By failing to hold Stevens accountable, she argued, the UW suggested to players that "they were invulnerable to charges of sexual assault."

Hunsinger represented Stevens. He also represented Alexander. He had previously represented Shyne when prosecutors were mulling criminal charges.

In June 2004, Roe deposed Neuheisel. What was your code of conduct for your players? she asked. "I just said it was going to be up to you not to embarrass yourselves, your families, or your institution," Neuheisel said. Once prosecutors elected not to charge Stevens, Neuheisel elected not to discipline him. "The program had been embarrassed, but given the prosecution's decision not to go forward, it looked as if Jerramy was not the reason for the embarrassment."

Roe deposed Hedges the same year. Hedges said that if a player was convicted of a felony, he was off the team. Roe asked Hedges how she interpreted a decision not to file charges against someone. "The person has been exonerated," Hedges said.

Roe deposed Jim Lambright. He was Neuheisel's predecessor and the coach who had recruited Stevens. Lambright said he now worked as a life coach, and that his last keynote was to a dental convention.

"The topic was coaching, dentistry, God, and life."

"Hmmm," Roe said.

Lambright said that while recruiting Stevens, a "definite consideration" was his family: "Both parents are teachers."

Roe deposed Keith Gilbertson. He had been offensive coordinator during the 2000 season, and had since become Washington's head coach. Gilbertson said that when Stevens was arrested, he didn't direct him to any lawyer. "That would be the head coach's role," he said. Roe asked Gilbertson who was now on his referral list, besides Mike Hunsinger. Gilbertson named four other lawyers and a judge he would tap for recommendations.

"I've known—got to meet a lot of attorneys here in the last twelve months," he said.

"Lucky you."

Roe asked Gilbertson if there's a public perception that football players get special protection.

"I don't know, but it is not true," Gilbertson said. "It's the other way."

When Marie filed suit, she identified herself only by her initials. That's not uncommon in litigation alleging sexual assault or molestation; plaintiffs in such cases often want to protect their privacy.

But in October 2003, the UW demanded that Marie's full name be disclosed in the court file. Its motion championed the public's right to know—and any qualifiers be damned. "It is axiomatic that lawsuits are public events . . . secrecy obstructs the public's view of government . . . centuries of law forbid secrecy (to any degree) in our judicial proceedings."

The UW's motion was both brazen and hypocritical. Two weeks earlier, the university had made the opposite argument in another lawsuit. In that case, the UW Medical Center and a second defendant paid $5.2 million to settle a claim alleging that an insulin pump used by tens of thousands of people was unsafe and responsible for the plaintiff's brain damage. The public's need to know was obvious, but the UW joined the other parties in getting the file sealed—the entire file, not just part of it. Their sealing motion extolled the importance of protecting the plaintiff's privacy.

The UW's motion galled Marie. After her false start in the fall of 2000, she attended a community college for five quarters, and returned to the UW after Stevens left. She transferred from pre-med to economics. "I was confident again, starting to get my groove back," she says. "I went back because I started there and I wanted to finish. I'm not a quitter." Now, she couldn't fathom what the UW would gain from making her name public. The university knew who she was. It could dig into her background all it wanted. Her claims would be tried in open court. But she didn't want other students staring at her, whispering about her. She worried some people might try to take her picture. She worried some people might try to hurt her.

When she had accused Stevens of rape, no one at the UW had told her she could file a complaint with the office that handled student affairs. No one had offered her any services. Now, indifference was being replaced by something worse. Marie wrote of the UW's motion: "I am dismayed that the University of Washington, where I am a student, would so deliberately and needlessly make my life difficult in this manner."

Ten days after it was filed, the judge denied the university's motion. To this day, Marie is identified in the court file only by her initials.

For Marie, pursuing the lawsuit wasn't an easy decision. It meant reopening the wounds and exposing herself to questions from lawyers for Stevens, the fraternity, the university. "I just wanted him to say: 'I took advantage of her. I did something I shouldn't have,'" she says. The tipping point was when Becky Roe talked about her other clients suing the university, alleging rape by football players. "As soon as she told me that, I was like, 'Let's do it. I can't stand hearing about one more woman going through this.'"

In 2004, three opposing lawyers interviewed Marie. "They just kept throwing questions at me, and I was poised and answered them." Afterward, Roe looked at Marie and said: "You're fucking amazing. God, you did good. I'm so proud of you." Word came back quickly from the opposing counsel: We want to settle.

That spring, the parties convened outside of court—with Marie in one room, Stevens in another, the two never seeing each other, the lawyers shuttling from one room to the next. By the end of the day, a settlement agreement had been reached. The agreement was confidential, barring anyone from disclosing its terms. But in a letter to the university's lawyer—obtained under a public-disclosure request—Hunsinger described part of the deal. The agreement allowed the UW to be dismissed from the case, while Stevens and the fraternity would settle.

Hunsinger's letter made clear how much Stevens wanted to avoid being questioned about what happened that night. "One of the elements of the settlement is that Jerramy not be required to participate in any other litigation involving the UW, specifically the lawsuits filed by Becky regarding Eric Shyne and Roc Alexander. He does not want to be contacted by anyone, let alone deposed, or testify at trial."

That June, Hunsinger sent Roe a check to settle the case on

behalf of Stevens and the fraternity. The amount written on the check? Three hundred thousand dollars. The settlement came with no admission on Stevens's part. Stevens "was adamant that he wasn't guilty of the alleged crime," Hunsinger says. Settling the civil suit "was a business decision. Jerramy was a professional football player, and he came to the conclusion—with the advice of his agent—that it would be a good idea for him to get this behind him, for his career."

Stevens is looking good. Real good. Tony Gonzalez good. Shannon Sharpe good. Tight-end-of-the-future good.

Stevens, it turned out, wasn't that good. He looked tough enough. Sometimes, when he'd make a play, he'd hold his arms out and you could read the tattoo that started on his right bicep and finished on his left: "ALWAYS HATED . . . NEVER FADED." The problem was, he didn't make a lot of plays. He had twenty-six catches in 2002. Six in 2003. Thirty-one in 2004. He wasn't much of a blocker. He dropped a lot of passes. He ran his mouth and drew penalties.

In 2005 his career appeared to be on the upswing. He caught forty-five balls in the regular season, including five for touchdowns, and helped the Seahawks advance to the Super Bowl for the first time. But before the title game, Stevens talked about the Steelers' Jerome Bettis returning to his hometown of Detroit: "It's a heartwarming story and all that, but it will be a sad day when he leaves without that trophy." Pretty innocuous, really. But the Steelers' Joey Porter lit up: "He's too soft to say something like that." Porter called Stevens "a first-round bust who barely made some plays this season."

In the Super Bowl, Stevens dropped three passes. Or maybe it was four, maybe five. Different people count it different ways. Safe to say, he wasn't the second coming of Tony Gonzalez or Shannon Sharpe. Bettis and the Steelers walked off with the trophy.

In 2006, Seattle played Oakland on Monday Night Football. Stevens head-butted and taunted a Raiders safety, drawing a personal foul. He tried to knee a defensive end in the groin. (At least that's what the NFL concluded after reviewing tape.) He dropped a touchdown pass. Finally, he got kneed in the testicles. The Raider who did it was fined $25,000. Stevens was fined $15,000. Statistics aren't kept on such matters, but Stevens may be the only NFL player to take a knee to the groin—and get fined. *Must have groined the other player in the knee*, one sportswriter said. After the game, the Raiders' Warren Sapp called Stevens a "sissy" and a "punk." "This dude has been a piece of shit since he got in this league and it's never going to change about him." "You wouldn't want him on your ball club. You wouldn't want to be around him."

Stevens wasn't real popular with his neighbors, either.

His rookie year, Stevens bought a top-floor condominium in Bellevue, east of Seattle, a place with cherry floors, granite counters, floor-to-ceiling windows. Although Stevens earned more than $1 million a year, his neighbors had to sue to make him pay his monthly condo dues of $420. He coughed up only after his bank account was frozen. His neighbors complained of loud parties deep into the night. Of fireworks set off from his deck. Of finding used condoms. Of vomit raining down from above.

Beginning in May 2006, police received five calls in eight months about noise from Stevens's condo, or about neighbors' windows being sprayed with who knows what. Calls came in at 11:42 p.m., 2:19 a.m., 2:53 a.m., 3:28 a.m., 3:40 a.m. Typically, two officers responded. One time, five did. Stevens paid a $250 fine. A week later, he paid another.

In March 2006, Stevens was pulled over for speeding and found to be driving with a suspended license. Prosecutors said they would forgo charges if he enrolled in a re-licensing program. One month later, Stevens was caught again, driving with a suspended license. He was convicted of a misdemeanor and sentenced to ninety days in jail—all suspended, on condition that he stay out of trouble for a year.

The month after that, Stevens was the guest of honor at the Spring Fun Fair in his hometown of Lacey, Washington. He autographed footballs. Posed for pictures. Cradled a baby.

In the 2006 season, Stevens caught twenty-two balls in eleven games. He still wasn't that good. But his five-year contract was up—and he was still big. He was still strong. He was still fast and full of potential. As a free agent, Stevens figured to land a contract of $10 million and up. All he had to do was stay out of trouble.

On March 13, 2007, just after two in the morning, a police officer in Scottsdale, Arizona, watched a gray Chrysler sedan make a U-turn, then turn right on red when the sign said not to. The officer began to follow. Three times, the Chrysler drifted over the curb line and back. Its speed dipped to twenty-five miles per hour. Popped back up to forty-five. Dipped back to twenty-five. The officer needed to jam his brakes to avoid rear-ending the car. When the driver turned right without signaling, the officer pulled the car over and called for backup. The driver was Jerramy Stevens. His eyes were bloodshot, watery, half-closed. His breath smelled of alcohol. His speech was slow and slurred.

Have you been drinking tonight?

A little.

What's a little mean?

Four or five margaritas.

Getting out of the car, Stevens dropped his cell phone and wallet. Asked to do a walk-and-turn, he staggered off the sidewalk and into a driveway, where he stumbled and nearly fell. He refused to do any further field tests. He also refused to take a breath test. Police arrested Stevens for DUI. In the wee hours, officers obtained a warrant to draw Stevens's blood. Nearly three hours had passed since he was pulled over, precious time for his body to metabolize alcohol. Still, his blood-alcohol level registered at .204 percent— two and a half times the legal limit. That night, Stevens lost millions of dollars. He went from NFL free agent to criminal defendant—a player with undeniable potential coupled with renewed questions of character.

Stevens's latest misstep triggered a quick run of bad headlines for the NFL. Two days after Stevens was arrested in Arizona, a judge in Illinois sentenced Terry "Tank" Johnson to 120 days in jail. Johnson, a Chicago Bears lineman, violated probation by keeping, in his home, two assault rifles, a hunting rifle, a .44 magnum, and two other handguns. Also in his home? Five hundred rounds of ammunition and his daughters, ages three and one. As a Bear, Johnson was arrested three times in thirteen months. But a judge released Johnson from house arrest in January 2007—so that he could play in the Super Bowl. The Bears eventually lost patience with Johnson and released him. But the Dallas Cowboys picked him up. "I believe in giving people second chances," a member of the Cowboys organization said.

Four days after Johnson was sentenced to jail, the *Florida Times-Union* ran a front-page story describing how Khalif Barnes, a Jacksonville Jaguars lineman, had cried racism when a sheriff's deputy pulled him over. Barnes called the deputy a white "KKK devil that hates all colored people." He called Jacksonville a "fucking hick town." He claimed he was arrested because he was black. Or because he was a Jaguar. Or because the deputy had a quota to fill. The deputy pulled Barnes over because he was driving 101 in a 60 mile-per-hour zone. Barnes was also drunk. His blood-alcohol level was one and a half times the legal limit.

Stevens, Johnson, and Barnes had more in common than this streak of bad publicity. All three had been teammates at Washington. All three had been on that 2001 Rose Bowl team, Johnson and Barnes as redshirt freshmen. All three had played under Neuheisel and gotten to see, up close, how little players suffered when they went off the rails.

Seven weeks after his DUI arrest, Stevens landed with another team. The Tampa Bay Buccaneers signed him—on the cheap—

for $600,000, which was $5,000 above the minimum for a player with his experience. "He's a good player," said general manager Bruce Allen. "He is a big, powerful, speedy tight end. He has had some off-the-field issues that have hampered him a bit. We had a very serious talk with him today. I think Jerramy Stevens is a good young man." The Seahawks' coach, Mike Holmgren, gave Stevens a good recommendation, Allen said. "Sometimes," Allen said, "you have to give people a chance."

In Arizona, Stevens was convicted of extreme DUI, which carries a mandatory minimum of thirty days in jail. A judge instead gave Stevens twelve days and suspended the other eighteen. The DUI conviction appears to have violated the conditions of Stevens's suspended sentence in King County—the ninety-day sentence for driving with a suspended license. But nobody in Washington flagged it, sparing Stevens the threat of serving more jail time back home.

In 2008, Tampa Bay re-signed Stevens to another one-year contract. This came after the *Seattle Times* wrote a long story about Stevens's off-field troubles, including his settlement of Marie's lawsuit. The Bucs' decision sparked "a talk-radio firestorm," the *Orlando Sentinel* wrote. "Our phones haven't stopped ringing since the Bucs announced Stevens is back," the WADE program director told the *Tampa Tribune*. "I know we are the flagship station for the Bucs, but this community is in an uproar." Fans created Web sites such as firejerramystevens.com and nojerramystevens.blog spot.com. They sold "Anti-Jerramy Apparel," including T-shirts, hats, and a handbag proclaiming "Fire Jerramy Stevens!" They passed the *Seattle Times*' story around on blogs and fan forums.

Ultimately, the Bucs stood by Stevens and banned any links to the story on the team's official message boards. The Web site moderator wrote: "The article brings up, to paraphrase, forcing someone into sexual activities. That topic is not allowed here."

Marie: "I think it was hardest to watch how it affected my dad. That was probably the hardest. It crushed him. He became distant. He kind of pulled away."

Marie's brother: "Dad was just a basket case. He was just a total basket case. I mean, I have kids now. And I know my dad thinks the same thing. We've never talked about this, ever. But I know as a parent, you feel that your sole responsibility in life is to protect your kids. I'm sure he feels he let her down."

Marie's mother: "They were very, very close, and he somehow feels he should have protected her. And I know, he told me, he has a lot of guilt. And I said, 'You shouldn't. We raised her right. We did everything we could, every ounce of love we had, we gave to her. And it's not your fault.' But there is part of him that won't be the same."

Maggie couldn't forgive herself for what happened that night—for not walking Marie into the sorority, for leaving Marie with other friends in the alley behind Pi Beta Phi. For a year, Maggie received counseling. She began taking antidepressants.

Maggie: "I was just dwelling on it and thinking about it all the time. Just thinking about what I could have done differently. What could have made it not happen.

"We've been very close since the first grade. She was part of our family, and I was part of hers. We went to elementary, middle, and high school together. She would come on family vacations with us, for the summers, and when my parents were away, I would stay at her place. It's almost even better than a sister relationship. What she feels, I feel I'm connected to. Maybe that's why it affected me the way that it did.

"To this day, I still blame myself. I should have walked her inside, up to her bed. And I know I can't do that to myself. But that's the big remorse, and it's been hard for me."

Marie's mother: "I know Maggie's had a terrible time. I talked to her, and I said, 'Sweetheart, you didn't do anything wrong. You were all young. If you have any guilt, just take a big hole and bury it. Because my daughter loves you, I love you, and there's no reason to hold any guilt anymore.'"

Like Marie, Maggie grew up cheering for the Huskies. Her parents met at the UW while freshmen. Her father and her father's father worked on the Husky scoreboard—her father kept the time, her grandfather the score. Her grandmother worked in the ticket office. But in 2001, Maggie refused to watch the Rose Bowl. "No. And I was pissed. And I was bitter that they won, that they were successful. It was not a good feeling at all."

A year or two after the Rose Bowl, Marie and Maggie were at the Rock Bottom brewery in Bellevue when they saw Stevens at another table.

Maggie: "I think there was a girl sitting with him, and Wilbur was there. And we decided to leave. And I don't know what got into me, I went over to him and told him that he was an asshole, and then I picked up his beer and threw it in his face. And he just sat there. He didn't do anything. And then I walked out. . . . It wasn't something that I thought about, it's not something I would normally do. I'm not a confrontational person, or anything like that. I just think that emotions were building up."

Marie's brother remembers sitting at Harborview that night, waiting to see his little sister. "The toughest part was just waiting. It seemed like forever."

"And how do you have a conversation with your sister about something like that? Especially when she doesn't know, she doesn't have a lot of answers. And you don't know what to say, or what the right thing is to say."

Marie asked her brother not to say anything to anybody. "She doesn't ask you for much, and out of respect, if she does ask, you honor that. I mean, it's been nine years and my sister and I have never spoken a word about it, in nine years. The only thing I ever said to her was, 'I believe you, and I'll be there for you.' That's the only thing I ever said.

"We never told my grandfather, because my grandfather paid for my sister's first year of college, and we worried about him feeling guilty. It was a gift.

"My wife didn't even know for the first five years.

"You contemplate, 'What can I do about it?' I'm not going to risk going to jail for the rest of my life for doing something stupid. I don't know if you can relate to this, but day in and day out, I work around a lot of people, and you are hearing people talk about this. The media coverage. And they are talking about it. During the whole event, people are talking about it. And they are saying, 'Oh, it's just some groupie, claiming to get raped.' And people I worked with were saying things like this."

In 2001, Marie's brother was in a restaurant. It was a Red Robin, or some chain joint like that. At the time, Stevens was back in the news for running his pickup into a retirement home. Some guys at a nearby table were talking about Stevens, and his history, and the allegation of rape the year before, and one of them said something like, "Another groupie got what she deserved."

"I grabbed him by the throat and lifted him up off the floor. I lifted him up out of his chair. I told him, 'You better shut your mouth right now. You don't know what you're talking about.' And he just looked at me, like, 'What are you doing?' And two of my buddies said, 'We've got to go, we've got to go.' And we left.

"You have so much rage build up inside you that you have to find a way to let that out."

Marie's roommate: "I first met Jerramy at a party at the UW. It is so hard for me to even think of ever being attracted to him. He was quiet and soft-spoken when I met him. But, obviously, there was a lot more to him than I knew about.

"The reason why I left the UW was partly because of the incident with Marie. The school did not seem the same afterwards. It was such an awful time. The response to Marie's situation was so crazy. It was very hard to see how differently people were towards her afterwards. Girls were all very sweet, at least the ones who knew her. But the football players all looked at her as a horrible person who made false accusations, instead of a victim.

"The incident brought a very tight bond between Marie and me. We were inseparable for many years afterwards. I don't ever regret leaving the U, it was the best decision for me. The incident did keep me from easily trusting anyone, especially men. It was harder for me to feel safe when I was out at the U at night."

The woman who received the May 8, 2000, e-mail from Stevens—the one that came on sweet and turned—says: "It's an e-mail that, to this day, still chokes me up. It was a horrible e-mail to receive."

After graduating, she moved to another state. She has returned to Seattle only twice. "Here's the deal. Obviously, Jerramy is a high-profile athlete. . . . I think he carries hostility and anger toward me for even having brought the e-mail to light. I'm definitely cautious of what I do when I go to Seattle. I'm worried about running into him. I think it would be a bad thing if I ran into him."

Nine years passed before she learned what Spencer Marona told police, before she learned that he had called her "a typical football groupie."

"Well, that's funny, because I only slept with him and Jerramy," she says. "I lost my virginity to Spencer."

Stevens's e-mail changed her, she says. "I do not approach things with the same assumption that people will be nice. I'm more aware of people's hidden ambitions, or hidden self."

Marie's mother: "I often wonder, nine years later, if he regrets what he did . . . if he personally regrets what he did.

"I think the worst thing was, the look in her eyes. I'll never forget that look, as long as I live. It honestly haunts me."

One night, Marie and her family ran into Spencer Marona at a Benihana restaurant in Seattle. "Her face went white, absolutely white," Marie's mother says of her daughter. "It was her twenty-first birthday. And Spencer was at the table, and it just ruined it. She went into the bathroom and started crying. And I said, 'You walk back in there with your head up high.'

"We had season tickets, my husband's parents had season tickets. And I'll never set foot in there again. I get the offers through the mail, and I just rip 'em up.

"You know, it's funny, because even to this day, I see her stare off into the distance, and I know she's someplace else. And she wasn't like that before this happened. So she kind of goes off, sometimes, and I know what she's thinking about. When you're a mom, and you have their blood flowing through your body, you know."

Marie finished her economics degree at the University of Washington and now holds a good job. "I had bigger hopes for myself than to let one person take it away from me. I couldn't let him take any more from me.

"When I've dated, it's always found its way in there. It interrupts. I'm so scared to tell people, in case they think I'm tainted, or whatever. That part is hard. It's not their business to know. But then they can't know who I am until I tell them.

"Now I second-guess people. It still affects me to this day. It was like my life changed in a minute.

"The day he left the Seahawks was the best day ever. I finally could go out and not worry about running into him. You know, when he was here, every time I would hear his name on the news, it would make me cringe. I never went to another Seahawks game while he was playing. People would say, 'You've never been to a Seahawks game!' and I would make something up, say that I didn't like football.

"It will always be with me. I try to learn from it, rather than let it get me down. My biggest thing is, I want other girls to be aware. That's the number one reason I'm here, because it's no fun to rehash. I hope that someday, when I can control my emotions more, that I can go into sororities, and speak to the girls, and say, 'This is me, and I'm exactly like you.'"

When the Game's Over

Jeremiah Pharms never came back for his dogs. When Paul Coleman, the Lynnwood cop, impounded two of the pit bulls in late December, that left two behind. Not long after, one of those two jumped the fence and was taken away. That left one holdout, a young male. For a month that dog stayed in Pharms's backyard, alone. Police couldn't remove him until Pharms's lease expired. The neighbor, Grace Lundeen, continued feeding the dog. Pharms's landlord dropped by to help. So did Coleman. The dog's adoptive caretakers even came up with a name for the terrier: Jack.

Coleman recommended that Pharms be charged with cruelty to animals, for abandoning the dogs. The Lynnwood prosecutor took a pass. Instead, Pharms faced more of the same—another misdemeanor charge of having too many animals.

One day, Coleman went to the house and discovered Pharms's wife, Franquell, loading furniture into a U-Haul truck. He told her about the charge against Jeremiah and gave her the court date. Franquell said Jeremiah would return—and that she hoped the judge was a Huskies fan.

At the end of January, Jack was impounded. Police described him as "very friendly," so his adoption prospects looked good. The landlord found dog shit all through the house. Garbage, too. And an unpaid utility bill of $324. "It was a mess," he says. The landlord estimated the damage to his place at $3,500. He contacted the uw's athletic department in hopes of garnishing Pharms's scholarship checks. But there were no more checks to be had.

Pharms was finished with school. For four and a half years he had struggled to remain eligible. Now, he was leaving the uw without a degree. After the Rose Bowl, Pharms stayed in California to get ready for the NFL draft.

In the spring of 2001, the Cleveland Browns' new head coach, Butch Davis, consulted Neuheisel about Pharms. Neuheisel's report glowed. A few days later, on April 22, the Browns selected Pharms in the draft's fifth round. The Browns portrayed Pharms as a character pick—a family man, responsible and mature. The media went along. The *Cleveland Plain Dealer*: "While his Washington teammates were out socializing on Friday and Saturday nights, Jeremiah Pharms was home changing diapers." The *Akron Beacon Journal*: "The Browns won't have to spend too much time teaching Jeremiah Pharms about commitment and maturity. Pharms . . . knows a little bit about those values. That comes from being married and having three children before his 23rd birthday."

Back in Seattle, Mike Lang, the prosecutor, read the coverage and cringed. Lang happened to be from Cleveland, which meant, of course, that he was a Browns fan. He knew his team had just stepped in it. "I said, 'If you only knew.' That's what I thought, 'If you only knew.'"

Pharms's agent figured his client was in position to sign a three-year contract worth $1 million, with a signing bonus of $140,000. But before Pharms could sign, his past took him down. In May 2001 he was finally charged with robbery for what happened that night in Sullivan's apartment. The filing came fourteen months after Sullivan was shot. Ten months after Pharms's fingerprint was identified. Eight months after the first DNA results came back.

Detectives Mudd and Magan flew to Sacramento to help make the arrest. Police figured it would be safer to have Pharms in the open—and Magan couldn't resist a ruse. Pretending to be a producer from KJR, a Seattle sports radio station, Magan called Pharms and asked if he could show up somewhere for an interview. Sure, Pharms said. Police busted him after he came outside. "The only thing he asked for was his mother and his agent," Magan says. "I felt bad for him. You're watching a guy's livelihood and career being flushed."

Four weeks later, the Browns released Pharms. Neuheisel told reporters that he knew nothing about the investigation. "I've been accused of knowing and not divulging, and I can categorically say that's false. I can only apologize and say that I was in the same company as everyone else who did not know, including the Cleveland Browns."

Jeffery Robinson, one of Seattle's most respected lawyers, represented Pharms. A Harvard Law graduate, Robinson had a polite demeanor and a soft voice, but he was about the last defense attorney any prosecutor wanted to see across the courtroom. When a Washington State Supreme Court justice was charged with DUI, she hired Robinson. She knew what everyone knew. "Jeff Robinson is, in my view, the best criminal defense lawyer in town," says Steve Fogg, who was prosecuting Pharms with Lang. "If you have Jeff Robinson on your side, and a remotely plausible defense, you have a chance of walking out of court a free man."

In court documents, prosecutors called the evidence against Pharms "overwhelming." But they cut a plea deal that sliced his sentence to a fraction of the nearly twenty years he could have faced. They didn't charge Pharms with attempted murder. They didn't charge him with first-degree assault. And on the robbery charge that they did file, they dropped a firearms enhancement that could have added five years to his sentence.

Robinson maintained that Pharms hadn't gone to Sullivan's apartment with a gun. He said the gun was Sullivan's, and that the two had argued, and that the gun went off. Pharms entered an Alford plea to the robbery charge. He didn't admit guilt, but acknowledged there was enough evidence to convict him. The plea amounts to a distinction without a difference; under the law, a conviction is a conviction. During a pre-sentence interview, Pharms told a corrections officer: "I don't think I should go to prison, but the Lord puts you in trials and tribulations throughout your life. I want to be a great person, professionally and personally. In order to see the top, sometimes you have to see the bottom."

In January 2002 a King County judge sentenced Pharms to

three years and five months in prison. "It's difficult to imagine a more serious robbery without it becoming an attempted-murder conviction," she said.

In prison, Pharms lifted weights and played dominoes. He worked as a janitor and groundskeeper. He completed a twelve-step program to improve moral reasoning. The Department of Corrections had Pharms fill out a questionnaire reflecting upon his life. The title was: "Rearview Mirror . . . A Thinking Report."

> I have accomplished many things in my life. But I am not proud because my family is struggling because everyone once depended on me and I let them down. And since a young boy the only thing I ever wanted to do is take care of my family. . . . Things started going bad for me when I began to sacrifice the well-being of my family by smoking marijuana. . . . What got me to this point in my life is not being able to deal properly with my emotions such as anger, pain, sadness and grief. Always feeling like I needed to smoke to deal with everything when in reality things were only getting worse. . . . I was two days away from being a millionaire and fulfilling a goal and dream to take care of my family for generations. And it was taken away because of a mistake.

Pharms had never gotten to know his father. He had vowed to do better with his own kids—and there were five of them now. "It kills me every day that I'm not with them," he wrote.

In prison, Pharms held tight to his goal of playing in the NFL. He wrote a letter to the *Post-Intelligencer*, saying: "I plan on turning my body into a machine. I am treating my time as a twenty-nine month long training camp." He signed the letter: "Jeremiah Pharms, #4, 2001 Rose Bowl champs."

Ted Miller, the sportswriter who covered Husky football for the *Post-Intelligencer*, interviewed Pharms in prison and wrote a long piece about him in January 2004. Pharms told Miller he had converted to Islam and was rebuilding his spirit and mind. He declined to discuss details of what happened inside Sullivan's apartment. But Miller's story recounted that night and asked a series of questions challenging the prosecution's case. "Why would he, a year away from a shot at the NFL, decide to rob a drug dealer at gunpoint, particularly one who likely would recognize him, mask or not? . . . How could his accomplice escape identification?" Miller's story described Sullivan's criminal history and posited: "Isn't it conceivable that a drug dealer with such a record would be a more likely person to own a gun than a UW football player with a generally clean record?"

The *Post-Intelligencer* story steamed Lang and Fogg, the two prosecutors. They drafted a letter to the newspaper's editor, but elected not to send it. "Mr. Miller's article implies that the system somehow allowed an innocent man to go to prison for a crime he did not commit. We want to be very clear about this: Mr. Pharms was guilty of robbing and shooting his victim." They posed a different question: Why would an NFL draftee—poised to sign a big contract, represented by "the best criminal defense team in King County"—plead guilty to a Class A felony, thereby incurring a lengthy prison sentence? "As it stands, Mr. Pharms is a lucky man; lucky that his victim didn't die, lucky that his victim wasn't permanently disabled, lucky we had mercy on him."

While serving his sentence, Pharms became eligible for work release. His work was football—playing for the Eastside Hawks, a semi-pro team in Everett. Twice he got in trouble for drinking with the team; one of those times he returned to his bunk "very drunk," prison records say.

In June 2004, Pharms was released from prison. He went on the state's equivalent of parole—subject to drug testing, restricted from leaving the state. Unable to join his wife and kids in Sacramento, Pharms moved in with a friend south of Seattle. Month after month, his urinalysis samples turned up dirty for marijuana. He was ordered into a drug-treatment program in the fall of 2004. But one month later he was kicked out for missing too many group sessions.

The Hawks belonged to the North American Football League—alongside the South Ogden Rhino-Raiders, the Bastrop County

Bulldogs, the Cedar Valley Vikings. In November 2004 the Hawks made it to the championship. Playing in Florida, they beat the Central Penn Piranha, finishing the season undefeated. For Pharms, the celebration was short-lived. He got in trouble for leaving the state without permission.

In 2005, Pharms played again for the Hawks—now the Everett Hawks, part of the National Indoor Football League. When a probation officer refused to let Pharms cross the state line for road games, Pharms despaired. "Football is my life," he said.

That June, Pharms was released from parole, meaning he could go anywhere he wanted—to be with his family in California, to be with his team on the road. Nine days later, the Hawks were scheduled to play a night game at home. The morning of the game, at a little after two, a state trooper pointed a speed gun at northbound traffic on Interstate 5. A Chevy Suburban busted past, doing eighty-six in a sixty. Because the road was wet, the trooper struggled to catch up. He called for help from another trooper up ahead.

The driver of the Suburban was Jeremiah Pharms. His eyes were watery and his breath smelled of alcohol. His blood-alcohol level was one and a half times the legal limit. The trooper handcuffed Pharms and took him in. Pharms was cooperative throughout. The trooper wrote: "Pharms offered to give me free tickets to the Everett Hawks football game, and I advised him that I appreciated the offer but I could not accept."

Charged with DUI, Pharms failed to appear in court. A judge issued a warrant for his arrest—a warrant that would remain in effect for years to come.

Pharms left the state and reunited with his family in California. Then he landed a spot with the New York Dragons in the Arena Football League. In August 2006, Ted Miller of the *Post-Intelligencer* wrote again about Pharms, after Franquell called to say how well her husband was doing. Miller, needing something to write about, figured this would make for an easy column. He wrote a feel-good piece about Pharms coaching his son's peewee league football team, about his enduring marriage to Franquell, about his determination to make the NFL.

He doesn't expect to become a star. He just wants his moment, or as he says, "just one NFL kickoff." Yet here's the most important part, the best good news. Pharms made a mess of his life but he cleaned it up and now he and those around him are happy and optimistic.

Notified that Pharms had an arrest warrant out for skipping on a DUI charge, the paper did a never-mind. "Pharms' journey toward redemption hasn't been as smooth as it was reported in Tuesday's P-I," Miller wrote. This addendum also noted that Pharms had paid only $50 of the $13,900 he owed in restitution from the robbery case. "I should have run his name," Miller says.

A year later, in August 2007, Pharms was talking to Franquell on the telephone. He was drinking. He became angry. He took a shotgun and fired it at the cell phone. The blast shattered the living room's glass door. At the time, four of Pharms's children were in the house, in other rooms. The oldest was ten, the youngest five.

Pharms was charged in Sacramento with two felonies: illegal possession of a firearm by a convicted felon, and discharging a firearm in a grossly negligent manner that could harm or kill. He pleaded guilty to the former charge; in February 2008, a judge sentenced him to two years and eight months in prison. "It was kind of a dumb case in a way—it was really juvenile what he did," the lead detective says. "To put your family in danger for something like that is really ridiculous."

A month after the Rose Bowl, Curtis Williams was moved from a medical center and into his brother David's home in central California. After playing football at Fresno State, David had parlayed his education into a management position at a medical-waste company. David had always been there for Curtis. He had taken Curtis in during high school, after their father had suffered a debilitating heart attack. David had been at the Stanford game when Curtis was injured. He went to the hospital afterward—and stayed. From the accident on, only one day passed when David wasn't with Curtis. His brother needed him, and David answered.

Before the injury, Curtis had been dating a woman named April. She would come to California and see him from time to time. His daughter, Kymberly, visited for two weeks in the summer of 2001. She was six. They ate together in his room and watched movies. Before he was paralyzed, Curtis called Kymberly twice a week. Now the calls tapered off to maybe once a month.

David would sit with Curtis and talk. "With anybody who gets injured, there's always that question. Why me? We would talk about that a little bit. . . . He missed seeing Kymberly. He missed April. . . . Sometimes I'd walk into the room, and he was crying. I'm sure he was thinking about what could have been. . . . Even though it hurt, he still kept a positive attitude about stuff. At least he'd try and work with it, and get up and get ready and do whatever he had to do each day. That's what I'm most proud of him for doing."

Curtis had no recollection of the play that left him paralyzed. His memories stopped at halftime of the Stanford game, and picked back up in the hospital.

A device was implanted in Curtis's chest to let him breathe for up to twelve hours without a respirator. In Seattle, the Curtis Williams Fund raised $400,000 to help with his care, with donations coming in even after his name began to fade from the sports pages. One fund-raising dinner generated $20,000; eight months later, a second dinner raised $30,000. Old teammates pitched in. Jerramy Stevens hosted a bowling tournament to raise money.

In February 2001, Blaine Newnham, the *Seattle Times* sports columnist, encouraged the UW to divert some of the money to Williams's child-support obligations. It was the decent thing to do, he wrote. But then Newnham went further. He recounted talking to Williams before the 2000 season, and asking why he had begun playing so well.

He focused on the impact of two people. Rick Neuheisel, who had come into his life and given him a chance to play, and Michelle Williams, who was now out of his life and had given him a chance to breathe.

Michelle Williams called The Seattle Times often to complain about Curtis and a university that would allow him to stay on scholarship even though she said he was abusive.

Friends of Curtis said Michelle was more abusive than he. It was a bad marriage.

Newnham's column said nothing of how Curtis had been charged, time and again, with assaulting Michelle. It said nothing of how Curtis had pleaded guilty to a felony and served two and a half months in jail. When Michelle read Newnham's column, she couldn't believe it. "A lot was written about what a great football player he was. With the other issues it was like, 'Don't ask, don't tell. Don't look, don't see.'"

There were still two assault charges pending against Williams, both dating from 1996. In September 2001, prosecutors dropped the first. A day later, they dropped the second. What purpose would have been served pursuing them now?

Neuheisel made sure that Williams remained part of Washington's football program. During the 2001 season, Williams sometimes called during team meetings to voice words of encouragement. The players gathered around and listened on speakerphone.

Williams scheduled a trip to return to Seattle in April 2002. He hadn't been there since the team departed for the Stanford game. About a week before leaving, his body temperature plunged. He became incoherent. David suggested the trip be postponed, but Curtis was determined to go. "He really wanted to get back, to see April and everybody," David says. "I think he wanted to say good-bye—or not to worry about him."

He was no longer the eighteen-year-old who arrived on campus with the responsibilities of a man twice his age, unprepared to shoulder them. The records in all those files—the police files, court files, prison files, UW files—do not flatter Williams. But people who knew him say he had changed even before that collision on the 6-yard line. "He had turned into a damn good person—and this is not putting a halo on him after he became a damn paraplegic," Mike Hunsinger says. "I really liked him."

Al Black, a sociology professor, told the *Seattle Times*: "In the beginning, he was . . . one of the more difficult kids. He came in and saw his life only in terms of football. The academic thing was not something he was into. I stepped on him all the time, and I'm not even sure Curtis liked me for most of the time. But when Neuheisel came in and Curtis started playing, he changed. Not only in terms of academics, but he wanted to be seen as an accomplished individual in all areas. He started asking himself all the time, 'Is this something that's going to allow me to be seen that way?' . . . He began to think of himself as a man and not just an athlete."

In Seattle, Williams was wheeled out for the ceremonial first pitch at a Mariners game. The crowd gave him a standing ovation. He reunited with teammates at the spring football game. He met with UW staff and made plans to complete his degree by taking correspondence courses. He attended a fund-raising dinner and told the people there: Touch me. Laugh with me. Don't be afraid. "I have to keep going on," Williams told one reporter. "But sometimes I've got to mourn the past."

Williams returned home at the end of April. A week later, the morning nurse arrived to find his body cold. Williams had died in the quiet of the night, sometime between midnight and dawn. His body shut down two days after his twenty-fourth birthday—and eighteen months after he crumpled on the football field.

Neuheisel was in Spokane when he learned of Williams's death. "I will always admire Curtis for his tremendous courage and for inspiring all of us to learn to persevere in tough times," Neuheisel said. "We always said that he was a warrior on the field. What we learned was that he was a warrior in life."

At Williams's funeral, some six hundred people filed into a Fresno church only blocks from the high school where he once played. The mourners included more than thirty current or former UW football players—Marques Tuiasosopo, Anthony Kelley, Jerramy Stevens, Anthony Vontoure—and a half-dozen coaches. A Husky helmet and pictures of Williams in uniform flanked the altar. Purple and gold flowers covered the casket. Inside the church, a video played of Williams landing one big hit after another.

Michelle and Kymberly attended the service. They were asked to sit behind Neuheisel and Hedges. Kymberly sent flowers, with a ribbon that said "Beloved" on one side and "Daddy" on the other. Her grandmother asked that the flowers be placed atop the casket. They were instead placed in the reception hall, next to the fried chicken.

At a graveside service afterward, Willie Hurst left two dog tags with Williams's body. Kelley left two copper bracelets from South Africa. Neuheisel took Williams's No. 25 jersey from atop the casket and presented it to Williams's parents.

Other gestures followed in the weeks and months and years to come. Hakim Akbar tattooed his left arm: RIP CW 25, next to an angel with wings. The UW painted Williams's number on the sidelines at Husky Stadium and awarded Williams a posthumous degree. The money raised for Williams's care was converted to scholarships and a $125,000 trust fund for his daughter.

In Alaska, Kymberly became a straight-A student. Her smile reminds her mother of Curtis. Not long ago, Kymberly said she couldn't remember what her father's voice sounded like. For years, Michelle had kept an old answering machine with Curtis's voice on it. But then she threw it away. "I would give anything for things to be different today," Michelle says. "For him not to be hurt. For him to be alive. For him to take part in the special things that Kymberly is doing. For him to be a part of her life. Like teaching her how to drive, or questioning the first guy who dated her."

One of Curtis's older brothers, J.D., played in the NFL for seven years. He told a reporter after Curtis's death: "It's a game that's given me everything, and it's taken everything away from him. I was with Curtis in the hospital when he actually woke up, and he asked, 'Why me?' But after awhile he got comfortable with his situation, and he said instead, 'Why not me?'" In 2006, J.D. became an assistant football coach at the University of Washington.

Curtis's younger brother, Paul, was a junior in high school when Curtis was paralyzed. At first, Paul wanted to give up football—but a conversation with Curtis changed his mind. "He told me he wanted to watch me play," Paul told a reporter. "I've been playing ever since, trying to make him proud." In 2007, Paul joined the NFL as a wide receiver with the Tennessee Titans.

Within a year of Curtis's death, both of his parents died. But not long after, his sister Donna had a little boy. She named him Curtis.

On May 31, 2002—eighteen days after Curtis Williams's funeral—Anthony Vontoure became delirious and began to hallucinate. In a Sacramento apartment, four friends tried to calm him. They tried holding his arms. They tried sitting on him. But Vontoure lashed out, punching, twisting, biting, screaming. He yelled things like: "I see green men with masks. They're coming to kill me."

One of the friends, Eldridge Walker, had known Vontoure for three years. Although Vontoure had said he was bipolar, Walker had never seen him take any medication. And Walker had never seen him flip out like this. At 3:46 a.m., Walker called 911.

For fifteen months, Vontoure had been adrift. In February 2001, a month after the Rose Bowl, Neuheisel announced that Vontoure had been dismissed from the team. Vontoure complained about the way that sounded. He told a reporter that he had reached an understanding with the coaches during the 2000 season that it would be his last.

When Vontoure left the UW, he was thirty-five credits shy of his bachelor's degree. After four years of school, he was nowhere close to graduating. He finished with a GPA of 2.00—just enough to stay eligible, down to the decimal point.

He signed up to play for Portland State, a Division I-AA school where he scrimmaged a couple of times and seemed comfortable enough. "And then September 11 happened," says Nigel Burton, an assistant coach. "Something triggered in him, and football was not as important as it had been." Vontoure became obsessed with the terrorist strikes. Nothing else mattered. He watched the coverage day and night. He dropped out of Portland State and eventually moved back to California.

When he attended Curtis Williams's funeral, Vontoure appeared devastated. "He was awful fond of Curtis," says Abner Thomas, Vontoure's mentor at the UW. "The team members don't know how deeply he cared about teammates. That was almost a religion to him."

Vontoure visited Seattle afterward and saw Anthony Kelley. He told Kelley he was like family. He told Kelley that he loved him. "I could see in his eyes that he was crying out to me for help, but really, he didn't know how to articulate that," Kelley says. "I just hugged him, let him know that, 'Whatever you need man, just don't hesitate to ask.'"

When Walker called 911 in Sacramento, three deputies responded. The call went out as a "5150"—alerting them that Vontoure might have mental problems. The officers assumed they would take him to a nearby mental-health hospital. The deputies handcuffed Vontoure and walked him outside. "He was yelling, 'Hey, everyone, look, they're trying to shoot me in the head,'" one officer recalled. "We were telling him, 'Anthony, we are not going to shoot you.'" When the deputies tried to pat Vontoure down for weapons, his pants fell, exposing him. They tried to pull his pants up and get him into the squad car. But Vontoure, drenched in sweat, began to struggle. Two deputies held onto his legs, while a third held his upper body. Vontoure's strength surprised them. The deputies holding onto his legs crashed into each other. "I was literally being thrown from side to side," one later wrote. A deputy radioed for backup.

For a moment, Vontoure seemed to calm down. On his knees, he said: "Okay, okay, let me pray, let me pray." For a few seconds, the deputies let him. But when they tried to get him into the car, the struggle resumed. Two more deputies arrived, bringing the number of officers to five. Still, that wasn't enough. A deputy radioed in. *We need leg shackles*. More deputies arrived.

With several deputies holding him down, Vontoure stopped struggling. One deputy stood up and said: Hey, this guy doesn't look so good. The officers rolled Vontoure over and checked for a pulse. There was none. They tried CPR and called for medics.

As medics attempted to resuscitate Vontoure, one deputy talked to Walker, the friend who had made the 911 call. Vontoure "had a look in his eye tonight," Walker told the deputy. It had just hit him that he wasn't going to make the NFL. Walker even feared that Vontoure might kill himself: "Because football is all he's got. That's all he knows how to do."

Less than an hour later, Vontoure was declared dead. He was twenty-two.

A detective looked inside Vontoure's blue Oldsmobile. On the dash he found a Huskies magazine from October 2000, the team's Rose Bowl year. In the apartment, the detective found a blanket and pillows, a backpack, a tennis ball and empty liquor bottles. A jacket hung over a chair. The detective described it: "Over the right chest is the number 23 in purple. Over the left chest is a 'W' with the word 'football' in purple embroidery."

At the funeral, held a week later, Vontoure's high school coach, Bob Ladouceur, spoke of Vontoure's big brown eyes, his beautiful smile, his gentle spirit, his knack for the big play, his infectious laugh. "I often heard it ringing throughout the locker room, all the way up to the coach's office. I would think to myself, 'There goes Anthony, he's on a roll.'" Ladouceur spoke of Vontoure's social conscience and his empathy—the suffering he absorbed over the deaths of his brother Chris and his teammate Curtis, his visceral reaction to 9/11. "Just as Anthony shared in others' joy, he shouldered others' pain—and he did this to a fault. Whether this was good or bad, I don't care, it was this quality I loved most about him."

Vontoure's father, Mike, took aim at the UW while remembering his son. "In high school, he played football for the love of the game, where the coaches and players were one family. Beyond high school, the family model for football dissolved." Mike Vontoure spoke of how his son had stuck by a friend that year when everyone else seemed to have abandoned him—an apparent reference to Jeremiah Pharms. Before Pharms was sentenced for robbery, Vontoure had written a letter to the court, saying how much he respected and admired his former teammate.

Anthony Kelley didn't attend Vontoure's funeral. "I couldn't afford to pay for a ticket," he says. The UW had flown all kinds of players to Curtis Williams's funeral. But not so for Vontoure's. "If they offered, I would have gone, but they didn't offer," Kelley says.

To Kelley's mind, the university's muted response to Vontoure's death spoke volumes. "Yes, he had his problems. But you sure didn't have too many issues with him when he was leaping across the field with one arm making interceptions and returning them for touchdowns. You can't be conditional in your support for players. That's the big thing. Being conditional in your support is what causes problems, it's what causes people to look back at their experience at the university, at whatever university they were at, and say, 'They weren't there for me. They were there just to use me.'"

The Sacramento County coroner concluded that Vontoure died from a sudden heart attack, triggered by "excited delirium" and "acute cocaine intoxication." In 2003, Vontoure's parents sued the county. They claimed the deputies used excessive force and asphyxiated their son. The lawsuit was settled two years later, for $20,000. The agreement called for the money to be given to De La Salle High School in order to create a scholarship in the Vontoure family name.

The winning streak that obsessed Vontoure kept getting longer. De La Salle's unbeaten string stretched to 126 games, to 138, to 150. Danny Ladouceur, the coach's son, became a wide receiver on the team. When Danny was younger, the Ladouceurs and

Vontoures lived near each other. Danny idolized Anthony. "He actually gave me a bicycle that got me into BMX racing," Danny says. Anthony was seven years older than Danny, but the two rode bikes together, played video games, listened to music. Danny saw all the sides of Anthony—generous, compassionate, angry, aggressive. At Anthony's funeral, Danny received permission from Anthony's family to wear No. 23—the same number Chris Vontoure wore, the same number Anthony wore. "It was really weird," Danny says. The first time he wore that jersey—"the very, very first play," he says—Danny returned a kickoff 89 yards for a touchdown. And Anthony's mom was there, watching.

On September 4, 2004, De La Salle traveled to Bellevue, just east of Seattle, to play Washington's best high school football team. It was Danny's senior season. Bellevue High School dismantled De La Salle 39–20—without throwing a single pass, without ever punting. A fourteen-year-old quarterback executed Bellevue's wing-T offense to near perfection.

The streak ended at 151 games. De La Salle's last loss had been in 1991. But this was a program that had not forgotten how to lose. "Act like gentlemen," Bob Ladouceur told his players. And they did. They offered no excuses. They congratulated Bellevue. They queued up and shook hands, the line so long it spanned the field. The De La Salle coaches said afterward: Remember. This is a game. That's all it is. This is a game.

Leather lungs together
With a Rah! Rah! Rah!
And o'er the land
Our loyal band
Will sing the glory
Of Washington forever.

The closing of "Bow Down to Washington"

Epilogue *All about the Wins*

To Washington fans, the team's dramatic run to the Rose Bowl promised the beginning of a new era. For years to come, blue-chip recruits would flock to Seattle. For years to come, the Huskies would compete for national championships. But the Rose Bowl season proved to be the beginning of the end. That *mystical, magical* season exposed a community's collective complicity and twisted values. That *mystical, magical* season dissolved into decline and ruin.

If winning is everything, what are we left with? Barbara Hedges was left with a sense of betrayal. After the Rose Bowl, she had worked so hard to keep her coach. She had checked around and discovered that in the salary sweepstakes, Neuheisel was falling behind. Florida's coach was pulling in $2.1 million a year. Oklahoma's was pulling in $2 million. Hell, even the coach at Minnesota—*Minnesota*—was making $1.3 million. This wouldn't do. Hedges fought to get her coach a big raise. She wrote the university's president, Richard McCormick: "As we both know, Rick Neuheisel is an exceptional person and coach. One only needs to see him out in the community to realize how valuable he is to the University."

The university jacked up Neuheisel's pay to $1.46 million a year, with incentives. His team responded with an 8-4 season. The next year, the UW reworked his contract again, giving him a $1.5 million loan that he wouldn't have to repay if he stayed long enough. The team went 7-6.

In 2003, Neuheisel was preparing for his fifth season at the UW when he got a call from Terry Donahue, the San Francisco 49ers' general manager. Would you be interested in coaching the 49ers?

Donahue asked. Neuheisel balked. So Donahue threw out a number: $2.25 million a year. Can't do it; I like my job, Neuheisel said. What if we went up? Donahue said. Say, $2.7 million? Neuheisel repeated the number out loud. His wife was in the room. Her eyes got big. I don't think I can do it, Neuheisel said. How about $3 million? Donahue said. Neuheisel flew down for an interview.

The 49ers didn't want the interview made public. Neither did Neuheisel. When the meeting wrapped up, Neuheisel expected to get a charter flight home. Instead, he was dropped at the airport, to fly commercial. In the gate area, he couldn't resist. He took out his cell phone. He called his mom and told her he had just interviewed with the 49ers. "It went well," he said. Six feet away from Neuheisel—just sitting there, listening—was John Levesque, a sports columnist for the *Seattle Post-Intelligencer*. Levesque was coming off vacation and happened to be taking the same flight home.

Back in Seattle, Neuheisel denied interviewing for the job. *I wasn't talking to the 49ers. I was playing golf with some buddies.* He went on the radio and lied. He issued a written statement and lied. He talked to newspaper reporters and lied. Levesque, after waiting a day, wrote what he had heard in the airport, and Neuheisel was busted. He admitted lying. He apologized for lying. He was put on notice by the university: No more lying. The 49ers never offered Neuheisel the job. Four months later, Neuheisel lied again.

NCAA investigators, having received an anonymous tip, asked Neuheisel if he had participated in a couple of high-stakes college basketball pools. All I did was watch, Neuheisel said. Hedges was in the room with Neuheisel and the investigators, her head swimming, her world falling apart. Questioned again later the same day, Neuheisel came clean. He admitted putting money down.

Long story short: The UW fired Neuheisel. Neuheisel sued the UW. He sued the NCAA. Discovery was a bloodbath. Neuheisel ducked and parsed. He didn't bet, he said. He didn't wager. He *contributed to a pool*. Sure, he might not get the money back. Or he might get back more. But to call that a bet? Neuheisel switched from defense to offense. *One only needs to see him out in the community to realize how valuable he is to the University.* Now, Neuheisel lashed out. He burned the university down.

Neuheisel wanted to know: Why was he being singled out when the UW teemed with scandal and lies? A doctor nicknamed "The Candy Man," "Dr. Feelgood," and "Pill Bill" doped up the softball team, illegally stockpiling Oxycontin and other painkillers and handing them out like Mentos. The UW's previous president, Richard McCormick, had engaged in an affair with an employee, and the university covered it up. An assistant basketball coach "apparently lied to the NCAA for weeks." Other coaches in the football program had participated in small-dollar basketball pools. On this last point, Neuheisel turned detective. He flew to Illinois and interviewed a former graduate assistant who had organized the pools, to gather names. "I told him that he needed to tell the truth. This was important to his career."

At trial, no one looked good—not Neuheisel, not the UW, not the NCAA. "The most stunning convergence of triangular ineptitude since Larry, Curly and Moe got together," Bud Withers wrote. The university's interim president said Neuheisel lacked an "integrity reflex." Neuheisel cried on the stand. The UW's compliance officer had written an e-mail saying it was okay to take part in pools—when, well, it wasn't. The NCAA had violated its own rules while investigating Neuheisel and failed to disclose its foul until the trial was halfway through. For a notoriously self-righteous organization that preaches the fine points of rules and timely disclosure, the irony was rich. Just before the case went to the jury, the parties settled. Neuheisel received $4.5 million—$2.5 million from the NCAA and $2 million from the University of Washington. Afterward, Neuheisel said: "I feel fully vindicated." Withers wrote: "Rick Neuheisel was blessed with good looks, a winning personality and not the vaguest whit of common sense."

Neuheisel's firing triggered fevered speculation. Who tipped off the NCAA? Conspiracy theorists flocked to Internet message boards, saying it must have been this person or that person. No one wanted to know more than Neuheisel. The day he was questioned by the NCAA, Neuheisel met with the university president, the president's special assistant, and Hedges at the president's home. Neuheisel wondered aloud: Who had it in for him? Who had turned him in? "He wanted to find out who did that," says Norm Arkans, the assistant who was there that night.

Using the alias of "Peter Wright"—the name of a famed British intelligence operative who had penned the international bestseller *Spycatcher*—the NCAA's tipster wrote investigators at least five e-mails in the spring of 2003. These e-mails provide a biographical sketch of the source (unless, of course, he—or she—was making these details up). The source said he had been an athlete in college. That he had graduated with a criminal justice degree. That he was pursuing a master's degree in counseling. That he used to participate in the pool, but it became too expensive. "Love to work for you one day," he told an NCAA investigator.

The source said of Neuheisel: "I have a firm ethical stance that what he did was wrong. To me, morally and ethically, I have a problem with an NCAA coach wagering on an NCAA event. . . . When will guys in his position learn that they're not invincible? Sad thing is that no matter what happens with him at UW, he will land on his feet somewhere. After all the infractions he committed at Colorado and some of the things he has done at UW, he will still have a job coaching somewhere and getting paid loads of money to do it. I feel it says a lot about our society."

After getting fired at Washington, Neuheisel worked as an assistant coach for the NFL's Baltimore Ravens. Then, in December 2007, UCLA announced its new head coach: Rick Neuheisel. The school's athletic director, Dan Guerrero, told reporters: "In the end it was all about 66 collegiate wins—a percentage that places him among the top active coaches in the country." Guerrero said Neuheisel would "start anew with a clean slate at his alma mater. He brings an energy, enthusiasm and a swagger that we needed."

Neuheisel signed a five-year contract worth between $1.25 million and $1.75 million a year, depending on incentives reached.

UCLA's 2008 opener was at home. Neuheisel was back in Rose Bowl Stadium, back where he coached Washington to the 2001 Rose Bowl, back where he quarterbacked UCLA to the 1984 Rose Bowl. UCLA played nationally ranked Tennessee in a game televised on ESPN. Trailing 21–17, the Bruins scored a touchdown with less than thirty seconds to go. "This is, according to the storybooks, supposed to be a dream night for Rick Neuheisel," announcer Mike Patrick said. "It's turning out that way." Tennessee tied the game as time expired, but UCLA prevailed in overtime, 27–24. "Rick Neuheisel has reawakened the echoes at UCLA," Patrick said. ESPN's sideline reporter grabbed Neuheisel after the game and asked him to describe his homecoming.

"Good to be back at UCLA, baby."

The roster for Washington's Rose Bowl team listed 107 players. Only Jerramy Stevens became a first-round draft pick—and he pretty much busted. Not one player became an NFL All Pro. All of which makes the team's 11-1 season more remarkable in retrospect. "It was my senior year, my fifth year," says Matt Fraize, an offensive lineman on the team. "We didn't have half the talent as in years before. But it was the perfect example of a team coming together."

In the years since, the players have gone every which way. Some managed to carve out careers in the NFL. Tuiasosopo became a backup quarterback for the Oakland Raiders and the New York Jets. Some players found a home in Canada's football league or in arena football. Others landed such jobs as chiropractor, UPS.driver, financial adviser, waiter, pharmaceutical salesman, cop. Matt Lingley, a linebacker, died in 2007. His work truck veered off a highway, slammed into a tree, and went up in flames. Marquis Cooper, another linebacker, died in 2009. He and two friends drowned when their fishing boat capsized off the coast of Florida.

Rock Nelson became a realtor. "If I wear my Rose Bowl ring,

it's such a conversation piece. People look at it. You'll meet them at an open house, start talking about Husky football, suddenly you're going out with them looking at real estate." As an offensive lineman, Nelson played one of football's most anonymous positions. Even so, people sometimes recognize him in the supermarket and say, "Hey, you're Rock Nelson."

"People really love Husky football," Nelson says.

Greg Carothers, the player who replaced Curtis Williams, bounced around NFL Europe before returning to the UW to finish his sociology degree. The first time around, he brushed off academics. "Here I am, having a silver spoon in my mouth, and I kind of shunned it." When he came back, he was twenty-six: "I was back in Kane Hall, with four hundred kids, feeling kind of old, but thinking, 'All right, I'm getting it done.'"

Reform has about as much staying power in football as it does in politics. With the UW's football and softball teams immersed in scandal, Barbara Hedges resigned as athletic director in 2004. Before stepping down, she had hired Keith Gilbertson to replace Neuheisel as the football team's head coach. In Gilbertson's first year, Washington went 6-6. In his second year the team collapsed, finishing an unthinkable 1-10, its first losing season in twenty-eight years. Gilbertson was a goner.

To replace Hedges as athletic director, the UW hired Todd Turner. He had been athletic director at Vanderbilt and was known for integrity. To replace Gilbertson as coach, Turner hired Tyrone Willingham, who had been fired at Notre Dame—and was known for integrity. The UW now had rectitude times two. What it didn't have was wins. In 2005 the team went 2-9. In 2006, 5-7. Willingham's third season tested the patience of fans accustomed to winning. As the Huskies staggered to a 4-9 record in 2007, fans wrote the coach and university administrators, offering their take on what needed to be done.

Ed Hansen, a multimillionaire lawyer, banker, and booster who had served three terms as mayor of Everett, sent an e-mail to UW president Mark Emmert offering $200,000 in scholarship funds if the coach and athletic director were fired. Other boosters threatened to pull financial support if the football program's fortunes didn't turn. The owner of a sporting goods company wrote: "You have me mutinying against this crap, and I am your money. I don't think I will be next year."

Fans lamented, beseeched, whined, and raged. "Fire Willingham NOW!!!!!!!!!!!!!!!!!" A 2004 graduate wrote: "Football, education, tradition, pride—these are the first four descriptors that come to my mind when thinking of UW; are future generations only going to think of one—education?" An elementary school teacher wrote: "We are Washington. At Washington you win football games or it just isn't Washington anymore." This teacher said he had bought his eight-month-old daughter a Husky cheerleader outfit, but now he would quit attending games or buying UW merchandise unless Willingham was fired. "Because now Husky Saturdays are days of sadness and why would I want my daughter to share that?"

Some fans resorted to name-calling. Willingham became "Willingfraud," "Willingloser," "Losingham." AD doesn't stand for athletic director, one fan wrote. It stands for "Always a Dildo." Some fans offered tips. "Dark purple, dark gold. Trust me . . . dark colors will begin a turnaround." To one fan, the answer lay with God: "I believe He wants to use you and the Huskies to bring glory to His name. If you and your staff will humble yourselves before the Lord, and seek His face—not just for the sake of your team, but for His glory—God will lift you up, and He will show Himself mighty through the Huskies."

"Where the HELL is the Tight END??????????????????????????????" another fan wrote.

At the end of the 2007 season, Turner was let go. He told reporters: "The message that our students hear, that our coaches hear, that our leadership hears from the general run-of-the-mill fan is that the only thing we really care about is how many games they win. And I have to look at that after 32 years of doing this and say, 'Wow, is that really what we are all about? Have I been that naïve all this period of time?' I have been spending all my time on the student-athlete experience and trying to create better lives for people and the proper place in higher education when all I should have been worrying about is how many games we've won. Why didn't I go to the NFL if that's all it's about?"

"Goodbye Turdner nice smelling ya!" one fan wrote.

The UW decided to bring Willingham back for a fourth season. Hearing that news, one fan wrote: "Today is the single worst day I have ever experienced as a Husky. My hope is gone, and that is truly sad. I am 24 . . ." In 2008 the Huskies went 0-12. Willingham was a goner, too.

The ripples from Washington's 2000 season extended for years. When the Huskies were in California, preparing for the Rose Bowl, a student equipment manager had sex with Roc Alexander, a freshman cornerback. It was consensual; no one questions that. But back in Seattle, she called the relationship off. Afterward, she alleges, Alexander forced his way into her dorm room and raped her. In 2004 she filed a lawsuit against Alexander. So did a second UW student, who also accused Alexander of rape. Alexander wasn't criminally charged in either instance. He denied the women's allegations, but settled both suits for an undisclosed sum.

Alexander joined the NFL in 2004 and played a few years for the Denver Broncos and Houston Texans.

The equipment manager also sued the UW, alleging it had violated Title IX, the federal law that forbids discrimination in educational programs. To prevail, she had to prove the university had treated her with "deliberate indifference," a daunting hurdle. A Superior Court judge tossed out her lawsuit before trial. The equipment manager appealed.

In 2008 a unanimous state appeals court revived her lawsuit—and with language to make the university shudder. When the equipment manager alerted the athletic department to the alleged assault, the department responded by sending her and Alexander to mediation. The department put her and Alexander in the same room—to talk it out. But an allegation of rape is not a matter to talk out. It is a matter for police to investigate.

The appellate court wrote that the equipment manager—identified in court records by her initials, S.S.—had provided "ample evidence" to warrant a trial, assuming her allegations were true. "A lack of appropriate discipline of her rapist . . . keeping the matter out of the public eye to avoid negative publicity . . . discouraging S.S. from filing a police report . . . repeatedly suggesting that S.S. leave her job with the football program while her rapist would remain . . ." The court listed twelve ways in which the UW had allegedly brushed aside the woman's claim, and strung them together in one sentence, a Faulknerian thunderclap 157 words long.

In the fall of 2009, the case went to trial. "Cover-up, betrayal, justice long denied—that is what this case is about," the equipment manager's lawyer, Becky Roe, told the jury. The jurors returned a verdict in favor of the UW—but not because they approved of the UW's actions. One juror, asked how the UW handled the rape allegation, said: "You want a quote? Piss poorly." Jurors found for the UW because the plaintiff's "educational environment" had not been sufficiently harmed. She remained in school, kept a high GPA, and graduated. Jurors acknowledged that it was a perverse result—the plaintiff was punished for being strong.

Richard McCormick, the UW president who had lectured football coach Jim Lambright on telling the truth, left the university in 2002 to become the president at Rutgers. A year later, the *Seattle Times* revealed that the university's regents had encouraged McCormick to leave after rumors surfaced of an affair he'd had with a woman in his administration. McCormick denied the affair in several interviews with the newspaper, but ultimately admitted the story was true. At Rutgers, McCormick oversaw a doubling of spending on football—from $7.5 million a year to $15.6 million—at the same time that classes were being canceled to cut costs. Under McCormick, Rutgers also concealed the football coach's full salary through a side deal that kept an extra $250,000 off the school's payroll. "If you want to have an outstanding program—and it was determined a long time ago that Rutgers wanted to do that—then you have to pay the price," McCormick told the *Newark Star-Ledger*. "You've got to pay to play, pardon the New Jersey expression."

At the UW, Eric Godfrey was promoted to vice-provost for student life. In 2007, he and other UW officials persuaded the state's governor and prison officials to remove registered sex offenders from homes near Greek Row—even though the offenders had lived there for years, without causing trouble. "We are trying to be preventive," Godfrey said. "All it takes is one incident." Godfrey is the same administrator who helped keep Curtis Williams on campus after Williams had served time for felony assault. And this is the same university that has repeatedly welcomed football recruits to campus despite criminal histories of violence. Newspaper accounts of this neighborhood purge tended to note the UW's interest in buying the homes where the sex offenders lived.

To replace Todd Turner as athletic director, Emmert hired Scott Woodward, whose background was in lobbying and public relations. Boosters cheered Emmert's choice. To replace Willingham as coach, Woodward hired Steve Sarkisian, the offensive coordinator at USC. The announcement was made in December 2008. As the UW's president, Emmert made about $900,000—one of the biggest financial packages in the country for the leader of a university. The university agreed to pay Sarkisian—who was thirty-four, and never before a head coach—twice as much, or about $1.85 million a year.

Sarkisian set to hiring a new staff. Within two weeks he lured Jim Michalczik away from California to be offensive coordinator. The UW agreed to pay Michalczik $350,000, the school's highest salary ever for an assistant coach.

The state's finances were in meltdown. Washington's budget deficit kept widening—to $3 billion, to $5 billion, to $8 billion. The state's public universities faced budget cuts of up to 20 percent. Students faced tuition increases of up to $1,000. In Pullman, the president of Washington State University volunteered to take a pay cut of $100,000. In Bellingham, the president of Western Washington University told faculty and students: "The budget situation is extraordinarily serious." To save money, Western Washington scrapped its football program.

At the UW the financial situation became so dire that the school shut its doors to new students wanting to start classes in the spring. But the university made an exception for athletes.

In January 2009—two months after the WSU president reduced his salary to $625,000—the UW landed a defensive coordinator. Sarkisian hired Nick Holt away from USC, where he had been in charge of the nation's best defense. But luring Holt to an 0-12 team wasn't easy. The UW agreed to pay him a staggering $2.1 million over three years—double what it was paying Michalczik, hired a month earlier at what was then a record for UW assistants. "I've been paying attention to the market pretty well," Woodward said. "The top coordinators in the country are making big figures. So, I had an idea that to get the best, you're going to have to pay."

The University of Washington had always defended its profligate spending on football by saying the athletic department paid its own way. Ticket sales and other revenue outpaced expenses. Taxpayers didn't take a hit. But now the UW was in Olympia, asking for $150 million in taxpayer money to renovate Husky Stadium. When WSU alumni objected, Husky booster Ron Crockett called them "fools." Lawmakers were less than enthused with the UW's sales pitch. They were trying to minimize the damage to essential state functions—schools, transportation projects, social services.

In 1925, *The Freshman* came out. It was a silent movie, starring Harold Lloyd. As Lloyd heads off to college, the screen turns to script: "The opening of the fall term at Tate University—a large football stadium with a college attached."

Eight decades later, in Seattle, the joke was still good.

NOTES

This book is based largely on public records. Many were generated as a result of criminal, civil, or ethics investigations and include police reports, depositions, declarations, forensic reports, court transcripts, and the like. Other documents run the gamut: personnel files; university archives; prison records; employment contracts; Pac-10 and NCAA investigative reports; e-mails to UW coaches and administrators; property records; student transcripts and other academic papers. We collected most of these documents by filing ninety-six public-records requests with twenty-seven agencies in Washington and California. Other documents were obtained from people connected to the story.

We also conducted extensive interviews. The people we interviewed include Maryann Parker; Mike Hunsinger; Mike Magan; Jeffery Mudd; Marie; Marie's mother; Marie's brother; Marie's friend Maggie; Sunny Rockom; Marie's roommate at Pi Beta Phi; Anthony Kelley; Kelley's wife, Tonya; Siya Manyakanyaka; Tom Williams; Sarah Winter; Norm Stamper; the student who received Jerramy Stevens's May 8, 2000, e-mail; Mark Larson; Michelle Williams; Michelle Williams's mother; David Williams; Jan Zientek; Douglas Smith; Eric Godfrey; Seyed Maulana; Robert Aronson; Rock Nelson; Mike Lang; Steve Fogg; Ron Crockett; Leo Poort; Chuck Heater; Terry Eidson; Bob Ladouceur; Danny Ladouceur; Mathew Clark; Bill Gagen; J. K. Scott; Abner Thomas; Wayne Moses; Donald Preston; Brian Beaky; Ralph Bayard; Greg Carothers; Hakim Akbar; Marques Tuiasosopo; Kerry Carter; Bud Withers; Ted Miller (he agreed to answer questions by e-mail); William Downing; Josh Dabbs; Grace Lundeen; Pharms's landlord in Lynnwood; Nigel Burton; Todd Turner; and Mark Emmert. This list is not exhaustive. We interviewed about twenty players and coaches from the 2000 team, as well as UW administrators, staff, professors, prosecutors, judges, police officers, boosters, players' relatives, journalists, and others. Some of these interviews were conducted while the authors were doing reporting for "Victory and Ruins," a series published in the *Seattle Times* in January 2008.

Extensive dialogue that appears in quotation marks is drawn from audiotapes or videotapes or from transcribed police statements, depositions, or court testimony; in these instances, we knew the words were verbatim. We generally avoided using quotation marks for extended dialogue that was recounted after the fact by one or more participants in interviews, police reports, or other documents.

In the following notes, we describe what documents or other records we used for each chapter, followed by more traditional citations of published sources. For documents, we have tried to include the identifying number assigned by the agency that generated the records. For police departments, these are typically incident or case numbers; for courts, cause numbers; and for other agencies, file numbers.

Abbreviations

DOC: Department of Corrections
KCDC: King County District Court
KCSC: King County Superior Court
SMC: Seattle Municipal Court
SPD: Seattle Police Department
UW: University of Washington
UWPD: University of Washington Police Department
WSP: Washington State Patrol

Prologue

The announcer quotes come from a videotape of ABC's broadcast of the Miami-Washington game. We discovered how many players Mike Hunsinger represented by doing background checks on each member of the team's roster. We reviewed our list with Hunsinger, who confirmed his role in each case. The "exonerate" quote comes from Neuheisel's June 18, 2004, deposition in a lawsuit filed against the UW (KCSC, 03-2-35567-4).

2 **A Husky crowd hits 135:** Rob Oller, "Huskies Fans Make Visitors Feel the Noise," *Columbus Dispatch*, September 15, 2007; Chris Dufresne, "The Places to Watch College Football," *Los Angeles Times*, September 20, 1996.

3 **joined a group of thirty-four businessmen:** Dan Raley, "Jones' Younger Brother Says He Will Play for UW," *Seattle Post-Intelligencer*, January 30, 1993; Jane Hadley and Dan Raley, "Endorser Group Organized to Pad Low James Salary," *Seattle Post-Intelligencer*,

January 29, 1993; Duff Wilson, "uw Finds 'Endorsers' List, but It's Four Years Old," *Seattle Times*, January 28, 1993.

3 **Mike's brother Bill gave summer jobs:** Eric Nalder, "Husky Football: What Went Wrong?" *Seattle Times*, January 25, 1993.

4 **"Not having him would change":** Blaine Newnham, "Tournament Losing Players, Prestige, but Not Enjoyment," *Seattle Times*, August 2, 2000.

4 **"good-natured giant":** Ted Miller, "Huskies Tight End Stays Focused on the Present," *Seattle Post-Intelligencer*, November 12, 1999.

1. Freeze

Documents: Mike Magan's personnel file (spd, 5094), including commendations and other background materials; police reports on the two attacks on the Tau Kappa Epsilon fraternity (spd, 99-201262 and 99-202797); the uw's internal investigation of the fraternity attacks, memorialized in an October 21, 1999, report from Ralph Bayard to Barbara Hedges; police records on the shooting of Sullivan (spd, 00-116928), including reports by detectives Mudd and Magan and witness accounts from Sullivan, Sullivan's roommates, and a neighbor; transcribed testimony of Nick Banchero at an Inquiry Judge Proceeding held October 27, 2000; crime-scene photos of Sullivan's bedroom and other parts of the apartment; a January 4, 2002, victim-impact statement from Sullivan (kcsc, 01-1-04360-5); a pre-sentencing report on Pharms.

Sullivan's perspective is drawn from statements he provided to police or prosecutors on four dates in 2000: March 14 (while in an ambulance going to the hospital); March 22 (this statement was tape-recorded and transcribed); March 31; and October 5. Sullivan was also interviewed by defense counsel, as described in the defendant's sentencing memorandum. The description of Sullivan's criminal history comes from records in kcsc, smc, and Chelan County Superior Court.

8 **Prosecutors refused to bring felony charges, a result:** Bud Withers, "Lack of Felony Charges in uw Football Fracas Angers Frat Parents," *Seattle Times*, July 13, 1999.

9 **But now his grades were so bad:** Ted Miller, "Ailing Shaw Decides to Leave Huskies," *Seattle Post-Intelligencer*, June 16, 2000. This

description is also based upon what Pharms told Sullivan on March 14, 2000, about failing his classes.

10 **"A man of mystery"**: Ted Miller, "Pharms Does His Talking on the Field," *Seattle Post-Intelligencer*, December 23, 1999. Pharms's media boycott started in the spring of 1999 and continued until August 2000—five months after the robbery of Sullivan, and shortly before the 2000 season began.

12 **his hair had long since turned gray**: Ann Rule, *The End of the Dream: The Golden Boy Who Never Grew Up* (New York: Pocket Star Books, 1999), 186.

12 **In 1997 the Seattle Police Department named him**: Kimberly A. C. Wilson, "Seattle Police Honor Four of Their Finest Officers," *Seattle Post-Intelligencer*, March 17, 1997.

12 **A fourth-generation cop**: Rule, *The End of the Dream*, 179.

12 **Magan made his biggest mark**: Rule, *The End of the Dream*, 255–59.

13 **In three years Magan solved eighty-five holdups**: Kimberly A. C. Wilson, "Ho, Hum; Bank Robbery Suspect Caught," *Seattle Post-Intelligencer*, April 13, 1999.

13 **"I guess you could say I have"**: K. A. C. Wilson, "Ho, Hum; Bank Robbery Suspect Caught."

13 **Pharms's case simply joined hundreds**: Ken Armstrong, Justin Mayo, and Steve Miletich, "The Cases Your Judges Are Hiding from You," *Seattle Times*, March 5, 2006.

2. Marie

This chapter was based on interviews with Marie, Marie's mother, and Marie's friend Sunny Rockom. We elected to protect Marie's privacy, but without resorting to the use of a false name. We did that by using her middle name: Marie. She does not go by Marie with family and friends; she uses her first name. We also used a middle name, Maggie, for Marie's friend since first grade. We avoided using any name for Marie's roommate at Pi Beta Phi, simply referring to her as Marie's roommate.

3. Fragments

Documents: Records from police and prosecutors pertaining to the investigation of Marie's allegation of rape (SPD, 00-254487), including notes of police interviews with Chris, the student who called 911 (interviewed on June 27 and August 2, 2000); statements provided by Marie on June 5 and June 8, 2000; the Certification for Determination of Probable Cause; a confidential decline letter written by prosecutors on October 31, 2000; and statements provided by Marie's roommate and her friends Maggie, Molly, Katie, Sterling, Jennifer, and Sunny. The dialogue between Jerramy Stevens and Spencer Marona comes from a description provided by Marona in a lengthy statement to police on July 27, 2000. That statement was taped and transcribed, and runs forty-three pages. The section on Sigma Chi draws on records obtained during discovery in a lawsuit filed against the fraternity (KCSC, 03-2-35567-4).

24 **The worst the university would do:** Marsha King, "UW Cracks Down on Drinking, Targeting Minors on Greek Row," *Seattle Times*, November 1, 1995; editorial, "Rules for Fraternities," *Seattle Times*, January 8, 1996.

25 **One time, three members were shot and wounded:** Ian Ith and Dave Birkland, "Shooting at Fraternity Injures 3 UW Students," *Seattle Times*, July 20, 2002.

4. Stirrings

This chapter relied heavily on interviews with Anthony Kelley, Tom Williams, Sarah Winter, and Robert Aronson. We also interviewed UW administrators about tutoring and other academic services provided to athletes, and drew upon an eleven-page letter that Aronson wrote to UW president Lee Huntsman on March 16, 2004. Lowell Cohn's book *Rough Magic: Bill Walsh's Return to Stanford Football* (New York: HarperCollins, 1994) was a terrific resource on Walsh, Williams, and the culture at Stanford vis-à-vis Washington.

29 **That's one reason his college teammates:** Cohn, *Rough Magic*, 60.

30 **he was All State in football, basketball, and baseball:** *Washington Football Media Guide 2000*, 84.

30 eighteen-hour days in a salmon cannery: Cohn, *Rough Magic*, 155.

30 a collective graduation rate of about 90 percent: Cohn, *Rough Magic*, 256–57.

30 While Jackie Sherrill, the Mississippi State coach: Richard Oliver, "Politically Incorrect; Jackie Sherrill Will Leave a Legacy That Will Be Remembered for as Many Negatives as Positives," *San Antonio Express-News*, November 26, 2003.

30 "We will not be a wildebeest": Cohn, *Rough Magic*, 114.

31 "The football players there have almost no contact": "Walsh Attacks Husky Program," *Seattle Times*, May 25, 1993. Walsh's comments were initially reported in the *Sacramento Bee* by columnist R. E. Graswich. When Walsh later apologized, he sent a case of wine—Napa Valley, white—to the UW coaching staff.

31 Only a third of Washington's players: Duff Wilson and Lily Eng, "A Matter of Degree—Husky Football Program Coming Up Anything but Roses Academically," *Seattle Times*, April 11, 1993.

31 Williams also sang in the gospel choir: Jorge Castillo, Efren Bonner, and Courtney Pannell, "Williams Lands the Job He's Always Wanted," *Yale Daily News*, February 6, 2009.

33 "Football was an outlet": Matthew Chernicoff, "A Diamond from the Rough," *The Daily of the University of Washington*, June 7, 2002.

34 "I don't know what I was thinking": Bud Withers, "Linebacker Snubs Michigan for UW," *Seattle Post-Intelligencer*, February 3, 1998.

35 Hakim Akbar's father was in prison: Bud Withers, "The Faith of Their Father," *Seattle Times*, November 3, 2000.

35 Omare Lowe, at age eight: Blaine Newnham, "High Times for Lowe, at Long Last," *Seattle Times*, September 13, 2001.

35 with a 3.97 high school GPA: Eric Sondheimer, "Scott Set to Enjoy Huskies; Burroughs Star Enjoys Everything," *Los Angeles Daily News*, January 21, 1997.

35 Ossim Hatem, a Muslim: John Blanchette, "Hatem Will Resume

Fasting to Observe Muslim Holy Period," *Spokane Spokesman-Review*, January 2, 2001.

35 **Ben Mahdavi, a Jew:** "The Chosen 1's; Gridiron Jews Poised for NFL Draft," *Jewish Chronicle*, April 24, 2003.

37 **When Allen was a teenager:** Stephen Manes and Paul Andrews, *Gates: How Microsoft's Mogul Reinvented an Industry—and Made Himself the Richest Man in America* (New York: Doubleday, 1993), 37–38.

38 **One NCAA report looked at all athletes:** Tom Farrey, "Black Athletes at the UW Face a Special Challenge—Graduate Rates Raise Concern," *Seattle Times*, November 28, 1993.

38 **"You get angry at a program":** Farrey, "Black Athletes at the UW Face a Special Challenge."

39 **The *Washington Post* found nearly three dozen:** Mark Schlabach, "Varsity Athletes Get Class Credit; Some Colleges Give Grades for Playing," *Washington Post*, August 26, 2004.

39 **The University of Georgia offered:** Rana Cash and Mark Schlabach, "No-brainer Final Exam Stings UGA," *Atlanta Journal-Constitution*, March 5, 2004.

5. Louisville Slugger

Documents: Police records of the Stevens investigation (SPD, 00-254487), including the incident report, follow-up reports, continuation sheets, consent for release of medical information, search-warrant records, and witness statements. The e-mail sent by Stevens on May 8, 2000, was found in the case file kept by King County prosecutors. (The earlier e-mail—the one sent to Stevens beforehand—was not in the file; we interviewed the woman involved in this e-mail exchange, and she did not remember what she wrote.) The exchange between Parker and the e-mail recipient comes from a report Parker wrote after interviewing the student on September 8, 2000. Much of Parker's background derives from her personnel file (SPD, 5085), which includes commendations, promotions, letters of praise, and other background materials.

For Stevens's early history we relied in part on high school yearbooks and records from the Thurston County Prosecuting Attorney's Office, the Thurston County Sheriff's Office (98-19259-6), the Lacey Police Department, and Thurston County Superior Court (98-1-01041-3). These records include investigative reports written by Detective Cliff Ziesemer and Captain Mark Curtis; transcribed police interviews of Jerramy Stevens (June 2, 1998), Van Buckingham (June 2, 1998), Brian Flowers (June 2, 1998), James Hoover (June 11, 1998), and other witnesses; a written statement from Flowers dated October 7, 1998; a letter to the sentencing judge written by Hoover; toxicology reports that showed marijuana in Stevens's system; and letters written by UW football coaches and community members to the prosecutor or judge. Stevens's high school GPA (3.12, to be precise) comes from a pre-sentencing report prepared by Stevens's attorney. We also relied on Stevens's file with the state DOC (789578), which included a Community Service Worker Questionnaire filled out on January 5, 1999.

The charges that Toalei Mulitauaopele faced after leaving UW were filed in KCSC and KCDC.

47 **picking the Huskies over BYU and Hawaii:** Bud Withers, "Marquee Names Escape Huskies," *Seattle Post-Intelligencer*, February 4, 1998.

49 **With a charge like this, bail would:** Elise Gee, "Party Dispute Ignited Fracas," *Olympian*, June 4, 1998.

50 **At age sixteen, Mulitauaopele helped:** Percy Allen, "The Case of Toalei Mulitauaopele," *Seattle Times*, December 1, 1996.

50 **The *Seattle Post-Intelligencer* wrote a profile:** Ted Miller, "Keeping a Grip on His Past," *Seattle Post-Intelligencer*, December 17, 1999.

50 **"He's a sweet, kind, gentle soul":** Joel Coffidis, "Quarterback for UW Spared," *Olympian*, August 8, 1998. (The quote appears in a cutline that runs with the story).

51 **"Don't let yourself or your family":** Coffidis, "Quarterback for UW Spared."

51 **On this same day, the *Post-Intelligencer*:** Bud Withers, "UW Recruit Awaits Ruling from Judge," *Seattle Post-Intelligencer*, August 7, 1998.

51 **"We don't give up on a player":** Bud Withers, "Freshman Gets His Act Together to Hit UW Stage," *Seattle Post-Intelligencer*, August 13, 1998.

53 **"soft-spoken, good-natured giant"**: Miller, "Huskies Tight End Stays Focused on the Present."

54 **"gregarious, happy personality"**: Bud Withers, "A Chance Nearly Thrown Away; After Brush with Law, Huskies' Stevens Looks to Future," *Seattle Times*, December 25, 1999.

6. Nothing but Ashes

Documents: Detective Mudd's reports and other documents in the SPD's file on the shooting of Sullivan, including a description of the search of Pharms's house and of his arrest; Mudd's personnel file (SPD, 5244); the fingerprint report, dated July 14, 2000, matching Pharms's right pinky with the print left on the car door; search warrant records, including the application, affidavit in support, and inventory; and a motion to seal the search-warrant records with a supporting affidavit signed by Mudd on June 28, 2000. That motion was filed in KCSC.

59 **A TV crew had set Mudd and his partner up:** Susan Paynter, "Degenerate Goes High-Tech with an Obscene Fax," *Seattle Post-Intelligencer*, July 1, 1991.

7. Face-off

Documents: Records from police and prosecutors pertaining to the rape allegation (SPD, 00-254487), including a fourteen-page chronology of Parker's investigation; the Certificate for Determination of Probable Cause (July 28, 2000); the Inventory and Return of Search Warrant (July 27, 2000); a forty-three-page transcription of the July 27, 2000, interview of Spencer Marona by Detective Rob Howard; a Statement Form by Detective Tim Fields describing the arrest and questioning of Jerramy Stevens; a July 31, 2000, letter from prosecutor Jim Rogers to Cellmark Diagnostics, requesting DNA testing; Report of Laboratory Examination, August 17, 2000, from Cellmark Diagnostics to Rogers, describing the results of the DNA testing; and a July 27, 2000, fax from Hunsinger's law office to the SPD.

Other details come from a June 18, 2004, deposition of Neuheisel and an April 4, 2004, deposition of Hedges, both of which were taken as part of Marie's lawsuit against the UW. Neuheisel, in his deposition, described learning about Stevens's arrest while playing golf; Randy Hart's role as go-between with police; how Hedges received updates from Satterberg and passed them along; and the conversation that Neuheisel had with Stevens after Stevens's arrest.

65 **First he grew his hair so long:** Ted Miller, "New-look Marona Is Ready for Action," *Seattle Post-Intelligencer*, April 19, 2000.

66 **He suffered one injury after another:** Gail Wood, "Robbins Frustrated by Recent Injuries," *Olympian*, December 27, 2001.

69 **His favorite vacation spot:** "Coaches Q&A," *Seattle Times*, November 15, 2001.

69 **"The tradition of Hunsinger as player counsel":** Bud Withers, "Huskies Unleash Their Lawyer," *Seattle Times*, May 31, 2005.

71 **Satterberg wrote Maleng's speeches and letters:** Stuart Eskenazi, "Satterberg Says He, Maleng Were 'True Partners,'" *Seattle Times*, October 16, 2007.

71 **with the *Post-Intelligencer* calling Stevens:** Ted Miller, "Huskies' Stevens Arrested, Booked," *Seattle Post-Intelligencer*, July 28, 2000.

71 **About a dozen of his teammates:** Anne Koch, "UW Tight End Free as Probe Continues," *Seattle Times*, July 29, 2000.

72 **A week after Stevens's arrest:** Newnham, "Tournament Losing Players, Prestige, but Not Enjoyment."

72 **Two days later, a *Seattle Times* story:** Bud Withers, "Clouds on Husky Horizon Involve Stevens, Juergens," *Seattle Times*, August 4, 2000.

73 **"An ongoing investigation has cast":** Ted Miller, "Return to Dominance? Despite Numerous Concerns, Rick Neuheisel and the Huskies Are Poised to Reclaim Their Position as Pac-10's Top Program," *Seattle Post-Intelligencer*, August 31, 2000.

73 **"The recent losses pale":** Nick Daschel, "No News Just Fine for UW," *Vancouver Columbian*, August 25, 2000.

73 **"Washington will have trouble finding":** Carter Strickland, "Pac-10 Conference Scouting Report," *Spokane Spokesman-Review*, August 24, 2000.

73 **One *Seattle Times* sportswriter did a story in Q&A format:** Bud

Withers, "Pac-10 Favorites Still Have Questions," *Seattle Times*, August 12, 2000.

73 **"He's a big part of our offense":** Daschel, "No News Just Fine for UW."

73 **Donohoe said there would be no decision:** Koch, "UW Tight End Free as Probe Continues."

73 **A week later, he said:** Withers, "Clouds on Husky Horizon Involve Stevens, Juergens."

73 **A couple of weeks later, he said:** Ted Miller, "Barton Transfer Looking Probable," *Seattle Post-Intelligencer*, August 16, 2000.

74 **Toward the end of August, Donohoe said:** Bud Withers, "Vontoure's Back with Team, Could Play in Idaho Opener," *Seattle Times*, August 29, 2000.

76 **He missed the next eight practices:** Ted Miller, "Marona Resolves His Personal Issues," *Seattle Post-Intelligencer*, August 17, 2000.

76 **"A personal issue":** Ted Miller, "Pharms No Longer Letting Game Do All the Talking," *Seattle Post-Intelligencer*, August 14, 2000.

76 **Marona "reportedly" was feeling "overwhelmed":** Miller, "Barton Transfer Looking Probable."

76 **"My mind's all right now":** Miller, "Marona Resolves His Personal Issues."

8. Taking the Field

Documents: Derrell Daniels's DUI records (KCDC, C00356891). The blood-alcohol content reading comes from a database kept by the WSP.

77 **"Washington has been on a giant pedestal":** Jim Moore, "Reality Will Hit Hard for Vandals, Price's Cougars," *Seattle Post-Intelligencer*, September 2, 2000.

78 **"When the pro scouts ask about Chad":** "Husky Football Team Prepares for Hurricanes," University of Washington press release, September 3, 2000.

79 **that required five stitches:** Jim Meehan, "No. 96 Takes On Special Meaning," *Spokane Spokesman-Review*, September 3, 2000.

79   The team's backup tight end: Ted Miller, "UW Doubles Up at Tight End," *Seattle Post-Intelligencer*, September 26, 2001.

79   "should be suddenly charged": Blaine Newnham, "Huskies' One-Man Offensive Show Could Use a Much Bigger Cast," *Seattle Times*, September 3, 2000.

80   "wasn't as hard as I thought": Jim Meehan, "Game Showed Vandals Still Have Work to Do," *Spokane Spokesman-Review*, September 5, 2000.

80   "Obviously, more people think": Ted Miller, "Huskies Open Season with 44–20 Win over Idaho," *Seattle Post-Intelligencer*, September 2, 2000.

80   "no nonsense" and a "straight shooter": Bert Sahlberg, "Frustration Mounts, but Not Skepticism," *Lewiston Morning Tribune*, November 1, 2001.

80   Cable instituted a three-strikes policy: Bud Withers, "Real Live Wire: Coach Tom Cable Brings Discipline, Fresh Approach to Idaho," *Seattle Times*, August 30, 2000.

81   "I feel like throwing up every day": Sahlberg, "Frustration Mounts, but Not Skepticism."

81   "We like everything about our program": Jim Meehan, "New Contract Has Given Cable Some Security," *Spokane Spokesman-Review*, October 30, 2001.

81   In 1999, he told a Seattle TV station: "No Felony Charges for Husky Players in UW Frat Melee," Associated Press, July 13, 1999.

9. Happily Ever After

Documents: SPD reports detailing calls to Williams's apartment on August 30, 1996 (96-393468), September 30, 1996 (96-441861), October 31, 1996 (96-488398), and November 17, 1996 (96-514741); UWPD reports for call on December 7, 1996 (96-908668); King County police reports for call on May 9, 1997 (97-116615); transcript of May 28, 1997, hearing in KCDC on misdemeanor assault charges; King County police reports for call on June 1, 1997 (97-138422), and accompanying court records for the felony assault charge (KCSC, 97-1-04958-6); September 2, 1997, presentencing report on Williams; transcript of September 19, 1997, hearing on misdemeanor assault charges in KCDC; court records for misdemeanor charges filed against Williams (KCDC, C03413 and CQ10118SH); Williams's academic file at the UW, including his transcript, an August 24, 1998, letter and memorandum from Lambright that presented the case for pulling Williams's scholarship, and a September 2, 1998, letter from Eric Godfrey to Williams; and Williams's DOC file (769531), including probation-violation reports, descriptions of counseling, and a detailed chronology of notes and observations from probation officers.

85 **At Bullard High School in Fresno:** *Washington Football Media Guide 2000*, 66.

85 **he chose the UW over USC:** Hugo Kugiya, "UW Taps California for Another Top Tailback," *Seattle Times*, January 24, 1996.

85 **"potential star":** "College Football Recruiting: How Northwest Schools Fared," *Vancouver Columbian*, February 8, 1996.

85 **When Curtis was seven, J.D. practiced baseball:** Richard Linde, "Funeral Service for Curtis Williams," May 13, 2002, 4malamute .com.

85 **"I don't like those high ones":** Linde, "Funeral Service for Curtis Williams."

86 **"He's an athlete":** Percy Allen, "Summer without Football Let Freshman Focus on Family," *Seattle Times*, August 17, 1996.

86 **"I was away from my daughter":** Allen, "Summer without Football Let Freshman Focus on Family."

93 **almost half the University of Rhode Island football team:** Jack Cavanaugh, "U. of Rhode Island Is Shaken by Players' Assault on Fraternity," *New York Times*, October 18, 1996.

93 **"This is not about football":** Bill Plaschke, "University Chief Benches Football Team as a Lesson," *Los Angeles Times*, October 26, 1996.

93 **Other members of Nebraska's 1995 championship team:** Steve Wieberg, "Nebraska: 'A Very Defining Case'; Did Players Get Away with Too Much?" *USA Today*, September 18, 1998.

98 **regained his eligibility by taking Swahili:** Glenn Dickey, "Hypocrites React to Walsh Comments," *San Francisco Chronicle*, June 16, 1993.

98 **"He'll be invited back":** Bud Withers, "Lambright Says Conditioning Still Needs Work," *Seattle Post-Intelligencer*, August 18, 1997.

98 **A sports columnist for the *Seattle Times*:** Blaine Newnham, "Talented Hooker a Sure Thing for '98," *Seattle Times*, December 25, 1997.

98 **"academic and unspecified off-field problems":** Bob Condotta, "UW Update: Safety Williams Back on Huskies' Roster," *Tacoma News Tribune*, September 25, 1998.

101 **Williams led the team in solo tackles:** *Washington Football Media Guide 2000*, 66.

10. The Twelfth Man

The quotes from Nessler, Griese, and Swann come from a videotape of ABC's broadcast of the Miami-Washington game.

102 **worth $30,000, easy:** Chris Dufresne, "Irish Know They Have Battle-tested QB," *Los Angeles Times*, September 7, 2000. The trophy, insured for $30,000, weighs a whopping 123 pounds.

103 **The stadium was built in 1920:** Dan Raley, "Aging Not So Gracefully; Officials: It's Time to Deal with Dilapidated Stadium," *Seattle Post-Intelligencer*, September 27, 2007.

103 **pooled $50 and $100 donations:** "Husky Stadium," gohuskies .com.

103 **To minimize the glare:** "Husky Stadium," gohuskies.com.

103 **first big college to install AstroTurf:** "Husky Stadium," gohuskies .com.

103 **the stadium shifted to FieldTurf:** Blaine Newnham, "FieldTurf's Fake Grass Grows on Neuheisel," *Seattle Times*, December 5, 1999.

106 **"embraced and passionately kissed":** Steve Miletich, Mike Carter, and Christine Willmsen, "Officers and Dancers Too Close for Comfort," *Seattle Times*, February 18, 2005.

107 **One regular in the 1950s and '60s:** Regina Hackett, "Jack David, the Man behind the Blue Moon Tavern, Dies at Age 90," *Seattle Post-Intelligencer*, January 16, 1999.

107 **"Dark, dark my light"**: Theodore Roethke, "In a Dark Time," in *The Collected Poems of Theodore Roethke* (Garden City NY: Doubleday, 1966), 239. One of Dylan Thomas's most famous lines is, of course, "Rage, rage against the dying of the light." One can only imagine these two men sharing a stiff drink in a dark bar.

108 **"They were yelping a bit"**: Jim Cour, "No. 15 Washington 34, No. 4 Miami 29," Associated Press, September 9, 2000.

108 **"Whose House? Dawgs' House!"**: Kevin Acee, "Huskies Have Last Howl, Top the 'Canes," *San Diego Union-Tribune*, September 10, 2000.

11. In Hiding

This chapter relies upon interviews with Marie, Marie's mother, Marie's brother, and Sunny Rockom. We also used records from two lawsuits against the University of Washington (KCSC, 03-2-35567-4 and 03-2-32273-3).

12. Taking a Pass

Documents: Detective Mudd's reports on the Sullivan shooting, including continuation sheets that provide a chronology of the investigation. Details about the Eric Shyne case come from SPD records (02-238650), the King County prosecutors' file, and court records (KCSC, 03-2-35567-4). The Tau Kappa Epsilon case draws on records from the SPD, the Seattle City Attorney's Office and SMC (366623, 366624, 366625). The description of the basketball-tournament brawl comes from a lawsuit filed against Pharms and several other defendants in the Municipal Court of Sacramento County (96AM02715). We used records from Pharms's DOC file (833475), which included his marriage certificate issued in Nevada on September 29, 1996. The passage about the fight in the student union building comes from UWPD records (98-903341). These include statements taken from Kenneth Washington, Washington's fifteen-year-old brother, Pharms, and seven other witnesses.

112 **"Washington's bandwagon is becoming crowded"**: Jim Cour, "Huskies Jump to No. 9 with Win over Miami," Associated Press, September 10, 2000.

114 **he could drop into a Dairy Queen**: Michael Paulson, "Unarresting

Style Has Not Kept Maleng from Locking onto Issues," *Seattle Post-Intelligencer*, July 26, 1996.

114 **Rise early, milk the cows:** Carlton Smith, "The Legal Leader Norm Maleng Polishes His Mr. Clean Image for Another Campaign for King County Prosecutor," *Seattle Times*, April 27, 1986.

114 **Maleng's love of certain phrases:** "Remembering Norm," *Washington Law and Politics*. The magazine's Web site offered remembrances of Maleng; a contribution from Dan Satterberg recounted some of Maleng's favorite sayings.

114 **Maleng believed she became an angel:** Levi Pulkkinen, "Maleng Remembered for Faith and Devotion to Family," *Seattle Post-Intelligencer*, June 2, 2007; Warren King, "Grief, Gratitude in Farewell," *Seattle Times*, June 3, 2007.

115 **he took a mediocre academic record:** O. Casey Corr, KING: *The Bullitts of Seattle and Their Communications Empire* (Seattle: University of Washington Press, 1996), 158.

115 **He played footsie with the *Seattle Times*:** Corr, KING, 158.

115 **he secretly tape-recorded conversations:** Corr, KING, 160.

115 **his successor found weird wiring in the desk:** Chris Bayley, "Maintain the Justice Model Norm Maleng Perpetuated," *Seattle Times*, June 1, 2007.

115 **Another rumor had it that he went easy:** Bayley, "Maintain the Justice Model Norm Maleng Perpetuated."

115 **"Fair Catch" by critics:** Chris Bayley, "Reflecting on the Time When Seattle Police Crossed the Line," *Seattle Times*, January 25, 2007.

116 **"confusing and conflicting statements":** Withers, "Lack of Felony Charges in UW Football Fracas Angers Frat Parents."

116 **"identification seemed to be a problem":** Withers, "Lack of Felony Charges in UW Football Fracas Angers Frat Parents."

117 **"Cream of the crop":** "College Football Recruiting: How Northwest Schools Fared," *Vancouver Columbian*, February 8, 1996.

117 **"The head of this freshman class":** Jim Moore, "Pharms a Force as UW Freshman," *Seattle Post-Intelligencer*, August 16, 1996.

117　penciled Pharms in as a backup strong safety: Percy Allen, "uw Has Fresh, Young Look—More Newcomers Will Get Chance to Play This Season," *Seattle Times*, August 15, 1996; Jim Moore, "Lambright Expects Pups to Contribute," *Seattle Post-Intelligencer*, August 15, 1996.

118　"He's the one who missed out": Joe Davidson, "Mother's Day Is Every Day; Pharms' Success a Reflection of Mom's Love, Faith," *Sacramento Bee*, January 12, 2001.

118　"She is the most special lady": Brian Beaky, "Putting Phamily Phirst," University of Washington game-day program, October 21, 2000.

118　"Pharms wore a purple No. 4 jersey": Percy Allen, "Freshman Pharms Steals Limelight as Huskies Open Football Practice," *Seattle Times*, August 16, 1996.

119　"Blessed with an unusual package of size": J. Moore, "Pharms a Force as uw Freshman."

119　"I knew I wouldn't be": Allen, "Freshman Pharms Steals Limelight as Huskies Open Football Practice."

119　"I'm usually really quiet": J. Moore, "Pharms a Force as uw Freshman."

119　Franquell had become pregnant in high school: Ted Miller, "Jail Term Also Tough on Wife," *Seattle Post-Intelligencer*, January 15, 2004.

121　"In reviewing the case, we discovered": Percy Allen, "Charges Won't Be Filed against 3 uw Players," *Seattle Times*, June 20, 1998.

121　"unsure whether Washington accurately identified": Allen, "Charges Won't Be Filed against 3 uw Players."

13. Narrowly Honest

The Neuheisel quotes come mostly from his deposition, taken June 24–25, 2004, as part of his lawsuit against the uw and the ncaa (kcsc, 03-2-34268-8). In that deposition Neuheisel describes his family, school, and coaching history. Details about Bradley Calkins's jet come from Neuheisel's written responses to ncaa allegations; the same document describes Neuheisel's recruitment of Andre Gurode and Matt Holliday. Other documents used for this chapter: depositions of Hedges taken June 21, 2004 (as part of KCSC, 03-2-34268-8), and April 4, 2004 (KCSC, 03-2-26969-7); deposition of Dick Tharp taken October 28, 2003, and January 16, 2004, for a lawsuit filed in U.S. District Court in Colorado (02-RB-2390); December 3, 2003, deposition of Mary Keenan taken as part of the same lawsuit in Colorado; Boulder Police Department reports (PCR97-19846); UW records showing contributions from individual donors to the athletic department; Neuheisel's employment contracts with the UW; Neuheisel's Annual Report of Outside Income for 2000; March 5, 1999, letter of reprimand from Hedges to Neuheisel; Washington State Executive Ethics Board records concerning investigations of Neuheisel's Nike contract (file No. 99-18) and the use of a private jet provided by Wayne Gittinger (No. 03-145); Hedges's performance evaluation of Neuheisel for July 1999–June 2000; Neuheisel's evaluation of the 1999 season.

122 **"Ri-cky, Ri-cky":** Blaine Newnham, "Washington Takes It to Colorado," *Seattle Times*, September 17, 2000.

122 **"I'm not about money":** Percy Allen, "Neuheisel, Now Possibly 2nd Highest Paid College Coach, Meets with Players," *Seattle Times*, January 11, 1999.

122 **"This is not a monetary decision":** Allen, "Neuheisel, Now Possibly 2nd Highest Paid College Coach, Meets with Players."

122 **"Salary is just not an issue":** Bud Withers, "No Rest for Top Dawg: UW's New Coach Hits Town with a Hefty To-do List," *Seattle Post-Intelligencer*, January 11, 1999.

122 **"All About Cash":** Bud Withers, "Phone Woes Make Coaches Scramble," *Seattle Times*, September 17, 2000.

122 **"Hey, Rick. Show me the money":** Lee Barfknecht, "Fans May Boo Neuheisel, but He Gets Hugs from Buffs," *Omaha World-Herald*, September 17, 2000.

122 **"Loyalty pays, but not":** Withers, "Phone Woes Make Coaches Scramble."

124 **"You become a little kid":** Ivan Maisel, "Buffalo Wing; Shades of Flutie as Colorado Wins on 64-yard Prayer," *Newsday*, September 25, 1994.

125 **"Judith Albino was charmed":** Mark Kiszla, "Buffs' Ascent Is Slick," *Denver Post*, September 17, 2000.

126 **He plays the guitar on stage:** Terry Frei, "Just Having Fun: Neuheisel's Image Is More Than Meets the Eye," *Denver Post*, August 24, 1997.

127 **"I was reading the rules":** Gail Wood, "Neuheisel Grilled by Lawyers; Six-hour Cross-examination Delves into Past," *Olympian*, February 16, 2005.

127 **After practice one day:** Percy Allen, "Education of a Coach—Is Neuheisel Really Slick Rick?" *Seattle Times*, January 17, 1999.

129 **Arnold would later remember:** Sandy Ringer, "Shocked Arnold Says UW Move 'Positive,'" *Seattle Times*, January 11, 1999.

131 **"The Colorado Buffaloes have no football coach":** Mark Kiszla, "Neuheisel Departure an Immediate Improvement," *Denver Post*, January 10, 1999.

132 **"I don't get it":** Richard Hoffer, "No Hard Feelings; Even after a Loss to Their Former Coach, Rick Neuheisel, Spurned Colorado Players Were Able to Forgive and Forget," *Sports Illustrated*, October 4, 1999.

132 **"What does that say about us":** Art Thiel, "Huskies Make Splash by Throwing Big Cash," *Seattle Post-Intelligencer*, January 12, 1999.

132 **"If I leave a job as good":** Thiel, "Huskies Make Splash by Throwing Big Cash."

132 **his decision was based on the "platform":** Jim Cour, "Huskies Athletic Director Surprises Seattle," Associated Press, January 10, 1999.

132 **"the beacon university in the West":** Cour, "Huskies Athletic Director Surprises Seattle."

132 **"I am hopeful this is":** B. G. Brooks, "CU Goodbye Short, Not-so-sweet," *Rocky Mountain News*, January 12, 1999.

133 **The average faculty member would make:** Angelo Bruscas, "Neuheisel's Salary 'Obscene' Complain UW Faculty Leaders," *Seattle Post-Intelligencer*, January 11, 1999.

133 **"Sort of obscene":** Bruscas, "Neuheisel's Salary 'Obscene' Complain UW Faculty Leaders."

133 **Oregon's athletic director suggested:** Percy Allen, "The Hiring of Rick Neuheisel—New Coaches Raise Pac-10 Salary Bar—Costs Could Affect League's Balance," *Seattle Times*, January 12, 1999.

133 **"Hedges just hired":** Tom Shatel, "Is the Joke on Huskies?" *Omaha World-Herald*, January 11, 1999.

133 **"a phony from the get-go":** Bob Kravitz, "What Did Huskies See in Neuheisel?" *Rocky Mountain News*, January 10, 1999.

133 **"the perfect Ken doll":** John Blanchette, "Huskies Usher in Neu Era," *Spokane Spokesman-Review*, January 12, 1999.

136 **"It's a triangular thing":** Bob Partlow, "Neuheisel's $1 Million Deal under Scrutiny," *Olympian*, September 12, 1999.

136 **"That's nothing more than":** Partlow, "Neuheisel's $1 Million Deal under Scrutiny."

136 **"I would say that there's been":** Allen, "Education of a Coach—Is Neuheisel Really Slick Rick?"

137 **The gold was a special mix:** Blaine Newnham, "Thar's Gold in Them Thar Uniforms," *Seattle Times*, January 14, 1999.

137 **"We're going back to gold!":** David Wilson, "Neuheisel's Image Sold Him to Washington," *Daily Nebraskan*, January 13, 1999.

137 **What was $20,000:** Newnham, "Thar's Gold in Them Thar Uniforms."

137 **He also blamed any confusion:** B. G. Brooks, "UW Reprimands Neuheisel, Assistants for Recruiting Violations," *Rocky Mountain News*, March 5, 1999.

138 **have a recruit fly in by seaplane:** "Firing Could Cost Neuheisel His Mansion," Associated Press, June 13, 2003.

138 **sixteen sets of French doors:** Jim Moore, "Slim Chance—Not None—for Cougars on Saturday," *Seattle Post-Intelligencer*, October 30, 2003.

139 **"must have NFL scouts drooling already":** Tom Kensler, "Neuheisel Reunites with His Old Buffs," *Denver Post*, September 17, 2000.

139 **"Neuheisel Rules, Neuheisel Rules"**: B. G. Brooks, "'Neu' Rules over CU Again; Huskies Fend Off Late Rally to Defeat Buffs for Second Straight Year," *Rocky Mountain News*, September 17, 2000.

139 **gave her a hug**: Bud Withers, "UW's Battle Cry; Emotions Flow after Huskies Beat Colorado," *Seattle Times*, September 17, 2000.

14. Scoreboard, Baby

Documents: Detective Parker's reports, including continuation sheets that detailed each step of her investigation. For Marie's history we drew upon two declarations signed by her and filed in separate lawsuits (KCSC, 03-2-35567-4 and 03-2-32273-3).

140 **"Jerramy Stevens is a go-to guy"**: Bud Withers, "More Rest for the Healthy, but Team Wary about Bye," *Seattle Times*, September 18, 2000.

140 **Stevens looked in one corner's eyes**: Miller, "Huskies Tight End Stays Focused on the Present."

140 **I'll be your limo driver**: Miller, "Huskies Tight End Stays Focused on the Present."

140 **"There is one storm cloud"**: Withers, "More Rest for the Healthy, but Team Wary about Bye."

140 **"More of the same"**: Bud Withers, "Tailbacks Aplenty, but Too Many?" *Seattle Times*, September 19, 2000.

143 **"The King County Prosecutor's Office said"**: Ted Miller, "Huskies Wary of Autzen Edge," *Seattle Post-Intelligencer*, September 26, 2000.

145 **"could get a hurricane downgraded"**: Jim Moore, "Dawg in Distress? This Lawyer Answers the Call," *Seattle Post-Intelligencer*, March 18, 2003.

147 **"He's not a good blocker"**: Nick Daschel, "Neuheisel's Fake Punt Fails to Fool Alert Ducks," *Vancouver Columbian*, October 1, 2000.

147 **"A determination on whether to file"**: Bud Withers, "Hooks Says He's Ready to Go, after Heart Scare," *Seattle Times*, October 3, 2000.

15. Carving Their Names

Documents: This chapter relied in part on archival research done in Special Collections at the University of Washington Libraries, looking through the files of past UW presidents. Records on Gil Dobie came from Accession No. 71-34, Box No. 113; Jim Owens, Accession No. 71-34, Box No. 42; and Don James, Accession No. 05-11, Box No. 4, and Accession No. 99-143, Box No. 2. Old letters and notes quoted in this chapter were found in these various files.

Those interested in learning more about the history of the UW's football program should check out Dick Rockne, *Bow Down to Washington: A Story of Husky Football* (Huntsville AL: Strode, 1975); Sam Farmer, *Bitter Roses: An Inside Look at the Washington Huskies' Turbulent Year* (Champaign IL: Sagamore Publishing, 1993); Jim Daves and W. Thomas Porter, *The Glory of Washington: The People and Events That Shaped the Husky Athletic Tradition* (Champaign IL: Sports Publishing, 2001); and Greg Brown, ed., *What It Means to Be a Husky* (Chicago: Triumph Books, 2007).

151 **$3,000 a year:** Rockne, *Bow Down to Washington*, 33.

152 **"No smile, no handshake":** Daves and Porter, *The Glory of Washington*, 49.

152 **"This means they only get to the tacklers":** Dave Caldwell, "Wise Crackers," *Dallas Morning News*, August 26, 1999.

152 **There, the story went, the players weren't much impressed:** "Boxing Lesson: Dobie Offered to Fight the Whole Darned Squad; Bishop Tells How Seattle Coach Gained Respect of North Dakota Aggies," *Seattle Post-Intelligencer*, November 23, 1916.

152 **Kid, you're a rotten quarterback:** Rockne, *Bow Down to Washington*, 34; Daves and Porter, *The Glory of Washington*, 49.

153 **"Our objection," team captain Louis Seagrave told:** "'U' Football Squad Goes on Strike; Suspension of Member Is Resented," *Seattle Post-Intelligencer*, November 23, 1916.

153 **"faculty mercy":** "Dobie and Suzzallo Agree That Coach Is Done at Washington," *Seattle Daily Times*, December 9, 1916.

153 **labeled Grimm's cheating an "indiscretion":** "'U' Football Squad Goes on Strike; Suspension of Member Is Resented."

153 **"I think a start has been made":** "Football Followers of City and on the Campus Regret Dobie's Leaving," *Seattle Post-Intelligencer*, December 10, 1916.

153 **"Do not permit Grimm to play":** "Football Strike Declared Off: Washington to Finish Season with Same Men," *Seattle Post-Intelligencer*, November 24, 1916.

154 **"He has not accepted in practice":** "Dobie and Suzzallo Agree That Coach Is Done at Washington."

154 **Word of the firing raced through the Greek houses:** "Coach Dobie Talks to Students at 2:30 a.m.; Hundreds of Varsity Men Cheer Football Wizard as He Reviews His Experiences and Counsels Loyalty," *Seattle Daily Times*, December 9, 1916.

154 **"The fair maids of the sororities":** "Coach Dobie Talks to Students at 2:30 a.m.

154 **"This is the happiest moment of my life":** "Coach Dobie Talks to Students at 2:30 a.m.

154 **"Fight 'em Dobie":** "Football Followers of City and on the Campus Regret Dobie's Leaving."

155 **Owens was introduced as thirty years old:** Rockne, *Bow Down to Washington*, 171.

156 **including the publishers of both daily newspapers:** Roscoe C. Torrance and Bob Karolevitz, *Torchy! The Biography and Reminiscences of Roscoe C. Torrance* (Mission Hill SD: Dakota Homestead, 1988), 150.

156 **One player remembers losing nearly fifteen pounds:** Carver Gayton, "Carver Gayton Reflects on the Jim Owens Statue at Husky Stadium, University of Washington," HistoryLink.org Essay 5745.

156 **At least six went to the hospital:** Gayton, "Carver Gayton Reflects on the Jim Owens Statue at Husky Stadium."

156 **"I remember one game":** Rockne, *Bow Down to Washington*, 188.

157 **In 1968, *Life* magazine described:** "On the Campus, Protest at Washington, a Loner at Niagara," *Life*, March 15, 1968.

158 **"Why don't the nine UW faculty members"**: Royal Brougham, "Just a Few Questions for Profs," *Seattle Post-Intelligencer*, February 20, 1971.

158 **"Now is not the time"**: Bob Condotta and Jon Savelle, "Black Leaders Say Plan to Honor UW Coach Reopens Painful Past," *Seattle Times*, October 25, 2003.

159 **"A tidy ship is a happy ship"**: Douglas S. Looney, "Mr. Flexibility; Because Don James Was Willing to Make Changes, Washington Is on the Brink of a National Title," *Sports Illustrated*, December 30, 1991.

159 **"alone, imperial, impassive"**: Looney, "Mr. Flexibility."

159 **In 1984, *Sports Illustrated* named the top three coaches**: Douglas S. Looney, "Inside Slant on the Colleges," *Sports Illustrated*, September 5, 1984.

159 **a banner headline in the *Seattle Times***: Tom Farrey and Eric Nalder, "Huskies' Hobert Got $50,000 Loan—Money from Businessman Spent in Spree; May Violate NCAA Rules, Lead to Sanctions," *Seattle Times*, November 5, 1992.

160 **"There's a lot of things that players do"**: Farrey and Nalder, "Huskies' Hobert Got $50,000 Loan."

160 **a *Los Angeles Times* investigation revealed**: Danny Robbins and Elliott Almond, "Washington: A Program Gone Awry?" *Los Angeles Times*, December 9, 1992.

160 **"We run too clean a program"**: Robbins and Almond, "Washington: A Program Gone Awry?"

161 **"It's like hearing that the pope quit"**: Ellis E. Conklin, "Doomsday for the Dawgs," *Seattle Post-Intelligencer*, August 23, 1993.

161 **"The whole deal was a conspiracy"**: Conklin, "Doomsday for the Dawgs."

16. Body and Soul

Documents: The Shane Fortney details come from a lawsuit filed in Snohomish County Superior Court (99-2-02568-5), as well as underlying litigation materials obtained from the UW. The settlement amount is provided in a Settlement Agreement & Release, signed December 4, 2000. Records about Chad Wright include court documents (KCSC, 96-2-26410-5 and 97-2-01535-9), a tort claim filed with the state's Division of Risk Management (36026640-02), and documents obtained from the UW, including a release signed April 26, 1999, that describes the settlement amount and terms.

168 **about all the team's back injuries:** Bud Withers, "Sore Spot; Back Injuries a Perplexing Part of UW Football," *Seattle Post-Intelligencer*, September 16, 1998.

169 **once ripped his shirt in half:** Ted Miller, "Huskies Assistant Weighs in with Record; Gillespie Reclaims Title: 'World's Strongest Man,'" *Seattle Post-Intelligencer*, December 19, 2000.

170 **"I love football, I love the guys":** Blaine Newnham, "One Good Leg, One Big Heart," *Seattle Times*, November 11, 1999.

170 **One had four shoulder surgeries:** Wood, "Robbins Frustrated by Recent Injuries."

171 **A study released in 2007:** Luciana Chavez, "Study of Concussions' Effects Grows; Injuries Can Have Lasting Ramifications," *News and Observer*, July 22, 2007; Alan Schwarz, "Study of Ex-NFL Players Ties Concussion to Depression Risk," *New York Times*, May 31, 2007.

171 **Mortality studies provide grim news:** Mark Zeigler and Ed Graney, "Supersizing the NFL," *San Diego Union-Tribune*, January 23, 2003.

171 **In 2006 one study found:** Thomas Hargrove, "Supersized in the NFL: Many Ex-Players Dying Young," Scripps Howard News Service, January 31, 2006.

17. Up, Down, In, Out

Documents: The description of the fight in Danville, California, comes from Contra Costa County Sheriff's Department records (97-00361), including incident reports and witness statements; transcript of proceedings in *State of California v. Anthony Vontoure, a minor* (Contra Costa County Superior Court, April 17, 18, 21, and 22, 1997), including testimony from Mathew Clark and twelve other witnesses; and a June 13,

2002, continuation report obtained from the Sacramento County Sheriff's Department (02-00440105D), in which Clark recounts the beating he received five years earlier. We obtained Vontoure's academic file from the UW; this file included his academic transcript, a personal essay he wrote to the UW, and a makeup assignment he received in his anthropology class. Vontoure's arrest involving the keg of root beer is described in UWPD reports (98-901571) and court records (KCDC, C02494). Neil Hayes's *When the Game Stands Tall: The Story of the De La Salle Spartans and Football's Longest Winning Streak* (Berkeley CA: Frog, Ltd., 2003) was an outstanding resource on the history and culture of Vontoure's high school program.

172 **"We decided we'd put him in"**: Bud Withers, "Huskies Pull Away Late, Top ASU in Turnover Fest," *Seattle Times*, October 15, 2000.

172 **"the ugliest football game in history"**: Dan Bickley, "In Defining Moment, a Study in Ineptitude," *Arizona Republic*, October 15, 2000.

173 **"An unbelievably gifted athlete"**: Erin Hallissy, "Gifted Athlete's Death a Mystery; Concord Star, Burdened by Grief for Brother, Died Resisting Officers," *San Francisco Chronicle*, July 8, 2002.

173 **The motto of the school:** Hayes, *When the Game Stands Tall*, 7.

174 **"He was a gifted athlete"**: Hayes, *When the Game Stands Tall*, 284.

174 **Mike Blasquez, an athletic trainer:** Hayes, *When the Game Stands Tall*, 284–86.

174 **The school had retired Chris's number:** Hayes, *When the Game Stands Tall*, 293.

174 **"selfish teens into selfless teammates"**: Hayes, *When the Game Stands Tall*, 11.

174 **"He has created a culture"**: Hayes, *When the Game Stands Tall*, 11.

174 **Each player fills out a commitment card:** Hayes, *When the Game Stands Tall*, 127.

175 **Vontoure, on his card:** Hayes, *When the Game Stands Tall*, 127.

181 **could be "sensational" in that role:** Bud Withers, "Offense Doesn't Impress Coaches—But Defensive Moves Hold Promise for UW," *Seattle Times*, April 25, 1999.

181 **"He's got moxie":** Bud Withers, "New Site Considered for UW Practice Facility," *Seattle Times*, April 16, 1999.

181 **"We welcome him back":** Landon Hall, "Washington 47, Oregon St. 21," Associated Press, October 9, 1999.

181 **"Both of those catches":** Danny O'Neil, "Vontoure Picks Up Shaky UW Defense," *Seattle Times*, October 31, 1999.

183 **"the pressure of what was expected":** Ted Miller, "'No Hard Feelings'; Former CB Vontoure Claims He Left Team on His Own Terms," *Seattle Post-Intelligencer*, April 4, 2001.

184 **After hearing of Vontoure's disciplinary problems:** Hayes, *When the Game Stands Tall*, 127.

18. Taking a Shot

186 **"She was a woman of such dignity":** Nick Perry, "Gates Family Legacy at UW Builds with New Regent," *Seattle Times*, September 23, 2006.

19. A Week in the Life

Documents: WSP records on the I-5 accident (1048297); a text of Maleng's prepared statement at the October 24, 2000, press conference; the King County prosecutors' confidential decline letter, dated October 31, 2000; the SPD records of its investigation of Marie's allegation of rape (00-254487); SPD records on the rape allegation against Eric Shyne (02-238650); records of the King County Prosecuting Attorney's Office in the Shyne case; the Washington Court of Appeals opinion in *State v. Al-Hamdani*, 109 Wn. App. 599, 36 P.3d 1103 (2001); RCW 13.40.077 (the Washington State statute that recommends prosecuting standards for charging decisions); and Parker's SPD personnel file, which includes the card that Parker received from Marie after Maleng's announcement.

188 **driving "like a maniac":** John Dodge, "Ex–River Ridge Football Star Has List of Run-ins with Law," *Olympian*, May 18, 2001.

189 **"It must be a gypsy's curse":** Jay Heater, "New Game, Same Bad

News Bears," *Contra Costa Times*, October 22, 2000; Danny O'Neil, "'Bad Stuff Just Kept Happening,'" *Seattle Times*, October 22, 2000.

189 **"When you win"**: Bud Withers, "California Buckles under Husky Hex Yet Again," *Seattle Times*, October 22, 2000.

191 **"I think what this case demonstrates"**: Bernard McGhee, "Prosecutors Drop Sex-Assault Charges against Jerramy Stevens," Associated Press, October 24, 2000.

191 **"From the beginning, I was assured"**: Bud Withers, "No Charges in Stevens Case," *Seattle Times*, October 25, 2000.

192 **"It has been a difficult time"**: McGhee, "Prosecutors Drop Sex-Assault Charges."

20. Love, Love, Love

Documents: SPD reports and witness statements on the fight between Jeremiah and Franquell the day before the Oregon game (99-415813); UWPD reports and witness statements on the fight in Husky Stadium (99-907606); court records of the misdemeanor assault charge filed against Franquell (KCDC, C00003702); the secrecy order in a civil proceeding that was improperly sealed (KCSC, 99-2-22826-0); a transcript of the Inquiry Judge Proceeding held October 27, 2000, including testimony from Tarah, Tarah's mother, and Nick Banchero; UWPD reports on Pharms driving with an expired license (98-900393), and court records about the accompanying misdemeanor charge (KCDC, C00003056).

196 **"I think it's great the UW"**: Stuart Eskenazi, "Homecoming King, Queen Trumped by Pair of 'Royals,'" *Seattle Times*, November 5, 2004.

21. I Can't Breathe

We reviewed a videotape of the Stanford-Washington game, which was broadcast on tape delay by Fox. Information about Williams's child-support obligations comes from a legal action the state filed against him (KCSC, 98-5-01933-7). That file is sealed, but we obtained a declaration of Curtis Williams dated January 19, 2001, and a handwritten Response to Petition filed on July 31, 1998.

207 **feared the county would condemn it:** Roy S. Johnson, "Ready for Kickoff," *Stanford Magazine*, September/October 2006.

212 **"Curtis! Don't you stop":** Kim Grinolds and Joe Kaiser, "Curtis Williams: Remembering the Man," October 1, 2004, Dawgman .com.

212 **Burton looked into Williams's eyes:** Ted Miller, "Waiting Game Begins for Williams; Timetable for Spinal-Cord Injury Recovery Uncertain," *Seattle Post-Intelligencer*, October 31, 2000.

212 **"He ain't moving, man":** Blaine Newnham, "On a Day of Husky Miracles, UW Left Praying for Another," *Seattle Times*, October 29, 2000.

213 **he was supposed to blitz:** Curt Rallo, "Paralyzed Teammate Returns to Cheer Huskies," *South Bend Tribune*, January 1, 2001.

215 **"Three perfect throws":** Greg Beacham, "No. 9 Washington 31, Stanford 28," Associated Press, October 28, 2000.

215 **"It's a bittersweet taste":** Bud Withers, "Emotions Tough to Tackle after Teammate's Injury," *Seattle Times*, October 29, 2000.

215 **"He's a warrior":** Newnham, "On a Day of Husky Miracles, UW Left Praying for Another."

216 **Williams blinked twice as fast:** Blaine Newnham, "Injury to Williams Has Hit Husky Squad Hard," *Seattle Times*, October 31, 2000.

216 **"I don't think there's any question":** Bud Withers, "Williams in 'Wait-and-See' Mode after Spinal Injury," *Seattle Times*, October 30, 2000.

22. Story Lines

We arrived at the 180,000 words by searching Withers's stories in Lexis-Nexis and totaling the word counts.

Documents: Withers's lawsuit against the *Post-Intelligencer*'s parent corporation (filed in U.S. District Court in Seattle, 1995CV00856-BJR), including performance evaluations and descriptions of his work ethic; a deposition of Rick Neuheisel, taken June 24–25, 2004, as part of his lawsuit against the UW and the NCAA (KCSC, 03-2-34268-8); comments posted on a *Seattle Times* Reader Response forum and other online sites responding to the series "Victory and Ruins," published January 27–30, 2008; UWPD reports on Silvers's confrontation with the parking attendant (99-900891), including statements from the attendant, Silvers, and an independent witness, and accompanying court records (KCDC, C00003929).

218 **the newspaper soundproofed the walls:** Michael Miner, "Tweedle-Rick and TweedleJay," *Chicago Reader*, August 8, 2003.

218 **"We wish Jay well":** Phil Rosenthal, "Mariotti: Love-Hate Even in Exit," *Chicago Tribune*, August 28, 2008.

220 **He confronted Lambright:** Bud Withers, "Citing Interests of Team, Lambright Defends Handling of Shehee's Injury," *Seattle Post-Intelligencer*, October 23, 1996.

221 **"I made a mistake":** Bud Withers, "UW Admits Mistake in Handling of Shehee Affair," *Seattle Post-Intelligencer*, October 24, 1996.

222 **"Are we supposed to cheer now?":** Lee Jenkins, "DB's Injury Hits Huskies Hard," *Orange County Register*, November 2, 2000.

222 **"Imagine its impact":** Newnham, "Injury to Williams Has Hit Husky Squad Hard."

223 **Miller profiled Elliot Silvers:** Ted Miller, "Caution: Short Fuse, Defender Beware; Huskies Offensive Lineman a Handful on Field, Exact Opposite off It," *Seattle Post-Intelligencer*, October 26, 2000.

224 **"In 1997, he served a 90-day jail term":** Withers, "Williams in 'Wait-and-See' Mode after Spinal Injury."

225 **"Number 25 wants us to":** Ted Miller, "Focus on Arizona Is Hard for Huskies, Still Feeling Weight of Absent Teammate," *Seattle Post-Intelligencer*, November 4, 2000.

226 **"You can't shake him":** Charles Durrenberger, "UA Notes," *Tucson Citizen*, November 6, 2000.

227 **"We just knew we had to":** Jim Cour, "No. 8 Washington 35, Arizona 32," Associated Press, November 4, 2000; Bud Withers, "Houdini Huskies: UW Pulls 'Cat out of Its Hat,' Escapes with Victory Again," *Seattle Times*, November 5, 2000.

23. California Fun

Documents: SPD reports on the investigation of Sullivan's shooting; transcript of the Inquiry Judge Proceeding held on November 17, 2000, including the testimony of Sam Blanche and Tarah; court records for the misdemeanor assault charges against Curtis Williams (KCDC, C00003413); a deposition of Rick Neuheisel taken June 18, 2004, in which he addresses his talk to the sociology class and the team's trip to the Playboy Mansion; the 2001 "University Participation Manual" distributed by the Pasadena Tournament of Roses to the UW and Purdue; a December 4, 2000, letter from the Tournament of Roses president to UW president Richard McCormick; Lynnwood Police Department records involving warnings, infractions or charges against Pharms concerning his dogs (Incident Nos. 00-11003, 00-6694, 00-11044), including statements from Grace Lundeen and Pharms's landlord, and veterinarian exam notes; court records of misdemeanor charges against Pharms for having too many dogs (Lynnwood Municipal Court, C00020126 and C00020128).

231 **"Coach, make sure those guys":** Steve Bergum, "Rose Bowl: Just Reward; Huskies Looking Forward to 'Treat of a Lifetime,'" *Spokane Spokesman-Review*, November 19, 2000.

232 **his wife gave him a bottle:** Nick Daschel, "UW's Rose Bowl Countdown Is Under Way," *Vancouver Columbian*, November 20, 2000.

232 **"I'm not calling it a suspension":** Ted Miller, "One for the Records; Domination of Cougars Paves Way to Rose Bowl," *Seattle Post-Intelligencer*, November 20, 2000.

233 **"I've always felt great":** Bud Withers, "Neuheisel Doubters Get Lost in Roses; But Vindication? Coach, AD Say No," *Seattle Times*, November 21, 2000.

233 **"Curtis wants the big prize":** Ted Miller, "Huskies' Williams Improving; Injured Safety Able to Move Shoulders," *Seattle Post-Intelligencer*, November 21, 2000.

233 **"I never want to use":** Miller, "Huskies' Williams Improving; Injured Safety Able to Move Shoulders."

234 **"No, you can't be the quarterback":** Ryan Nickum, "U. Washing-

ton Football Coach's Comments Offend Some Students," *The Daily of the University of Washington*, December 4, 2000.

234 **"You guys are terrible"**: Nickum, "U. Washington Football Coach's Comments Offend Some Students."

234 **"the wrong kind of girl"**: Nickum, "U. Washington Football Coach's Comments Offend Some Students."

234 **"I'd expect it from my freshmen students"**: Nickum, "U. Washington Football Coach's Comments Offend Some Students."

234 **This student wanted to speak up**: Nickum, "U. Washington Football Coach's Comments Offend Some Students."

234 **"probably the best class"**: Nickum, "U. Washington Football Coach's Comments Offend Some Students."

235 **"After issuing the standard thanks"**: Art Thiel, "Alas, Neuheisel Just Too Slick," *Seattle Post-Intelligencer*, June 6, 2003.

235 **"I'm all for it"**: Bob Condotta, "A Long Route: Street Life to Rose Bowl to South Africa," *Tacoma News Tribune*, December 18, 2000.

236 **"Kelley's Tale"**: Blaine Newnham, "Kelley's Tale: From 'Hood to U District," *Seattle Times*, December 28, 2000.

236 **"His Bed of Roses"**: Fred J. Robledo, "His Bed of Roses; Academics, Not Game, Bowl Highlight for Kelley," *Los Angeles Daily News*, December 23, 2000.

236 **"Sit down!"**: Ryan Nickum, "U. Washington Coach's Comments Become Lesson in Sociology Class," *The Daily of the University of Washington*, December 5, 2000.

236 **"I ran onto the field"**: Andrew Baggarly, "Rose Cures Ills for Neuheisel," *Riverside Press-Enterprise*, December 24, 2000.

237 **had done something "not acceptable"**: Ted Miller, "Vontoure Will Play in Rose Bowl; Cornerback Won't Participate in pre-Christmas Events," *Seattle Post-Intelligencer*, December 16, 2000.

238 **"He will just be practicing"**: José Miguel Romero, "Vontoure Rejoins Huskies," *Seattle Times*, December 16, 2000.

238 **"would really be difficult"**: Miller, "Vontoure Will Play in Rose Bowl."

238 **"We have a lot of architectural majors"**: Dwight Perry, "Sideline Chatter," *Seattle Times*, December 26, 2001.

239 **"It's a tourist attraction"**: Larry Stewart, "Morning Briefing; In a Way, They Are Both Meat Markets," *Los Angeles Times*, December 23, 2000.

239 **"There's always going to be criticism"**: Stewart, "Morning Briefing; In a Way, They Are Both Meat Markets."

239 **"I wouldn't know how to act"**: Bud Withers, "'Dream Season' Helps Stevens Focus on Field," *Seattle Times*, December 24, 2000.

239 **"I know what happened"**: Ted Miller, "From Under Suspicion to Under Microscope," *Seattle Post-Intelligencer*, December 30, 2000.

239 **"It was unfortunate that I"**: Bob Condotta, "A Dream Season after a Nightmare Start," *Tacoma News Tribune*, December 27, 2000.

239 **"I would defend him in all terms"**: Condotta, "A Dream Season after a Nightmare Start."

240 **hopping a ride with a producer**: Ted Miller, "A Life Cut Short; Death of Former UW Star in Police Custody Leaves Many Questions Unanswered," *Seattle Post-Intelligencer*, July 23, 2002.

240 **confined to his hotel room**: Steve Springer, "Rose Bowl Daily Report: Washington; Hospital Trip Provides Perspective," *Los Angeles Times*, December 28, 2000.

243 **"might always be known"**: Janie McCauley, "Hedges, Huskies Anticipating the Rose Bowl on New Year's Day," Associated Press, December 28, 2000.

243 **"a stroke of genius"**: McCauley, "Hedges, Huskies Anticipating the Rose Bowl on New Year's Day."

243 **"It seems that everything she touches"**: McCauley, "Hedges, Huskies Anticipating the Rose Bowl on New Year's Day."

243 **"Naturally, he's getting an automatic raise"**: Ted Miller, "Neuheisel's Contract Comes Up Roses, Too," *Seattle Post-Intelligencer*, December 29, 2000.

243 **"She'd go to chemotherapy"**: Gabe Lacques, "Notebook: Huskies' First Play Is for Peggy," *Los Angeles Daily News*, January 1, 2001.

244 **"Our team will know he's watching"**: Blaine Newnham, "Williams Will Attend Rose Bowl," *Seattle Times*, December 31, 2000.

24. A Mystical, Magical Day

Documents: Nike contracts (the language about "contrast" appeared in a five-year contract Neuheisel signed with Nike while at the University of Colorado, and in a proposed contract at the UW that became the subject of a state ethics investigation described in chapter 13); the "University Participation Manual"; and UW financial records providing an annual breakdown of ticket sales and contributions to the football program.

245 **The billboard wasn't there**: Mike Schneider, "Rose Bowl Takes Cue from Sunshine Network in Use of Virtual Ads," Associated Press, December 31, 1998.

246 **"It was for the national interest"**: Mark Magnier, "China Abuzz over Lip-syncing Singer," *Los Angeles Times*, August 13, 2008.

246 **the anchorman for the U.S. team**: Brent Hunsberger, "Nike, Speedo Brands Battle for Exposure," *Oregonian*, August 14, 2008.

247 **"It's not going to be AT&T"**: Jeff Wilson, "It's the Rose Bowl, Presented by AT&T," Associated Press, June 26, 1998.

247 **ABC had paid $525 million**: Chris Perkins, "Bowl Series to Keep Calculators Busy," *Fort Lauderdale Sun-Sentinel*, August 28, 1998.

249 **when his cell phone rang**: Blaine Newnham, "With a Wave of the Wand, Neuheisel and Huskies Go on Wild Ride," *Seattle Times*, January 7, 2001.

250 **Neuheisel and his wife had visited**: Bud Withers, "A Little Faith Leads Huskies to Rose Bowl," *Seattle Times*, November 20, 2000.

252 **Purdue's tailback, Montrell Lowe**: Helene Elliott, "Purdue Is Prepared to Take Lowe Road," *Los Angeles Times*, December 25, 2000. Lowe's comment referring to Washington was: "They're very athletic, very physical, which is surprising for a Pac-10 team."

252 **"To be on the sidelines"**: Steve Springer, "Huskies' Past Shares the Present," *Los Angeles Times*, January 2, 2001.

252 **"The Huskies are one, one deal"**: Springer, "Huskies' Past Shares the Present."

254 **Neuheisel knew better**: Bud Withers, "He Knew Tui Had Time," *Seattle Times*, January 3, 2001.

256 **"On three!"**: "Rose Bowl Spotlight; Real Lowe Down on Purdue," *Los Angeles Times*, January 2, 2001.

256 **He believed celebration was lost**: Nick Daschel, "Q&A with Rick Neuheisel," *Vancouver Columbian*, August 18, 2002.

257 **to give the game's commemorative coin**: Ivan Maisel, "Passion Play," *Sports Illustrated*, January 8, 2001.

257 **"This win is for Curtis"**: "Huskies Rise in Honor of Williams," *Torrance Daily Breeze*, January 2, 2001; Jim Cour, "Paralyzed Safety Watches Huskies Beat Purdue," Associated Press, January 2, 2001.

257 **"kept a promise to a fallen comrade"**: David Leon Moore, "Washington Rolls in Rose," *USA Today*, January 2, 2001.

257 **"A magic carpet ride"**: Gail Wood, "Huskies Quiet Brees to Roll to Rose Bowl Win over Purdue," *Olympian*, January 2, 2001.

257 **"It's not about the trophy"**: Bud Withers, "Amazing Ride to Last a Lifetime for Huskies," *Seattle Times*, January 3, 2001.

257 **"mystical, magical season"**: Bud Withers, "Happy Neuheisel Calls Win 'Huge,'" *Seattle Times*, January 2, 2001.

257 **"The Washington Huskies are back"**: Jim Cour, "Huskies Are Back after Bowl Bans, Coaching Turmoil," Associated Press, January 2, 2001.

257 **"with a finger as long as a rose"**: Bill Plaschke, "Huskies Deserve the Top Billing If Sooners Stumble," *Los Angeles Times*, January 2, 2001.

258 **"We have to go"**: Brown, *What It Means to Be a Husky*, 438.

258 **After the final whistle**: Brown, *What It Means to Be a Husky*, 438, 463.

258 **"It was a great investment":** Ruth Schubert, "A Hush-Hush Homecoming for Happy Huskies," *Seattle Post-Intelligencer*, January 3, 2001.

25. Climbing the Hill

We reviewed a video recording of Anthony Kelley's speech introducing Archbishop Desmond Tutu.

261 **It was freewheeling and raucous:** Declan Walsh, "Making Amends for Apartheid: The Resurrection of District Six," *The Independent*, March 15, 2004.

261 **"unexceptional black settlement":** Bill Keller, "Guguletu Journal; A Brutalized Generation Turns Its Rage on Whites," *New York Times*, December 7, 1993.

262 **Amy Biehl's parents and sister Kim had visited Intshinga:** The Amy Biehl Foundation Web site, www.amybiehl.org.

268 **Bill Gates Sr. donated $5,000:** Gina Kim, "Girls from a Ghetto Touch Family's Heart," *Seattle Times*, June 16, 2002.

269 **"has found his passion":** Ted Miller, "Change for the Good; Huskies' Kelley Finds His Calling—Helping Kids," *Seattle Post-Intelligencer*, December 25, 2002.

269 **"Wearing green, orange and black":** Kim, "Girls from a Ghetto Touch Family's Heart."

271 **"The truth of the matter is they have two responsibilities":** John Boyle, *Everett Daily Herald*, April 6, 2008.

26. Always Hated, Never Faded

Documents: SPD records (01-207148) and court records (SMC, 401175) on the crash into the retirement home; police and court records on speeding tickets or warnings written by the WSP and the Cheney, Clyde Hill, and Bellevue police departments; WSP records on the negligent-driving citation (13295560); Medina Police Department records on the arrest on suspicion of DUI (Incident No. 03M0178) and the accompanying court records (Kirkland Municipal Court, 29891M); audio recording of the sentencing hearing in the Medina case; court records in lawsuits filed by four women accusing UW football players of rape (KCSC, 03-2-26969-7, 03-2-

35567-4, and 04-2-04660-2); depositions of Neuheisel (June 18, 2004), Hedges (April 4, 2004), Jim Lambright (August 6, 2004) and Keith Gilbertson (June 28, 2004) in lawsuits filed against the UW (KCSC, 03-2-35567-4 and 03-2-26969-7); a lawsuit filed against the UW and Medtronic, Inc., that was improperly sealed (KCSC, 02-2-16649-1); May 23, 2004, letter from Mike Hunsinger to counsel for the UW, laying out terms of the settlement for Marie's lawsuit; June 17, 2004, letter from Hunsinger to Marie's attorney, saying a check for $300,000 is enclosed (Note: That amount covers the amount paid by both Stevens and the fraternity; we do not know how much each party paid toward that total); property records from the King County Department of Assessments (parcel No. 0293950730); court records of the lawsuit filed against Stevens by his condo association (KCSC, 04-2-19725-2); minutes of Astoria at Meydenbauer Bay Homeowners' annual meeting held March 22, 2007, discussing fines and pending lawsuit against Stevens; Bellevue police records on noise and other complaints concerning Stevens's condominium (BI0705675, BI0715330, BPD00649307, BPD00649607, BPD00649707, BPD08125006, BPD07695706, BPD04356806, BPD08390406, BPD03298506, case No. 07-1128); police and court records on the stops in 2006 for driving with a suspended license (WSP, C00602522, and Bellevue Police Department, BC0143378); Scottsdale, Arizona, Police Department reports on the 2007 arrest on suspicion of DUI (07-07670).

272 **Stevens was "so good" last season:** Blaine Newnham, "Stevens Shelved QB Dream, Became Defense's Nightmare," *Seattle Times*, April 15, 2001.

273 **called at home in the wee hours:** Withers, "Huskies Unleash Their Lawyer."

273 **"to discuss the importance of behavior":** Lewis Kamb, "Huskies Star Charged in Hit-and-Run," *Seattle Post-Intelligencer*, May 5, 2001.

273 **"How can the UW justify":** Staff editorial, "Football Program Should Drop Player," *The Daily of the University of Washington*, May 9, 2001.

274 **"I'm not a bad person":** Bud Withers, "Stevens: 'I'm Not a Bad Guy,'" *Seattle Times*, August 18, 2001.

274 **"It breaks my heart":** Nick Daschel, "Stevens Tries to Elude Cloud of Controversy," *Vancouver Columbian*, August 19, 2001.

274 **"I think Jerramy has made great strides":** John Sleeper, "Huskies Star Stevens Says He'll Shape Up: It's Worth It . . . Literally," *Everett Daily Herald*, August 18, 2001.

274 **"that was a worthy punishment":** Janie McCauley, "Washington Tight End Held Out of Starting Lineup," Associated Press, September 8, 2001.

274 **"It's behind him now":** Bud Withers, "Stevens Penalty: Sit Out the Opening Half," *Seattle Times*, September 9, 2001.

274 **"If dreams come true":** David Andriesen, "Stevens Turning Pro; Huskies Tight End Leaving Team Early, Hopes to Be a Raider," *Seattle Post-Intelligencer*, January 11, 2002.

274 He **"promised himself, his family":** Janie McCauley, "Washington's Stevens to Leave School Early for NFL," Associated Press, January 11, 2002.

275 **"People make mistakes":** Percy Allen, "Once More, Holmgren Gambles on Greatness," *Seattle Times*, April 21, 2002.

275 **"I graduated from college":** Clare Farnsworth, "Meet the Seahawks: Jerramy Stevens," *Seattle Post-Intelligencer*, August 3, 2002.

275 **"He's huge. And he can run":** Clare Farnsworth, "Stevens Comes up Big—and Fast—in Hawks Debut," *Seattle Post-Intelligencer*, May 4, 2002.

275 **"He's so smart":** Steve Kelley, "Stevens Looks Like a Great Catch," *Seattle Times*, August 2, 2002.

275 **"Stevens is looking good":** Kelley, "Stevens Looks Like a Great Catch."

282 **"It's a heartwarming story and all that":** John Blanchette, "Stevens, Porter 'Bring It On' with Silly Barbs," *Spokane Spokesman-Review*, February 2, 2006.

283 **"sissy" and a "punk":** Art Thiel, "Stevens' Antics, Misplays Put Seahawks at Great Risk," *Seattle Post-Intelligencer*, November 8, 2006.

283 **"This dude has been":** Gregg Bell, "NFL Fine Latest Proof Seahawks'

Stevens Isn't Exactly Beloved," Associated Press, November 9, 2006.

283 **"You wouldn't want him":** Josh Dubow, "Brayton, Stevens Fined by NFL, but Avoid Suspensions," Associated Press, November 9, 2006.

284 **guest of honor at the Spring Fun Fair:** Gail Wood, "Hometown Hero; Seahawks' Stevens Visits with His Fans in South Sound," *Olympian*, May 21, 2006.

285 **"I believe in giving people second chances":** Clarence E. Hill Jr., "Tank Vows to Do Right Thing," *Fort Worth Star-Telegram*, September 20, 2007.

285 **"KKK devil that hates":** Paul Pinkham, "Jaguars Player Rants on Videotape," *Florida Times-Union*, March 21, 2007.

286 **"He's a good player":** Danny O'Neil, "Ex-Hawk Stevens Finds New Home in Tampa Bay," *Seattle Times*, April 30, 2007.

286 **"you have to give people a chance":** Joe Henderson, "Stevens' Talent Apparently Justifies Risk," *Tampa Tribune*, May 1, 2007.

286 **"a talk-radio firestorm":** Chris Harry, "Jerramy Stevens Catching More Heat Than Passes," June 3, 2008, OrlandoSentinel.com.

286 **"Our phones haven't stopped ringing":** Ira Kaufman, "Stevens' Signing Results in Uproar," *Tampa Tribune*, June 4, 2008.

27. Ripples

This chapter relies on interviews with Marie; Marie's mother; Marie's brother; Maggie; Marie's roommate at Pi Beta Phi; and the woman who received Stevens's May 8, 2000, e-mail.

28. When the Game's Over

Documents: Lynnwood Police Department records concerning Pharms's dogs (00-11003) and accompanying court records (Lynnwood Municipal Court, C00020128); January 3, 2001, letter from Pharms's sports agent, Lee Kolligian, to Pharms's lawyer, describing the kind of NFL contract Pharms would likely have signed; court records in Pharms's robbery case (KCSC, 01-1-04360-5); Pharms's January 2, 2002, pre-sentence investigation report; Pharms's DOC file (833475), including details about work release, disciplinary findings, drug-test results, and an offender chronological report with extensive notes about Pharms from correctional officers; draft of a letter from Lang and Fogg to the *Seattle Post-Intelligencer* (the letter was never sent; Lang provided a copy to the authors); WSP reports and accompanying court records for Pharms's 2005 arrest on suspicion of DUI (Everett District Court, C00583221); court records for Pharms's 2007 felony charges in California (Sacramento County Superior Court, 07F10319), and a District Attorney's Cover Sheet summarizing the case; Sacramento County Sheriff's Department reports on Vontoure's death and the events preceding it (02-0044010SD); Vontoure's academic transcript at the UW; text of Bob Ladouceur's comments at Vontoure's funeral, found at http://presenting-in-heaven.com/Anthony/Service.html; Sacramento County Coroner's Final Report of Investigation regarding Vontoure's death (02-2636); court records of the lawsuit filed by Vontoure's parents (Sacramento County Superior Court, 04AS00781).

294 **Neuheisel's report glowed:** Mary Kay Cabot, "More Charges May Await Pharms," *Cleveland Plain Dealer*, May 4, 2001.

294 **"While his Washington teammates were out socializing":** Susan Vinella, "Jeremiah Pharms," *Cleveland Plain Dealer*, April 23, 2001.

294 **"The Browns won't have to spend":** Brian Windhorst, "Pharms Feeds on Playing in NFL; Versatile Washington Standout Committed to Making Browns, Putting Food on Table for His Growing Family," *Akron Beacon Journal*, April 23, 2001.

295 **"I've been accused of knowing":** Danny O'Neil, "Neuheisel Comments on Arrests of Players," *Seattle Times*, May 8, 2001.

296 **"It's difficult to imagine":** Tracy Johnson, "Ex-UW Linebacker Pharms Sent to Prison for Robbery," *Seattle Post-Intelligencer*, January 12, 2002.

296 **He wrote a letter to the *Post-Intelligencer*:** Ted Miller, "Strong, Silent Jeremiah Pharms, Who Went to the Rose Bowl with the UW in 2000, Seeks a Second Chance at Life and Football after Getting out of Prison," *Seattle Post-Intelligencer*, January 15, 2004.

296 **wrote a long piece about him:** Miller, "Strong, Silent Jeremiah Pharms." Miller, who was hired by espn.com in 2008 to cover the Pac-10, has been critical of a four-part series the authors wrote in

the *Seattle Times* about the 2000 Huskies. For his take on that se-ries—and on the evidence in the Pharms case—readers can go to a blog posting of Miller's at http://blog.seattlepi.com/sportsrant /archives/130731.asp. Some players from the 2000 team were also critical of the series. Their reactions can be found at http://derek johnsonbooks.wordpress.com/2008/07/21/the-2000-washington-huskies-respond-to-the-seattle-times/.

299 **"He doesn't expect to become a star"**: Ted Miller, "Pharms Holds onto Dreams," *Seattle Post-Intelligencer*, August 22, 2006.

299 **"Pharms' journey toward redemption"**: Ted Miller, "Ex-Huskies DE Faces Warrant on DUI," *Seattle Post-Intelligencer*, August 26, 2006.

300 **Curtis had no recollection of the play:** Laura Vecsey, "One Special Life; Ex-Husky Gave Us Answers to Questions We Couldn't Ask," *Seattle Post-Intelligencer*, May 7, 2002.

300 **One fund-raising dinner generated $20,000:** "Curtis Williams, 1978–2002," *Seattle Times*, May 7, 2002.

300 **Jerramy Stevens hosted a bowling tournament:** Jim Moore, "Ste-vens' Sister Says There's a Positive Side to Troubled Seahawks Tight End," *Seattle Post-Intelligencer*, May 30, 2003.

301 **"He focused on the impact of two people"**: Blaine Newnham, "UW Needs to Show the Care, Giving of Community," *Seattle Times*, February 1, 2001.

302 **Al Black, a sociology professor:** Les Carpenter, "Williams Changed, Grew before Teacher's Eyes," *Seattle Times*, May 7, 2002.

302 **Touch me. Laugh with me:** Vecsey, "One Special Life."

302 **"I have to keep going on"**: Ted Miller, "Williams' Life Celebrated at UW Service; Nearly 2,000 Attend Memorial for Huskies Strong Safety," *Seattle Post-Intelligencer*, May 15, 2002.

302 **"I will always admire Curtis"**: Janie McCauley, "Paralyzed Wash-ington Safety Curtis Williams Dies," Associated Press, May 6, 2002.

303 **"It's a game that's given me everything"**: Bob Condotta, "CW's Brother Comes to Husky Stadium," *Seattle Times*, October 2, 2002.

304 **"he wanted to watch me play"**: Bob Condotta, "Football Remains Focus for Williams Family," *Seattle Times*, September 13, 2006.

304 **he had reached an understanding with the coaches:** Miller, "Former CB Vontoure Claims He Left Team on His Own Terms."

307 **"In high school, he played football"**: Miller, "A Life Cut Short."

308 **"Act like gentlemen":** Hayes, *When the Game Stands Tall*, 361.

308 **This is a game:** Hayes, *When the Game Stands Tall*, 366.

Epilogue

Documents: June 29, 2001, memo from Hedges to Richard McCormick about Neuheisel's salary; Neuheisel's June 24–25, 2004, deposition, in which he recounts his conversations with Terry Donahue and describes the steps he took to investigate other coaches participating in basketball pools; Hedges's June 21, 2004, deposition; a September 23, 2004, deposition of Norm Arkans, a UW vice-president; court records in Neuheisel's lawsuit against the UW and the NCAA (KCSC, 03-2-34268-8); e-mails to NCAA officials between April and August 2003; e-mails sent by Ed Hansen and other UW boosters and fans during Washington's 2007 football season (we obtained about a thousand e-mails pursuant to a public-records request); the Washington Court of Appeals 2008 ruling in the lawsuit against the UW over its handling of Roc Alexander (*S.S. v. Alexander et al.*, 143 Wn. App. 75, 177 P.3d 724).

For the *S.S. v. UW* trial, we interviewed four jurors after the verdict was returned.

312 **"It went well," he said:** John Levesque, "I Know What I Heard: UW Fans Should, Too," *Seattle Post-Intelligencer*, February 12, 2003.

312 **Levesque, after waiting a day:** Levesque, "I Know What I Heard."

313 **had engaged in an affair:** Steve Miletich, "UW Regents Pressured President to Leave," *Seattle Times*, November 2, 2003.

313 **"The most stunning convergence":** Bud Withers, "Lack of Common Sense Resounded in Trial," *Seattle Times*, March 13, 2005.

313 **"I feel fully vindicated":** Steve Kelley, "Like a Lucky Dawg, Neuheisel Finds Great Fortune," *Seattle Times*, March 8, 2005.

313 **"Rick Neuheisel was blessed with good looks":** Withers, "Lack of Common Sense Resounded in Trial."

314 **"In the end it was all about 66 collegiate wins":** Ken Peters, "UCLA Hires Rick Neuheisel," Associated Press, December 29, 2007.

315 **worth between $1.25 million and $1.75 million:** Brian Dohn, "Neuheisel Can Make $500K in Bonuses," *Los Angeles Daily News*, May 24, 2008.

317 **"The message that our students hear":** Bob Condotta, "Ousted Athletic Director: Is Winning the Only Thing?" *Seattle Times*, December 12, 2007.

319 **A year later, the *Seattle Times* revealed:** Miletich, "UW Regents Pressured President to Leave."

319 **oversaw a doubling of spending on football:** Ted Sherman and Josh Margolin, "Rutgers Football: A Game of Secrets; University Reluctant to Detail Expenditures," *Newark Star-Ledger*, December 7, 2008.

319 **Rutgers also concealed the football coach's full salary:** Josh Margolin and Ted Sherman, "Rutgers Hid Part of Its Deal with Schiano; Coach Got Extra $250,000 per Year," *Newark Star-Ledger*, July 22, 2008.

320 **"We are trying to be preventive":** Nicole Brodeur, "Landlady Could Teach UW a Lesson," *Seattle Times*, October 9, 2007.

321 **"The budget situation is extraordinarily serious":** Nick Perry, "Bottom Falls Out for Colleges," *Seattle Times*, November 23, 2008.

321 **"I've been paying attention to the market":** Don Ruiz, "Intensity Comes with a Price," *Tacoma News Tribune*, January 7, 2009.

321 **Husky booster Ron Crockett called them "fools":** Jim Brunner, "Cougars Try to Sack UW Request," *Seattle Times*, December 2, 2008.

INDEX

Marie, 66; academic record of, 17;
effects of alleged rape on, 109–11,
287, 289, 290–92; and family
relationships, 27–28, 109–11, 287–
89, 290–91; friendships of, with
football players, 18–19, 25, 56, 66;
friends of, 23, 27, 287–88, 289–90;
and injuries, 21, 23, 27, 28, 45; at
the "Jacked Up" party, 22–23; and
lawsuit against Stevens and the UW,
278–82; leaving the UW, 109–10;
and memories, 21–22, 23–24, 26–
27, 41; personality of, 17–18; and
rape investigation, 41–42, 56–57,
64–65, 66–68, 74–75, 190, 194–95;
and sexual-assault exam, 27–28
Mariotti, Jay, 218
Marona, Spencer, 22–23, 25–26, 27,
76, 290, 291; friendship of, with
Marie, 18; and rape investigation,
65–68
Maulana, Seyed, 97–98
McCartney, Bill, 125, 127
McCormick, Richard, xi, 52, 221,
319–20; affair of, 313, 319; and
Barbara Hedges, 243, 311
McElhenny, Hugh, 207
McMahon, Rose, 142, 143
Mead, Clint, 161–62
media: and Curtis Williams, 86, 96,
98, 165–66, 300–301; and Jeremiah
Pharms, 113, 118–19, 294, 296–97,
298–99; and Jerramy Stevens,
53–54, 70, 71, 73–74, 140, 143–44,
239, 272, 273–74; and Rick
Neuheisel, 72–73, 124–25, 131–32,
136–37, 221–22, 252–53, 256, 257;
and sportswriters, 217–24, 257–58;
and Sullivan robbery investigation,
59–60
Merrill Gardens retirement center,
272–73
Mertel, Charles, 99–100
Michalczik, Jim, 320, 321

Miller, Ted, 222–23, 224, 233, 296–
97, 298–99
Milus, Ron, 94, 180
Molly (friend of Marie), 22, 23, 27
Moon, Warren, 207, 255, 276
Moore, Jim, 221
Moppins, Franquell. *See* Pharms,
Franquell (Mrs. Jeremiah Pharms)
Moses, Wayne, 182, 209
Mudd, Jeffery, xi, 59; and Sullivan
robbery investigation, 15, 16,
58–63, 112, 202, 228, 230, 242–43,
294
Mulitauaopele, Toalei, 50

Naeole, Chris, 127
Nalder, Eric, 221
NCAA, 130, 144, 160–62, 312–14;
and academic standards, 33–34,
37–38; and recruiting violations,
126–27, 137
Nelson, Rock, ix, 102–3, 120, 139,
315–16; injuries of, 167–71, 212
Nessler, Brad, 1, 102, 104, 108
Neuheisel, Rick, x, 50, 122–23,
233, 239–40, 269; and Anthony
Vontoure, 172, 173, 181, 183,
184, 237–38; attending UCLA,
123–24; childhood of, 123; and
Curtis Williams, 100–101, 215–16,
225, 227, 231, 244, 249–50, 257,
301, 302, 303; and discipline,
81–82, 127, 136–37, 138–39,
273; firing of, by the UW, 312–14;
and fund-raising, 138; and golf,
68–69, 72; hiring of, by the UW,
127–28, 129–33; and Holiday Bowl
controversy, 235; and Husky fans,
104, 108, 122, 225; and Husky
uniforms, 137; interviewing with
the San Francisco 49ers, 311–12;
and Jeremiah Pharms, 200; and
Jerramy Stevens, 4, 69, 72–73, 74,
189–90, 192, 273, 274, 278–79;